Honey
So Sweet

1

Story and Art by
Amu Meguro

Contents

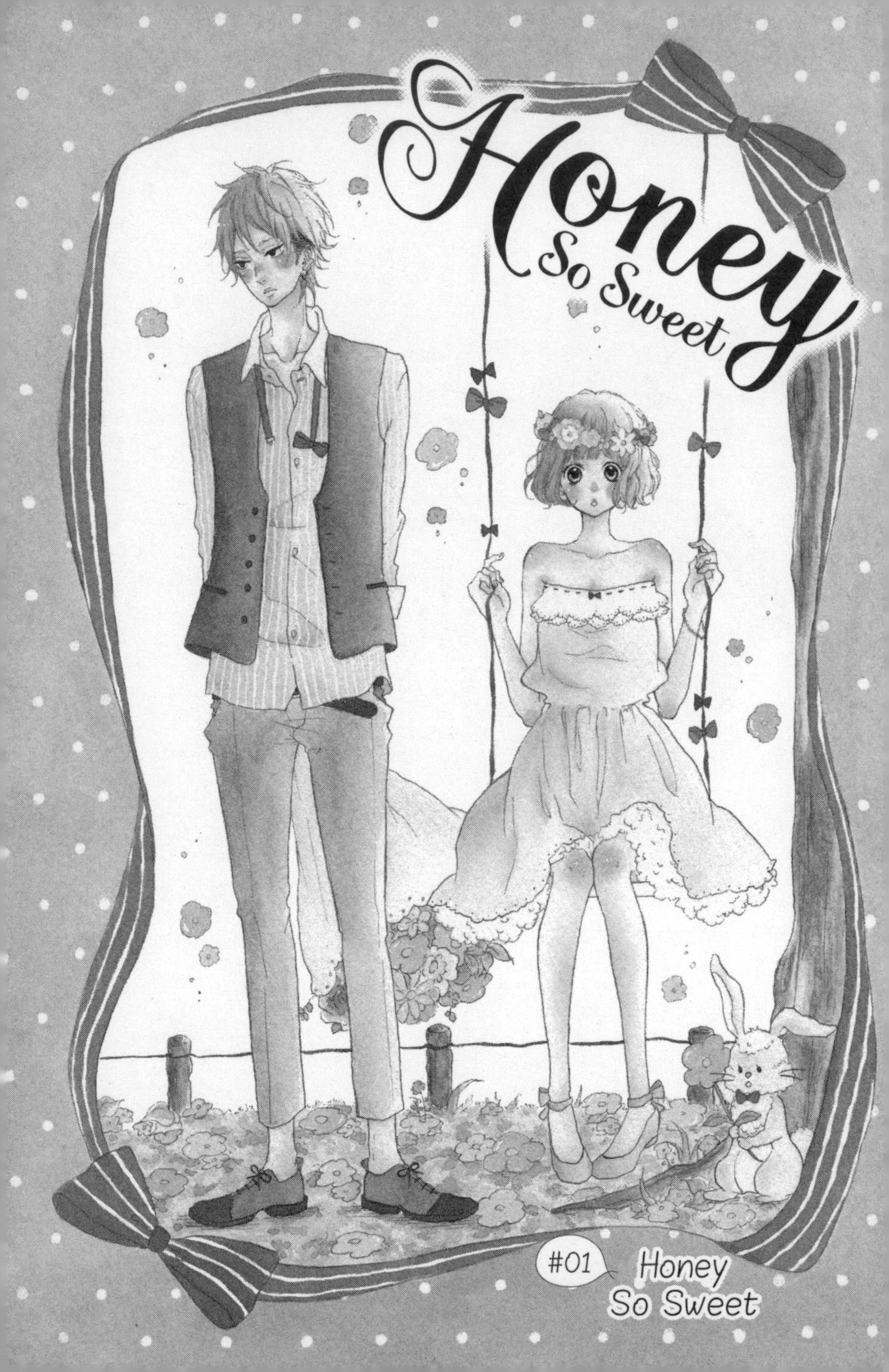
Honey
So Sweet
#01
Honey
So Sweet

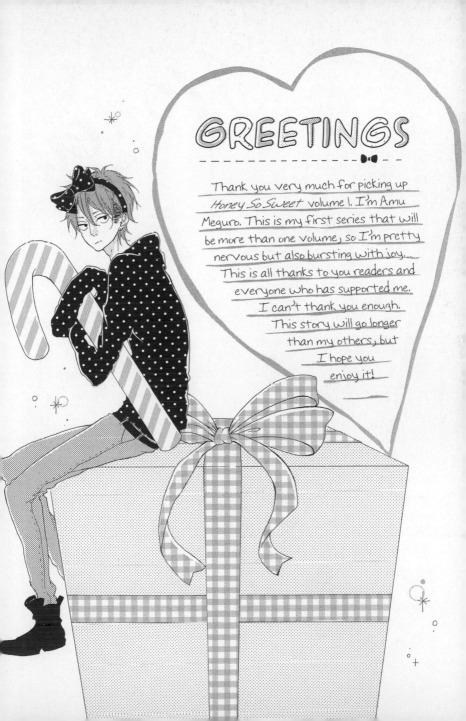

GREETINGS

Thank you very much for picking up *Honey So Sweet* volume 1. I'm Amu Meguro. This is my first series that will be more than one volume, so I'm pretty nervous but also bursting with joy. This is all thanks to you readers and everyone who has supported me. I can't thank you enough. This story will go longer than my others, but I hope you enjoy it!

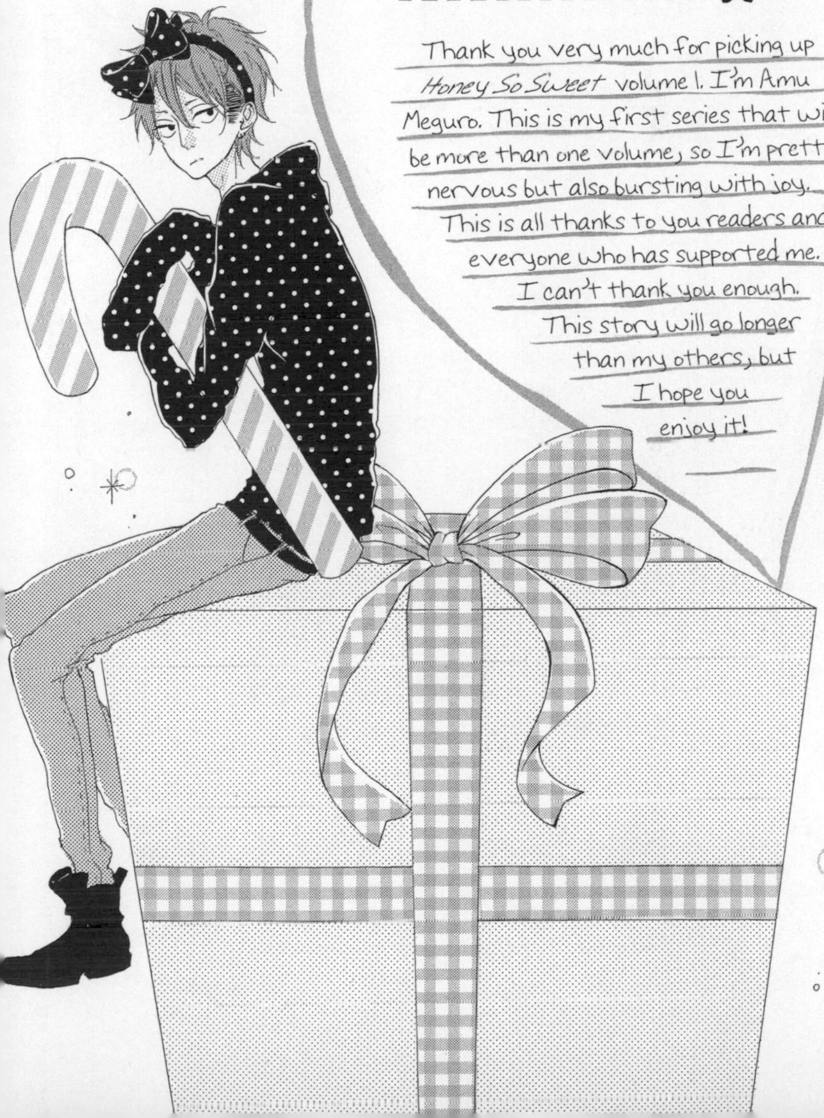

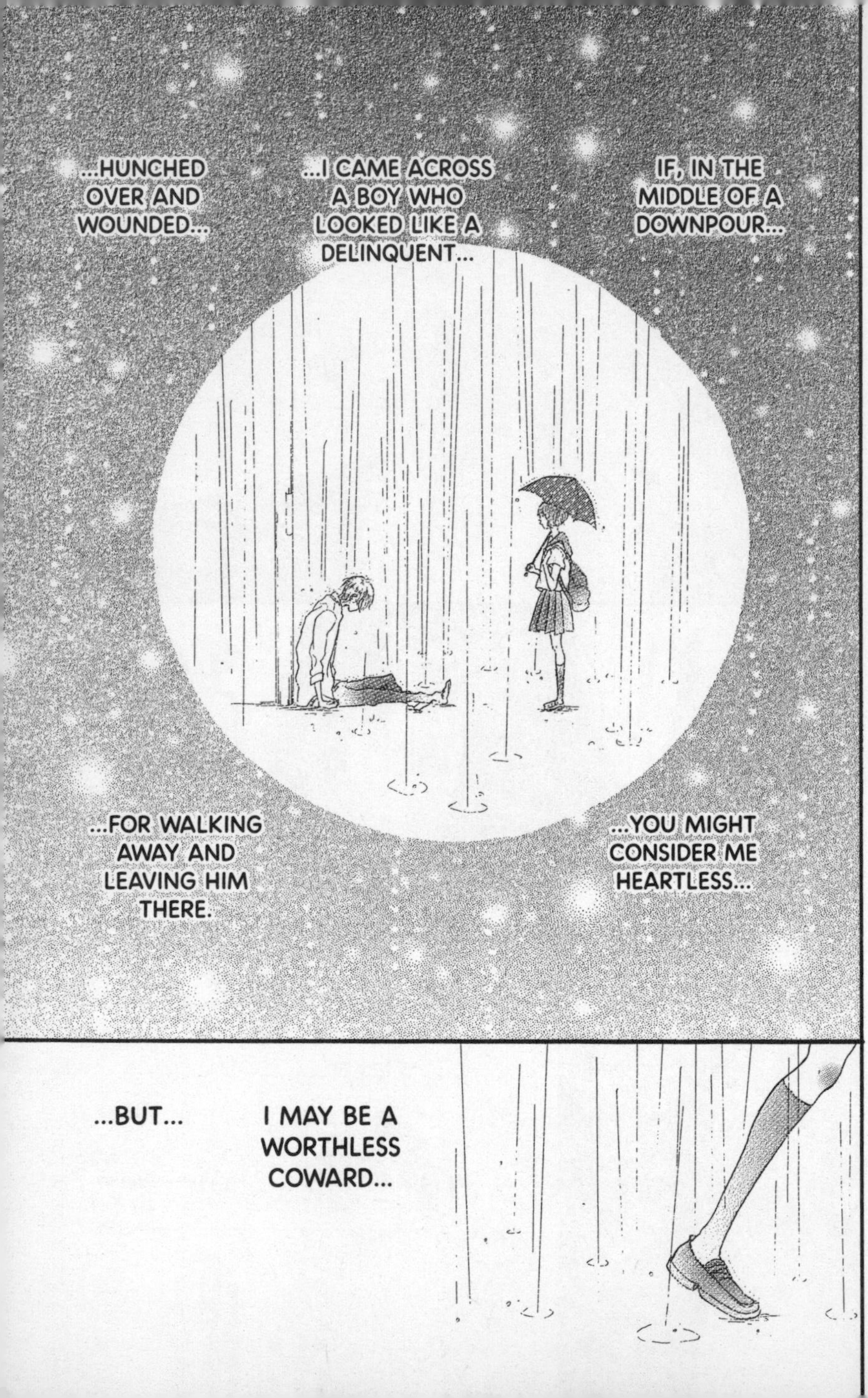
IF, IN THE MIDDLE OF A DOWNPOUR...
...I CAME ACROSS A BOY WHO LOOKED LIKE A DELINQUENT...
...HUNCHED OVER AND WOUNDED...
...YOU MIGHT CONSIDER ME HEARTLESS...
...FOR WALKING AWAY AND LEAVING HIM THERE.
I MAY BE A WORTHLESS COWARD...
...BUT...

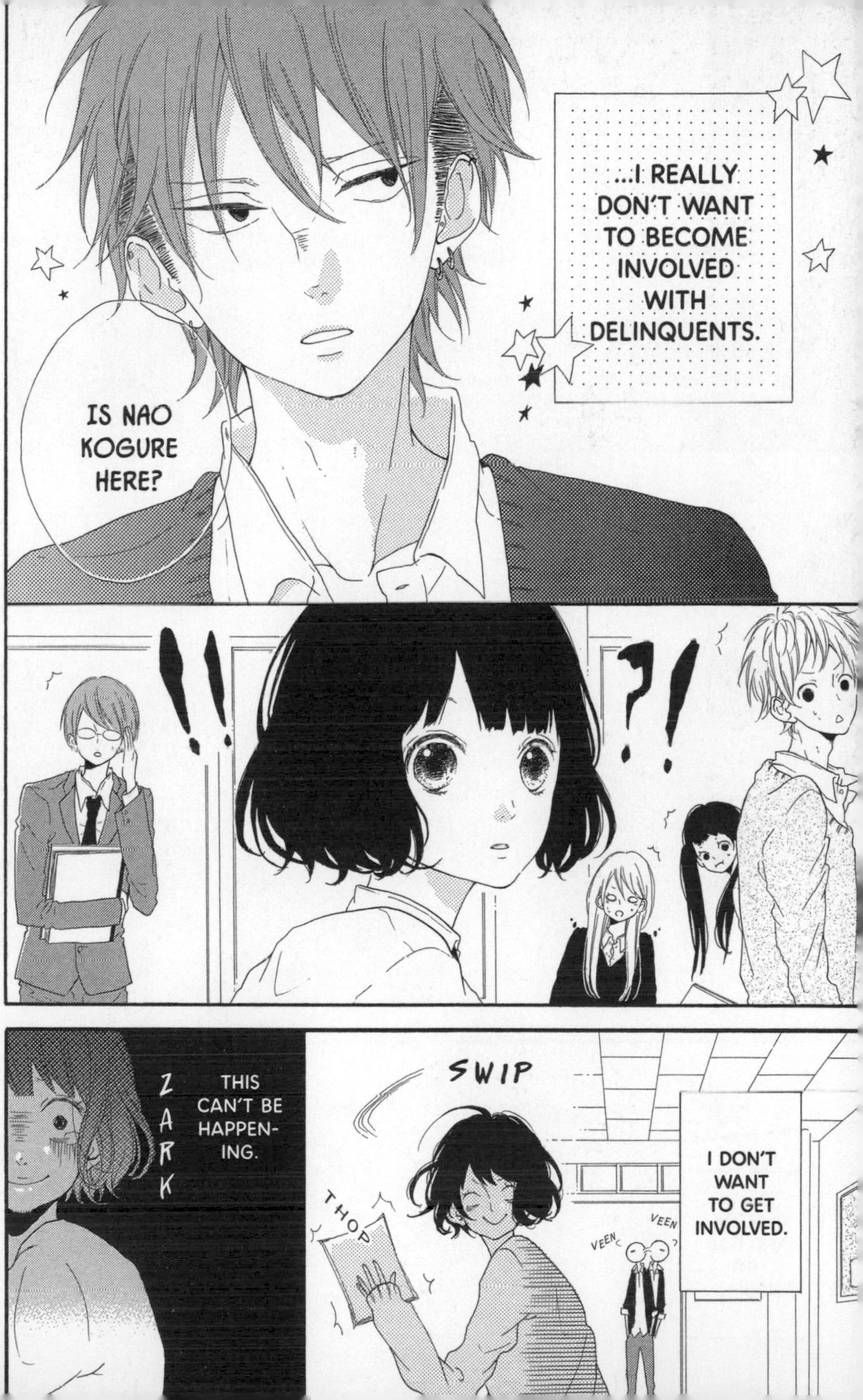
...I REALLY DON'T WANT TO BECOME INVOLVED WITH DELINQUENTS.
IS NAO KOGURE HERE?
?!
!!
SWIP
I DON'T WANT TO GET INVOLVED.
VEEN
VEEN
THOP
ZARK
THIS CAN'T BE HAPPENING.

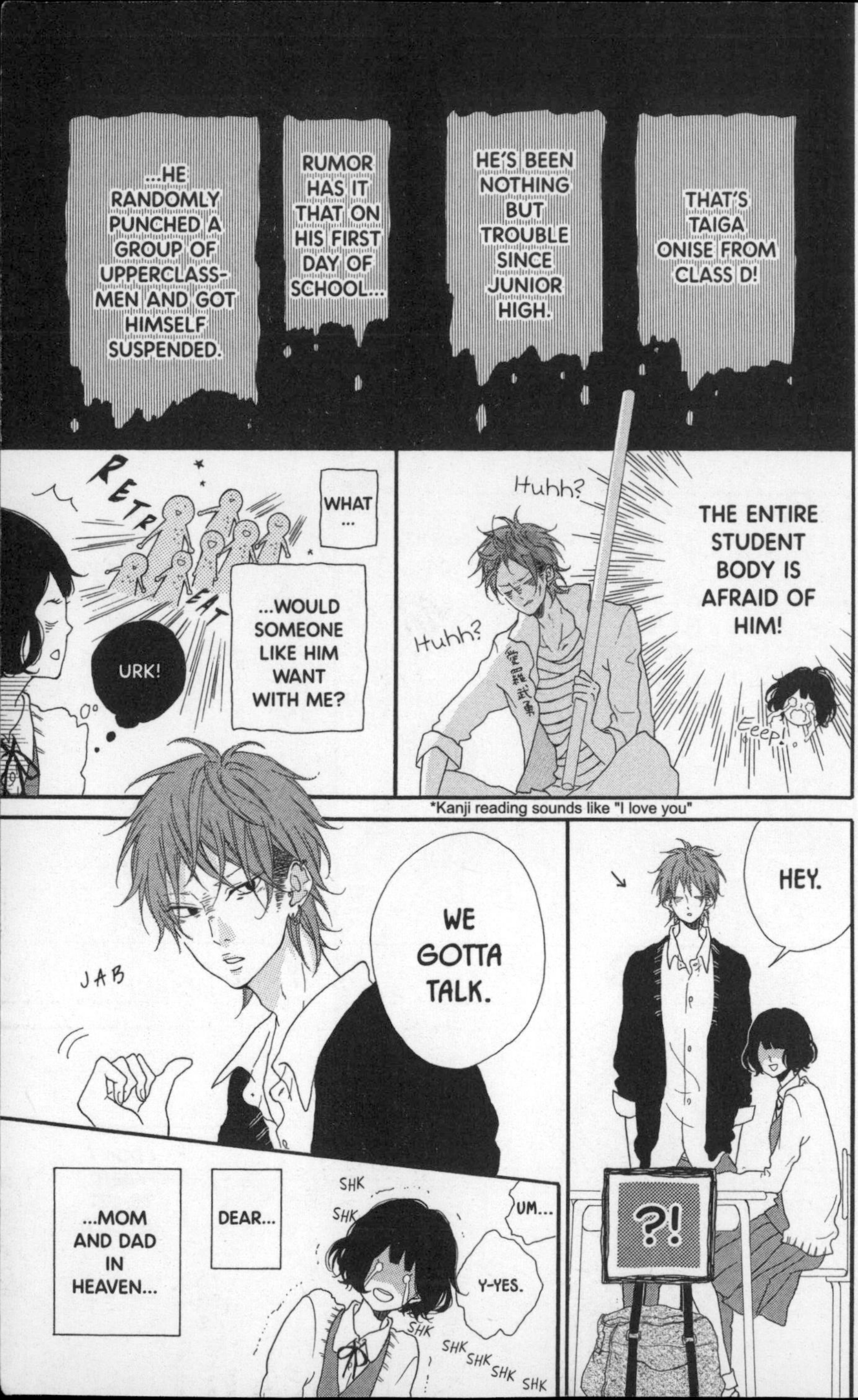
THAT'S TAIGA ONISE FROM CLASS D!
HE'S BEEN NOTHING BUT TROUBLE SINCE JUNIOR HIGH.
RUMOR HAS IT THAT ON HIS FIRST DAY OF SCHOOL...
...HE RANDOMLY PUNCHED A GROUP OF UPPERCLASS-MEN AND GOT HIMSELF SUSPENDED.
Huhh?
THE ENTIRE STUDENT BODY IS AFRAID OF HIM!
Huhh?
Eeep!
WHAT...
...WOULD SOMEONE LIKE HIM WANT WITH ME?
RETREAT
URK!
*Kanji reading sounds like "I love you"
HEY.
?!
WE GOTTA TALK.
JAB
UM...
Y-YES.
SHK SHK SHK SHK SHK SHK SHK
DEAR...
...MOM AND DAD IN HEAVEN...

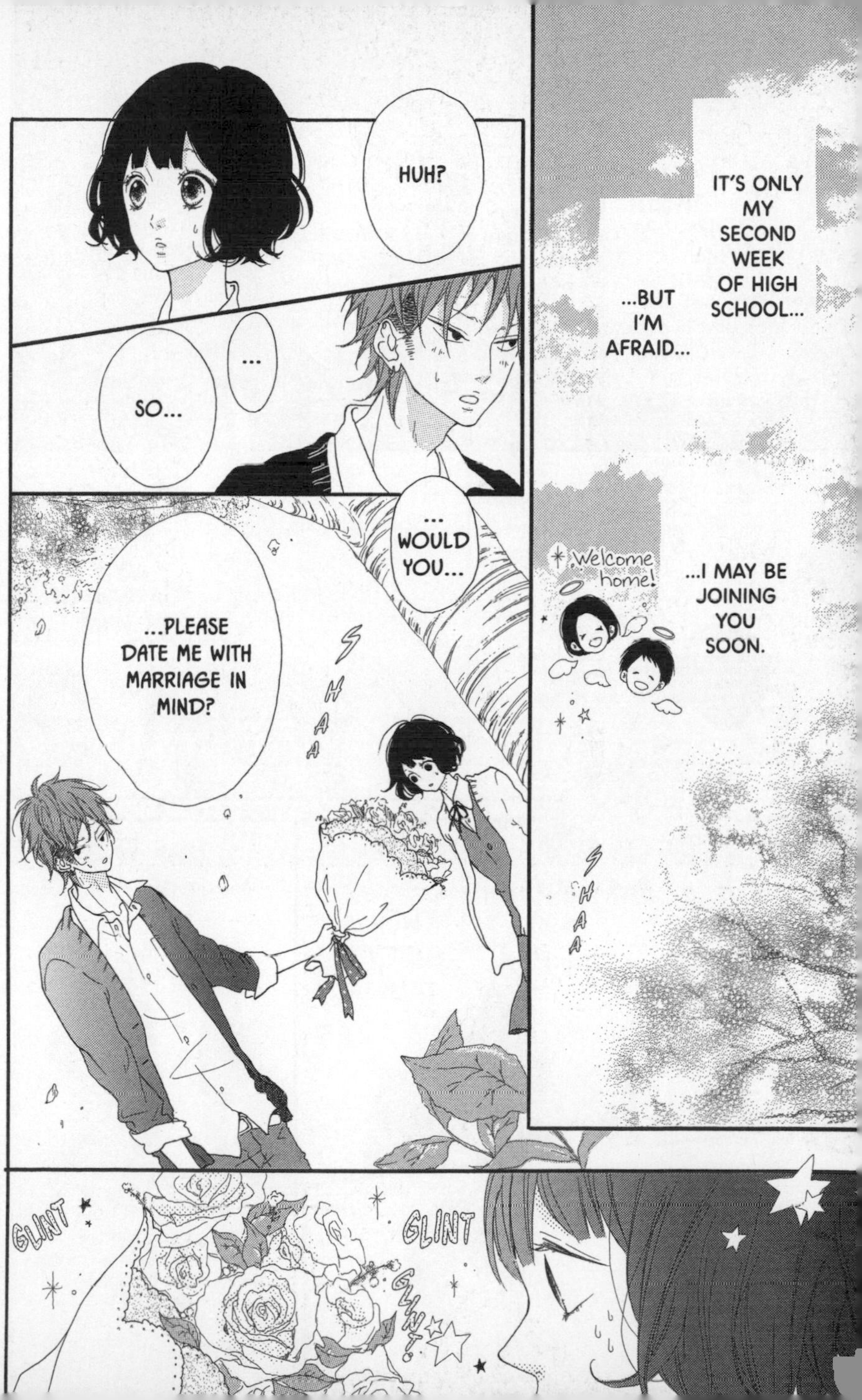
IT'S ONLY MY SECOND WEEK OF HIGH SCHOOL...
...BUT I'M AFRAID...
Welcome home!
...I MAY BE JOINING YOU SOON.
SHAA
HUH?
...
SO...
... WOULD YOU...
...PLEASE DATE ME WITH MARRIAGE IN MIND?
SHAA
GLINT
GLINT!
GLINT

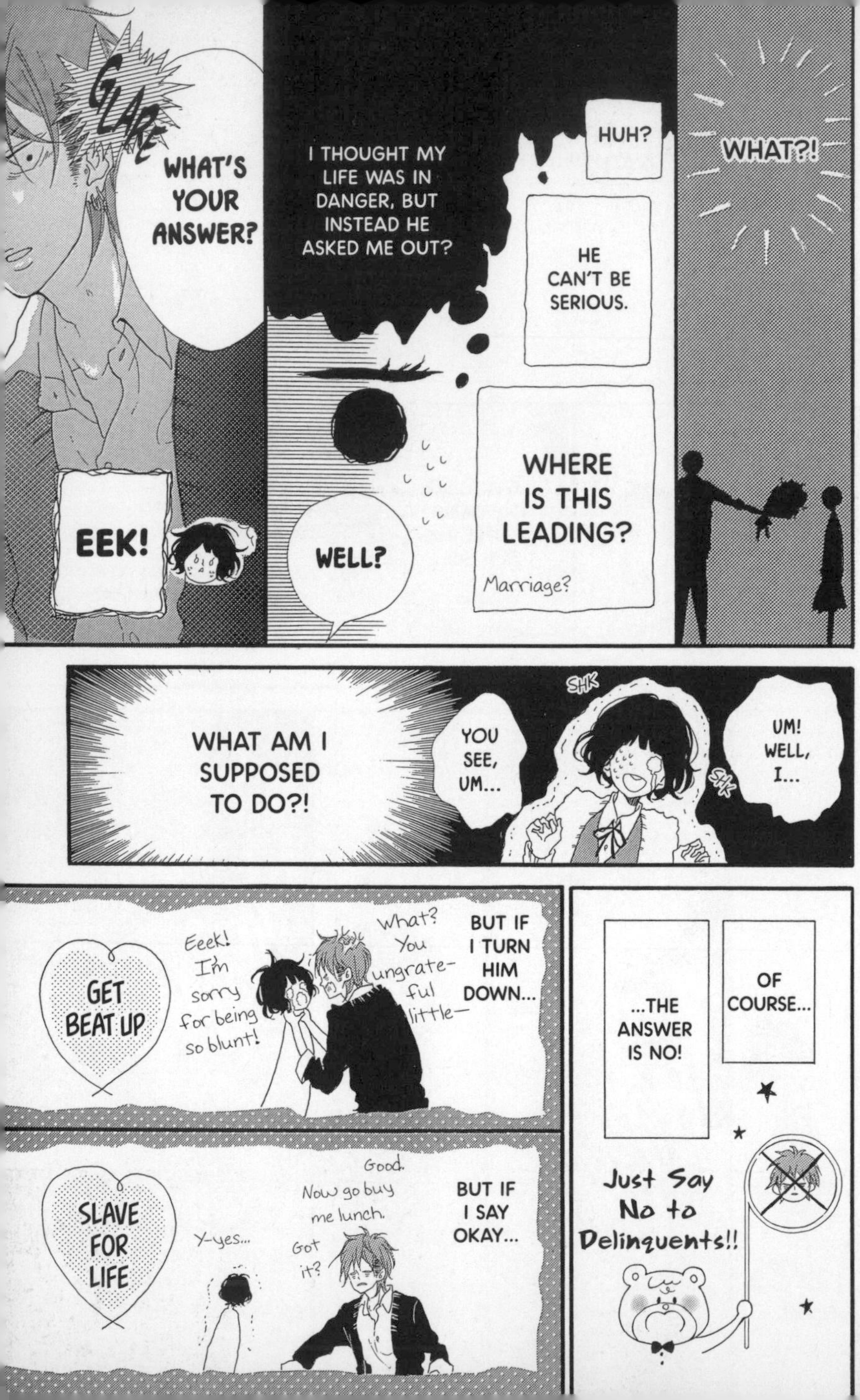
WHAT?!
HUH?
I THOUGHT MY LIFE WAS IN DANGER, BUT INSTEAD HE ASKED ME OUT?
HE CAN'T BE SERIOUS.
WHERE IS THIS LEADING?
Marriage?
WELL?
WHAT'S YOUR ANSWER?
GLARE
EEK!
UM! WELL, I...
SHK
SHK
YOU SEE, UM...
WHAT AM I SUPPOSED TO DO?!
OF COURSE...
...THE ANSWER IS NO!
Just Say No to Delinquents!!
BUT IF I TURN HIM DOWN...
What? You ungrate-ful little—
Eeek! I'm sorry for being so blunt!
GET BEAT UP
BUT IF I SAY OKAY...
Good.
Now go buy me lunch.
Got it?
Y-yes...
SLAVE FOR LIFE

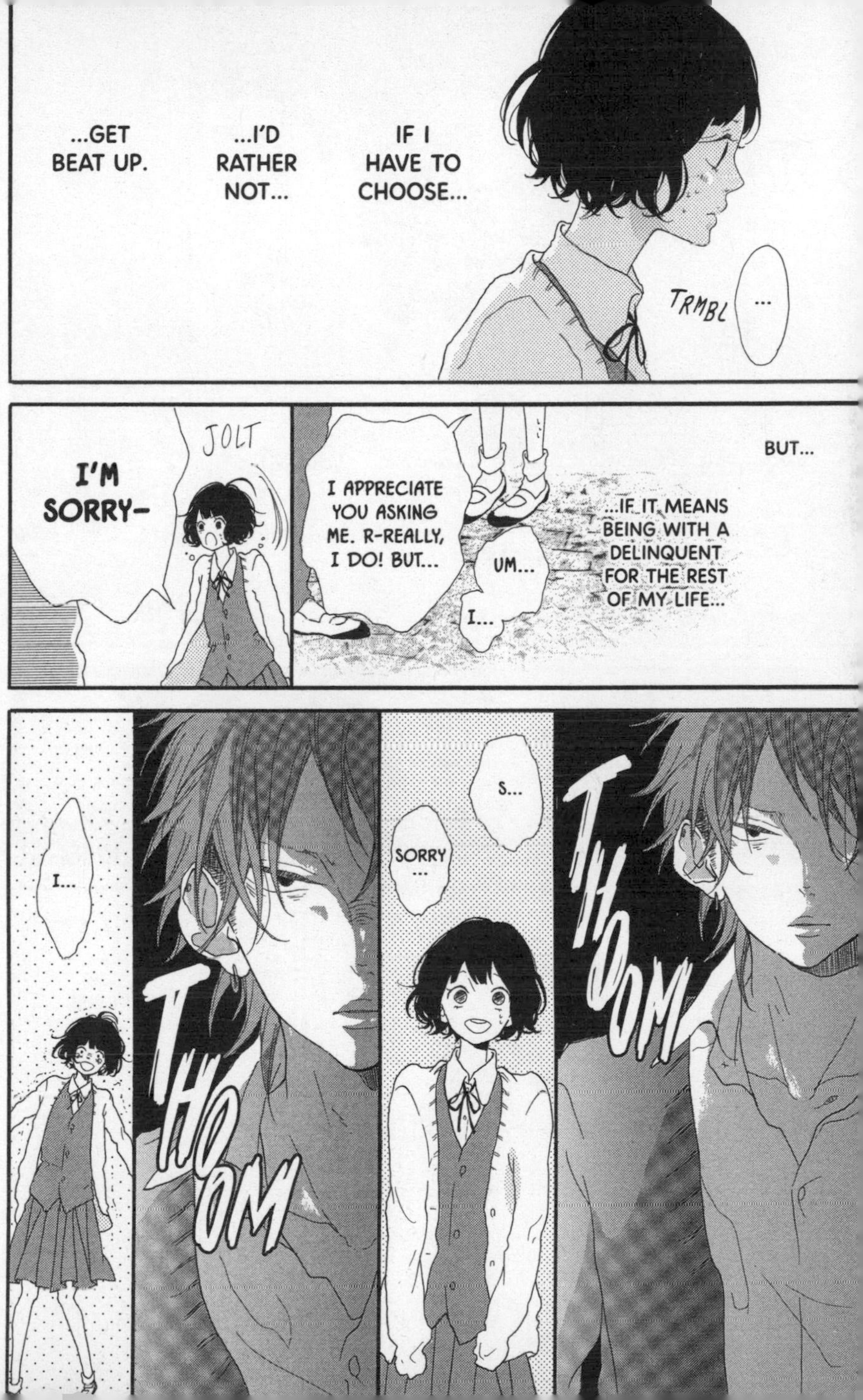
IF I HAVE TO CHOOSE...
...I'D RATHER NOT...
...GET BEAT UP.
TRMBL
...
BUT...
...IF IT MEANS BEING WITH A DELINQUENT FOR THE REST OF MY LIFE...
UM...
I APPRECIATE YOU ASKING ME. R-REALLY, I DO! BUT...
I...
JOLT
I'M SORRY–
THOOM
S...
SORRY...
THOOM
I...

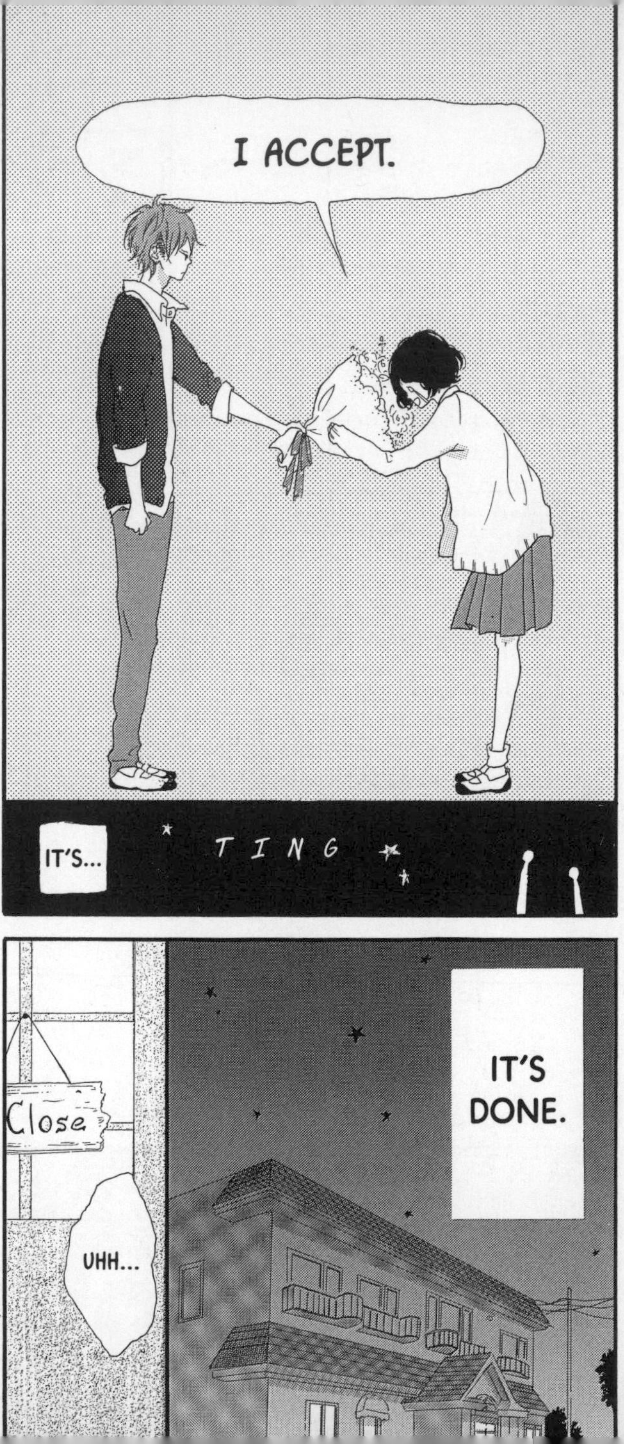
I ACCEPT.
TING
IT'S...
IT'S DONE.
Close
UHH...
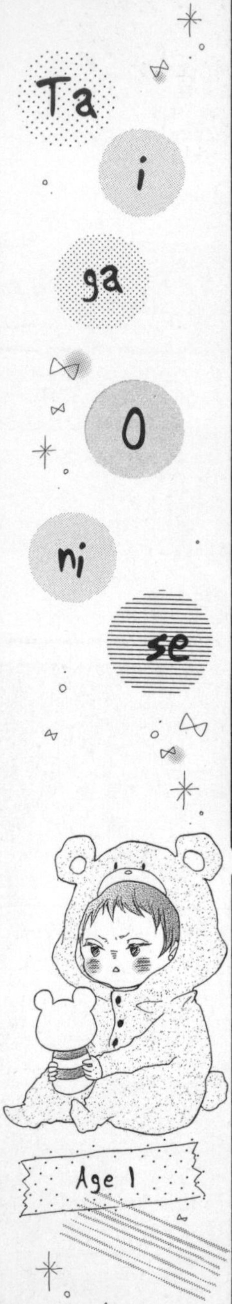
Ta i ga O ni se
Age 1

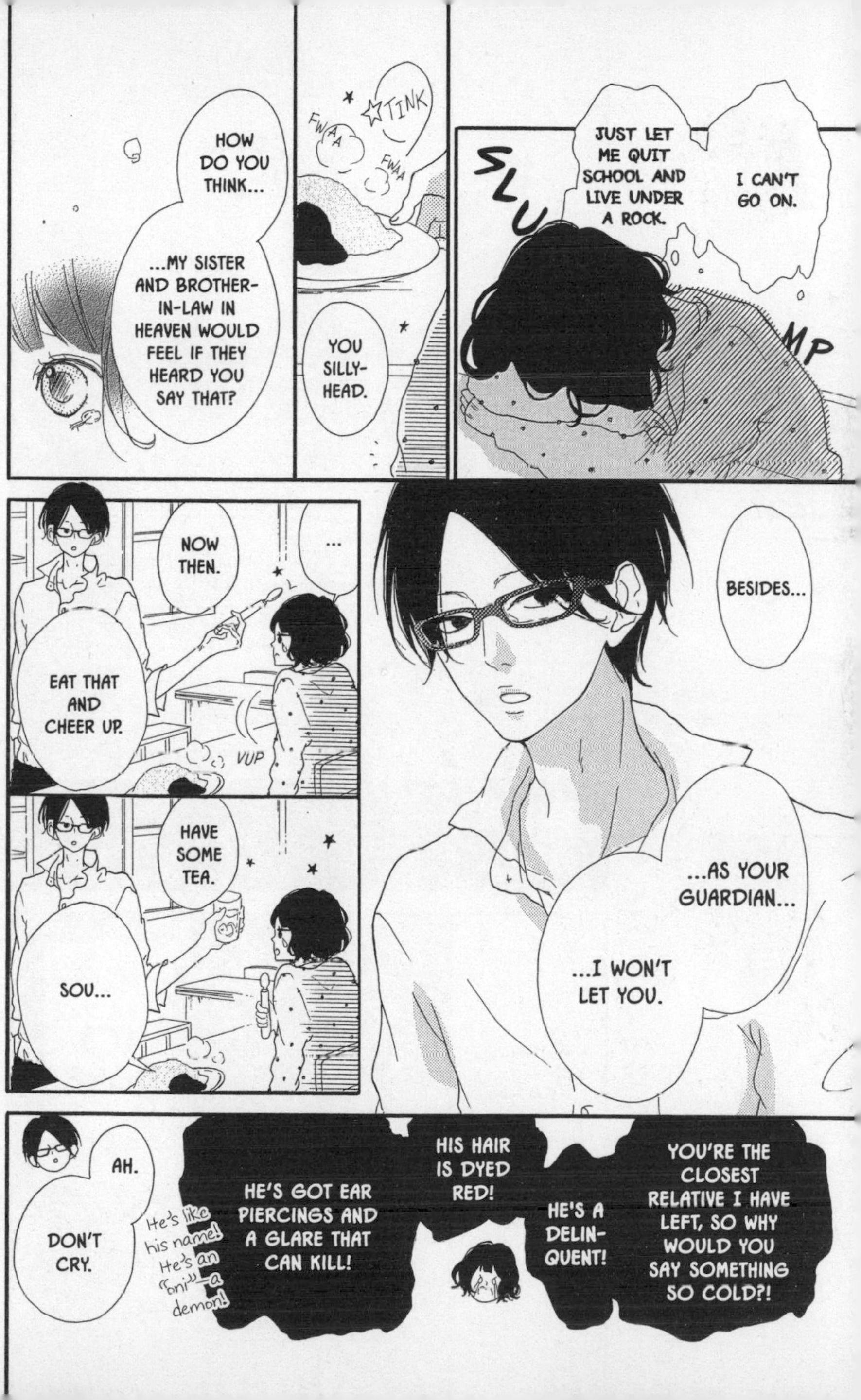
I CAN'T GO ON.
JUST LET ME QUIT SCHOOL AND LIVE UNDER A ROCK.
SLUMP
TINK
FWAA
FWAA
YOU SILLY-HEAD.
HOW DO YOU THINK...
...MY SISTER AND BROTHER-IN-LAW IN HEAVEN WOULD FEEL IF THEY HEARD YOU SAY THAT?
BESIDES...
...AS YOUR GUARDIAN...
...I WON'T LET YOU.
...
NOW THEN.
EAT THAT AND CHEER UP.
VUP
HAVE SOME TEA.
SOU...
YOU'RE THE CLOSEST RELATIVE I HAVE LEFT, SO WHY WOULD YOU SAY SOMETHING SO COLD?!
HE'S A DELIN-QUENT!
HIS HAIR IS DYED RED!
HE'S GOT EAR PIERCINGS AND A GLARE THAT CAN KILL!
He's like his name! He's an "oni"—a demon!
AH.
DON'T CRY.

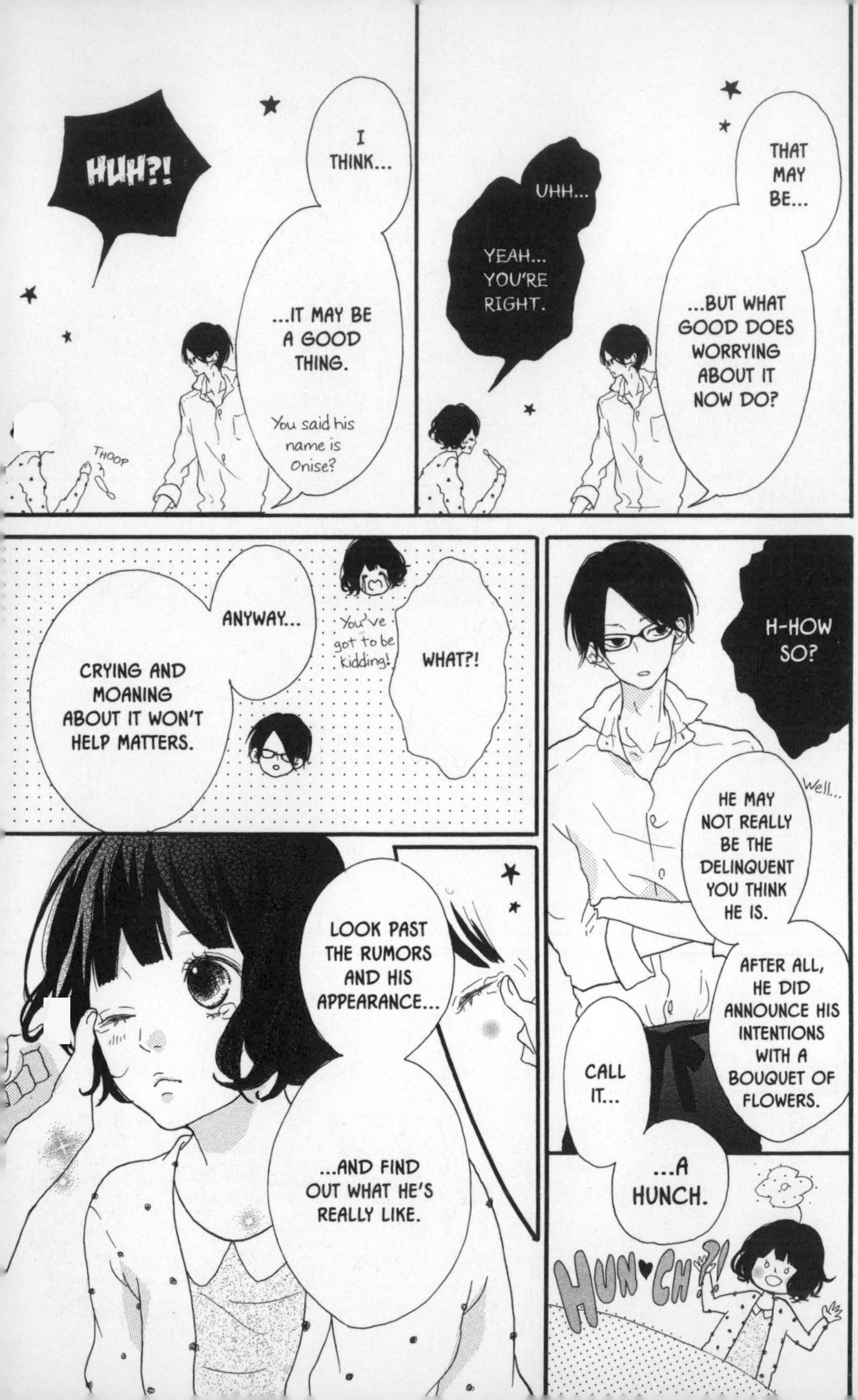
THAT MAY BE...
...BUT WHAT GOOD DOES WORRYING ABOUT IT NOW DO?
UHH...
YEAH... YOU'RE RIGHT.
I THINK...
...IT MAY BE A GOOD THING.
You said his name is Onise?
HUH?!
THOOP
H-HOW SO?
Well...
HE MAY NOT REALLY BE THE DELINQUENT YOU THINK HE IS.
AFTER ALL, HE DID ANNOUNCE HIS INTENTIONS WITH A BOUQUET OF FLOWERS.
CALL IT...
...A HUNCH.
HUN♥CH?!
WHAT?!
You've got to be kidding!
ANYWAY...
CRYING AND MOANING ABOUT IT WON'T HELP MATTERS.
LOOK PAST THE RUMORS AND HIS APPEARANCE...
...AND FIND OUT WHAT HE'S REALLY LIKE.

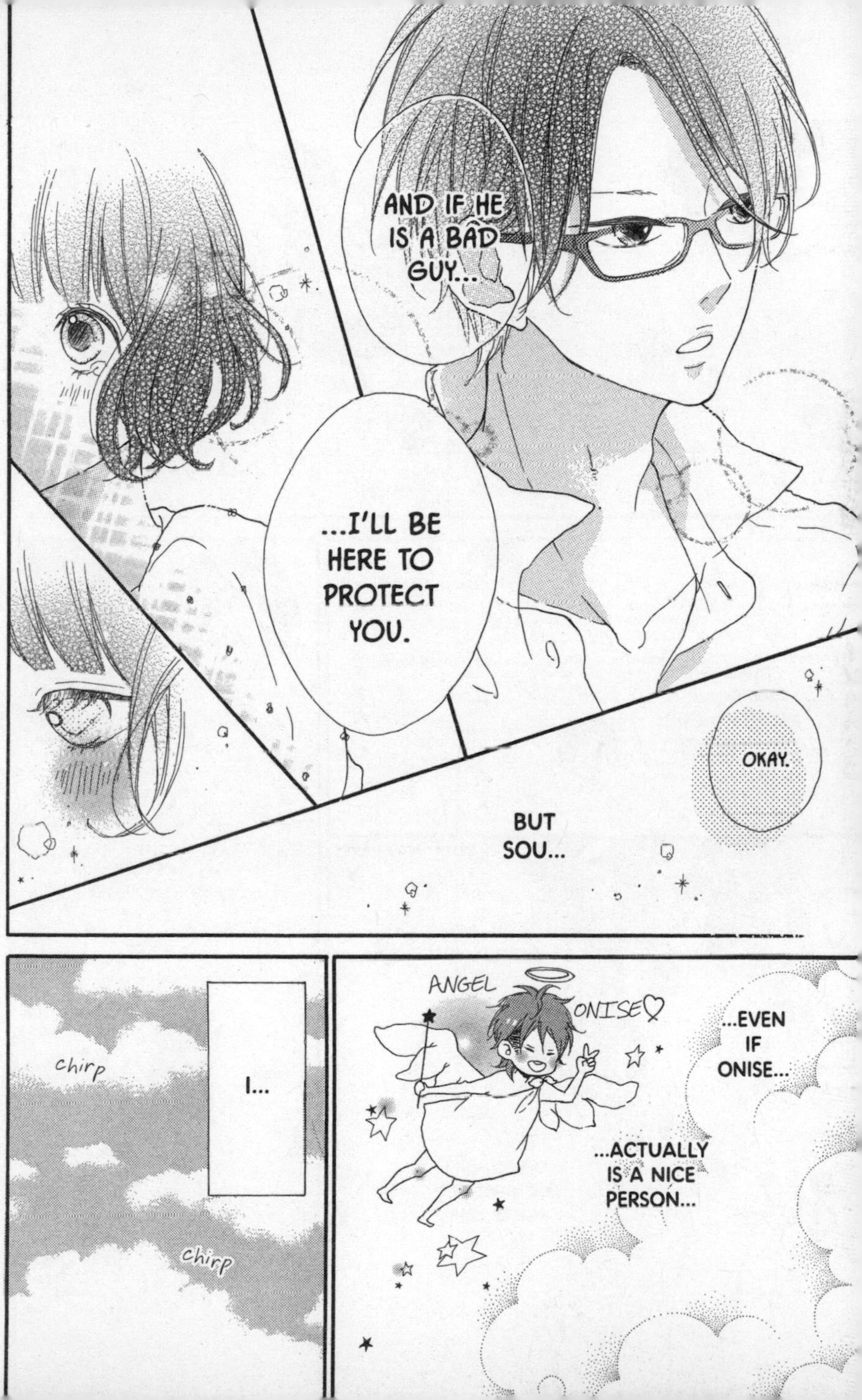
AND IF HE IS A BAD GUY...
...I'LL BE HERE TO PROTECT YOU.
OKAY.
BUT SOU...
ANGEL ONISE♡
...EVEN IF ONISE...
...ACTUALLY IS A NICE PERSON...
chirp
I...
chirp

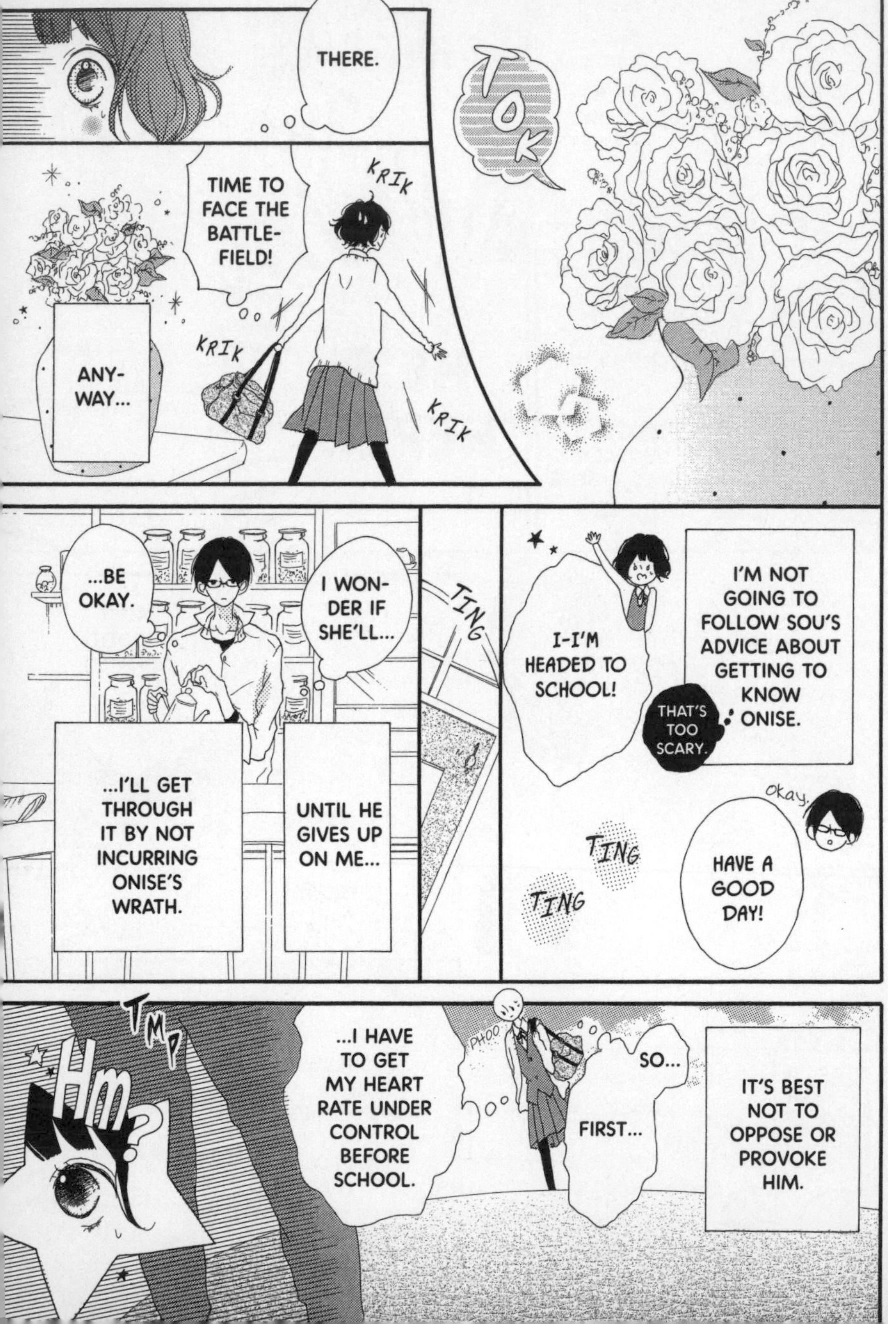
TOK
THERE.
KRIK
TIME TO FACE THE BATTLE-FIELD!
ANY-WAY...
KRIK
KRIK
I'M NOT GOING TO FOLLOW SOU'S ADVICE ABOUT GETTING TO KNOW ONISE.
THAT'S TOO SCARY.
I-I'M HEADED TO SCHOOL!
Okay.
HAVE A GOOD DAY!
TING
TING
TING
I WON-DER IF SHE'LL...
...BE OKAY.
UNTIL HE GIVES UP ON ME...
...I'LL GET THROUGH IT BY NOT INCURRING ONISE'S WRATH.
IT'S BEST NOT TO OPPOSE OR PROVOKE HIM.
SO...
FIRST...
PHOO
...I HAVE TO GET MY HEART RATE UNDER CONTROL BEFORE SCHOOL.
TMP
Hm?

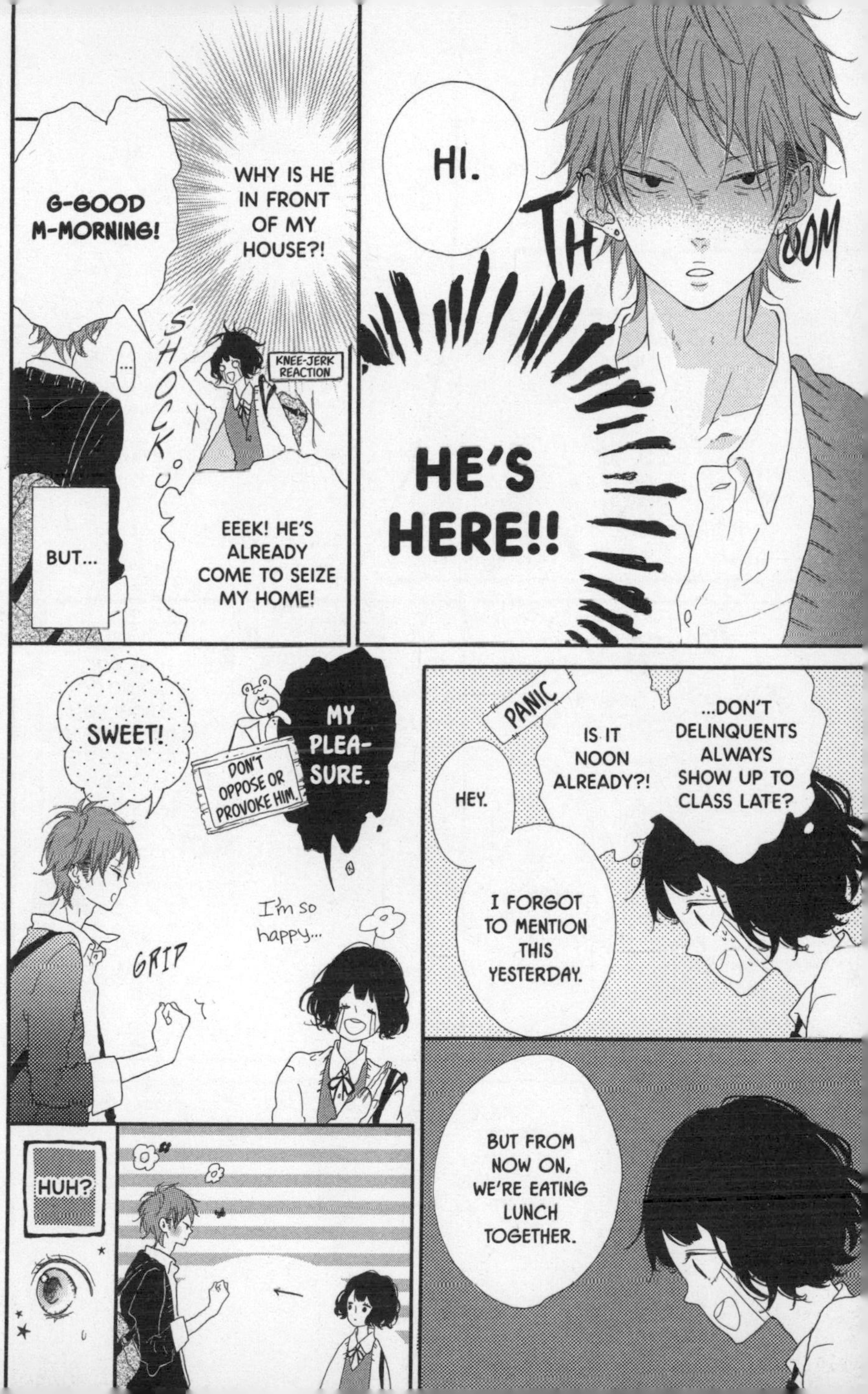
HI.
THOOM
HE'S HERE!!
WHY IS HE IN FRONT OF MY HOUSE?!
G-GOOD M-MORNING!
SHOCK
KNEE-JERK REACTION
...
EEEK! HE'S ALREADY COME TO SEIZE MY HOME!
BUT...
...DON'T DELINQUENTS ALWAYS SHOW UP TO CLASS LATE?
IS IT NOON ALREADY?!
PANIC
HEY.
I FORGOT TO MENTION THIS YESTERDAY.
MY PLEA-SURE.
DON'T OPPOSE OR PROVOKE HIM.
SWEET!
I'm so happy...
GRIP
BUT FROM NOW ON, WE'RE EATING LUNCH TOGETHER.
HUH?

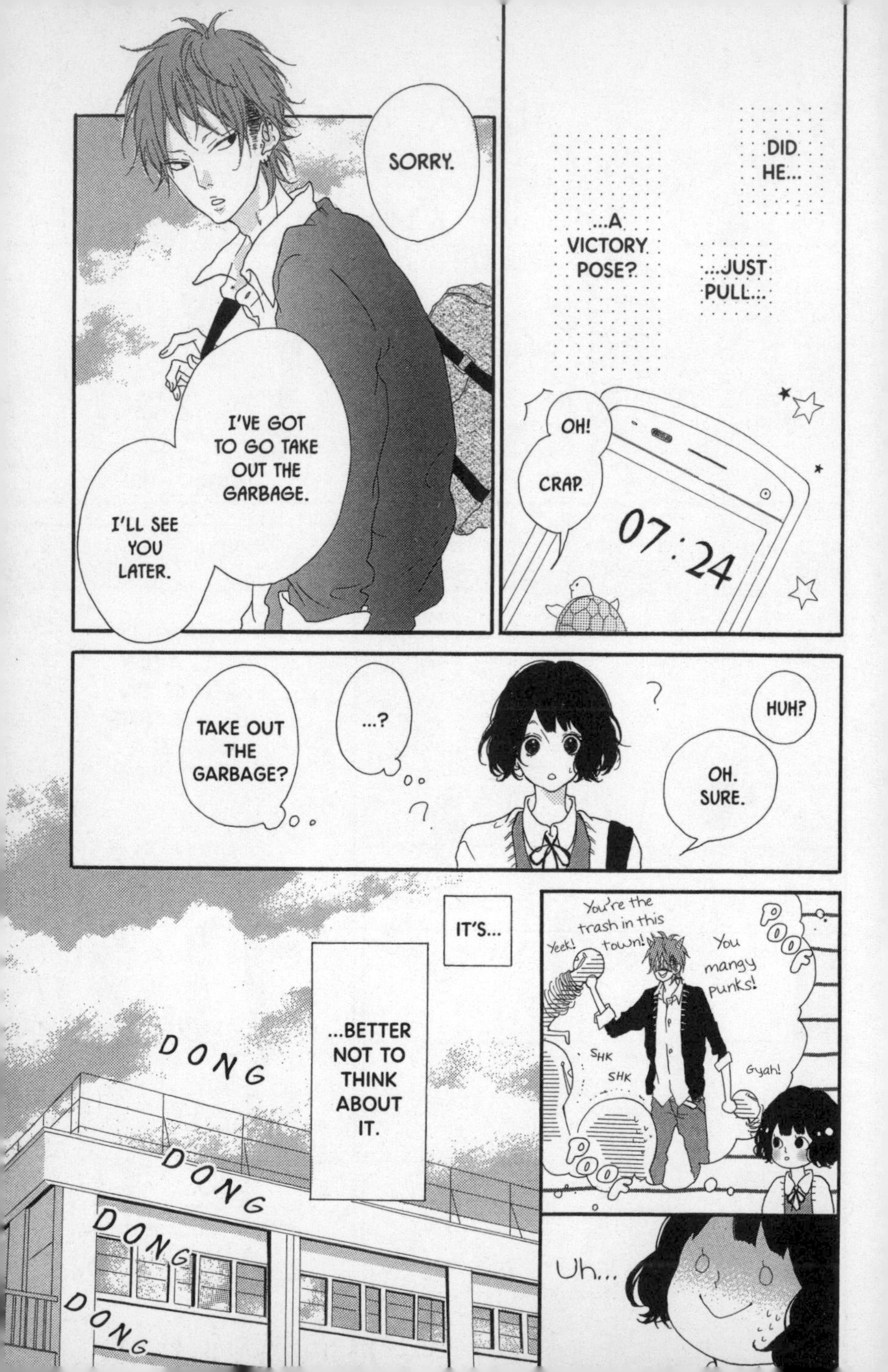
DID HE...
...JUST PULL...
...A VICTORY POSE?
OH!
CRAP.
07:24
SORRY.
I'VE GOT TO GO TAKE OUT THE GARBAGE.
I'LL SEE YOU LATER.
HUH?
OH. SURE.
...?
TAKE OUT THE GARBAGE?
POOF
You're the trash in this town!
You mangy punks!
Yeek!
SHK
SHK
Gyah!
POOF
Uh...
IT'S...
...BETTER NOT TO THINK ABOUT IT.
DONG
DONG
DONG
DONG

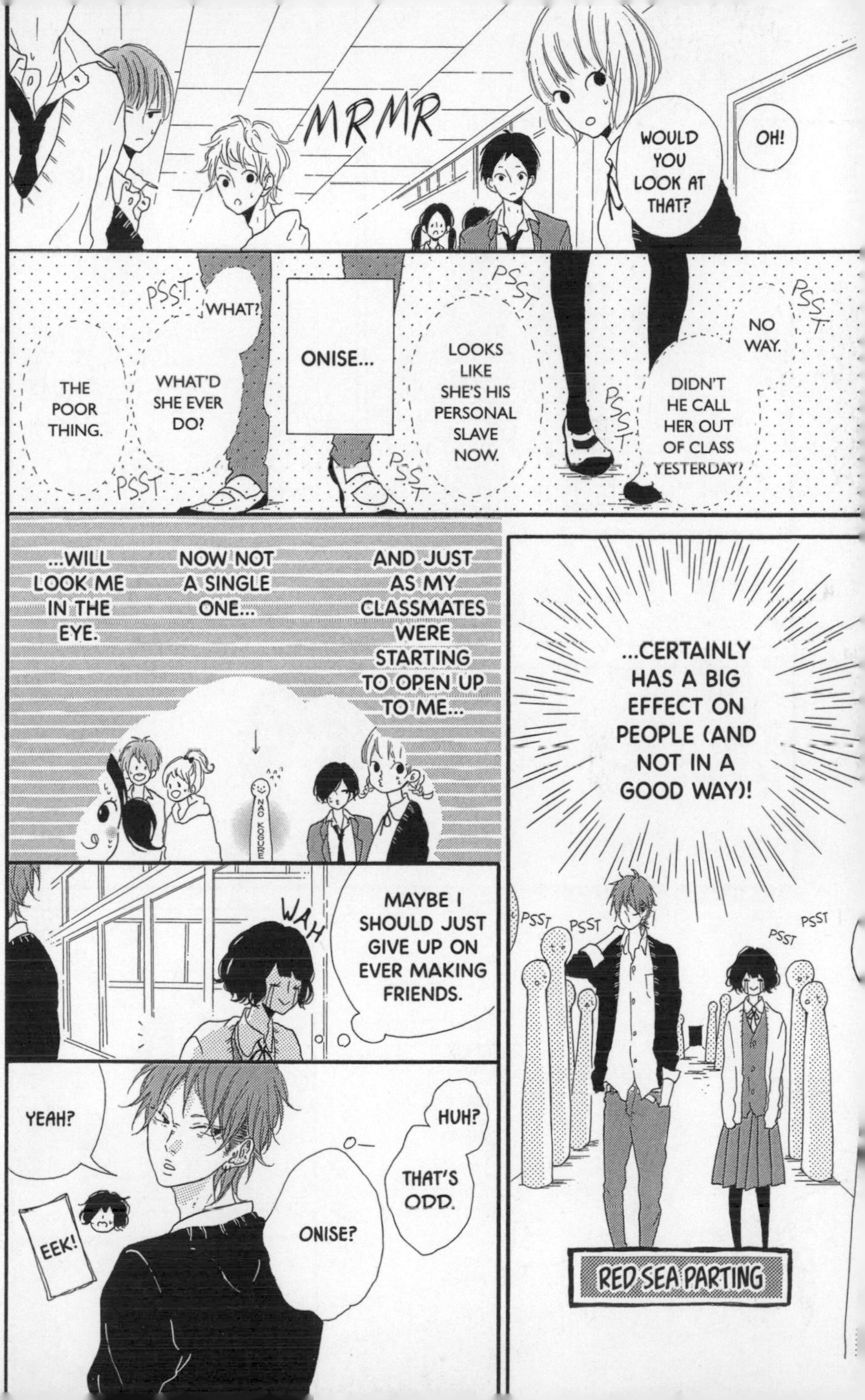
OH!
WOULD YOU LOOK AT THAT?
MRMR
PSST
NO WAY.
PSST
DIDN'T HE CALL HER OUT OF CLASS YESTERDAY?
PSST
LOOKS LIKE SHE'S HIS PERSONAL SLAVE NOW.
PSST
ONISE...
PSST
WHAT?
WHAT'D SHE EVER DO?
THE POOR THING.
PSST
...CERTAINLY HAS A BIG EFFECT ON PEOPLE (AND NOT IN A GOOD WAY)!
PSST
PSST
PSST
PSST
RED SEA PARTING
AND JUST AS MY CLASSMATES WERE STARTING TO OPEN UP TO ME...
NOW NOT A SINGLE ONE...
...WILL LOOK ME IN THE EYE.
NAO KOGURE
MAYBE I SHOULD JUST GIVE UP ON EVER MAKING FRIENDS.
WAH
HUH?
THAT'S ODD.
ONISE?
YEAH?
EEK!

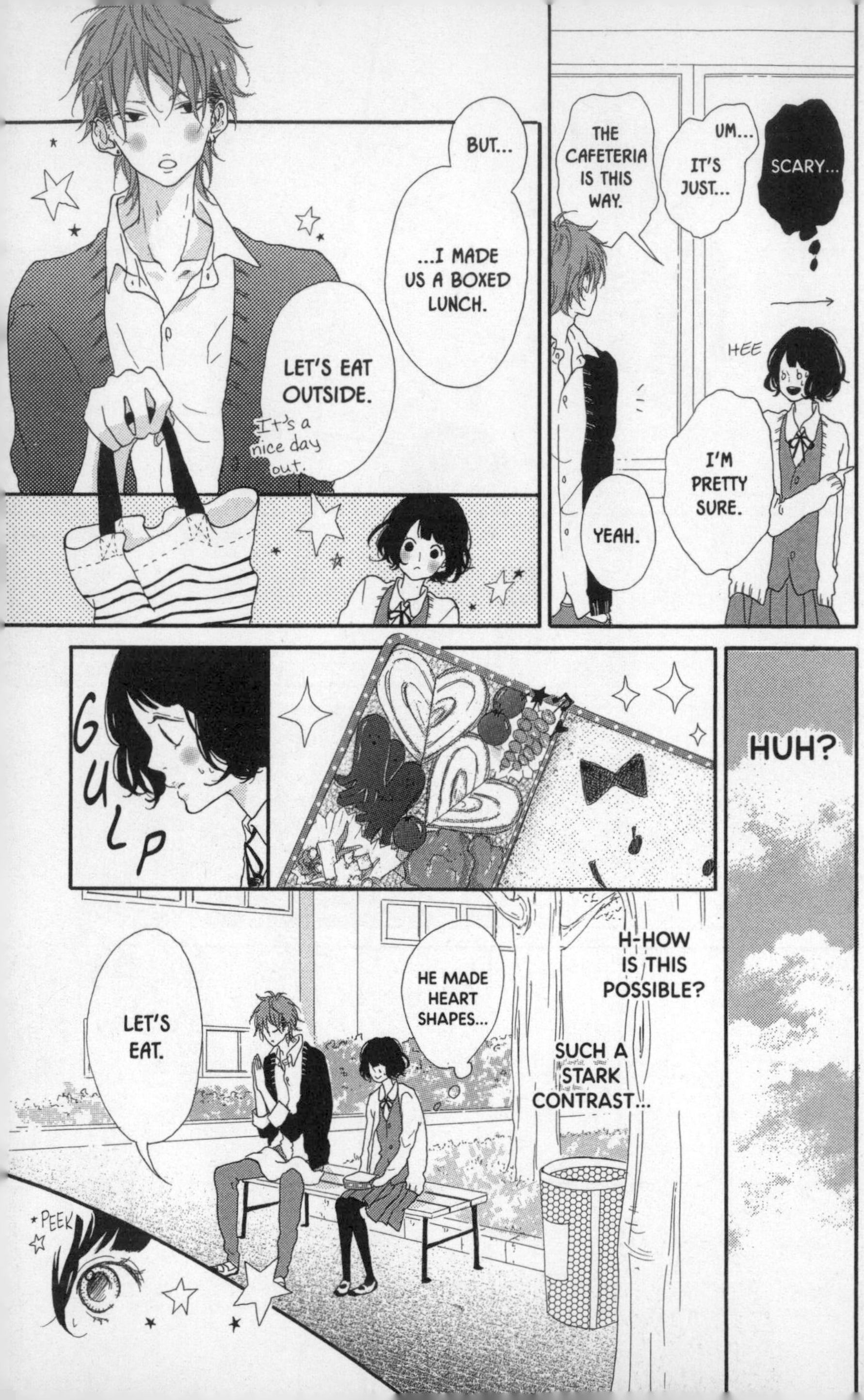
SCARY...
UM... IT'S JUST...
THE CAFETERIA IS THIS WAY.
HEE
I'M PRETTY SURE.
YEAH.
BUT...
...I MADE US A BOXED LUNCH.
LET'S EAT OUTSIDE.
It's a nice day out.
HUH?
GULP
H-HOW IS THIS POSSIBLE?
SUCH A STARK CONTRAST...
HE MADE HEART SHAPES...
LET'S EAT.
PEEK

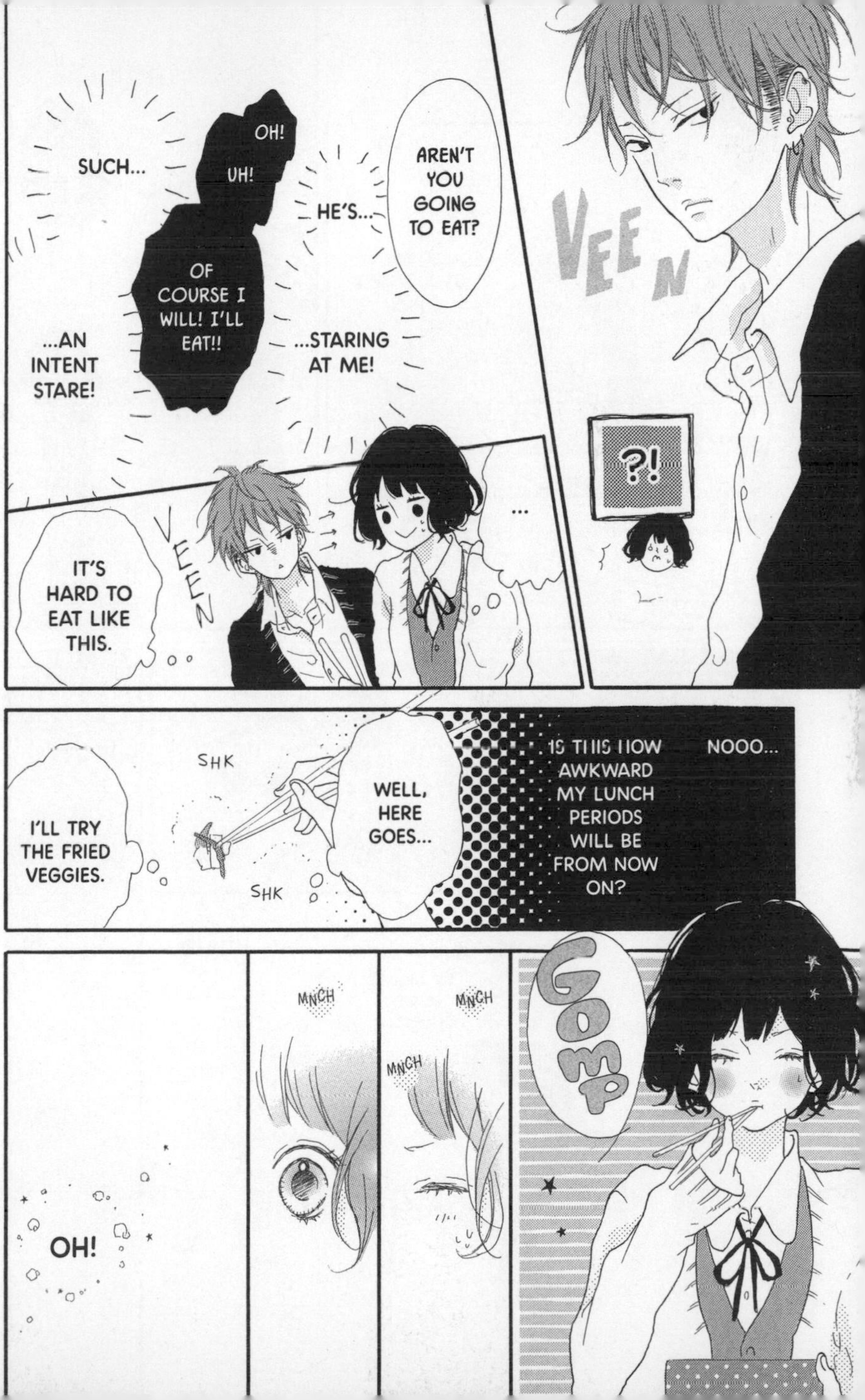
VEEN
?!
AREN'T YOU GOING TO EAT?
HE'S...
...STARING AT ME!
SUCH...
...AN INTENT STARE!
OH!
UH!
OF COURSE I WILL! I'LL EAT!!
...
VEEN
IT'S HARD TO EAT LIKE THIS.
NOOO...
IS THIS HOW AWKWARD MY LUNCH PERIODS WILL BE FROM NOW ON?
WELL, HERE GOES...
SHK
SHK
I'LL TRY THE FRIED VEGGIES.
GOMP
MNCH
MNCH
MNCH
OH!

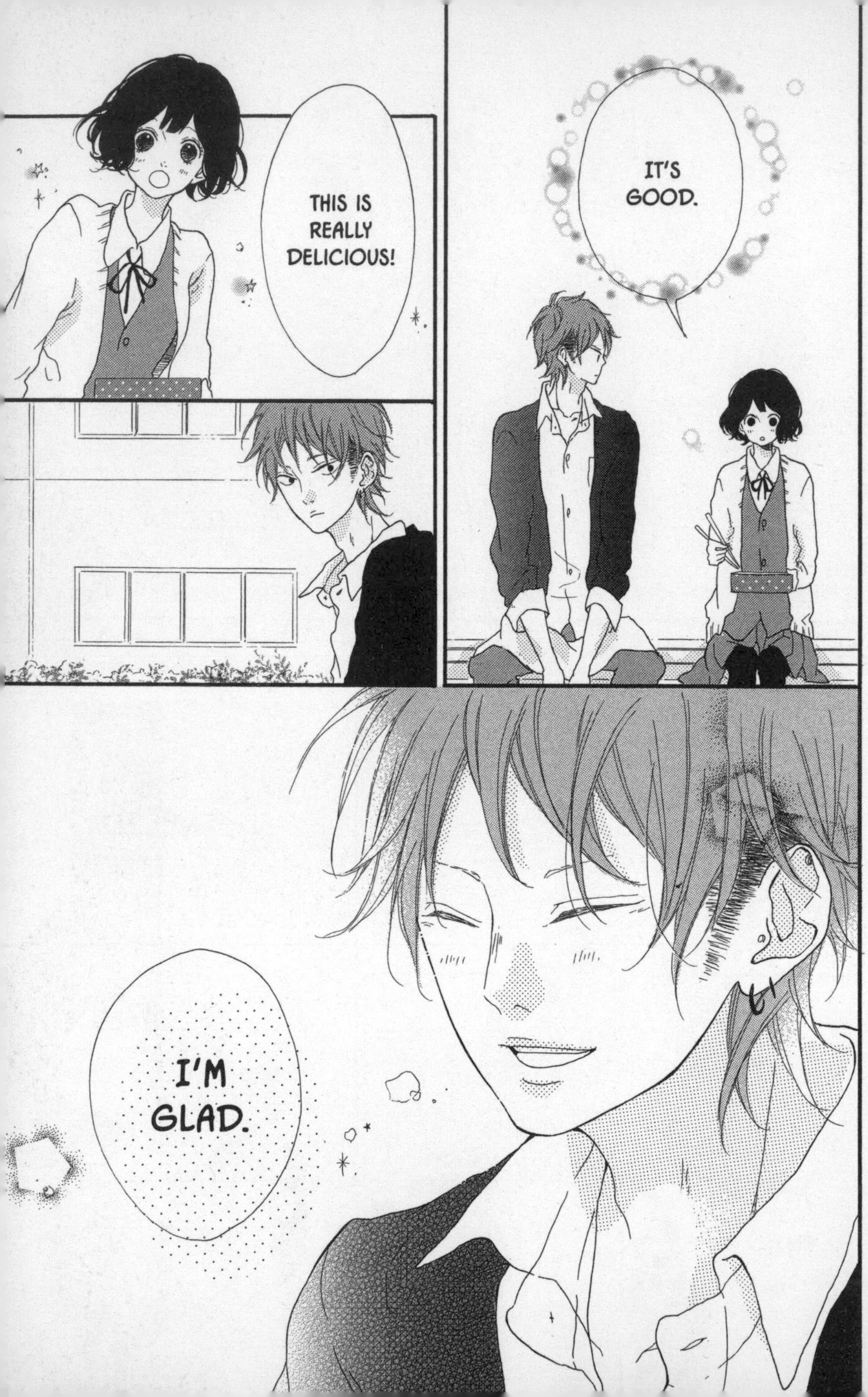
IT'S GOOD.
THIS IS REALLY DELICIOUS!
I'M GLAD.

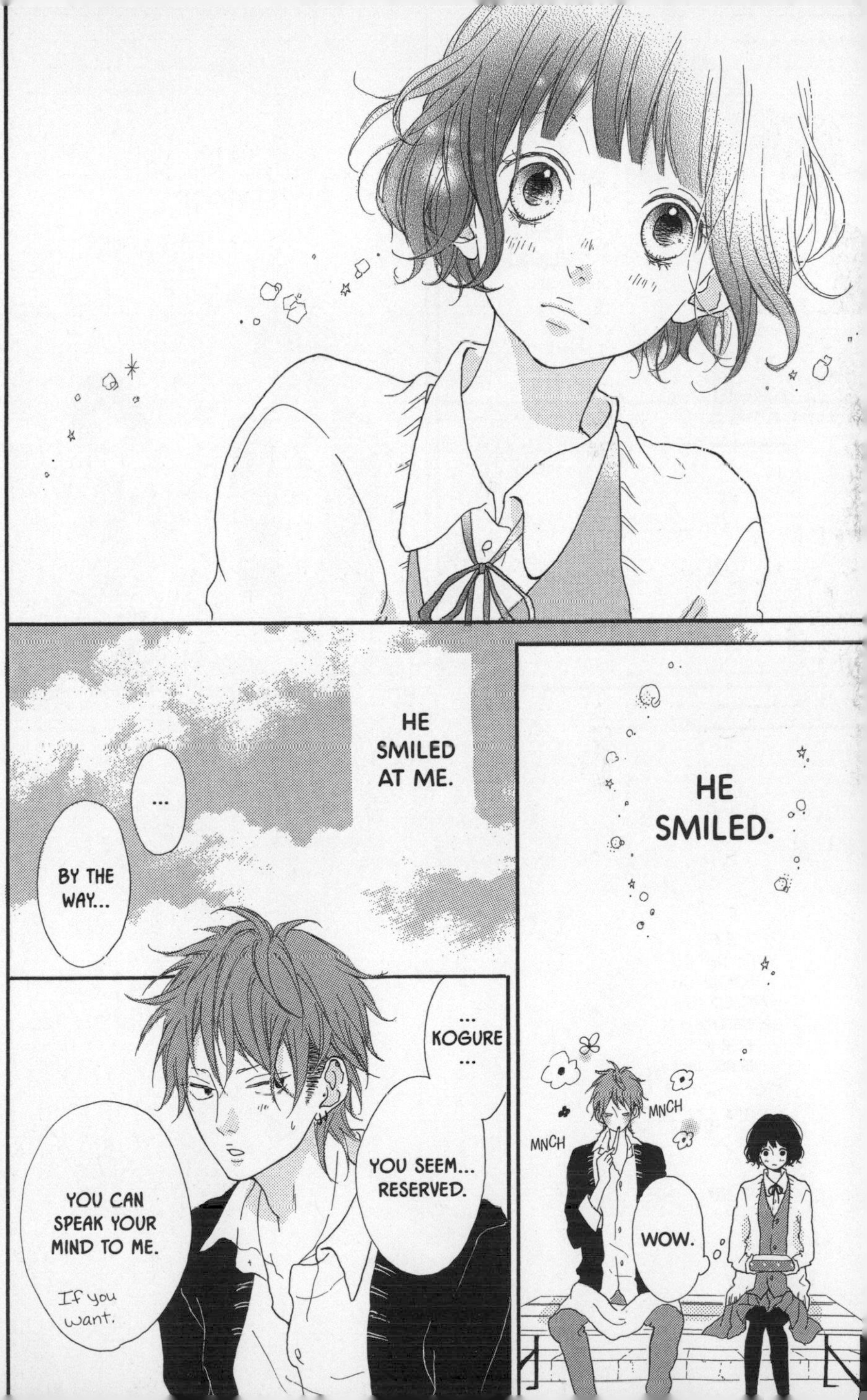
HE SMILED.
MNCH
MNCH
WOW.
HE SMILED AT ME.
...
BY THE WAY...
... KOGURE ...
YOU SEEM... RESERVED.
YOU CAN SPEAK YOUR MIND TO ME.
If you want.

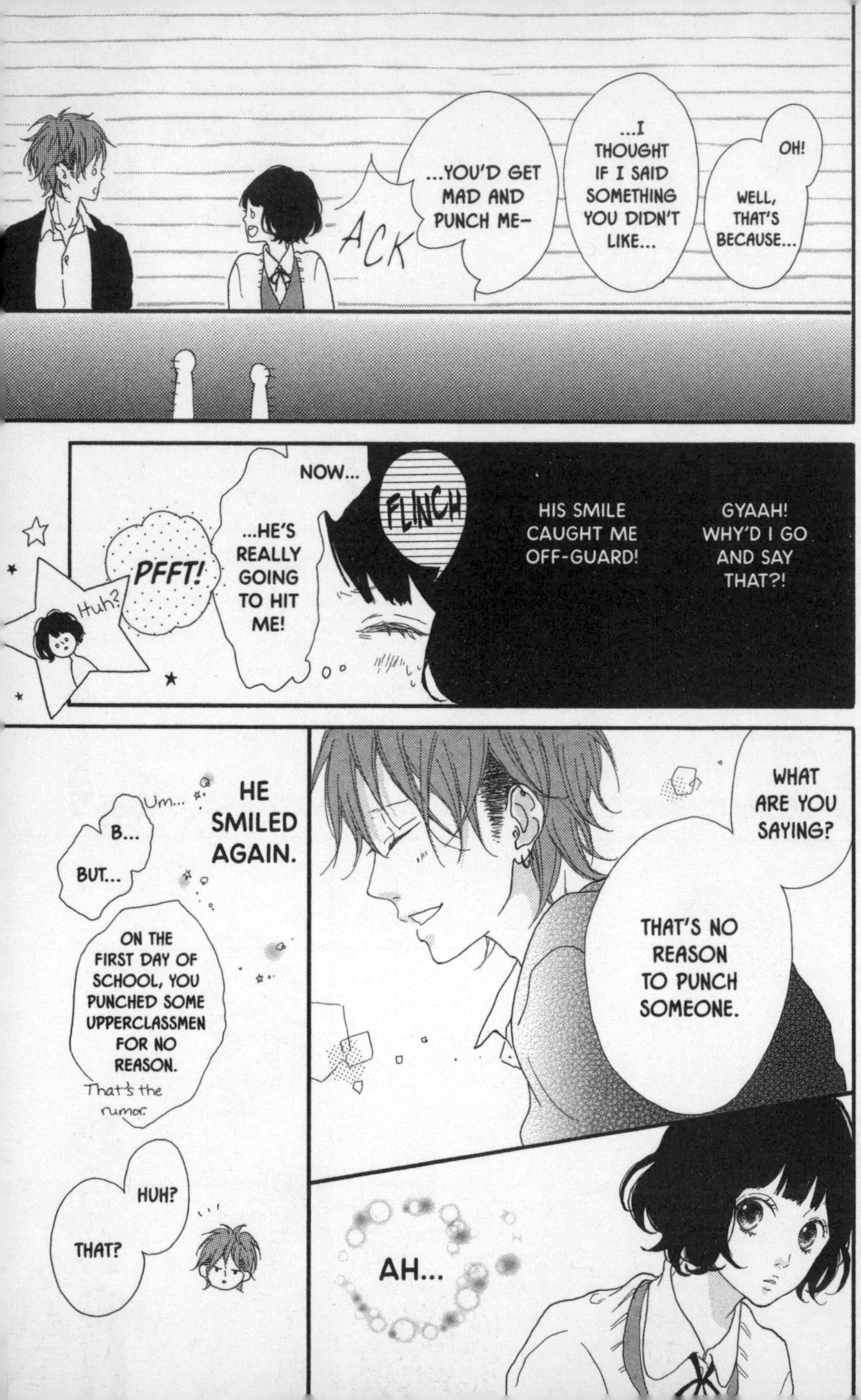
OH!
WELL, THAT'S BECAUSE...
...I THOUGHT IF I SAID SOMETHING YOU DIDN'T LIKE...
...YOU'D GET MAD AND PUNCH ME—
ACK
GYAAH! WHY'D I GO AND SAY THAT?!
HIS SMILE CAUGHT ME OFF-GUARD!
FLINCH
NOW...
...HE'S REALLY GOING TO HIT ME!
PFFT!
Huh?
WHAT ARE YOU SAYING?
THAT'S NO REASON TO PUNCH SOMEONE.
AH...
HE SMILED AGAIN.
Um...
B... BUT...
ON THE FIRST DAY OF SCHOOL, YOU PUNCHED SOME UPPERCLASSMEN FOR NO REASON.
That's the rumor.
HUH? THAT?

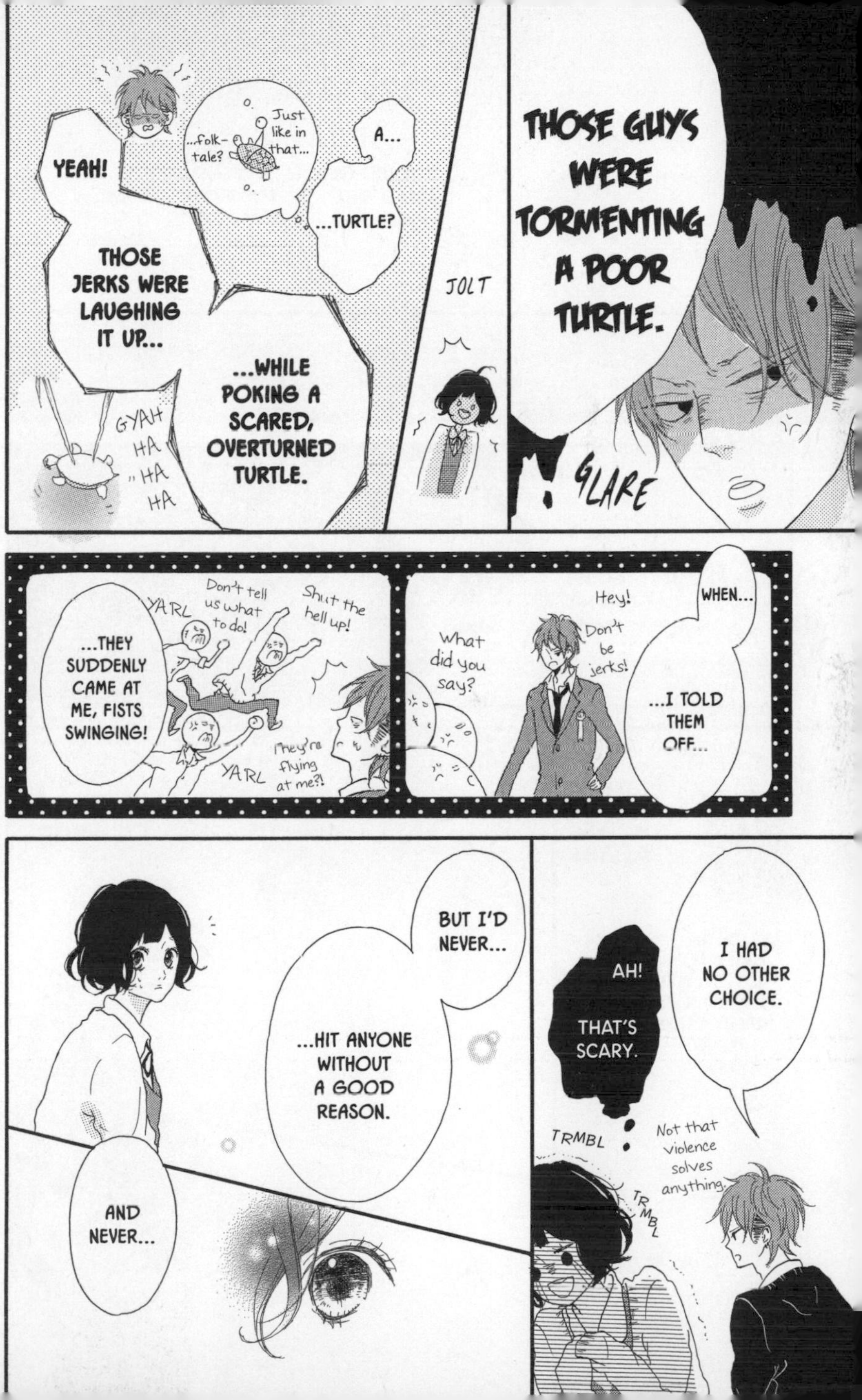
THOSE GUYS WERE TORMENTING A POOR TURTLE.
GLARE
JOLT
A...
...TURTLE?
Just like in that...
...folk-tale?
YEAH!
THOSE JERKS WERE LAUGHING IT UP...
...WHILE POKING A SCARED, OVERTURNED TURTLE.
GYAH HA HA HA
WHEN...
...I TOLD THEM OFF...
Hey! Don't be jerks!
What did you say?
Shut the hell up!
Don't tell us what to do!
YARL
...THEY SUDDENLY CAME AT ME, FISTS SWINGING!
They're flying at me?!
YARL
I HAD NO OTHER CHOICE.
AH! THAT'S SCARY.
Not that violence solves anything.
TRMBL
TRMBL
BUT I'D NEVER...
...HIT ANYONE WITHOUT A GOOD REASON.
AND NEVER...

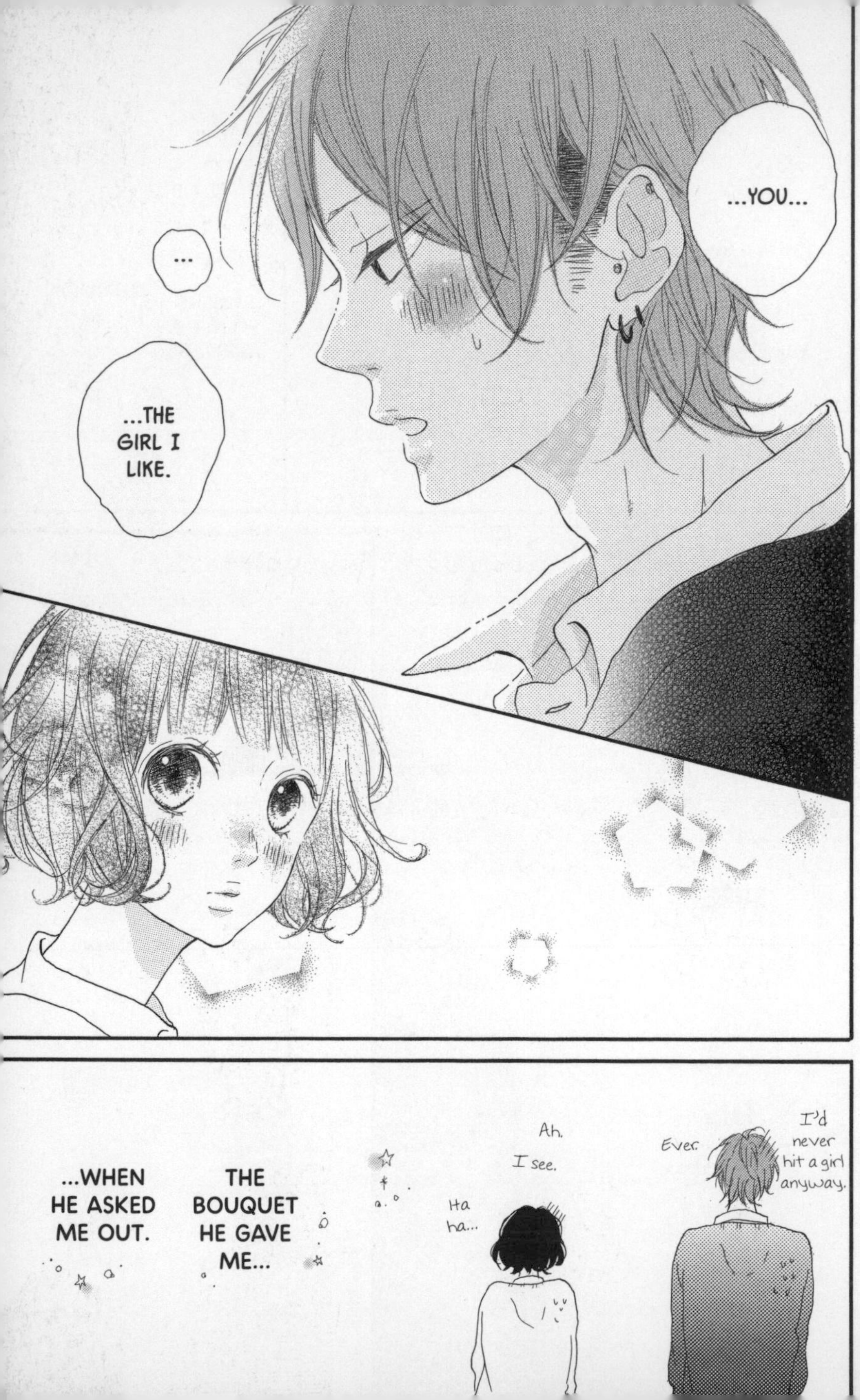
...YOU...
...
...THE GIRL I LIKE.
I'd never hit a girl anyway.
Ever.
Ah.
I see.
Ha ha...
THE BOUQUET HE GAVE ME...
...WHEN HE ASKED ME OUT.

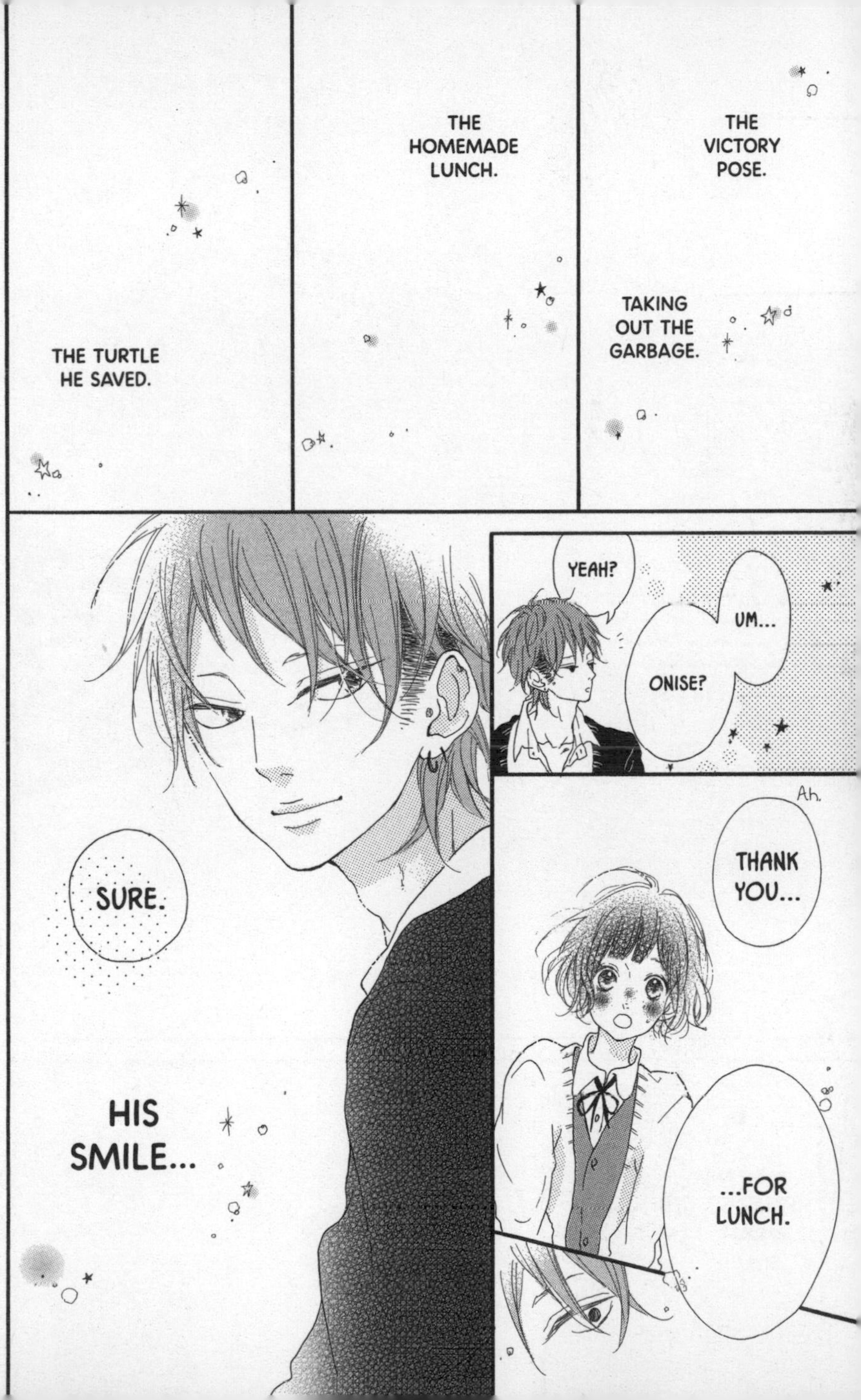
THE VICTORY POSE.
TAKING OUT THE GARBAGE.
THE HOMEMADE LUNCH.
THE TURTLE HE SAVED.
UM...
ONISE?
YEAH?
Ah.
THANK YOU...
...FOR LUNCH.
SURE.
HIS SMILE...

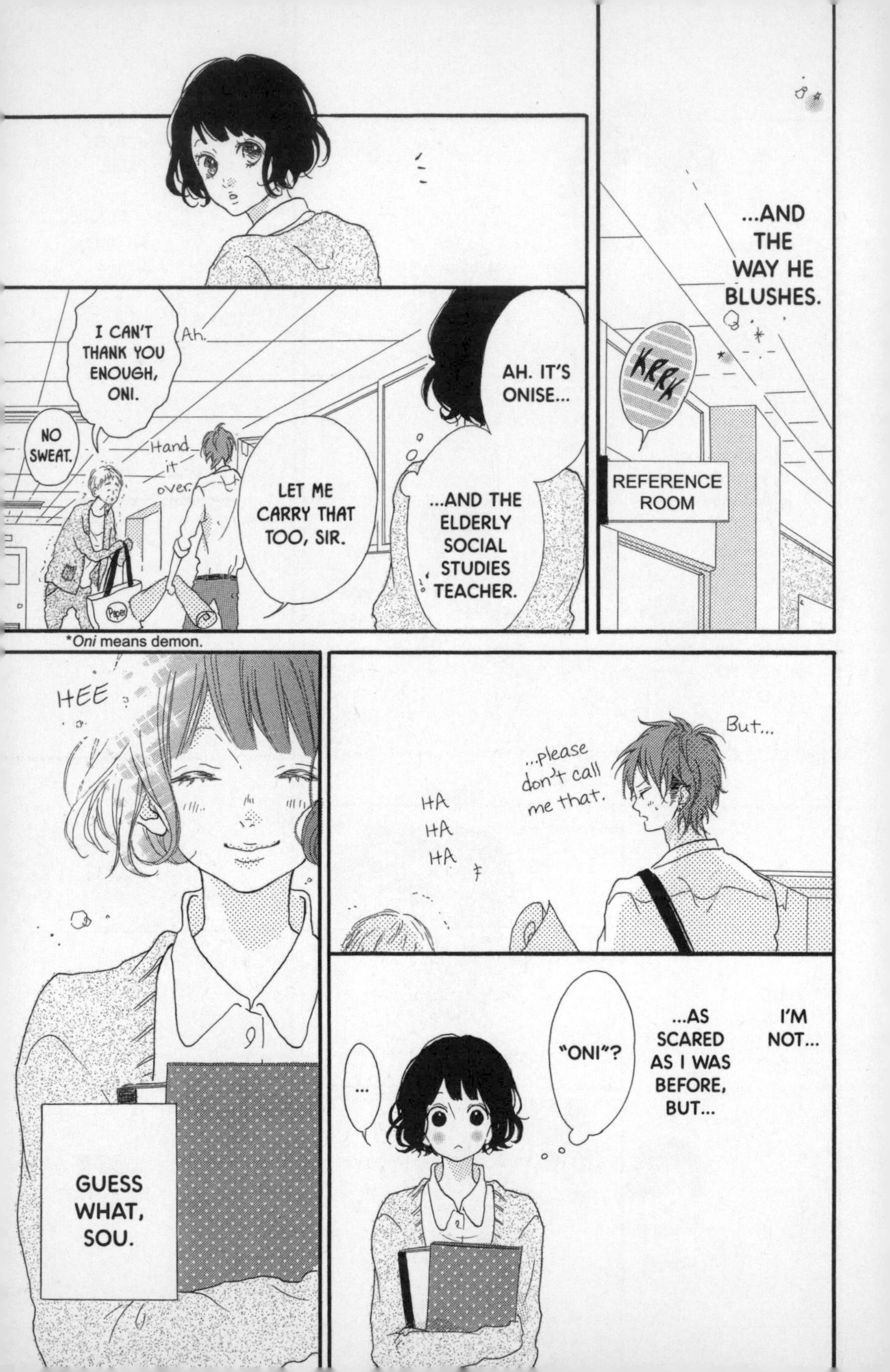
...AND THE WAY HE BLUSHES.
KRRK
REFERENCE ROOM
AH. IT'S ONISE...
...AND THE ELDERLY SOCIAL STUDIES TEACHER.
LET ME CARRY THAT TOO, SIR.
Ah.
I CAN'T THANK YOU ENOUGH, ONI.
Hand it over.
NO SWEAT.
But...
...please don't call me that.
HA HA HA
I'M NOT...
...AS SCARED AS I WAS BEFORE, BUT...
"ONI"?
...
HEE
GUESS WHAT, SOU.

*Oni means demon.

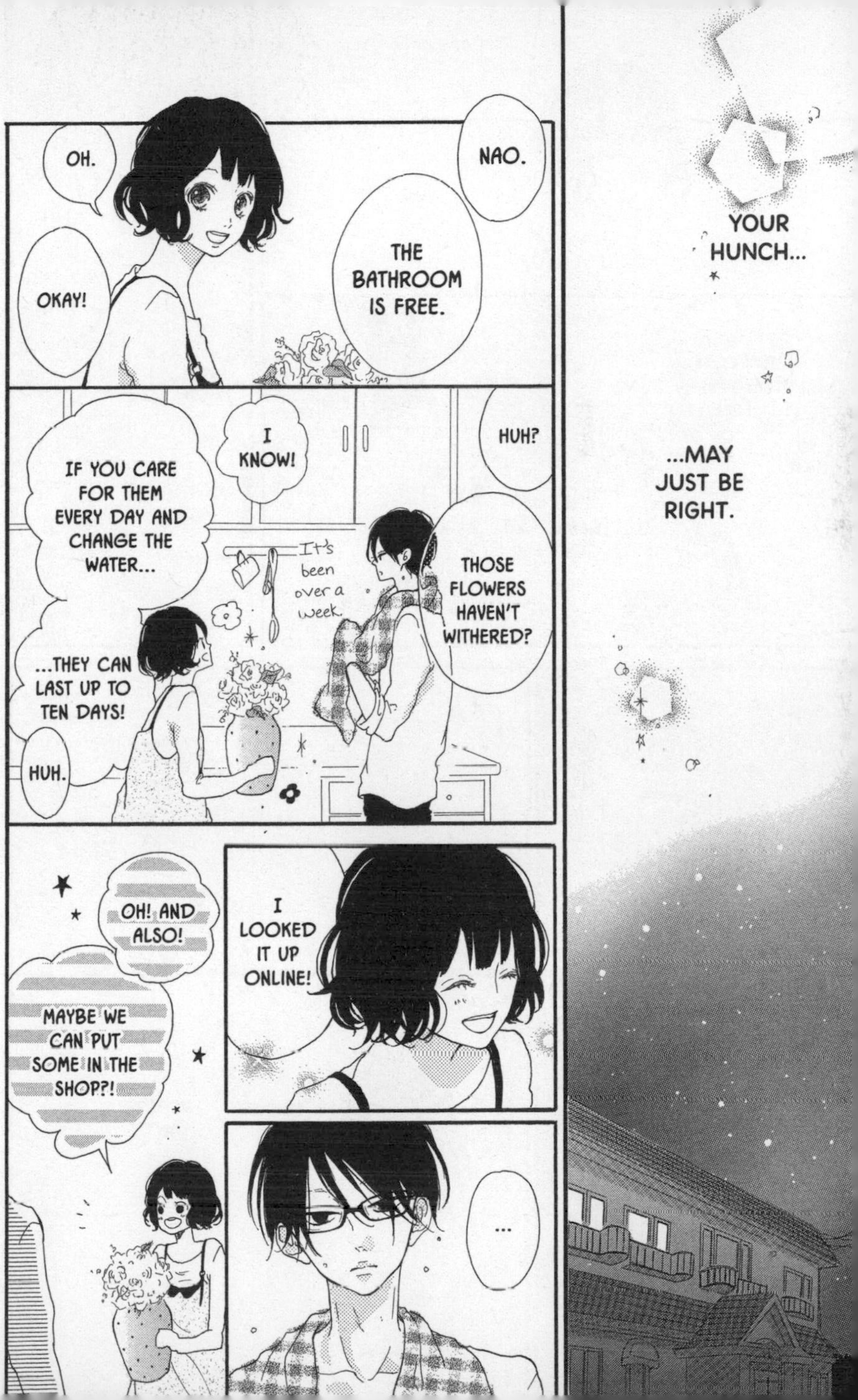
YOUR HUNCH...
...MAY JUST BE RIGHT.
NAO.
THE BATHROOM IS FREE.
OH.
OKAY!
HUH?
THOSE FLOWERS HAVEN'T WITHERED?
It's been over a week.
I KNOW!
IF YOU CARE FOR THEM EVERY DAY AND CHANGE THE WATER...
...THEY CAN LAST UP TO TEN DAYS!
HUH.
I LOOKED IT UP ONLINE!
OH! AND ALSO!
MAYBE WE CAN PUT SOME IN THE SHOP?!
...

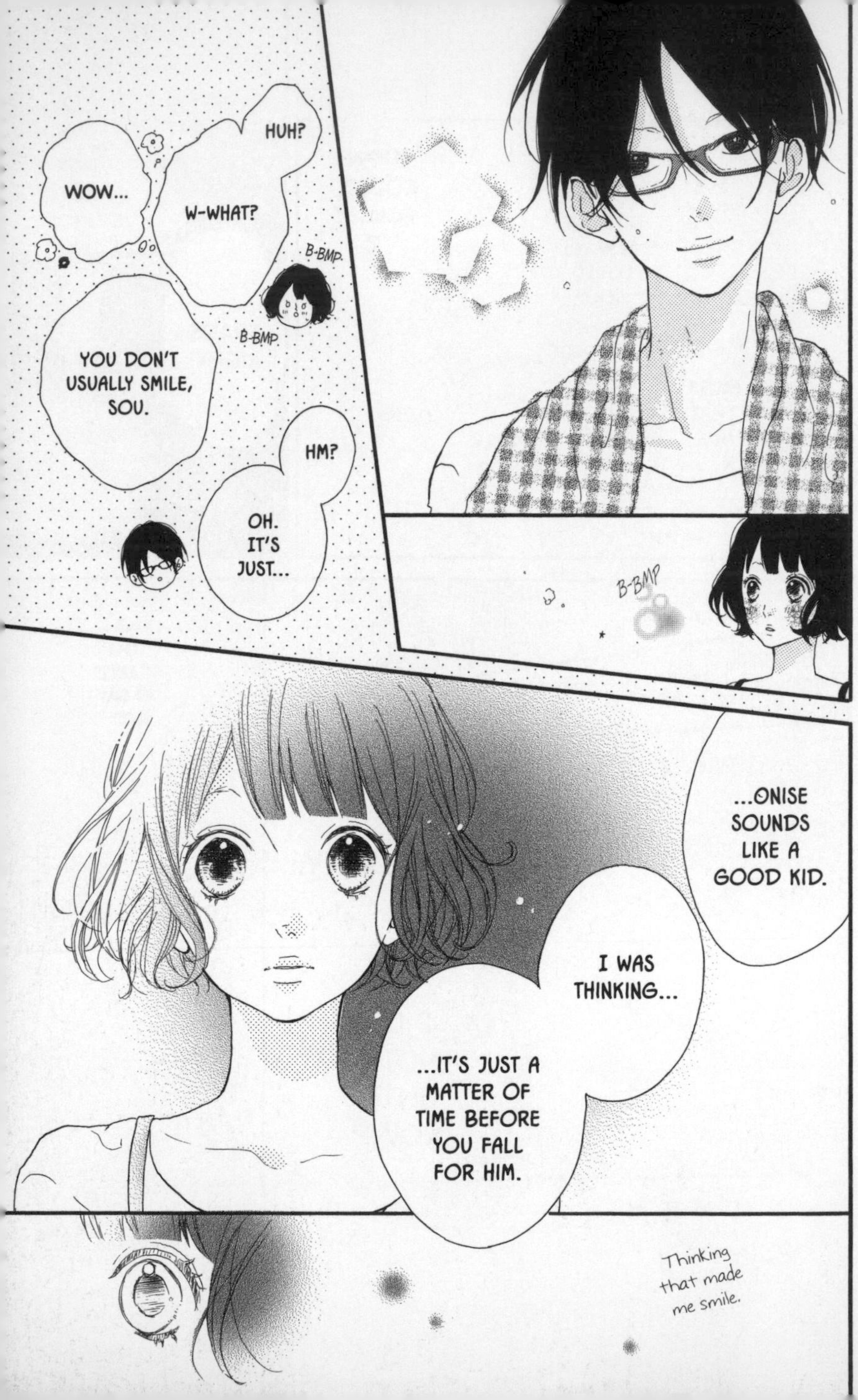
B-BMP
HUH?
WOW...
W-WHAT?
B-BMP.
B-BMP
YOU DON'T USUALLY SMILE, SOU.
HM?
OH. IT'S JUST...
...ONISE SOUNDS LIKE A GOOD KID.
I WAS THINKING...
...IT'S JUST A MATTER OF TIME BEFORE YOU FALL FOR HIM.
Thinking that made me smile.

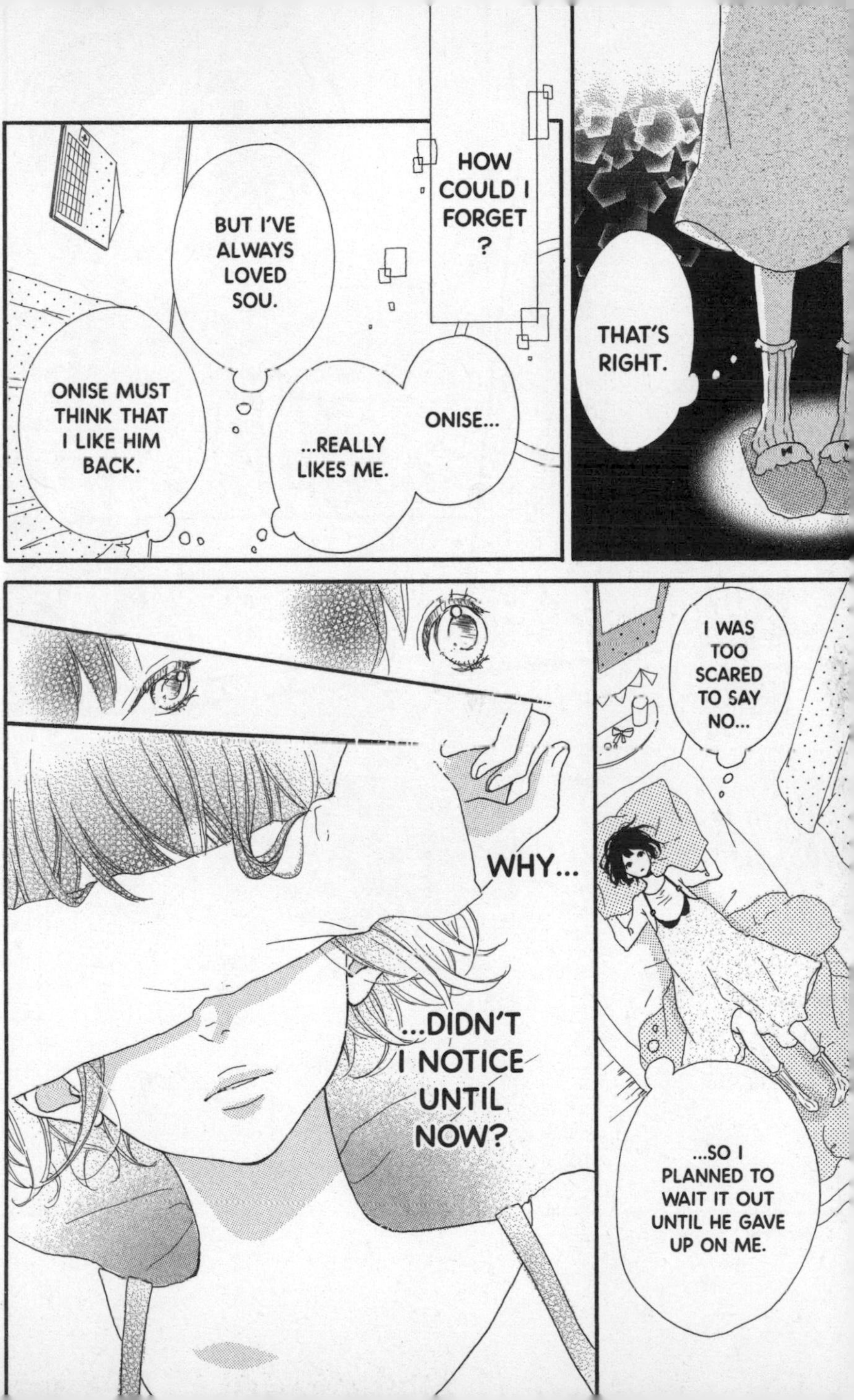
THAT'S RIGHT.
HOW COULD I FORGET ?
ONISE...
...REALLY LIKES ME.
ONISE MUST THINK THAT I LIKE HIM BACK.
BUT I'VE ALWAYS LOVED SOU.
I WAS TOO SCARED TO SAY NO...
...SO I PLANNED TO WAIT IT OUT UNTIL HE GAVE UP ON ME.
WHY...
...DIDN'T I NOTICE UNTIL NOW?

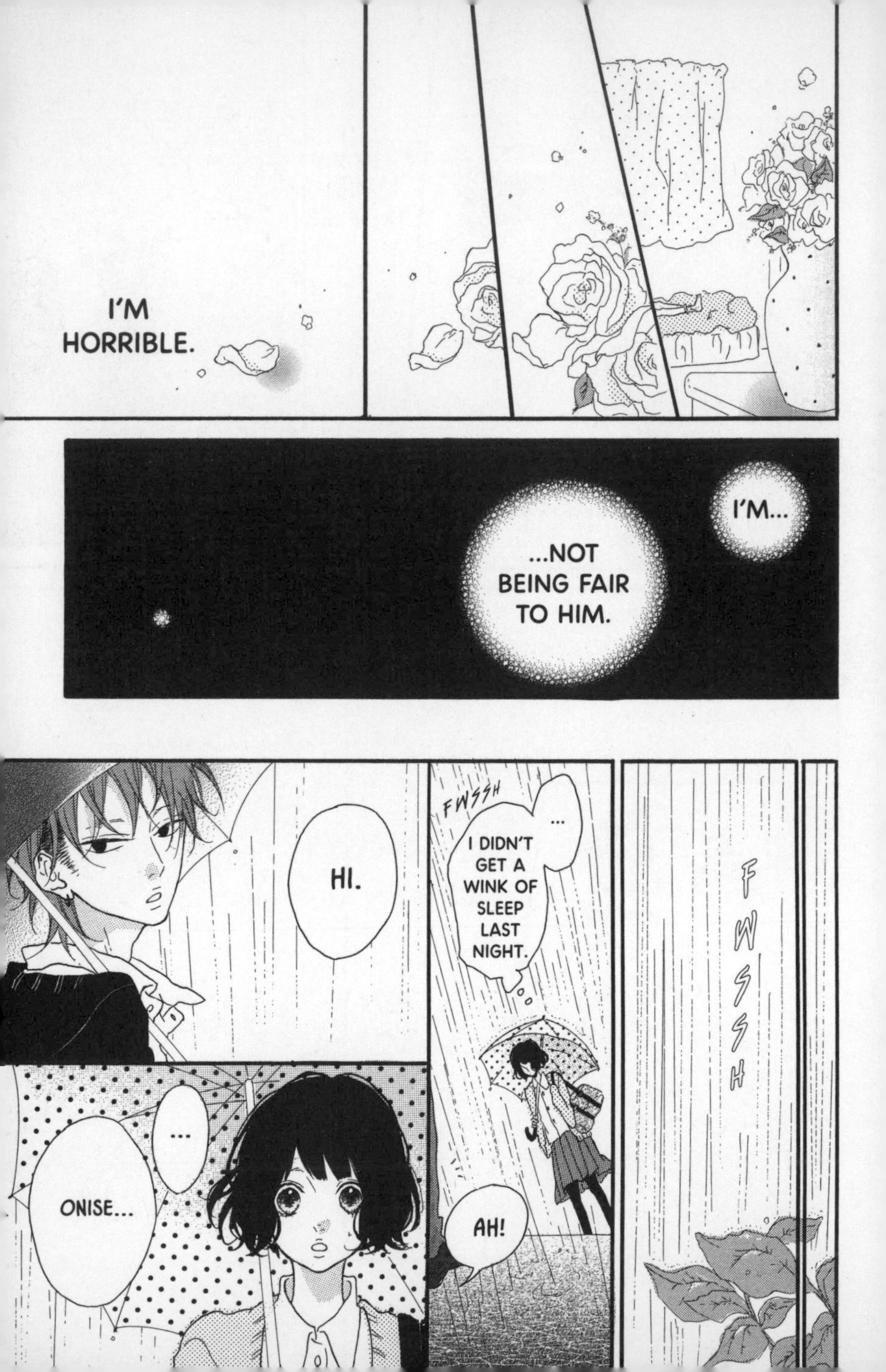
I'M HORRIBLE.
I'M...
...NOT BEING FAIR TO HIM.
FWSSH
FWSSH
...
I DIDN'T GET A WINK OF SLEEP LAST NIGHT.
AH!
HI.
...
ONISE...

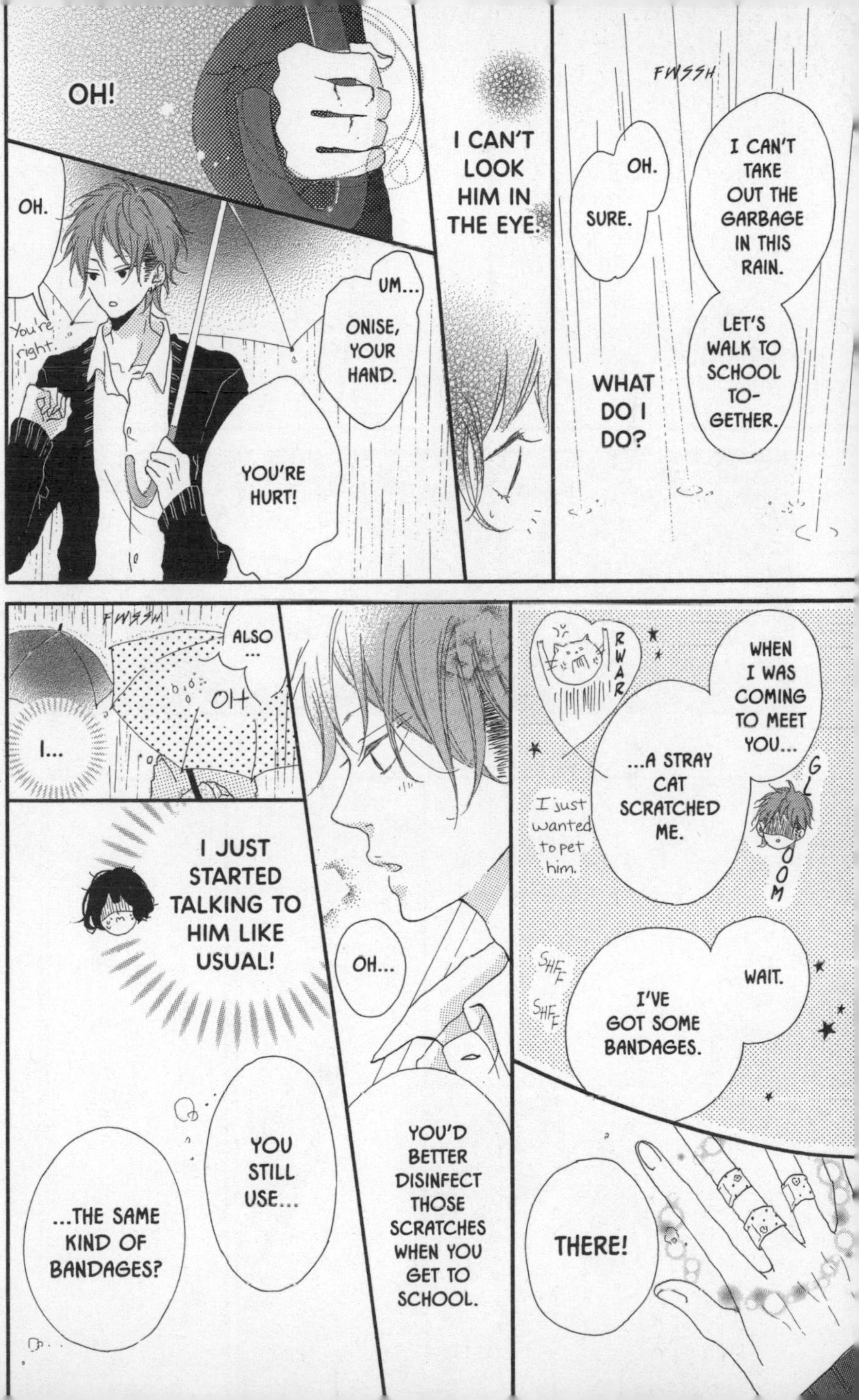
FWSSH
OH.
SURE.
I CAN'T TAKE OUT THE GARBAGE IN THIS RAIN.
LET'S WALK TO SCHOOL TO-GETHER.
WHAT DO I DO?
I CAN'T LOOK HIM IN THE EYE.
OH!
OH.
You're right.
UM...
ONISE, YOUR HAND.
YOU'RE HURT!
WHEN I WAS COMING TO MEET YOU...
RWAR
...A STRAY CAT SCRATCHED ME.
I just wanted to pet him.
GLOOM
WAIT.
I'VE GOT SOME BANDAGES.
SHFF
SHFF
THERE!
OH...
YOU'D BETTER DISINFECT THOSE SCRATCHES WHEN YOU GET TO SCHOOL.
FWSSH
ALSO...
OH
I...
I JUST STARTED TALKING TO HIM LIKE USUAL!
YOU STILL USE...
...THE SAME KIND OF BANDAGES?

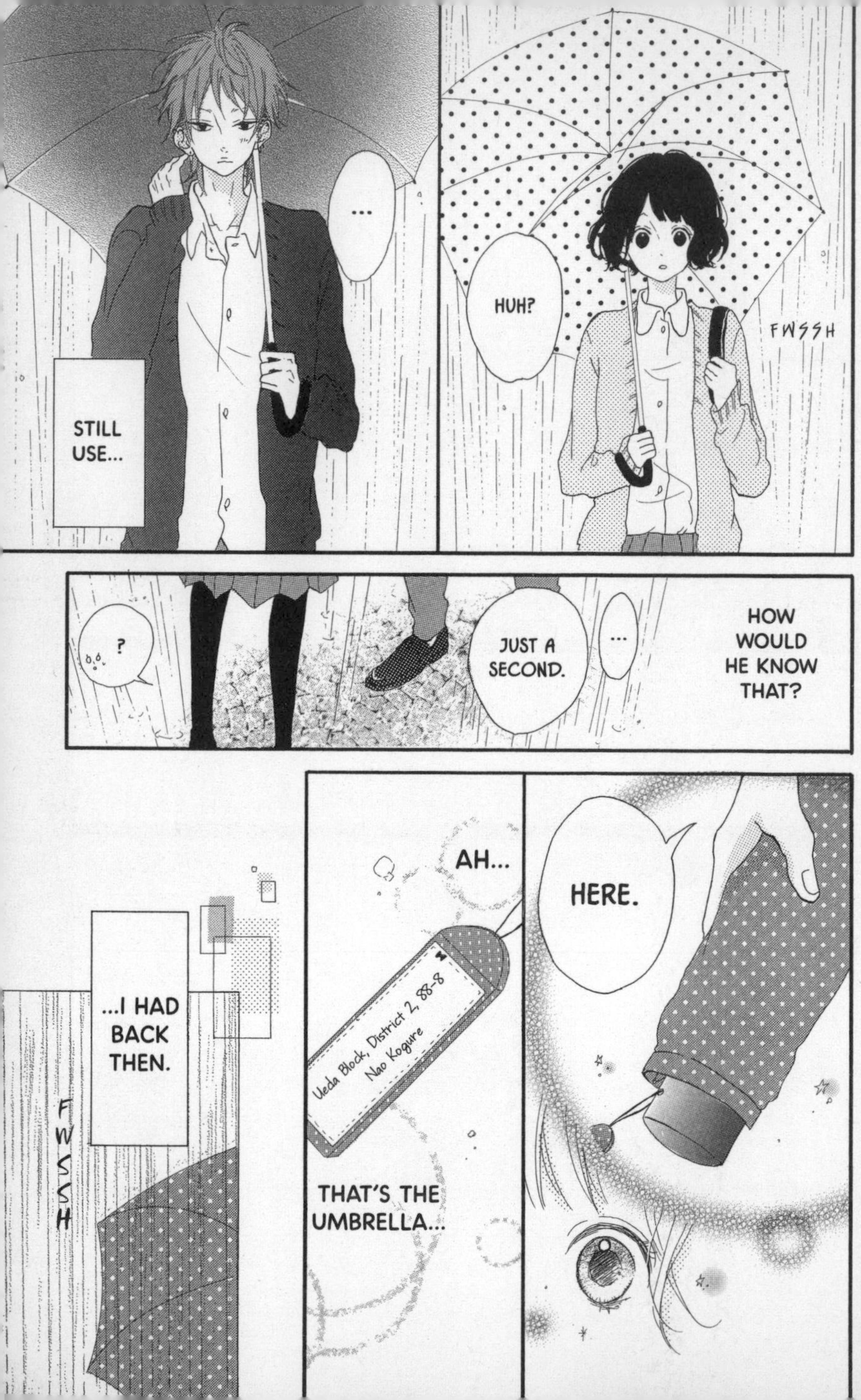
HUH?
FWSSH
...
STILL USE...
HOW WOULD HE KNOW THAT?
...
JUST A SECOND.
?
HERE.
AH...
Ueda Block, District 2, 88-8
Nao Kogure
THAT'S THE UMBRELLA...
...I HAD BACK THEN.
FWSSH

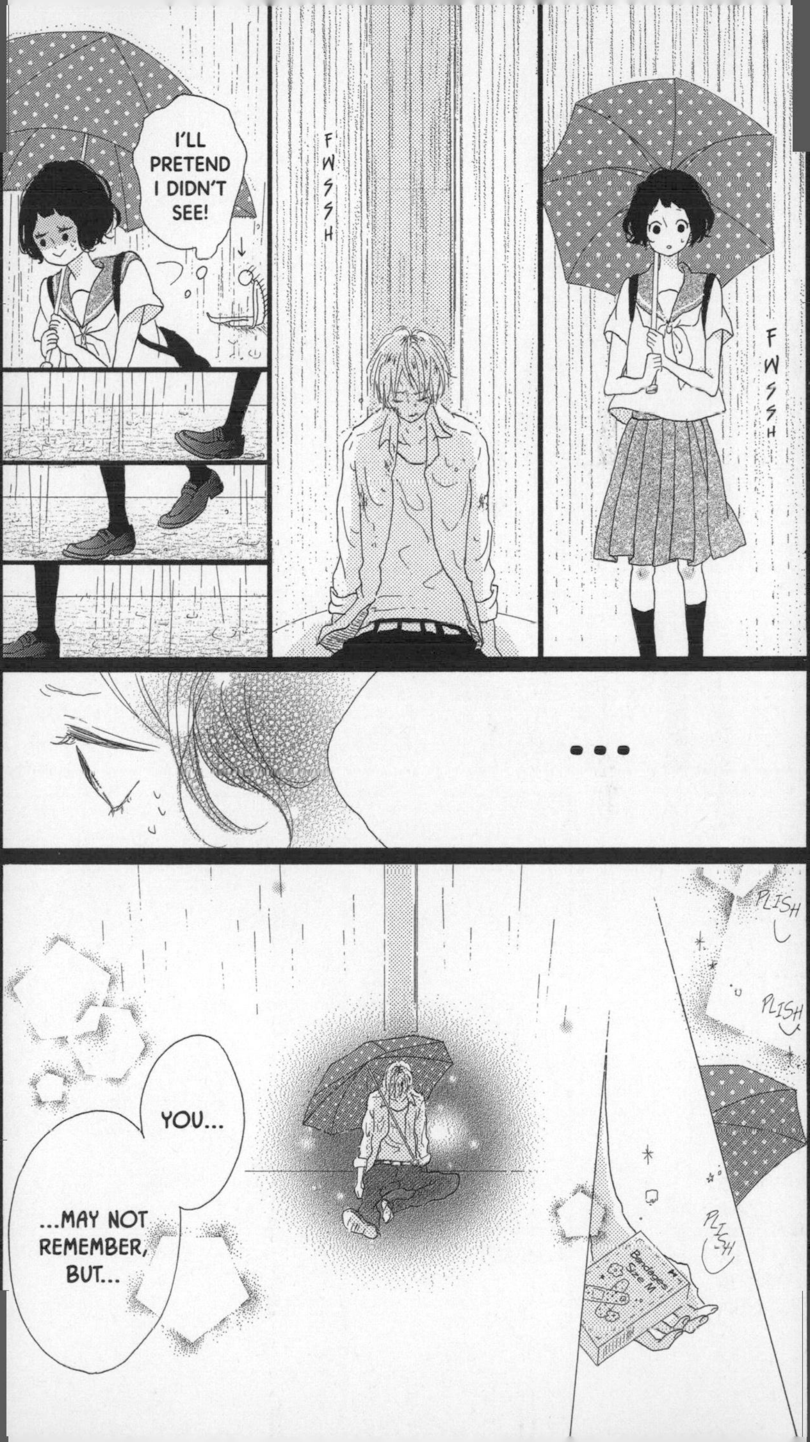
FWSSH
FWSSH
I'LL PRETEND I DIDN'T SEE!
...
PLISH
PLISH
PLISH
Bandages Size M
YOU...
...MAY NOT REMEMBER, BUT...

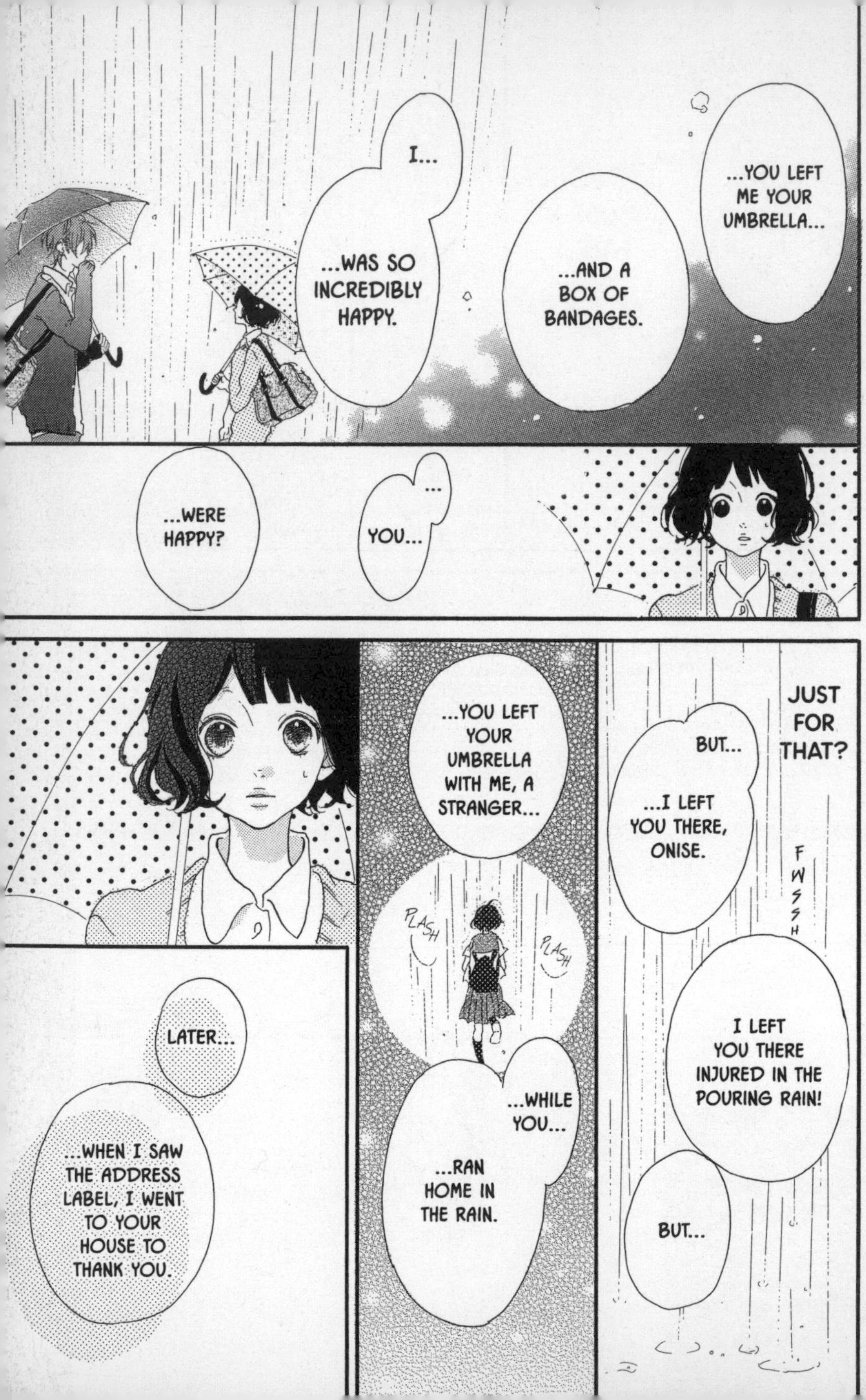
...YOU LEFT ME YOUR UMBRELLA...
...AND A BOX OF BANDAGES.
I...
...WAS SO INCREDIBLY HAPPY.
...
YOU...
...WERE HAPPY?
JUST FOR THAT?
BUT...
...I LEFT YOU THERE, ONISE.
FWSSH
I LEFT YOU THERE INJURED IN THE POURING RAIN!
BUT...
...YOU LEFT YOUR UMBRELLA WITH ME, A STRANGER...
PLASH
PLASH
...WHILE YOU...
...RAN HOME IN THE RAIN.
LATER...
...WHEN I SAW THE ADDRESS LABEL, I WENT TO YOUR HOUSE TO THANK YOU.

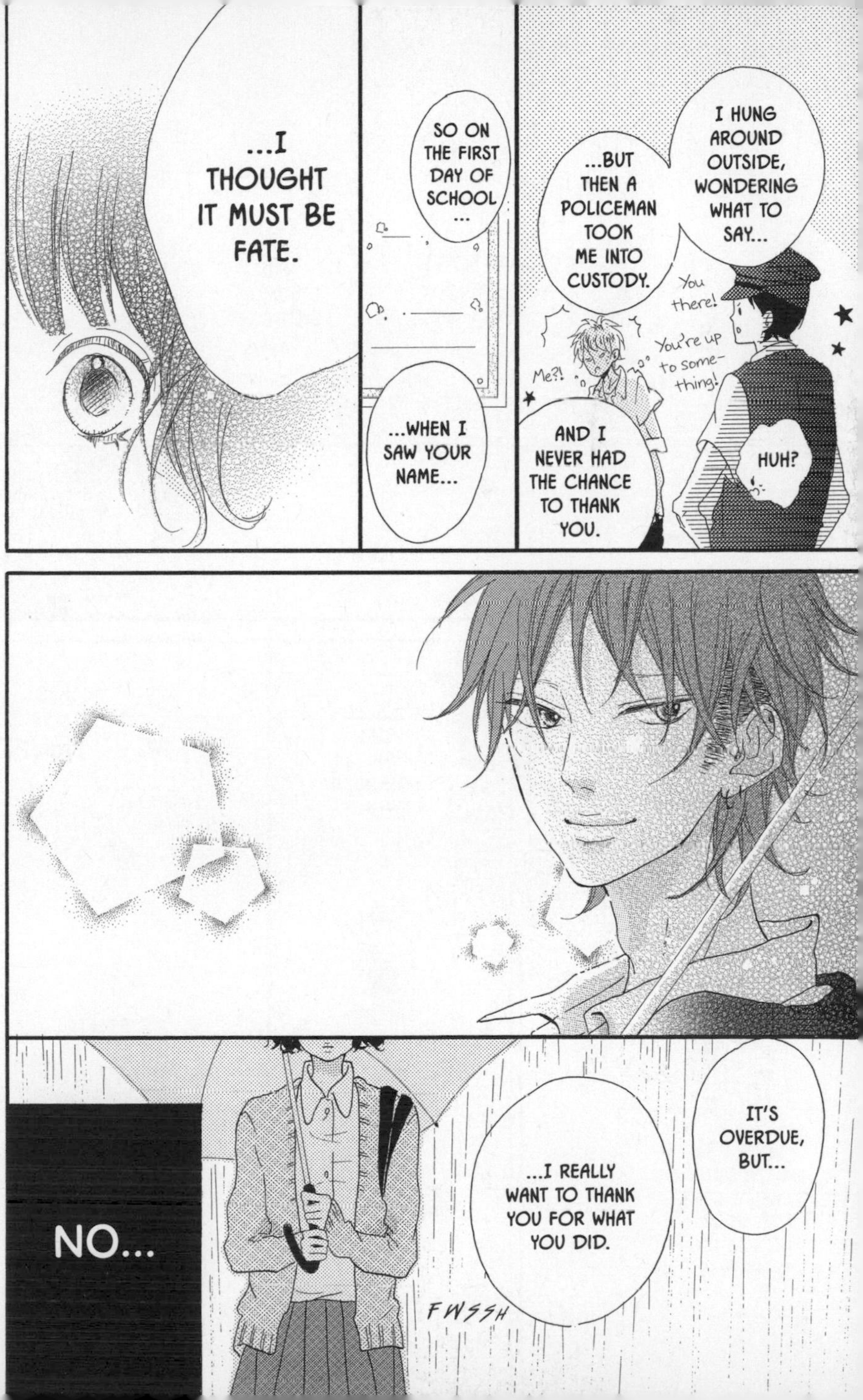
I HUNG AROUND OUTSIDE, WONDERING WHAT TO SAY...
...BUT THEN A POLICEMAN TOOK ME INTO CUSTODY.
You there!
You're up to some-thing!
Me?!
HUH?
AND I NEVER HAD THE CHANCE TO THANK YOU.
SO ON THE FIRST DAY OF SCHOOL...
...WHEN I SAW YOUR NAME...
...I THOUGHT IT MUST BE FATE.
IT'S OVERDUE, BUT...
...I REALLY WANT TO THANK YOU FOR WHAT YOU DID.
FWSSH
NO...

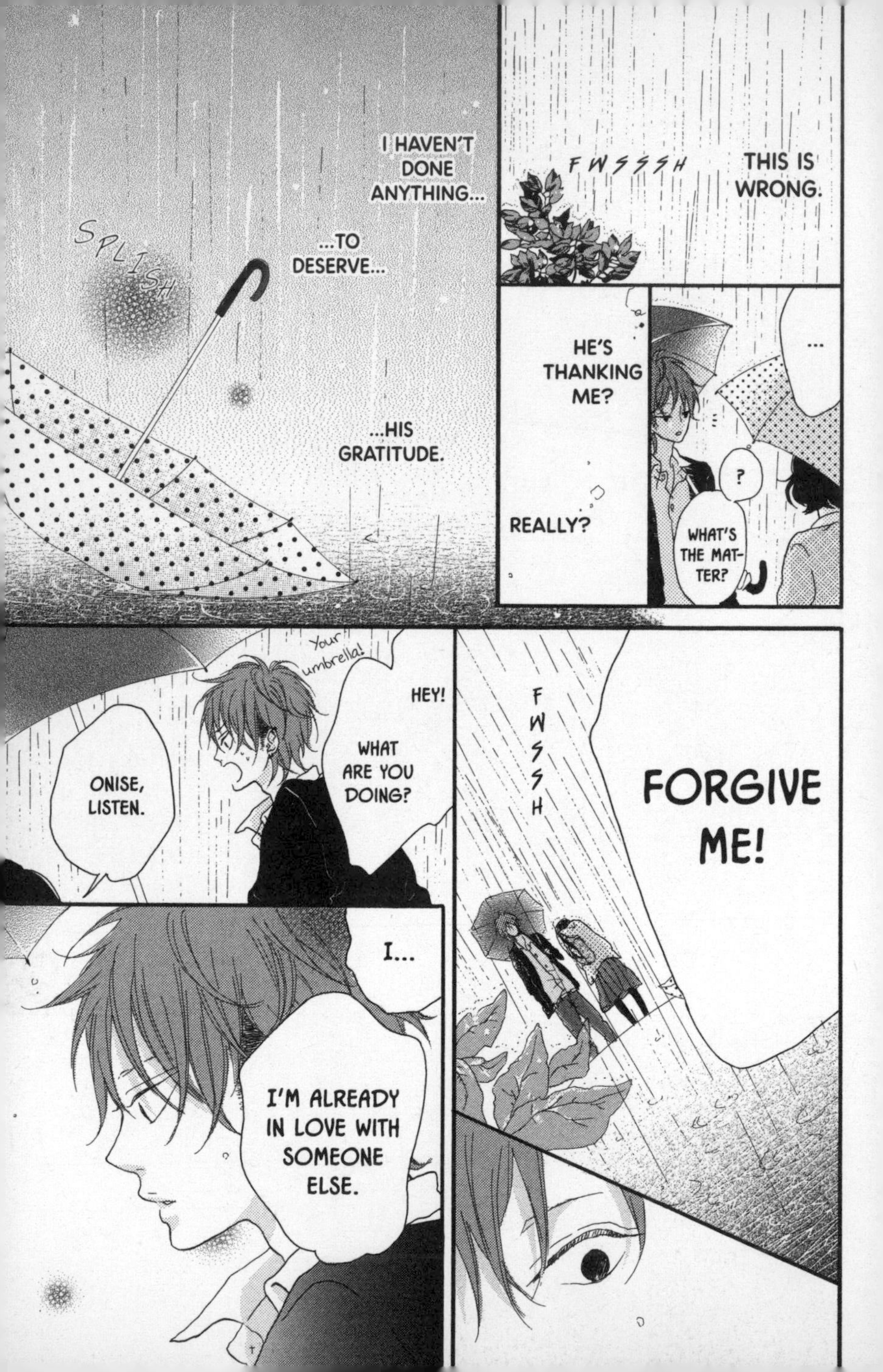
FWSSSH
THIS IS WRONG.
...
?
WHAT'S THE MATTER?
HE'S THANKING ME?
REALLY?
I HAVEN'T DONE ANYTHING...
...TO DESERVE...
...HIS GRATITUDE.
SPLISH
FORGIVE ME!
FWSSH
HEY!
Your umbrella!
WHAT ARE YOU DOING?
ONISE, LISTEN.
I...
I'M ALREADY IN LOVE WITH SOMEONE ELSE.

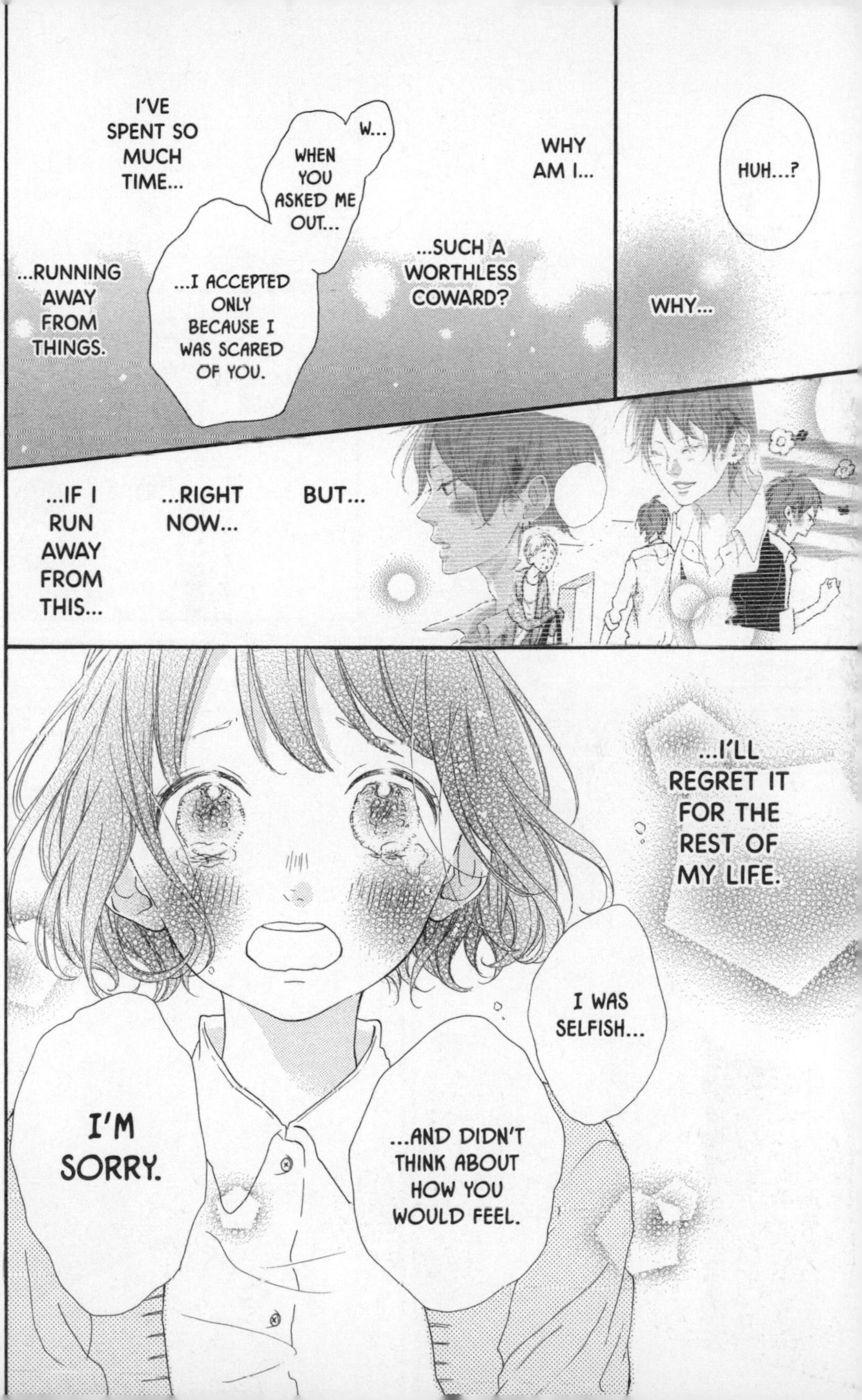
HUH...?
WHY...
WHY AM I...
...SUCH A WORTHLESS COWARD?
I'VE SPENT SO MUCH TIME...
...RUNNING AWAY FROM THINGS.
W...
WHEN YOU ASKED ME OUT...
...I ACCEPTED ONLY BECAUSE I WAS SCARED OF YOU.
BUT...
...RIGHT NOW...
...IF I RUN AWAY FROM THIS...
...I'LL REGRET IT FOR THE REST OF MY LIFE.
I WAS SELFISH...
...AND DIDN'T THINK ABOUT HOW YOU WOULD FEEL.
I'M SORRY.

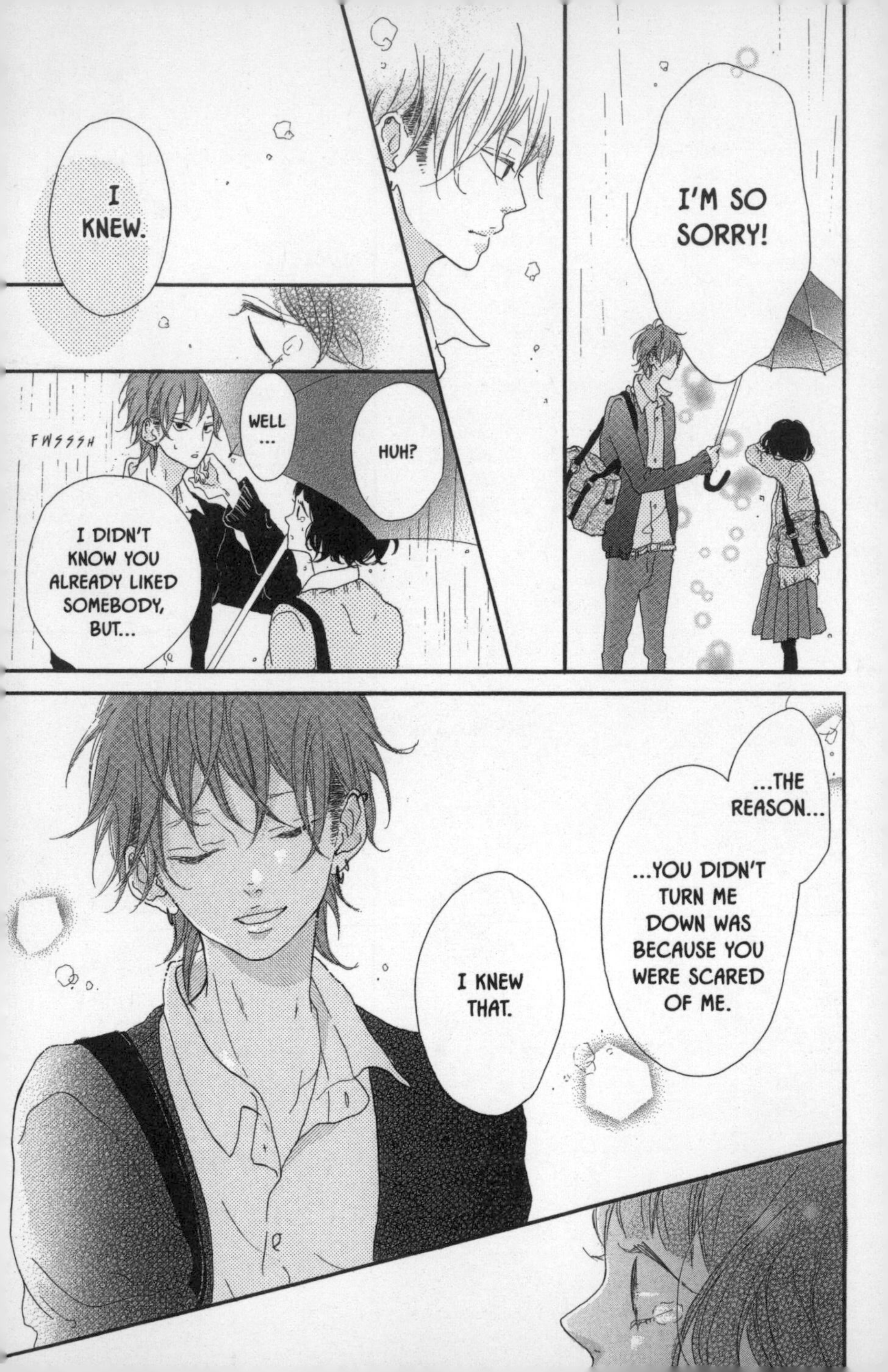
I'M SO SORRY!
I KNEW.
HUH?
WELL...
I DIDN'T KNOW YOU ALREADY LIKED SOMEBODY, BUT...
FWSSSH
...THE REASON...
...YOU DIDN'T TURN ME DOWN WAS BECAUSE YOU WERE SCARED OF ME.
I KNEW THAT.

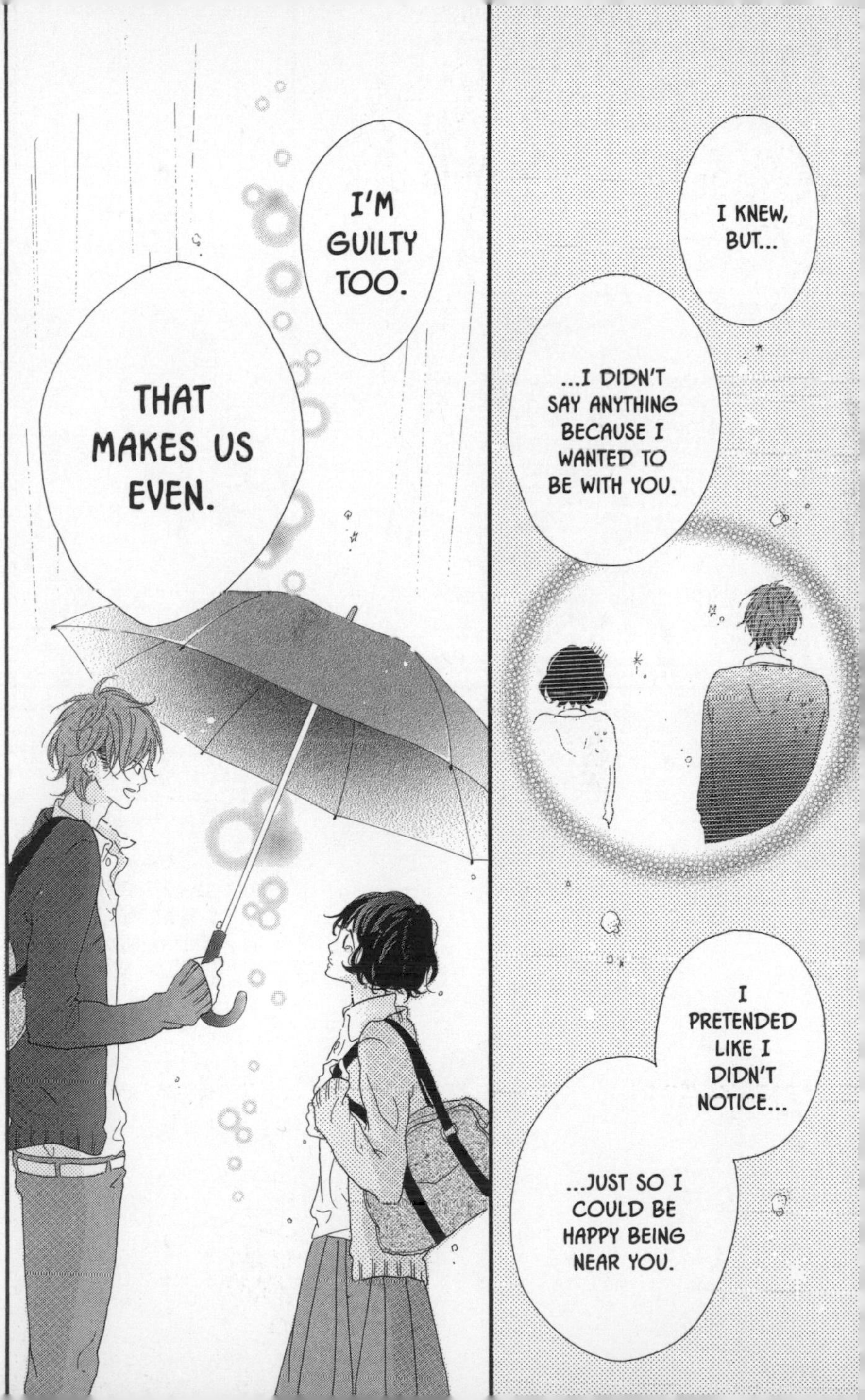
I KNEW, BUT...
...I DIDN'T SAY ANYTHING BECAUSE I WANTED TO BE WITH YOU.
I PRETENDED LIKE I DIDN'T NOTICE...
...JUST SO I COULD BE HAPPY BEING NEAR YOU.
I'M GUILTY TOO.
THAT MAKES US EVEN.

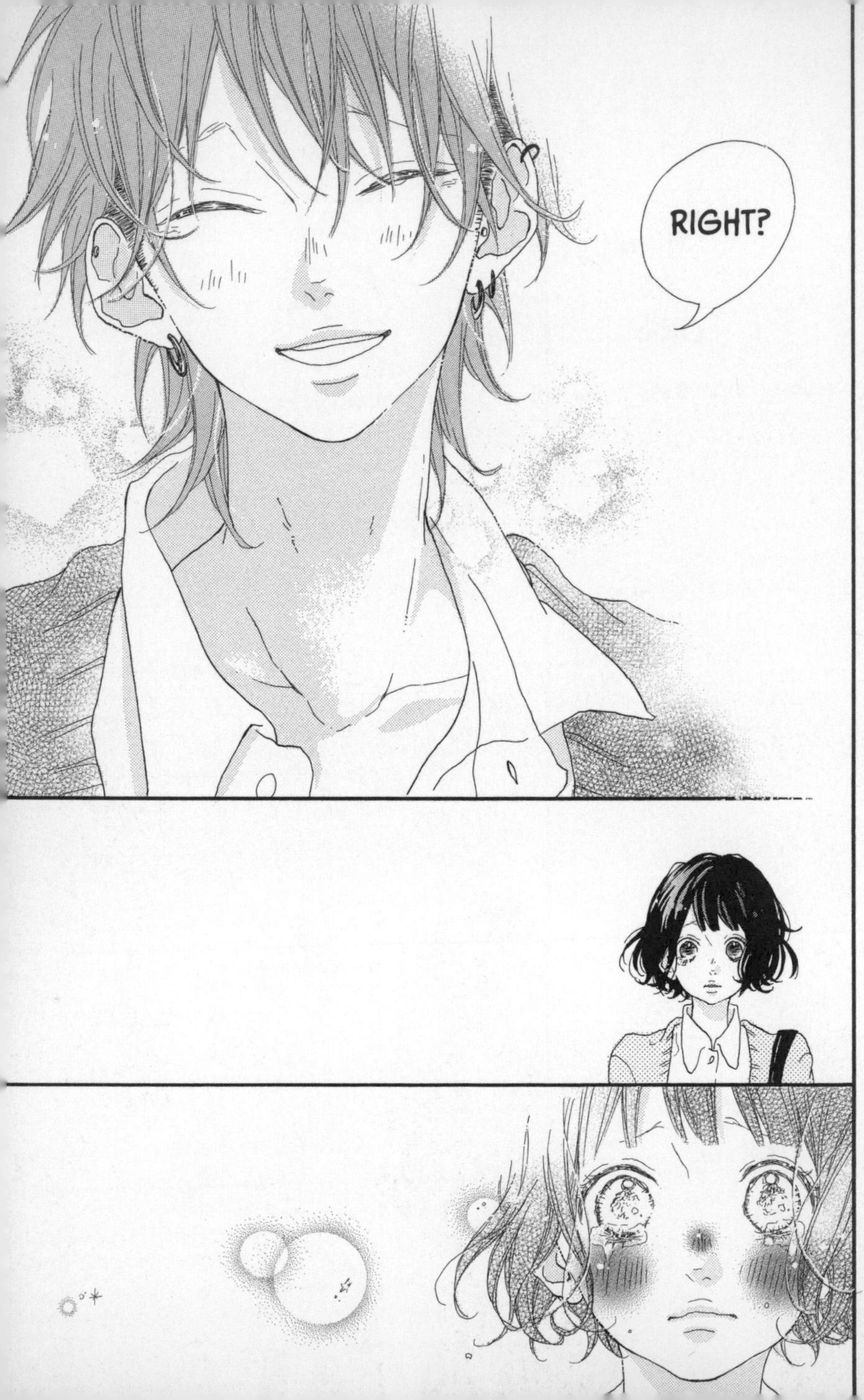
RIGHT?

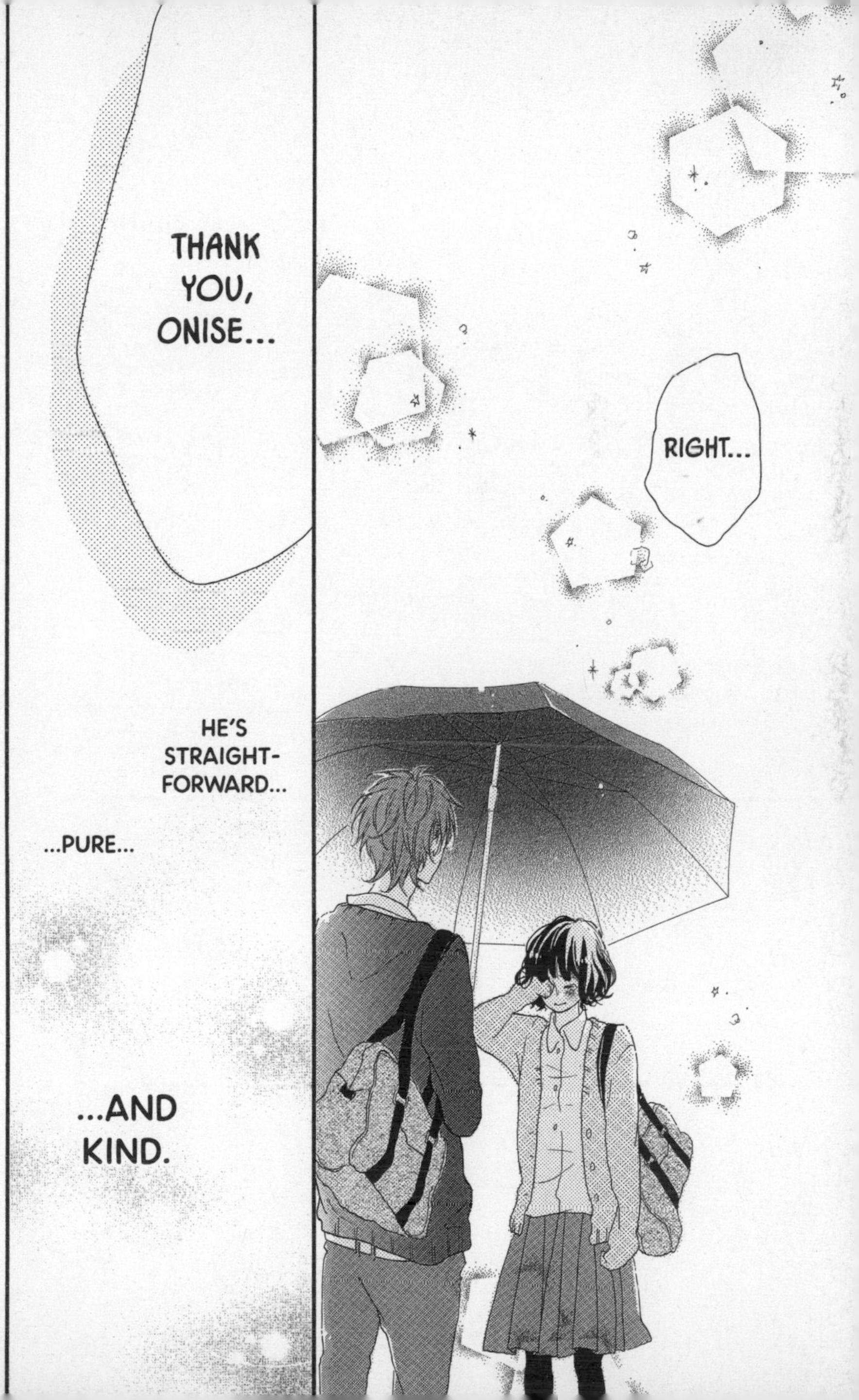
RIGHT...
THANK YOU, ONISE...
HE'S STRAIGHT-FORWARD...
...PURE...
...AND KIND.

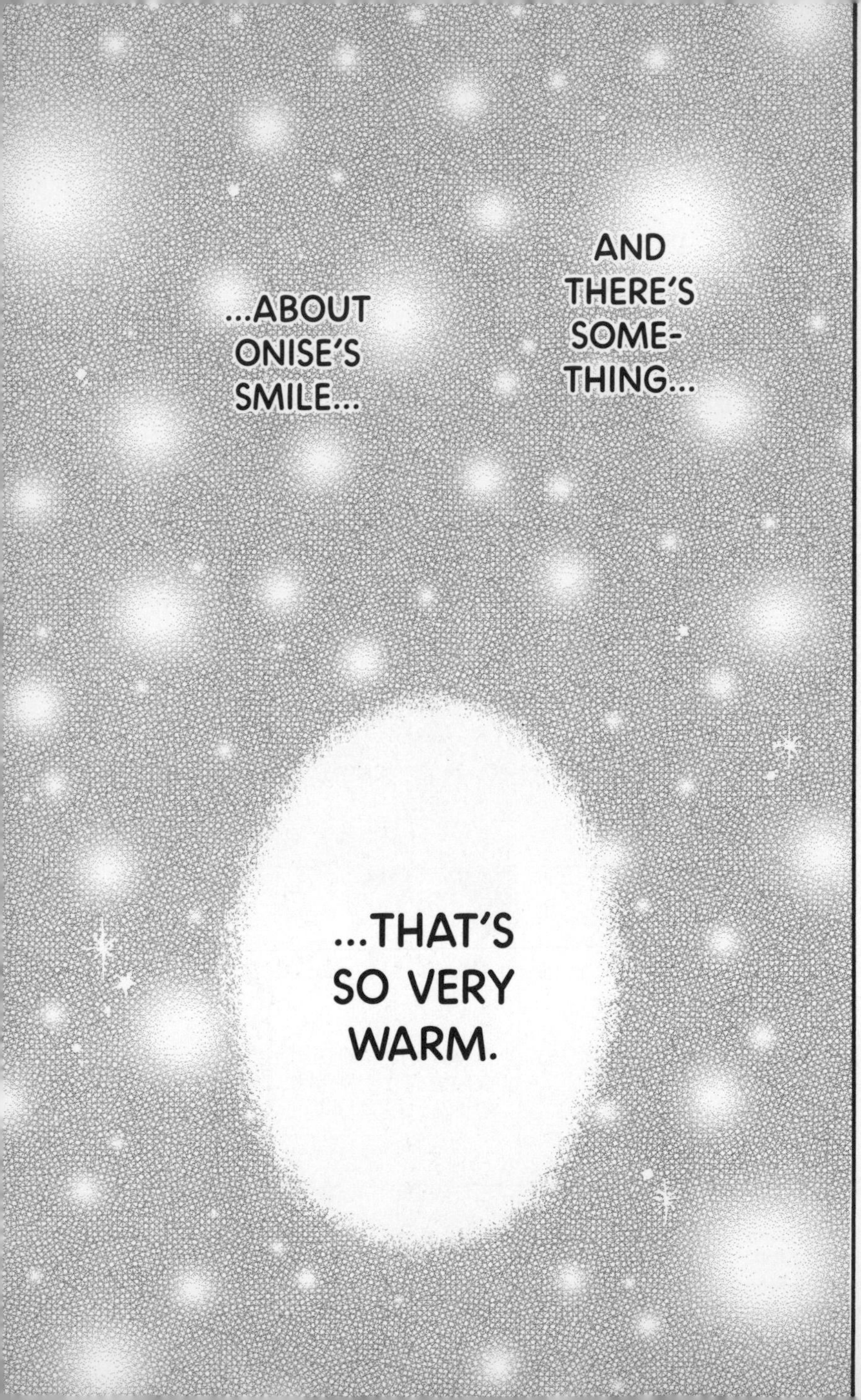
AND THERE'S SOME-THING...
...ABOUT ONISE'S SMILE...
...THAT'S SO VERY WARM.

At the Flower Shop

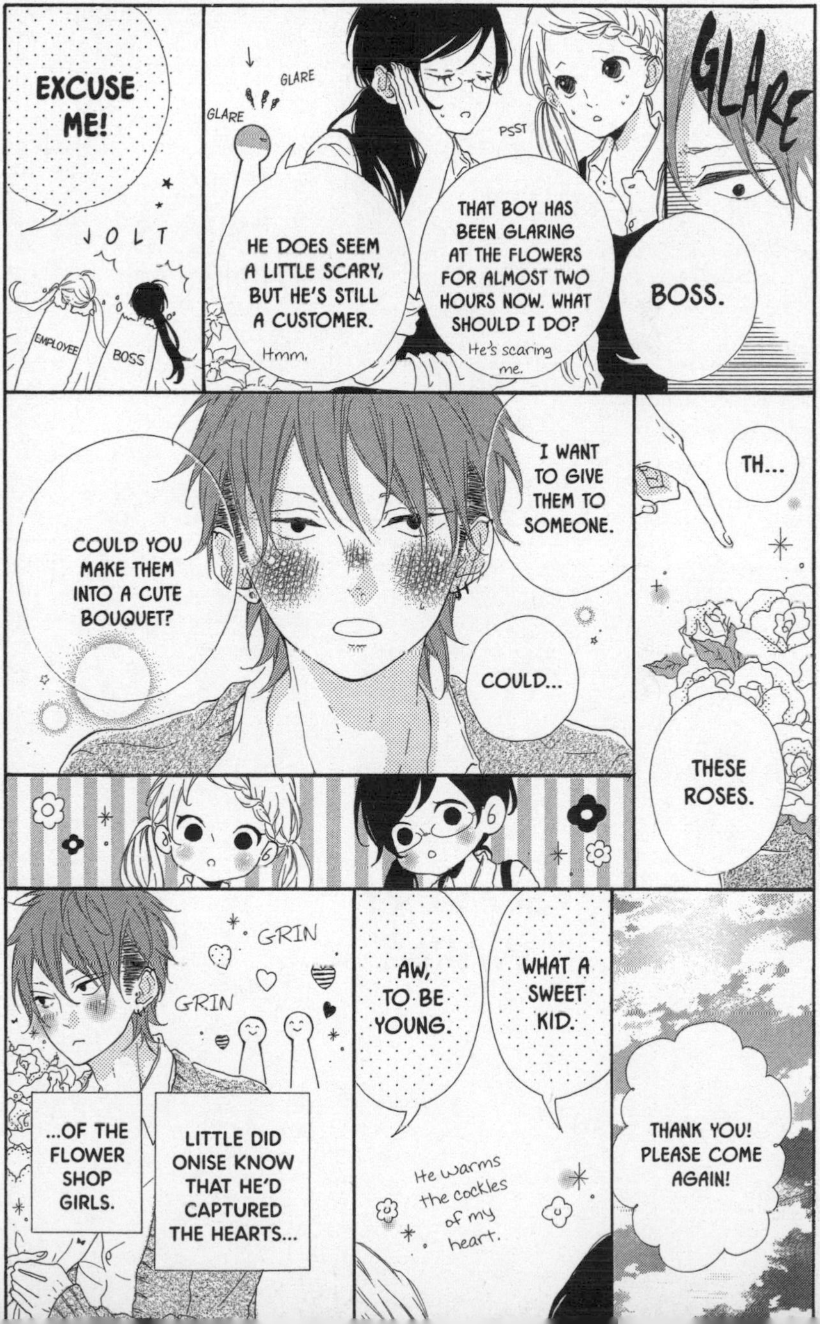
GLARE
BOSS.
THAT BOY HAS BEEN GLARING AT THE FLOWERS FOR ALMOST TWO HOURS NOW. WHAT SHOULD I DO?
PSST
He's scaring me.
GLARE
GLARE
HE DOES SEEM A LITTLE SCARY, BUT HE'S STILL A CUSTOMER.
Hmm.
EXCUSE ME!
JOLT
EMPLOYEE
BOSS
TH...
THESE ROSES.
I WANT TO GIVE THEM TO SOMEONE.
COULD...
COULD YOU MAKE THEM INTO A CUTE BOUQUET?
THANK YOU! PLEASE COME AGAIN!
WHAT A SWEET KID.
AW, TO BE YOUNG.
He warms the cockles of my heart.
GRIN
GRIN
LITTLE DID ONISE KNOW THAT HE'D CAPTURED THE HEARTS...
...OF THE FLOWER SHOP GIRLS.

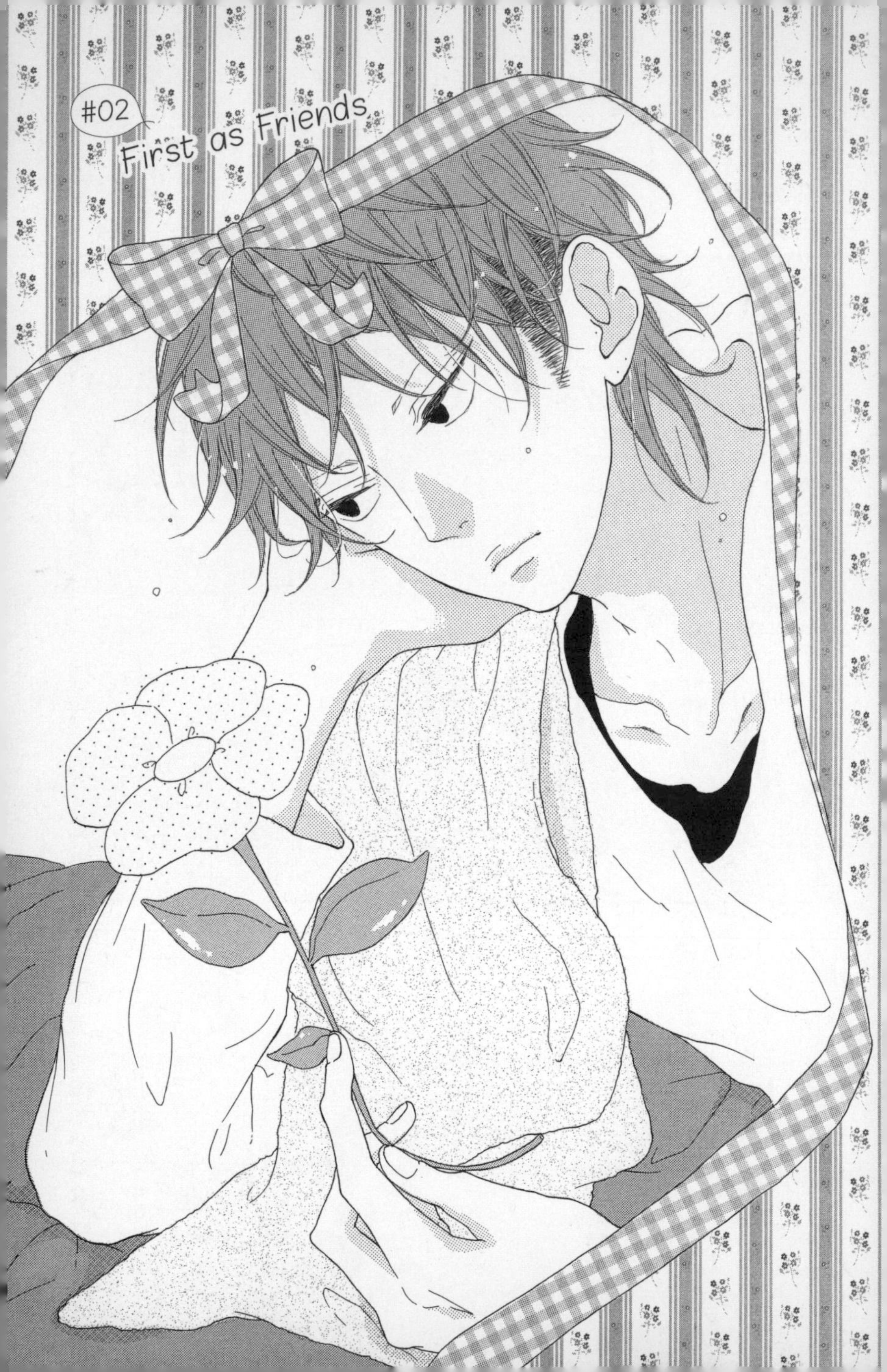
#02
First as Friends

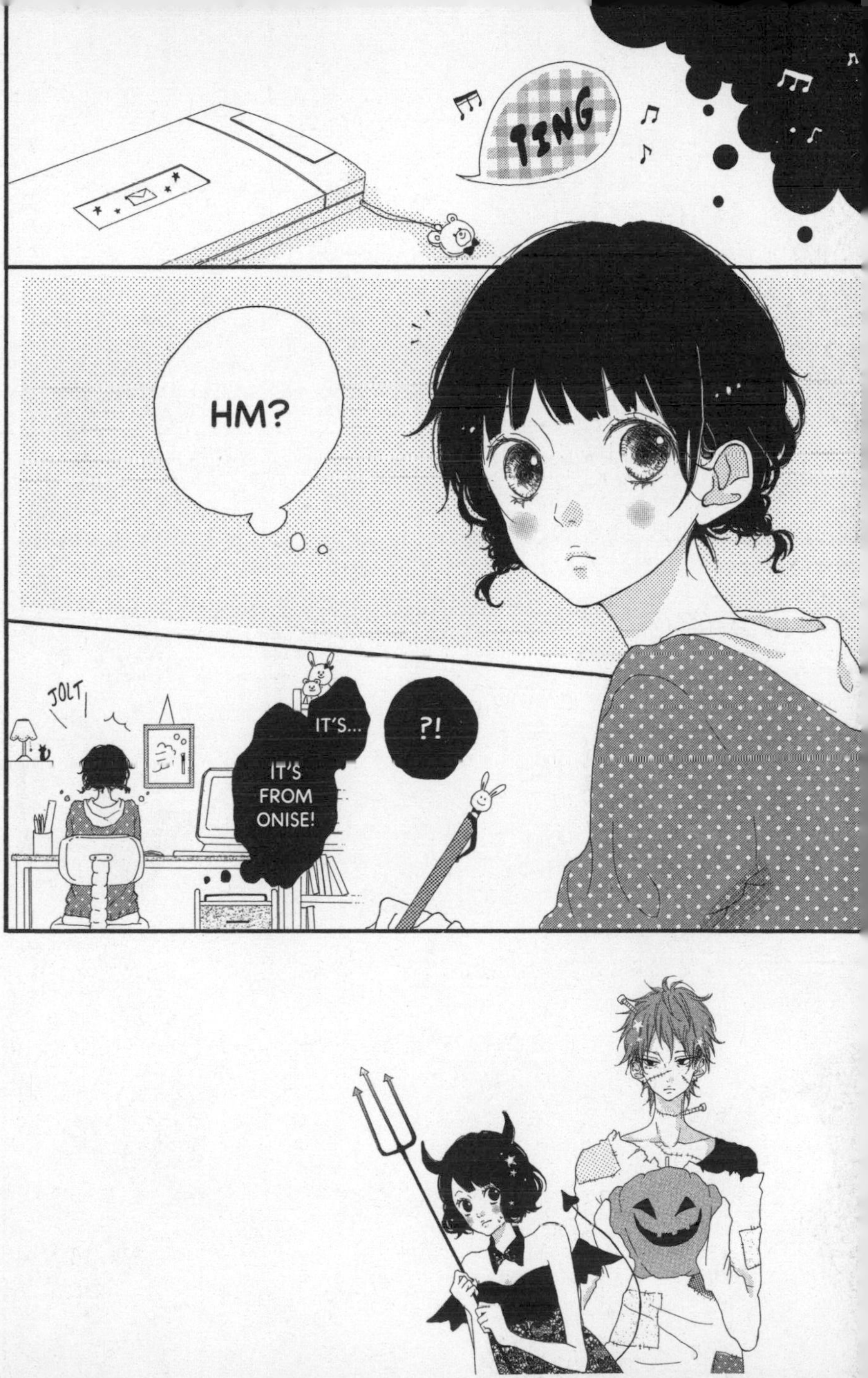
TING
HM?
?!
IT'S...
IT'S FROM ONISE!
JOLT

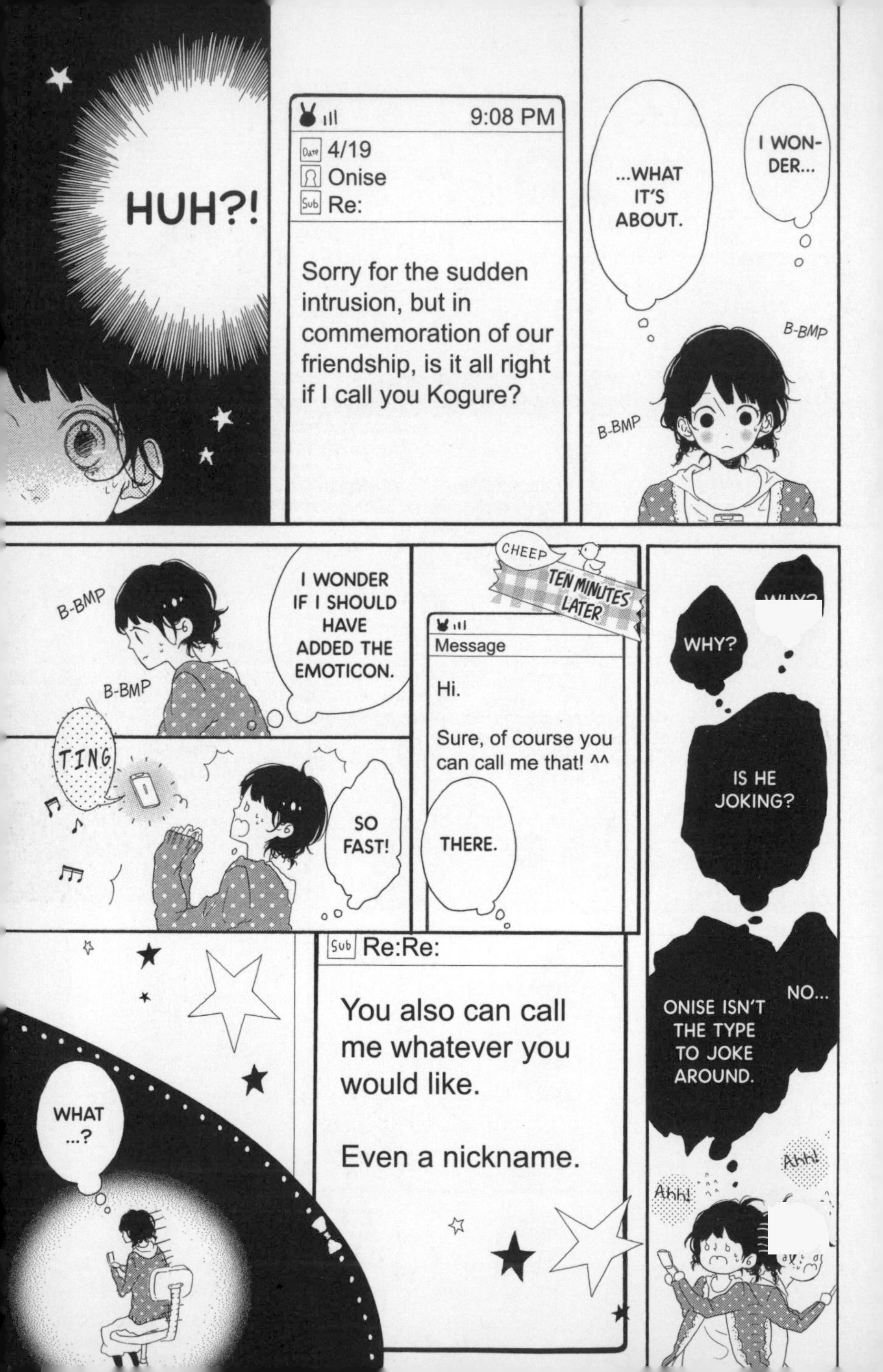
I WON-DER...
...WHAT IT'S ABOUT.
B-BMP
B-BMP
9:08 PM
Date 4/19
Onise
Sub Re:
Sorry for the sudden intrusion, but in commemoration of our friendship, is it all right if I call you Kogure?
HUH?!
WHY?
IS HE JOKING?
NO...
ONISE ISN'T THE TYPE TO JOKE AROUND.
Ahh!
Ahh!
CHEEP
TEN MINUTES LATER
Message
Hi.
Sure, of course you can call me that! ^^
THERE.
I WONDER IF I SHOULD HAVE ADDED THE EMOTICON.
B-BMP
B-BMP
SO FAST!
TING
Sub Re:Re:
You also can call me whatever you would like.
Even a nickname.
WHAT ...?

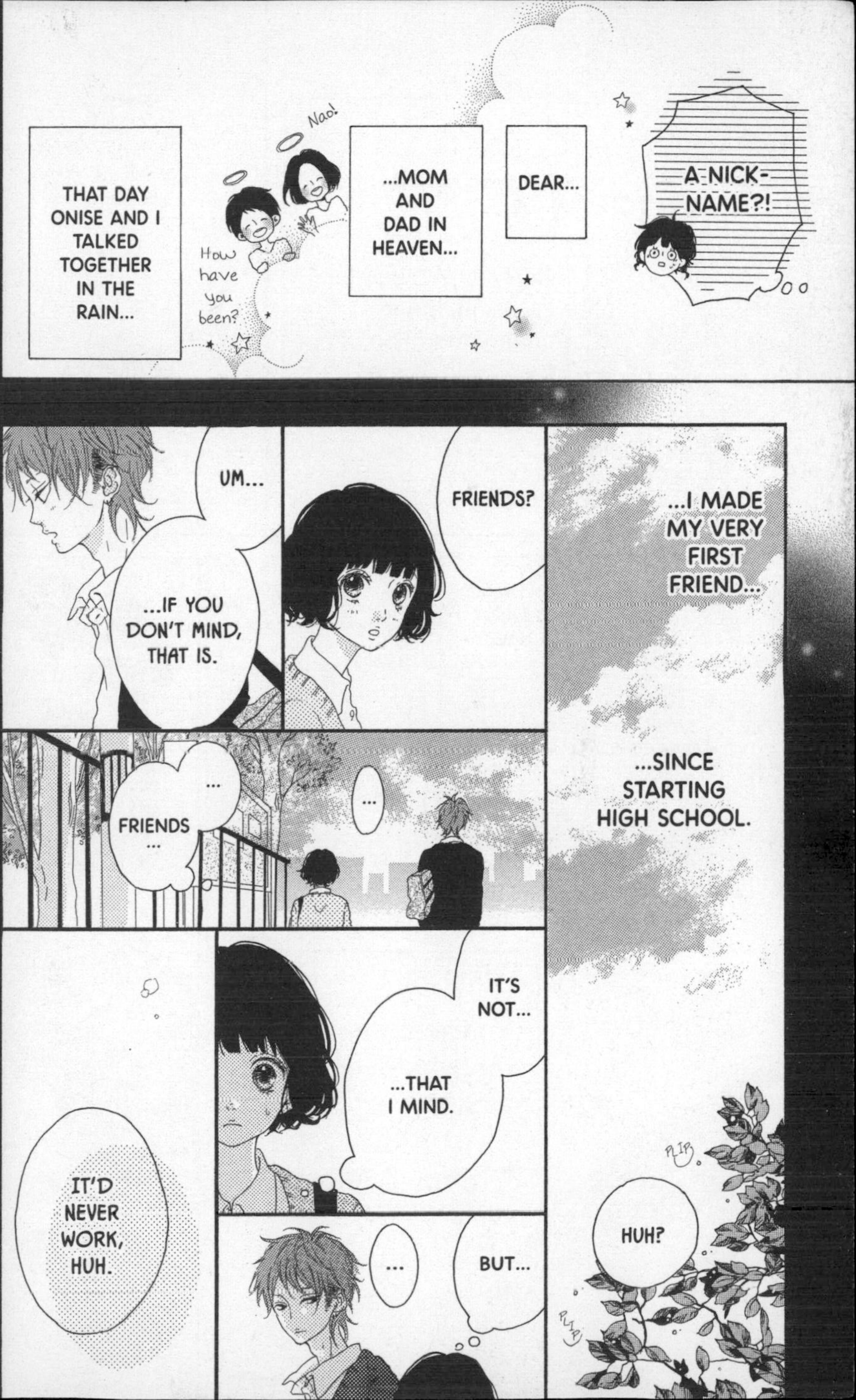
A NICK-NAME?!
DEAR...
...MOM AND DAD IN HEAVEN...
Nao!
How have you been?
THAT DAY ONISE AND I TALKED TOGETHER IN THE RAIN...
...I MADE MY VERY FIRST FRIEND...
...SINCE STARTING HIGH SCHOOL.
FRIENDS?
UM...
...IF YOU DON'T MIND, THAT IS.
...
... FRIENDS ...
IT'S NOT...
...THAT I MIND.
IT'D NEVER WORK, HUH.
HUH?
PLIP
BUT...
...
PLIP

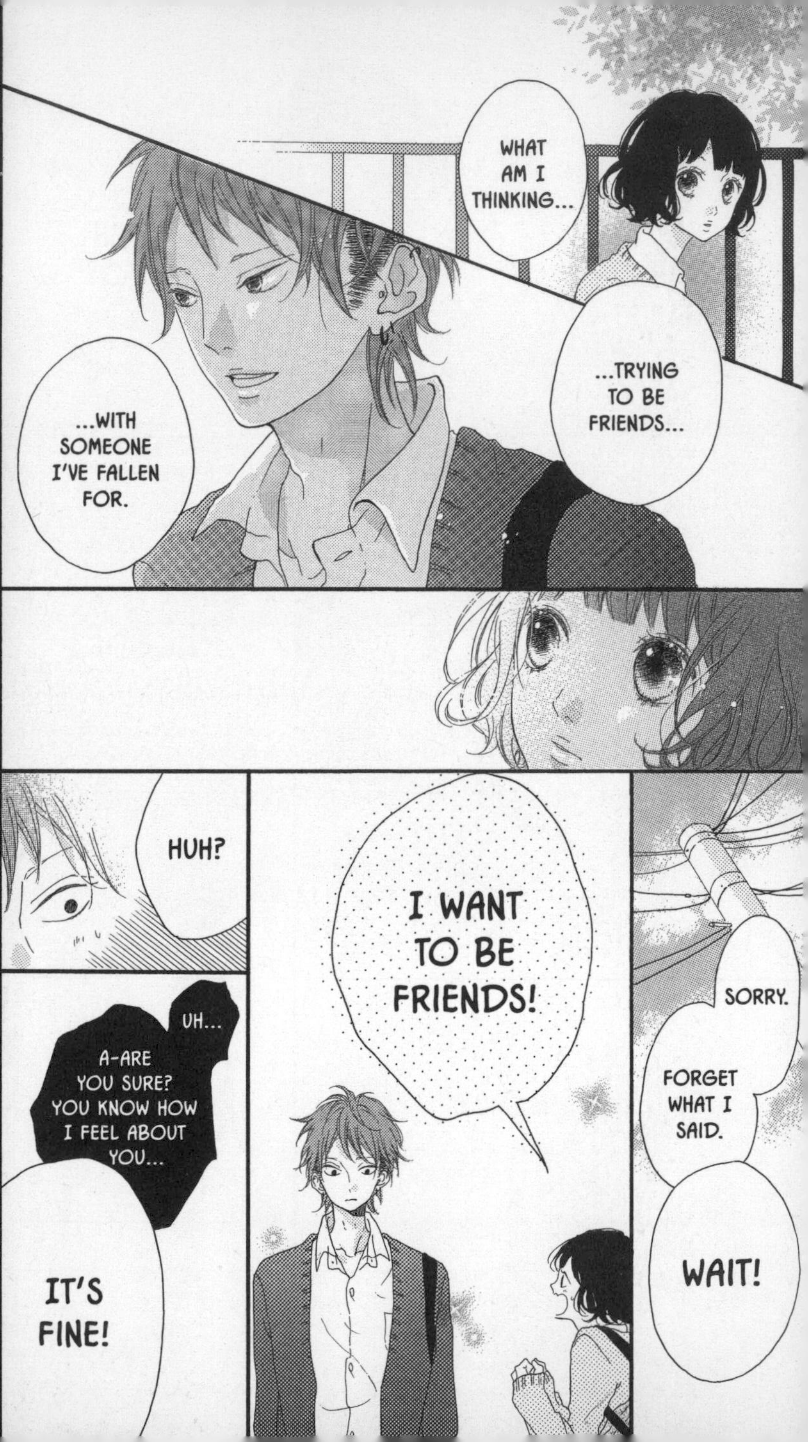
WHAT AM I THINKING...
...TRYING TO BE FRIENDS...
...WITH SOMEONE I'VE FALLEN FOR.
SORRY.
FORGET WHAT I SAID.
WAIT!
I WANT TO BE FRIENDS!
HUH?
UH...
A-ARE YOU SURE? YOU KNOW HOW I FEEL ABOUT YOU...
IT'S FINE!

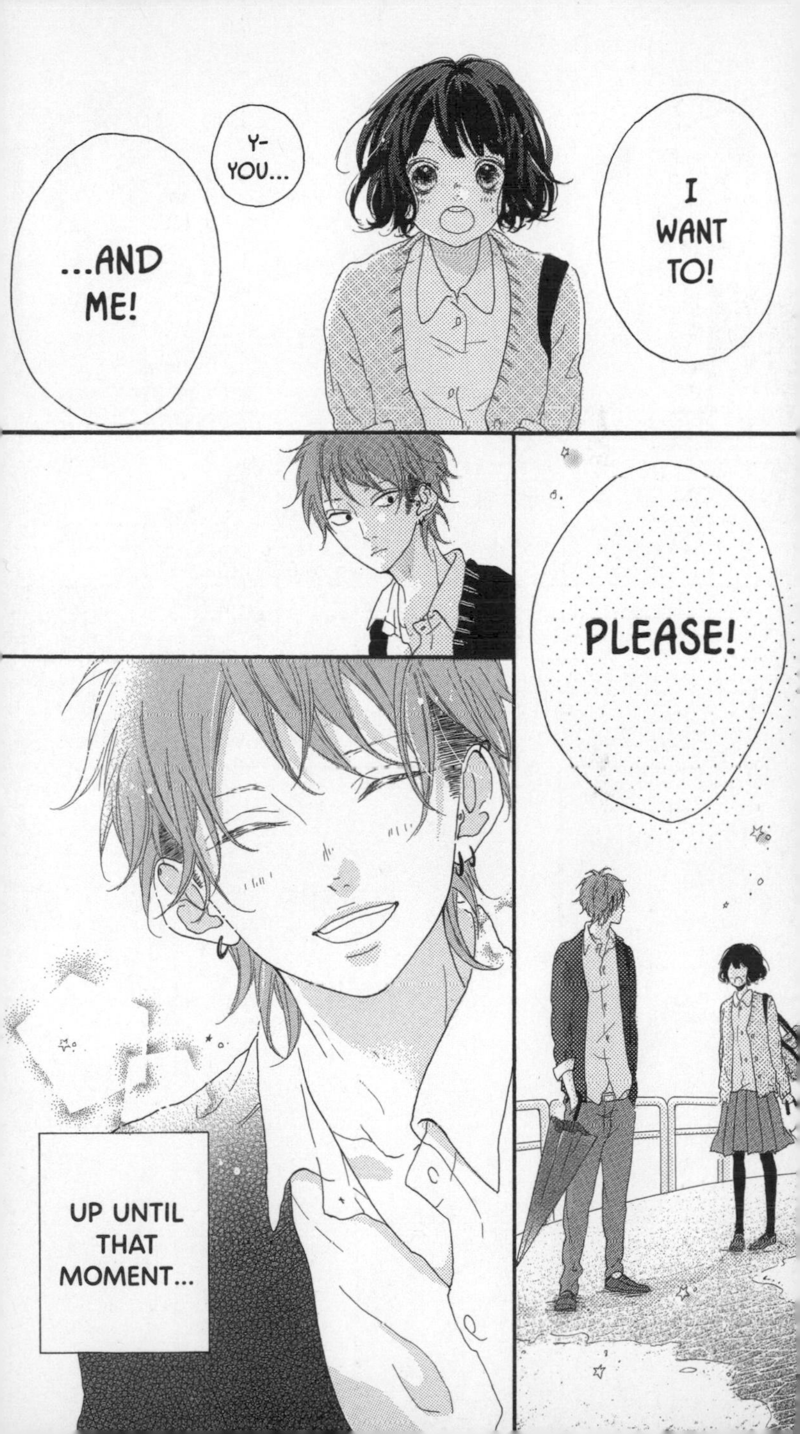
I WANT TO!
Y- YOU...
...AND ME!
PLEASE!
UP UNTIL THAT MOMENT...

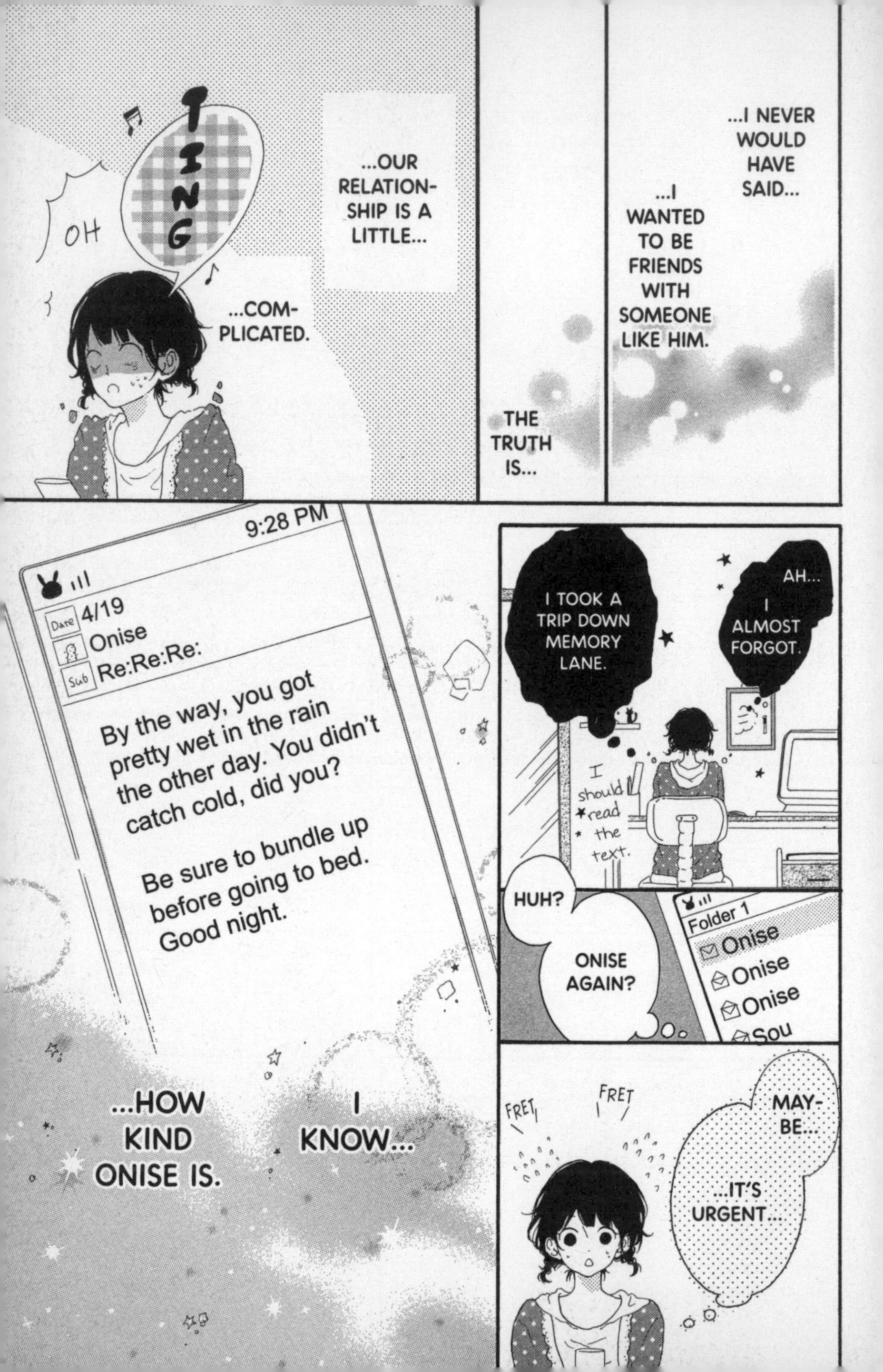
...I NEVER WOULD HAVE SAID...
...I WANTED TO BE FRIENDS WITH SOMEONE LIKE HIM.
THE TRUTH IS...
...OUR RELATIONSHIP IS A LITTLE...
TING
OH
...COMPLICATED.
AH... I ALMOST FORGOT.
I TOOK A TRIP DOWN MEMORY LANE.
I should read the text.
Folder 1
Onise
Onise
Onise
Sou
HUH?
ONISE AGAIN?
MAY-BE...
...IT'S URGENT...
FRET
FRET
9:28 PM
Date 4/19
Onise
Sub Re:Re:Re:
By the way, you got pretty wet in the rain the other day. You didn't catch cold, did you?
Be sure to bundle up before going to bed. Good night.
I KNOW...
...HOW KIND ONISE IS.

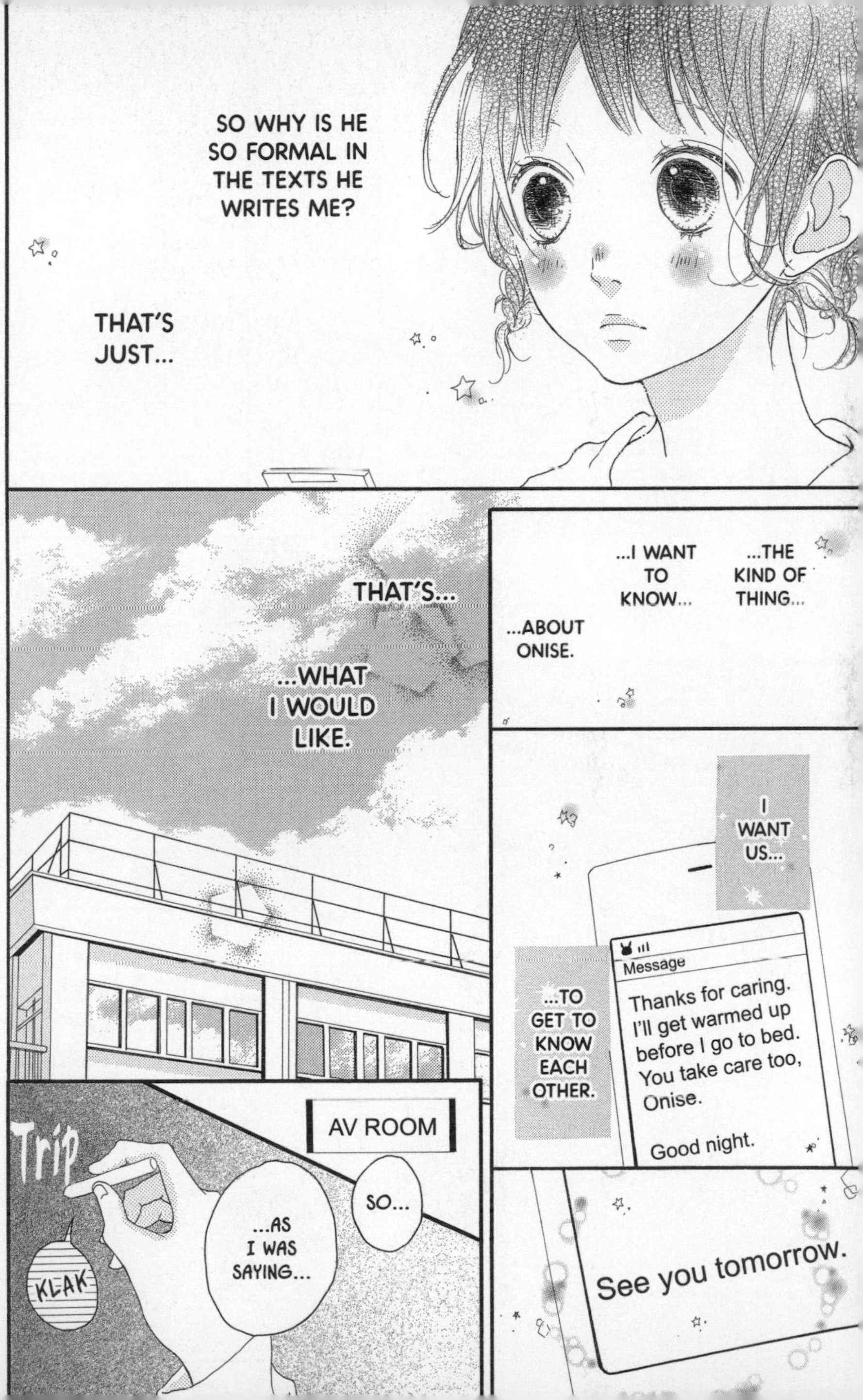
SO WHY IS HE SO FORMAL IN THE TEXTS HE WRITES ME?
THAT'S JUST...
...THE KIND OF THING...
...I WANT TO KNOW...
...ABOUT ONISE.
I WANT US...
...TO GET TO KNOW EACH OTHER.
Message
Thanks for caring. I'll get warmed up before I go to bed. You take care too, Onise.
Good night.
See you tomorrow.
THAT'S...
...WHAT I WOULD LIKE.
AV ROOM
SO...
...AS I WAS SAYING...
Trip
KLAK

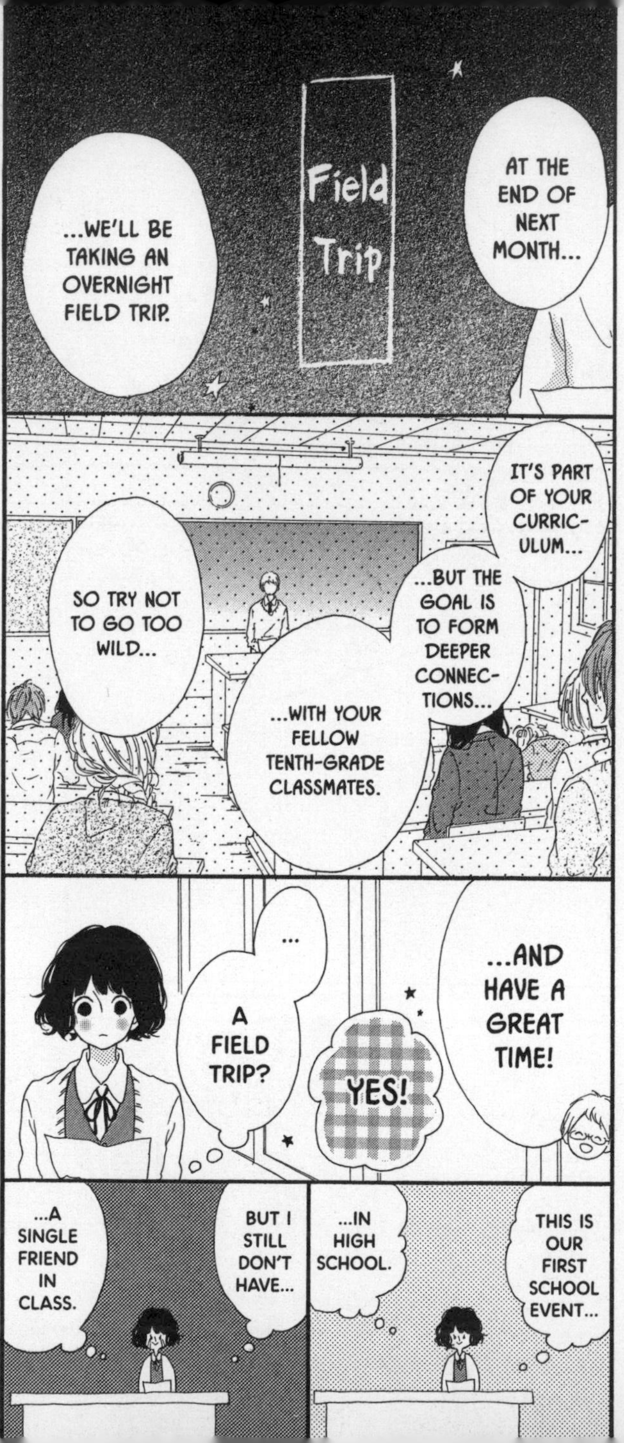
AT THE END OF NEXT MONTH...
Field Trip
...WE'LL BE TAKING AN OVERNIGHT FIELD TRIP.
IT'S PART OF YOUR CURRIC-ULUM...
...BUT THE GOAL IS TO FORM DEEPER CONNEC-TIONS...
...WITH YOUR FELLOW TENTH-GRADE CLASSMATES.
SO TRY NOT TO GO TOO WILD...
...AND HAVE A GREAT TIME!
YES!
...
A FIELD TRIP?
THIS IS OUR FIRST SCHOOL EVENT...
...IN HIGH SCHOOL.
BUT I STILL DON'T HAVE...
...A SINGLE FRIEND IN CLASS.
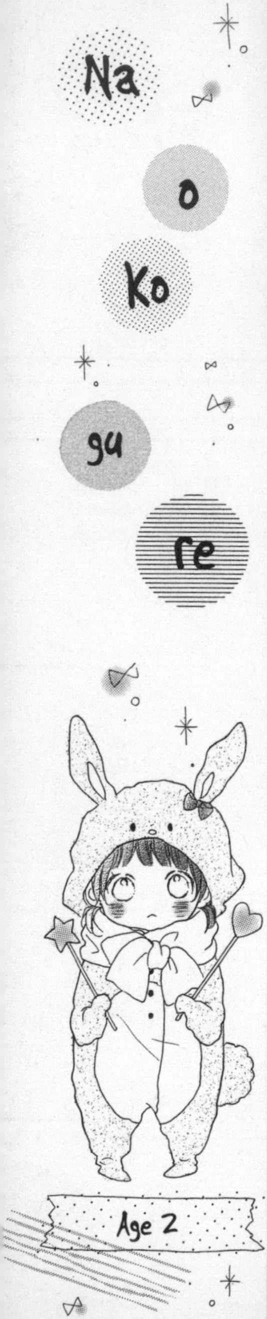
Na o Ko gu re
Age 2

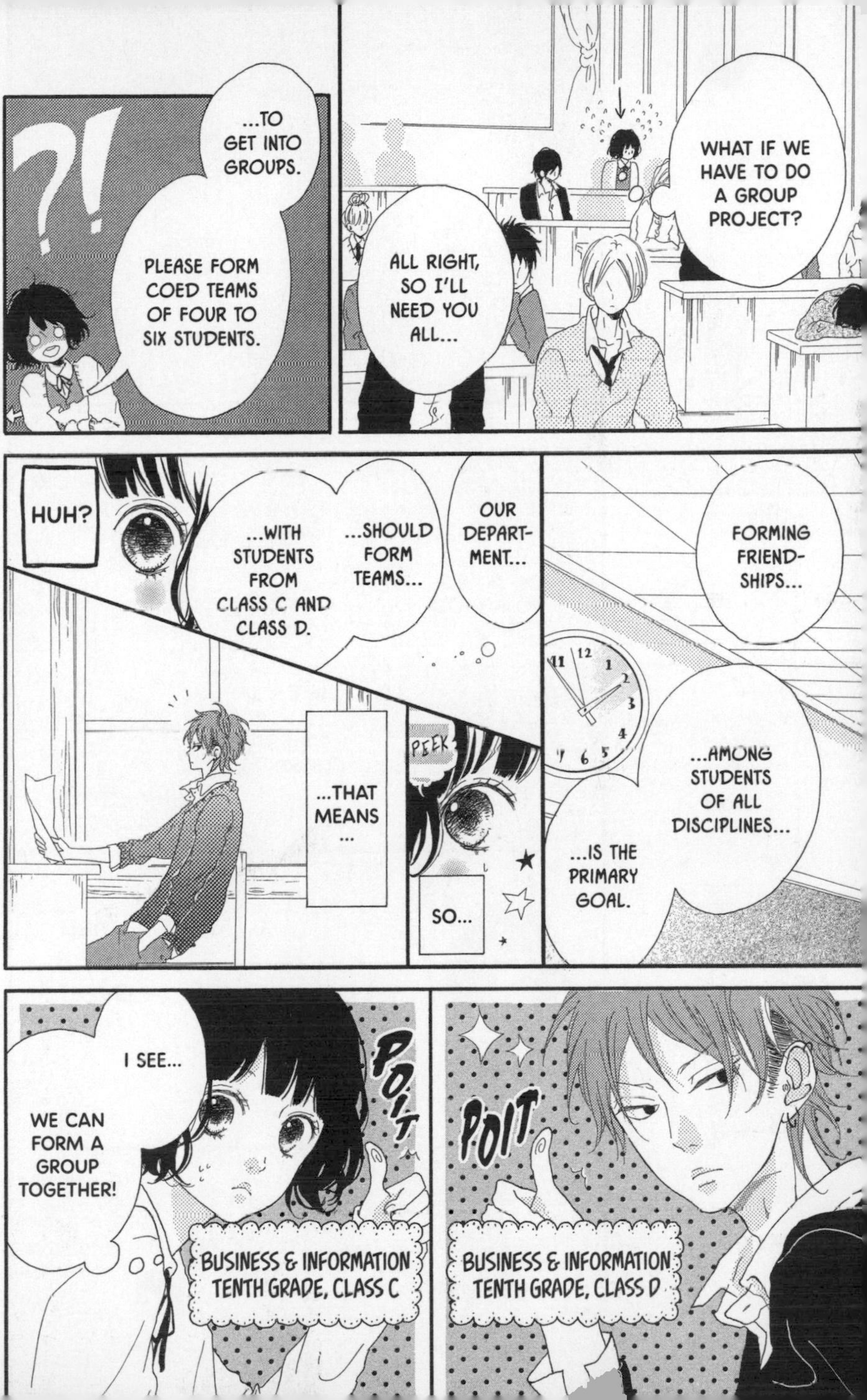
WHAT IF WE HAVE TO DO A GROUP PROJECT?
ALL RIGHT, SO I'LL NEED YOU ALL...
...TO GET INTO GROUPS.
PLEASE FORM COED TEAMS OF FOUR TO SIX STUDENTS.
?!
FORMING FRIEND-SHIPS...
...AMONG STUDENTS OF ALL DISCIPLINES...
...IS THE PRIMARY GOAL.
OUR DEPART-MENT...
...SHOULD FORM TEAMS...
...WITH STUDENTS FROM CLASS C AND CLASS D.
HUH?
PEEK
SO...
...THAT MEANS ...
POIT
BUSINESS & INFORMATION TENTH GRADE, CLASS D
I SEE...
WE CAN FORM A GROUP TOGETHER!
POIT
BUSINESS & INFORMATION TENTH GRADE, CLASS C

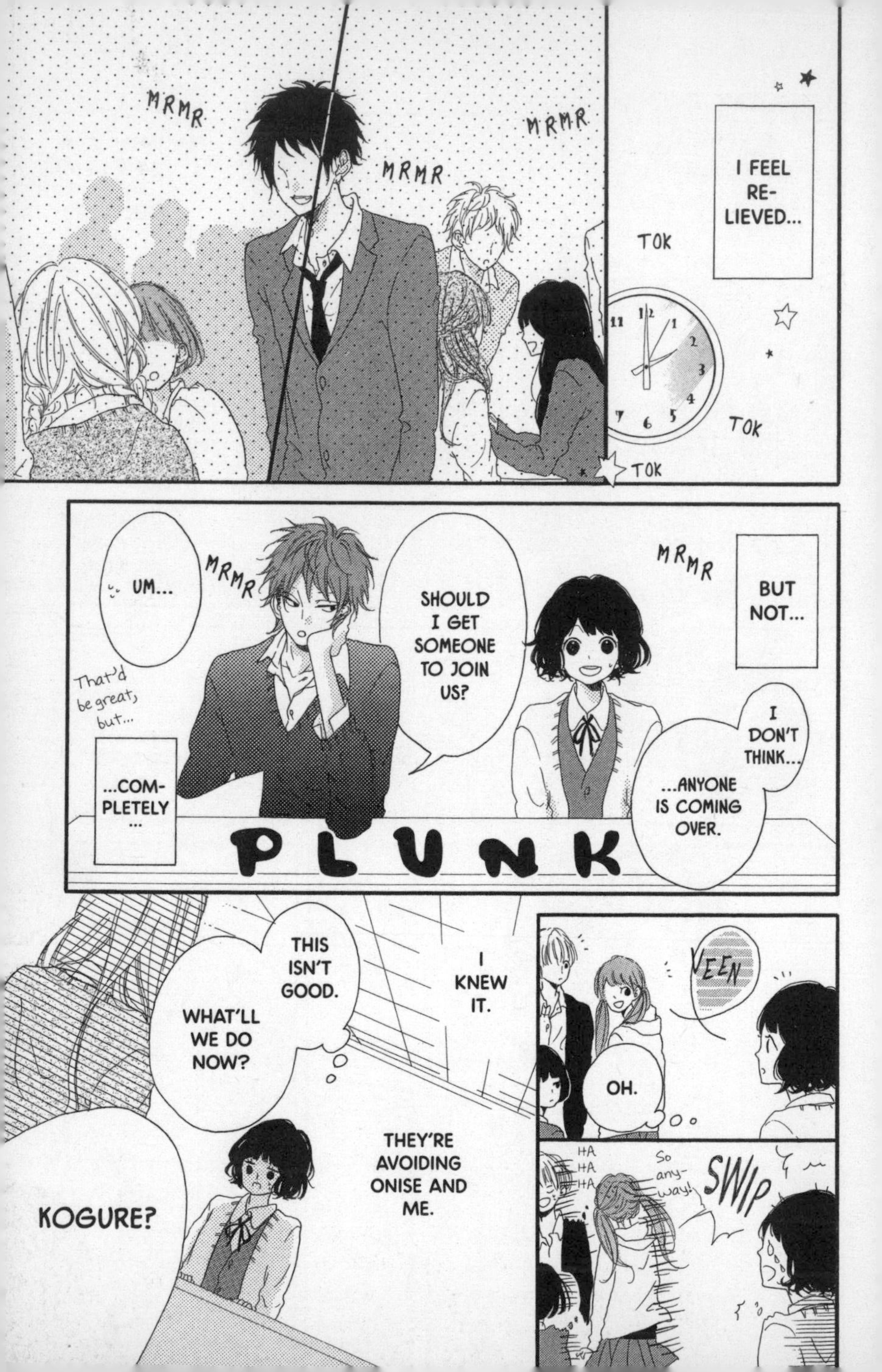
I FEEL RE-LIEVED...
TOK
TOK
TOK
MRMR
MRMR
MRMR
BUT NOT...
MRMR
I DON'T THINK...
...ANYONE IS COMING OVER.
SHOULD I GET SOMEONE TO JOIN US?
PLUNK
MRMR
UM...
That'd be great, but...
...COMPLETELY ...
VEEN
OH.
SWIP
So any-way!
HA
HA
HA
I KNEW IT.
THIS ISN'T GOOD.
WHAT'LL WE DO NOW?
THEY'RE AVOIDING ONISE AND ME.
KOGURE?

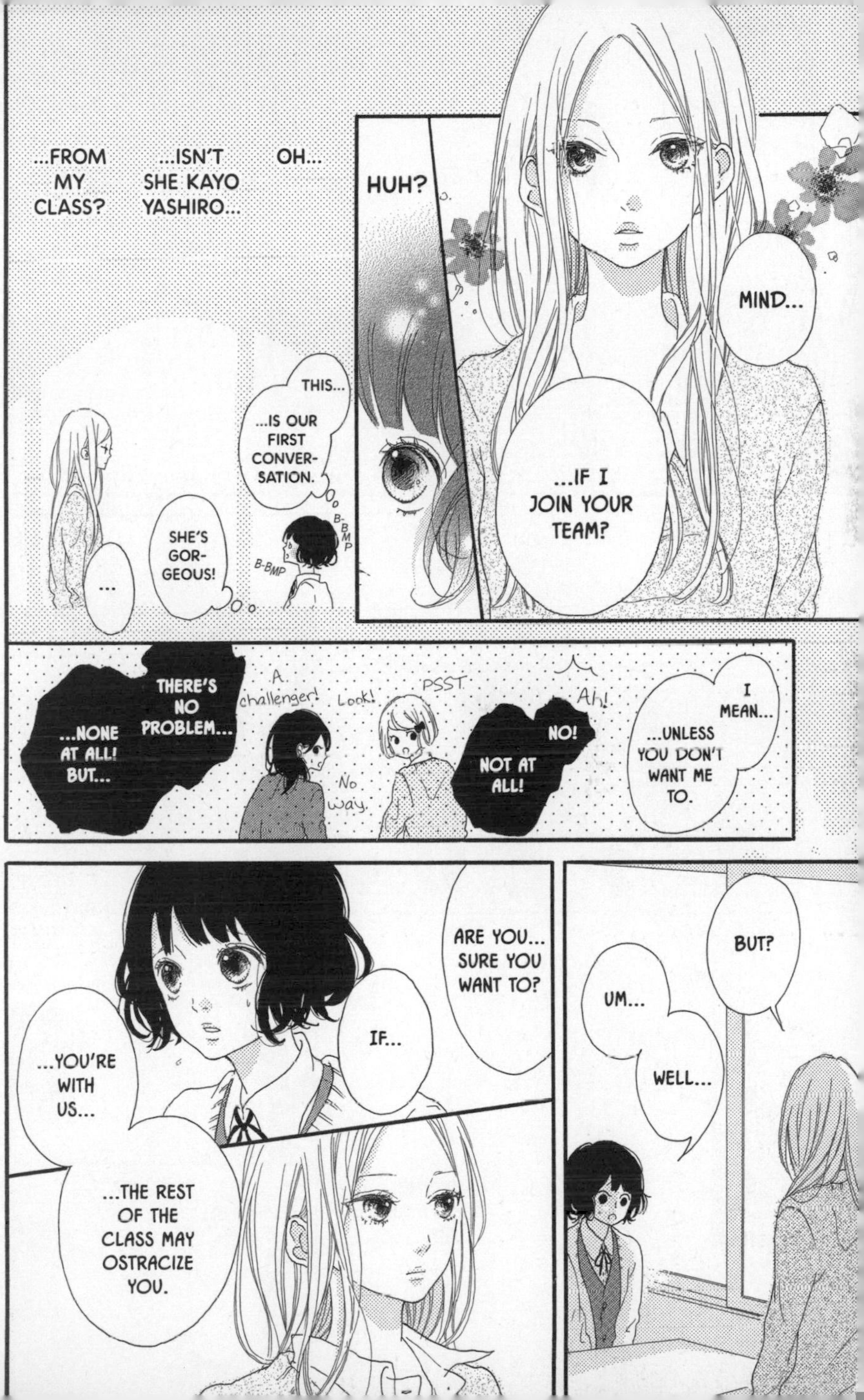
MIND...
...IF I JOIN YOUR TEAM?
HUH?
OH...
...ISN'T SHE KAYO YASHIRO...
...FROM MY CLASS?
THIS...
...IS OUR FIRST CONVERSATION.
B-BMP
B-BMP
SHE'S GORGEOUS!
...
I MEAN...
...UNLESS YOU DON'T WANT ME TO.
Ah!
NO!
NOT AT ALL!
PSST
Look!
A challenger!
No way.
THERE'S NO PROBLEM...
...NONE AT ALL! BUT...
BUT?
UM...
WELL...
ARE YOU... SURE YOU WANT TO?
IF...
...YOU'RE WITH US...
...THE REST OF THE CLASS MAY OSTRACIZE YOU.

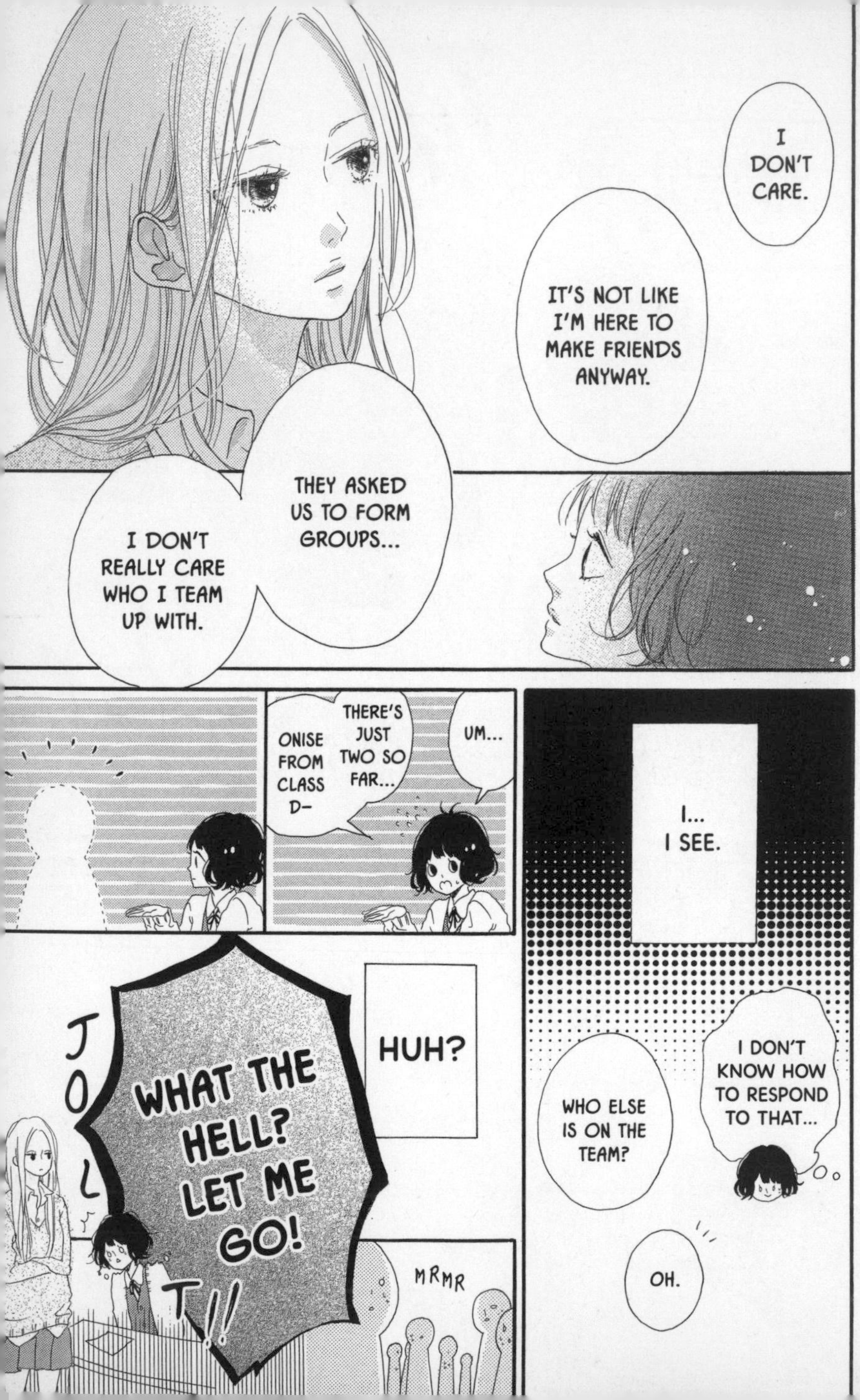
I DON'T CARE.
IT'S NOT LIKE I'M HERE TO MAKE FRIENDS ANYWAY.
THEY ASKED US TO FORM GROUPS...
I DON'T REALLY CARE WHO I TEAM UP WITH.
I... I SEE.
I DON'T KNOW HOW TO RESPOND TO THAT...
WHO ELSE IS ON THE TEAM?
OH.
UM...
THERE'S JUST TWO SO FAR...
ONISE FROM CLASS D-
HUH?
JOLT!!
WHAT THE HELL? LET ME GO!
MRMR

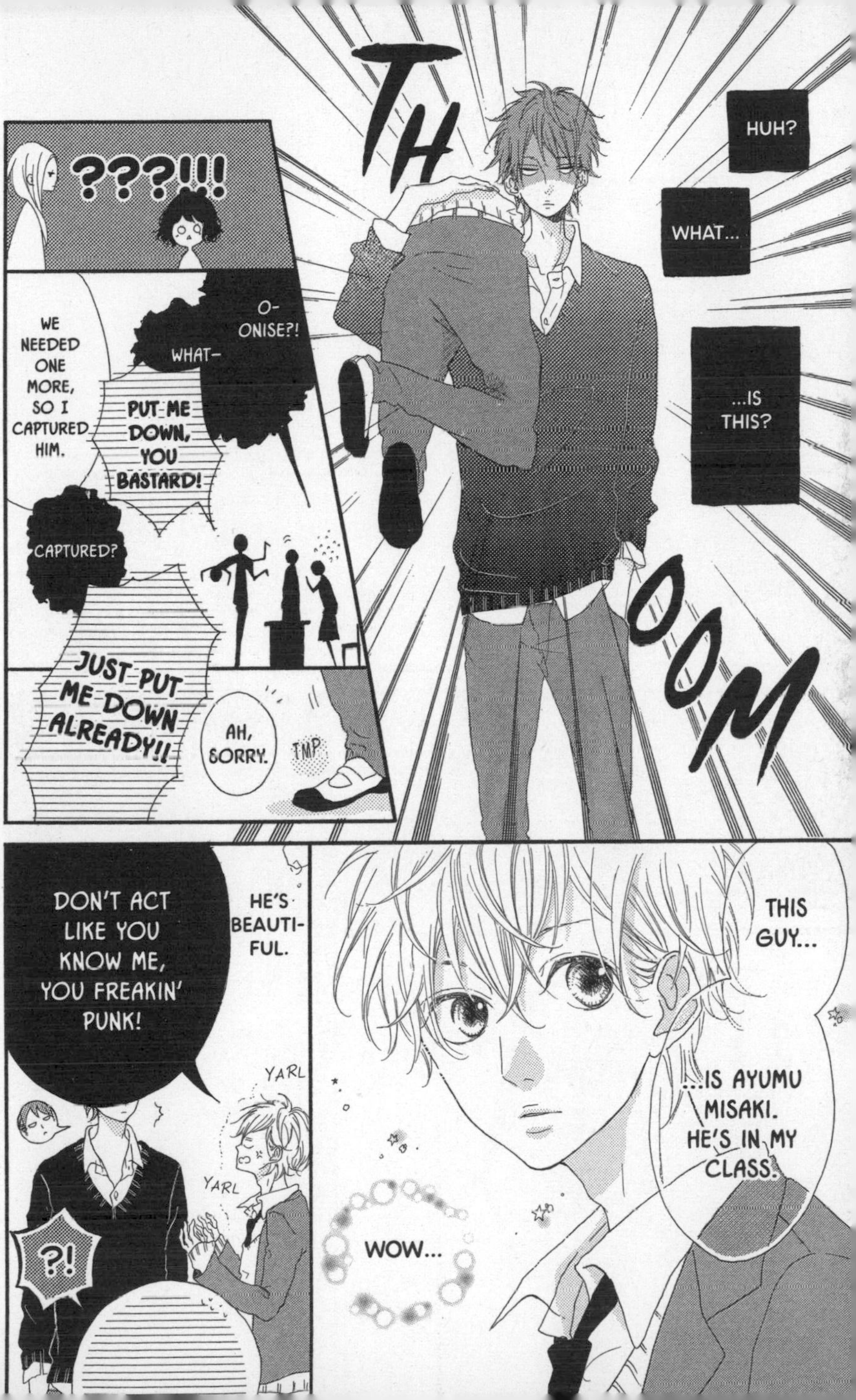

HUH?
WHAT...
...IS THIS?
THOOM
???!!!
O-ONISE?!
WHAT—
WE NEEDED ONE MORE, SO I CAPTURED HIM.
PUT ME DOWN, YOU BASTARD!
CAPTURED?
JUST PUT ME DOWN ALREADY!!
AH, SORRY.
TMP
THIS GUY...
...IS AYUMU MISAKI. HE'S IN MY CLASS.
WOW...
HE'S BEAUTIFUL.
DON'T ACT LIKE YOU KNOW ME, YOU FREAKIN' PUNK!
YARL
YARL
?!

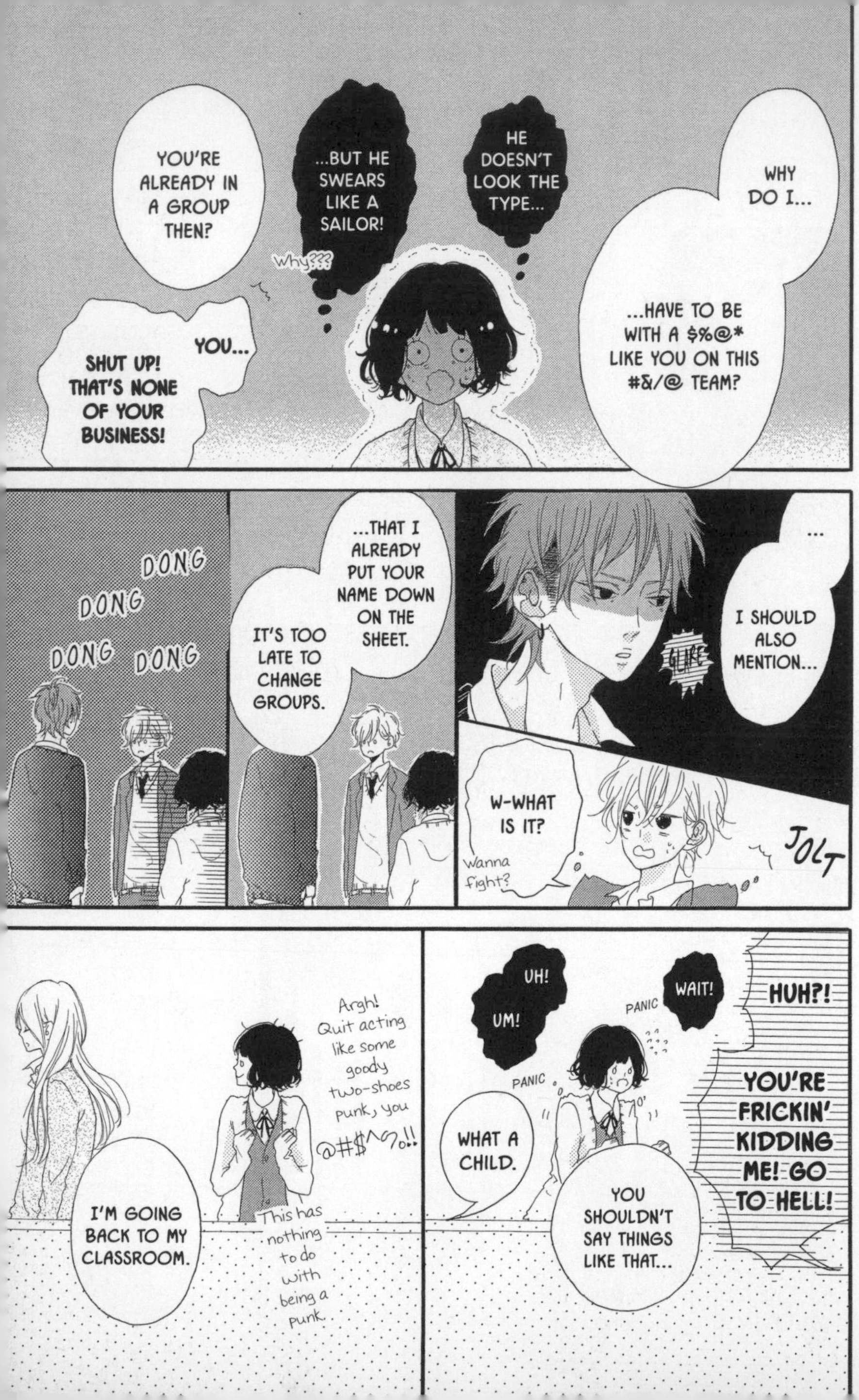
WHY DO I...
...HAVE TO BE WITH A $%@* LIKE YOU ON THIS #&/@ TEAM?
HE DOESN'T LOOK THE TYPE...
...BUT HE SWEARS LIKE A SAILOR!
Why???
YOU'RE ALREADY IN A GROUP THEN?
YOU...
SHUT UP! THAT'S NONE OF YOUR BUSINESS!
...
I SHOULD ALSO MENTION...
GLARE
JOLT
W-WHAT IS IT?
Wanna fight?
...THAT I ALREADY PUT YOUR NAME DOWN ON THE SHEET.
IT'S TOO LATE TO CHANGE GROUPS.
DONG
DONG
DONG
DONG
HUH?!
YOU'RE FRICKIN' KIDDING ME! GO TO HELL!
WAIT!
PANIC
UH!
UM!
PANIC
YOU SHOULDN'T SAY THINGS LIKE THAT...
WHAT A CHILD.
Argh! Quit acting like some goody two-shoes punk, you @#$^%!!
I'M GOING BACK TO MY CLASSROOM.
This has nothing to do with being a punk.

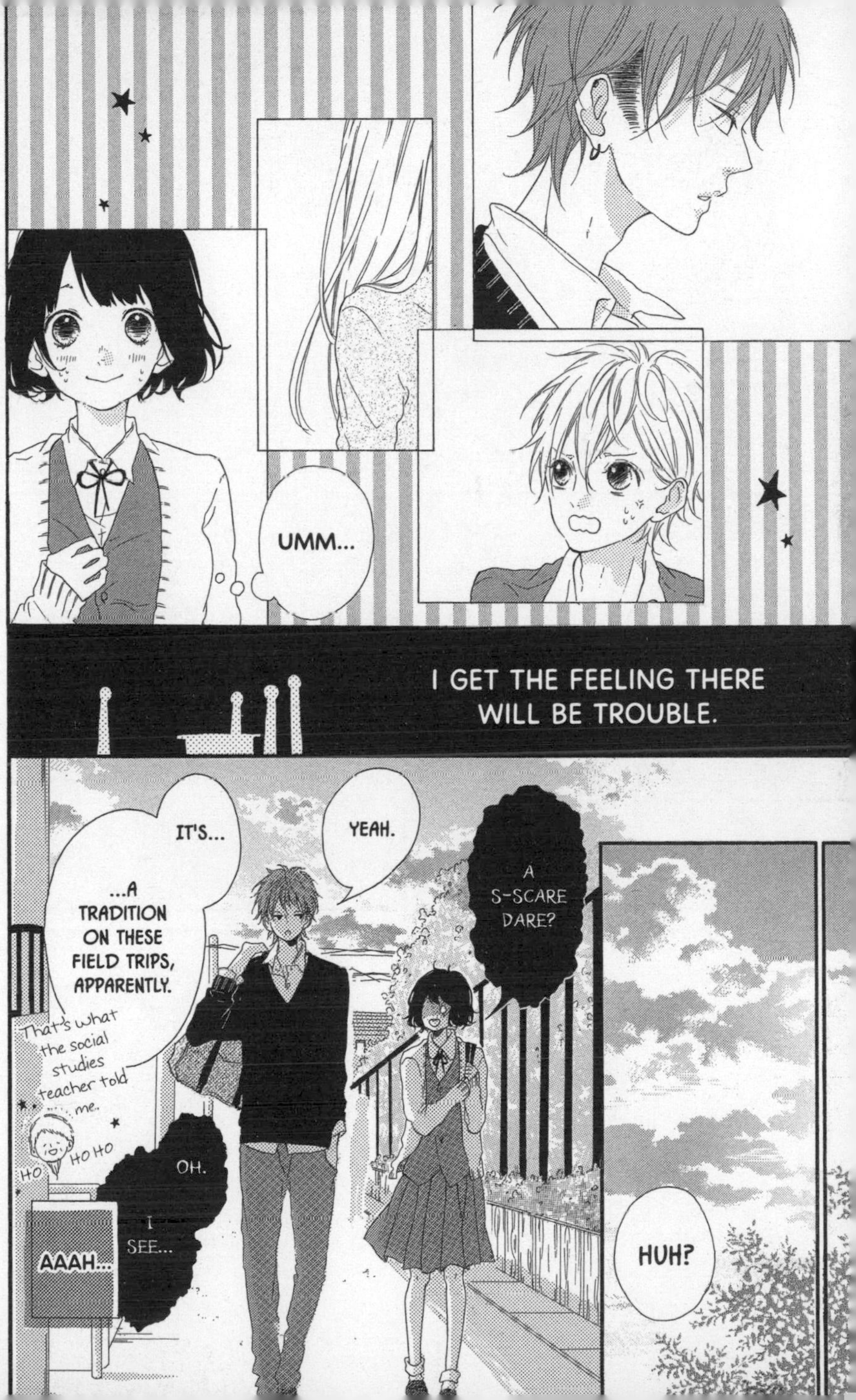
UMM...
I GET THE FEELING THERE WILL BE TROUBLE.
HUH?
A S-SCARE DARE?
YEAH.
IT'S...
...A TRADITION ON THESE FIELD TRIPS, APPARENTLY.
That's what the social studies teacher told me.
HO HO HO
OH.
I SEE...
AAAH...

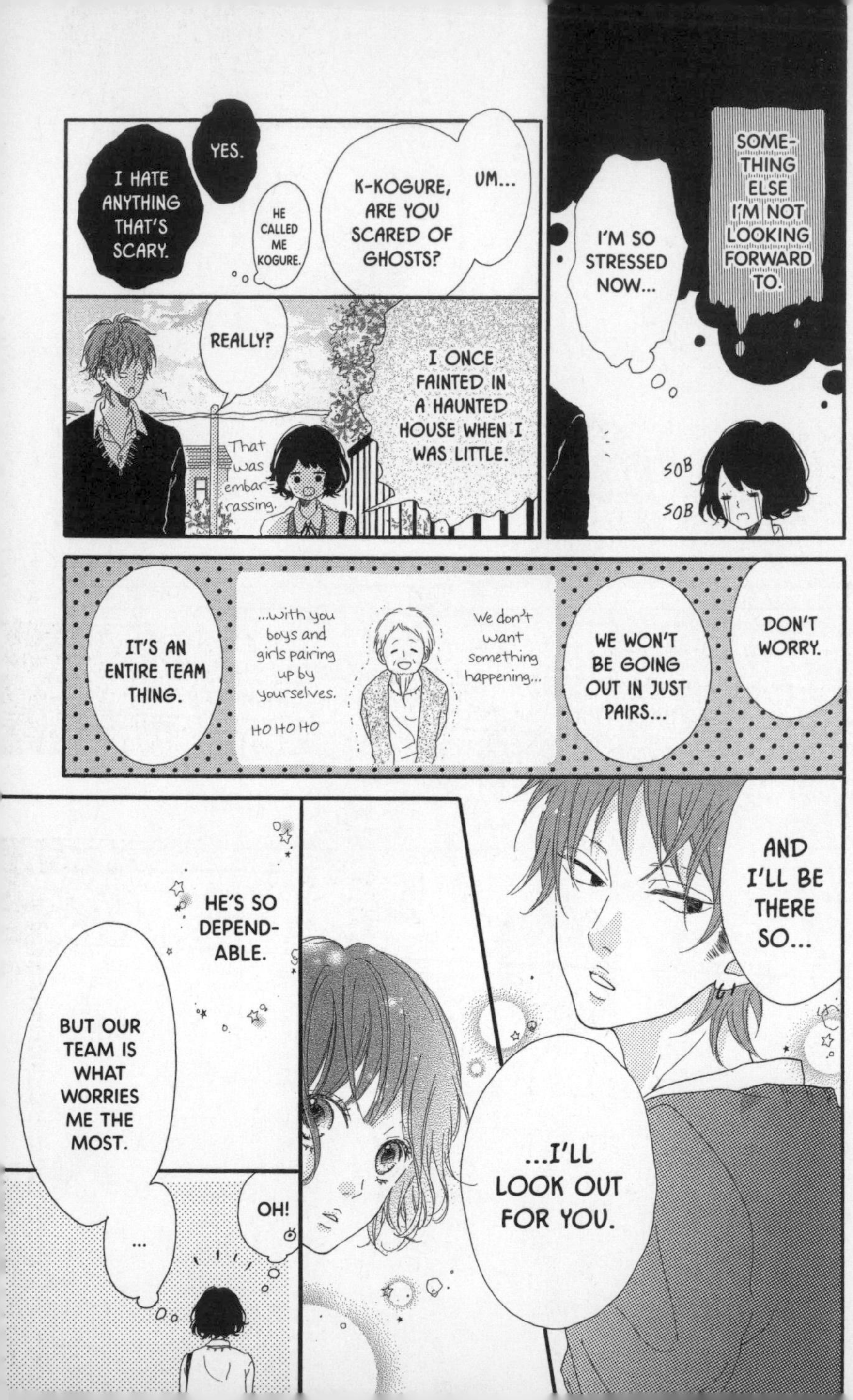
SOME-THING ELSE I'M NOT LOOKING FORWARD TO.
I'M SO STRESSED NOW...
SOB
SOB
UM...
K-KOGURE, ARE YOU SCARED OF GHOSTS?
HE CALLED ME KOGURE.
YES.
I HATE ANYTHING THAT'S SCARY.
I ONCE FAINTED IN A HAUNTED HOUSE WHEN I WAS LITTLE.
REALLY?
That was embar-rassing.
DON'T WORRY.
WE WON'T BE GOING OUT IN JUST PAIRS...
We don't want something happening...
...with you boys and girls pairing up by yourselves.
HO HO HO
IT'S AN ENTIRE TEAM THING.
AND I'LL BE THERE SO...
...I'LL LOOK OUT FOR YOU.
HE'S SO DEPEND-ABLE.
BUT OUR TEAM IS WHAT WORRIES ME THE MOST.
OH!
...

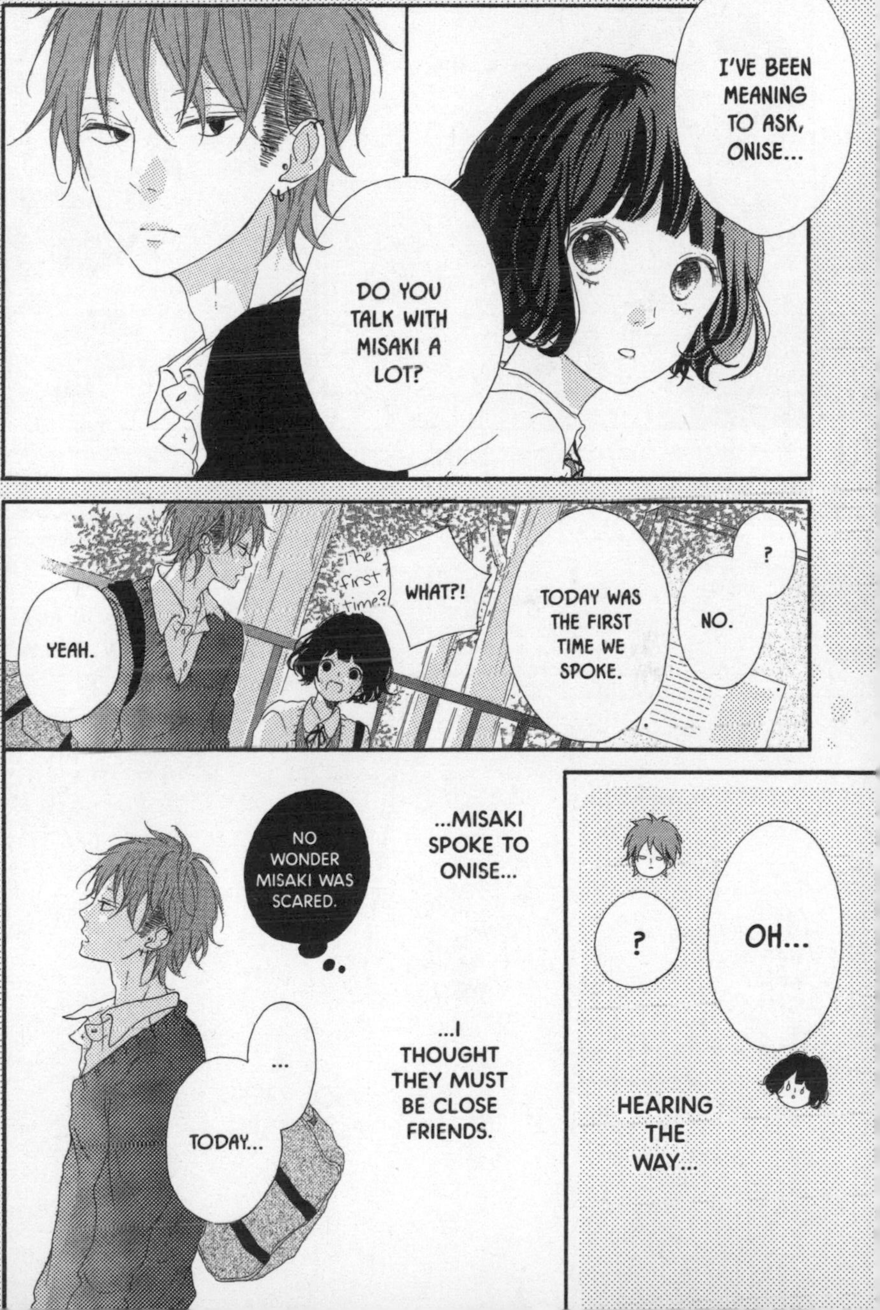
I'VE BEEN MEANING TO ASK, ONISE...
DO YOU TALK WITH MISAKI A LOT?
?
NO.
TODAY WAS THE FIRST TIME WE SPOKE.
WHAT?!
The first time?
YEAH.
OH...
?
HEARING THE WAY...
...MISAKI SPOKE TO ONISE...
...I THOUGHT THEY MUST BE CLOSE FRIENDS.
NO WONDER MISAKI WAS SCARED.
...
TODAY...

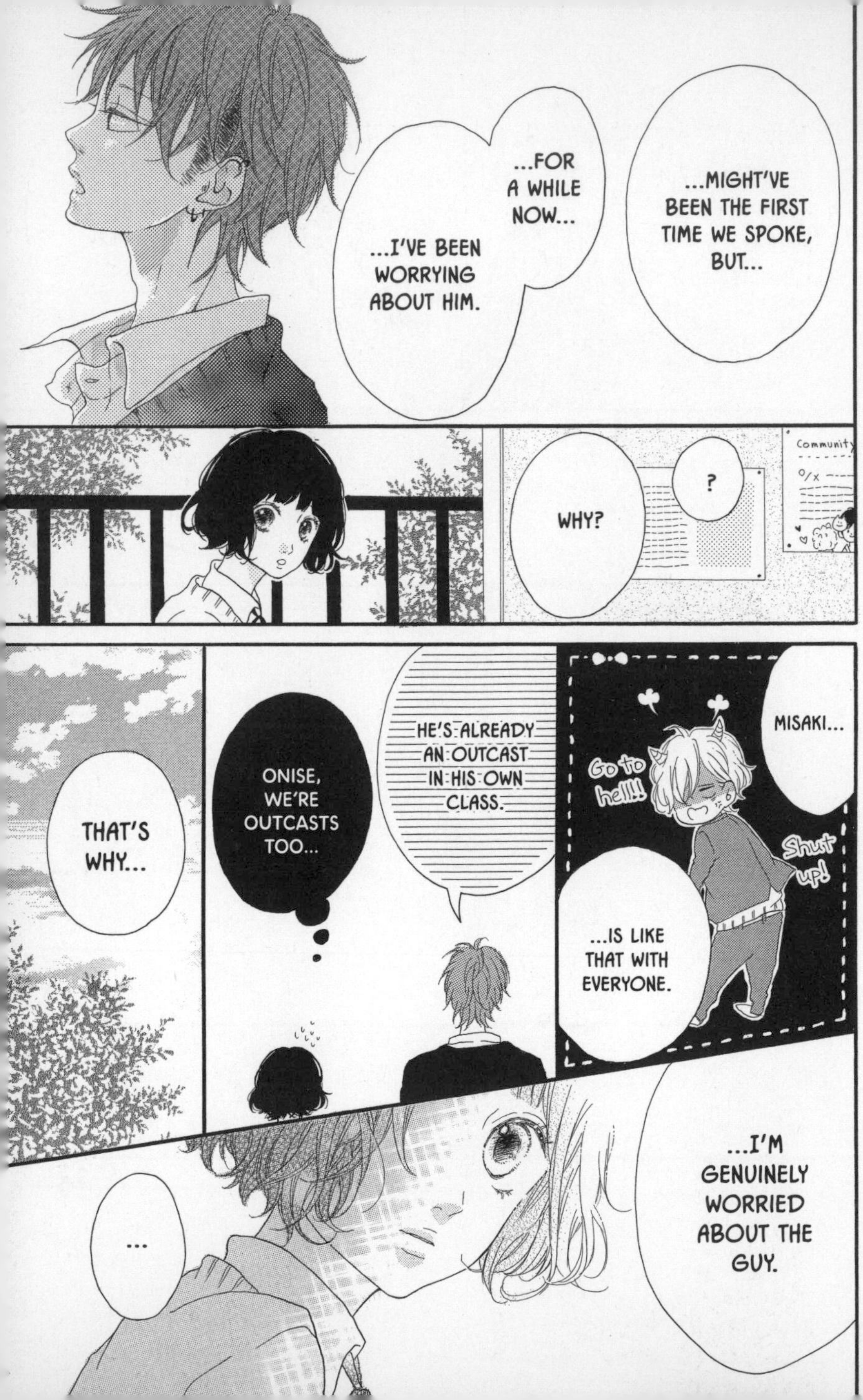
...MIGHT'VE BEEN THE FIRST TIME WE SPOKE, BUT...
...FOR A WHILE NOW...
...I'VE BEEN WORRYING ABOUT HIM.
Community
?
WHY?
MISAKI...
Go to hell!!!
Shut up!
...IS LIKE THAT WITH EVERYONE.
HE'S ALREADY AN OUTCAST IN HIS OWN CLASS.
ONISE, WE'RE OUTCASTS TOO...
THAT'S WHY...
...I'M GENUINELY WORRIED ABOUT THE GUY.
...

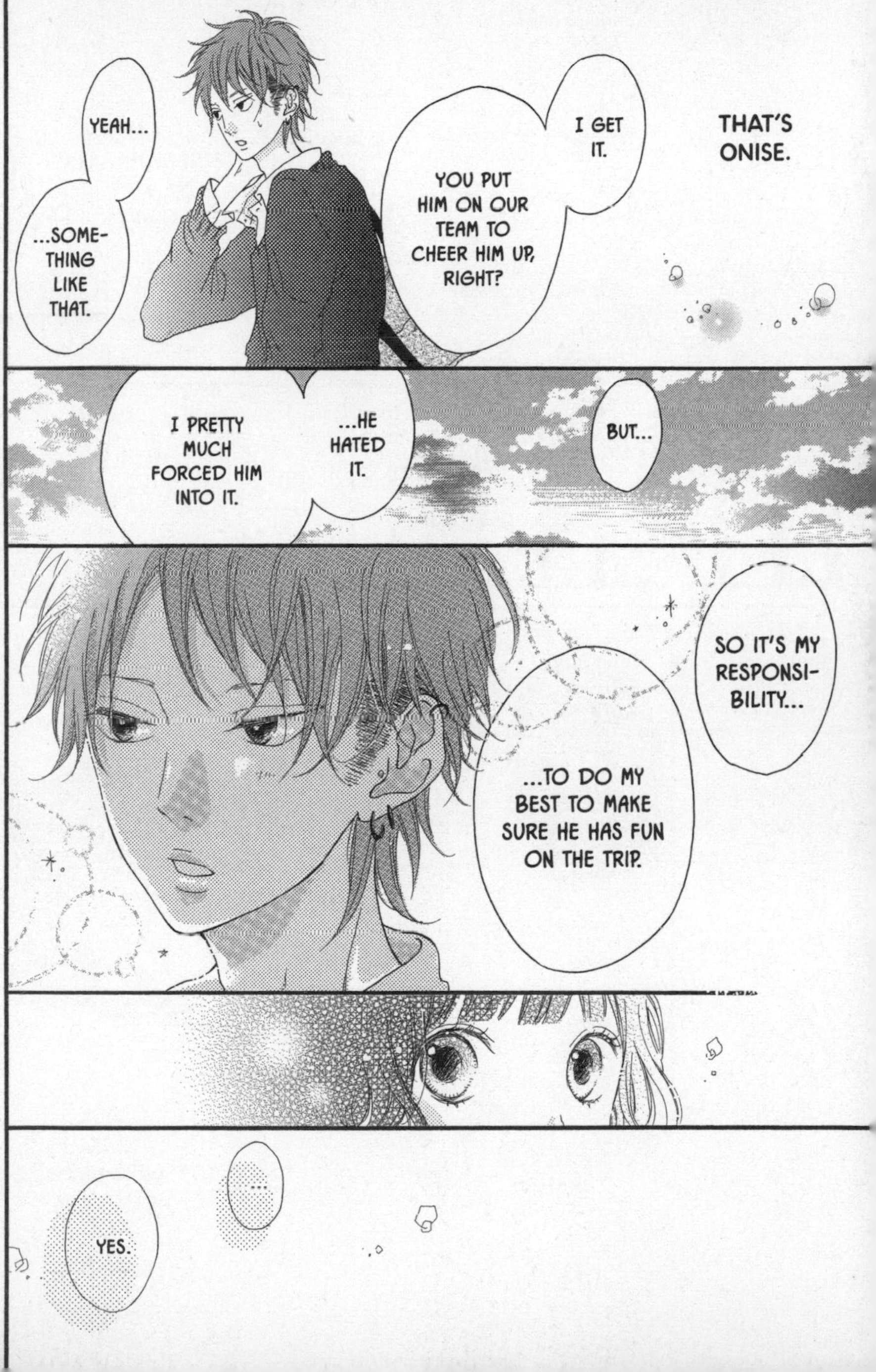
THAT'S ONISE.
I GET IT.
YOU PUT HIM ON OUR TEAM TO CHEER HIM UP, RIGHT?
YEAH...
...SOME-THING LIKE THAT.
BUT...
...HE HATED IT.
I PRETTY MUCH FORCED HIM INTO IT.
SO IT'S MY RESPONSI-BILITY...
...TO DO MY BEST TO MAKE SURE HE HAS FUN ON THE TRIP.
...
YES.

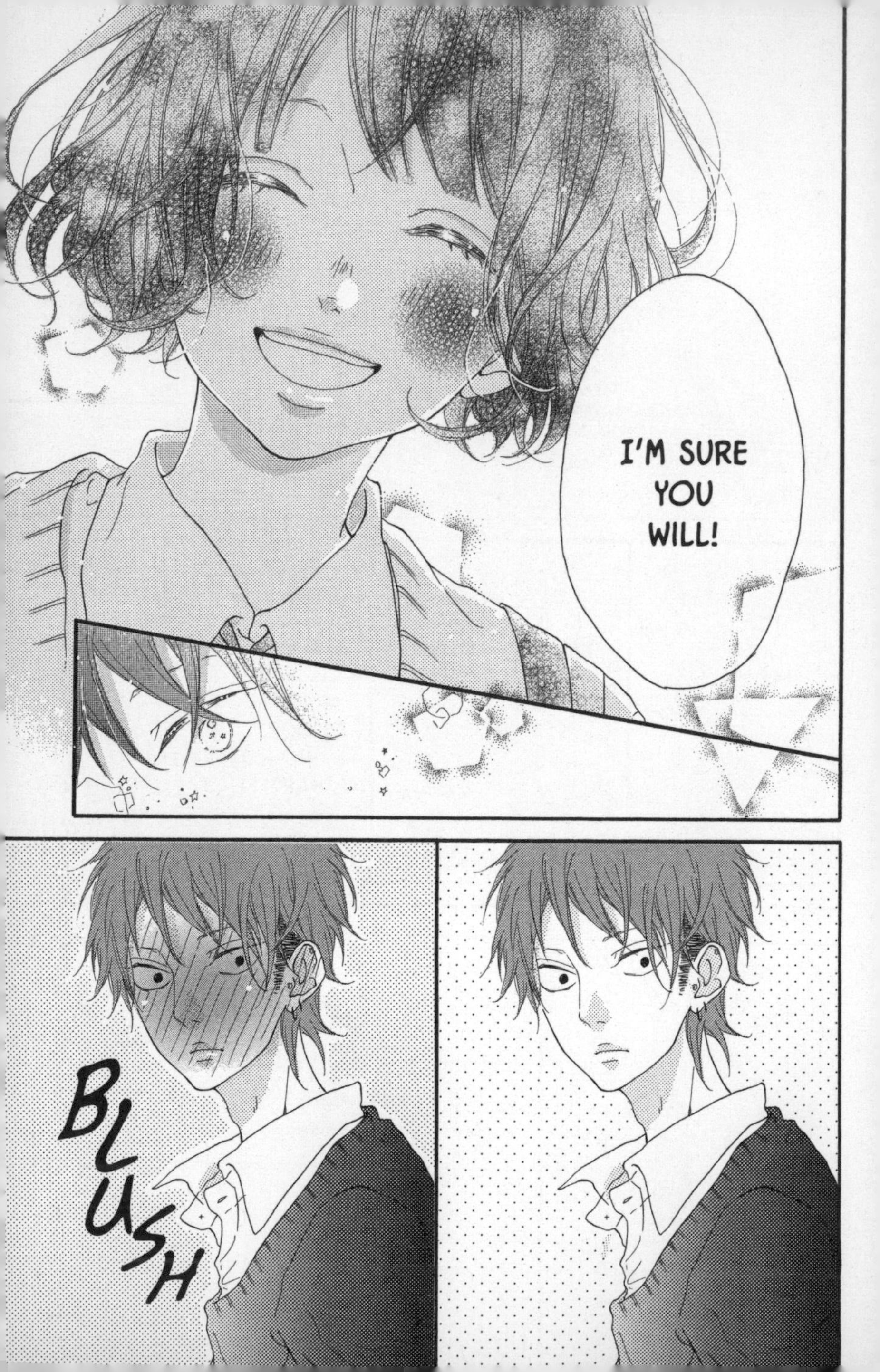
I'M SURE YOU WILL!
BLUSH

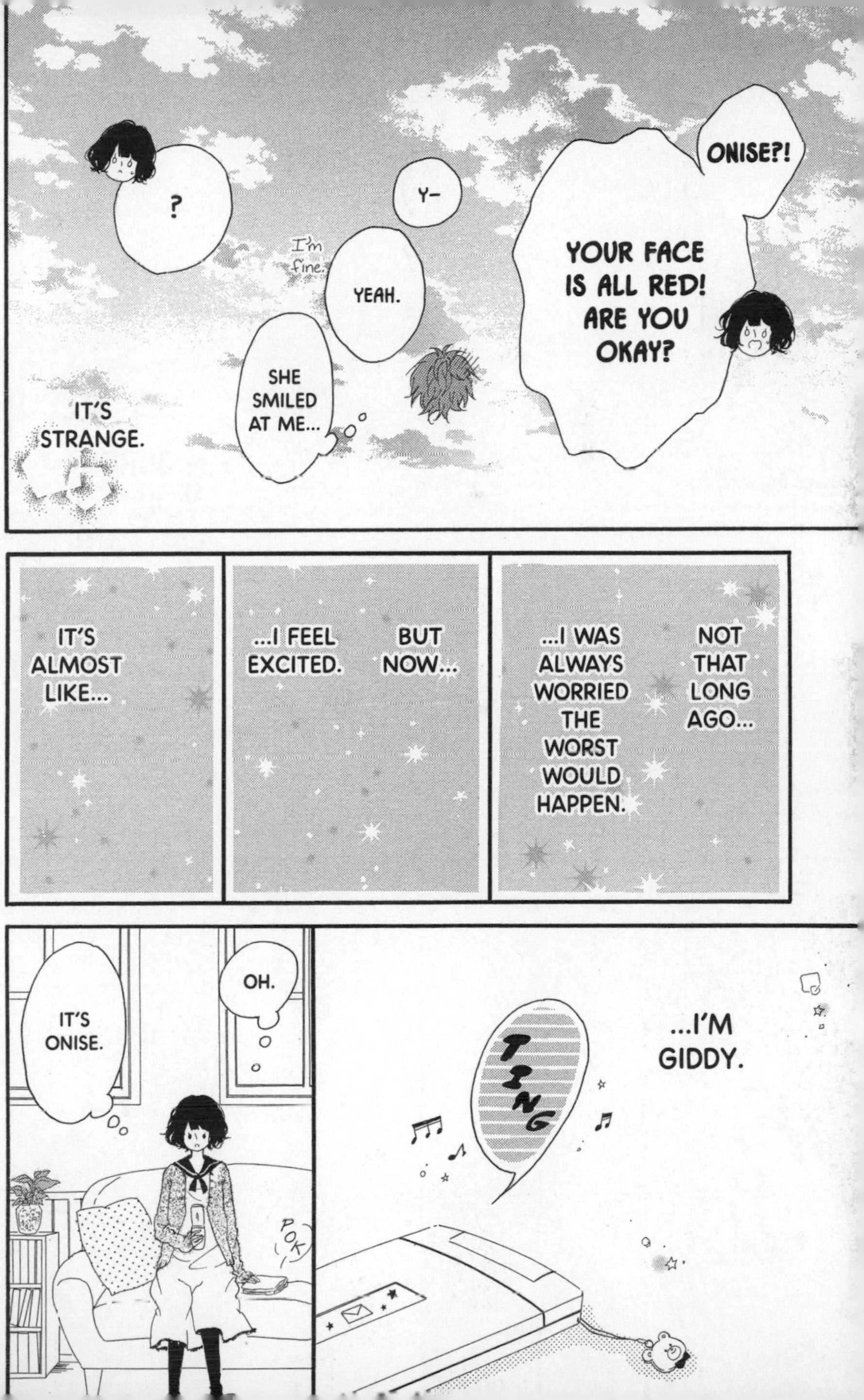
ONISE?!
YOUR FACE IS ALL RED! ARE YOU OKAY?
Y-
?
I'm fine.
YEAH.
SHE SMILED AT ME...
IT'S STRANGE.
NOT THAT LONG AGO...
...I WAS ALWAYS WORRIED THE WORST WOULD HAPPEN.
BUT NOW...
...I FEEL EXCITED.
IT'S ALMOST LIKE...
...I'M GIDDY.
TING
OH.
IT'S ONISE.
POK

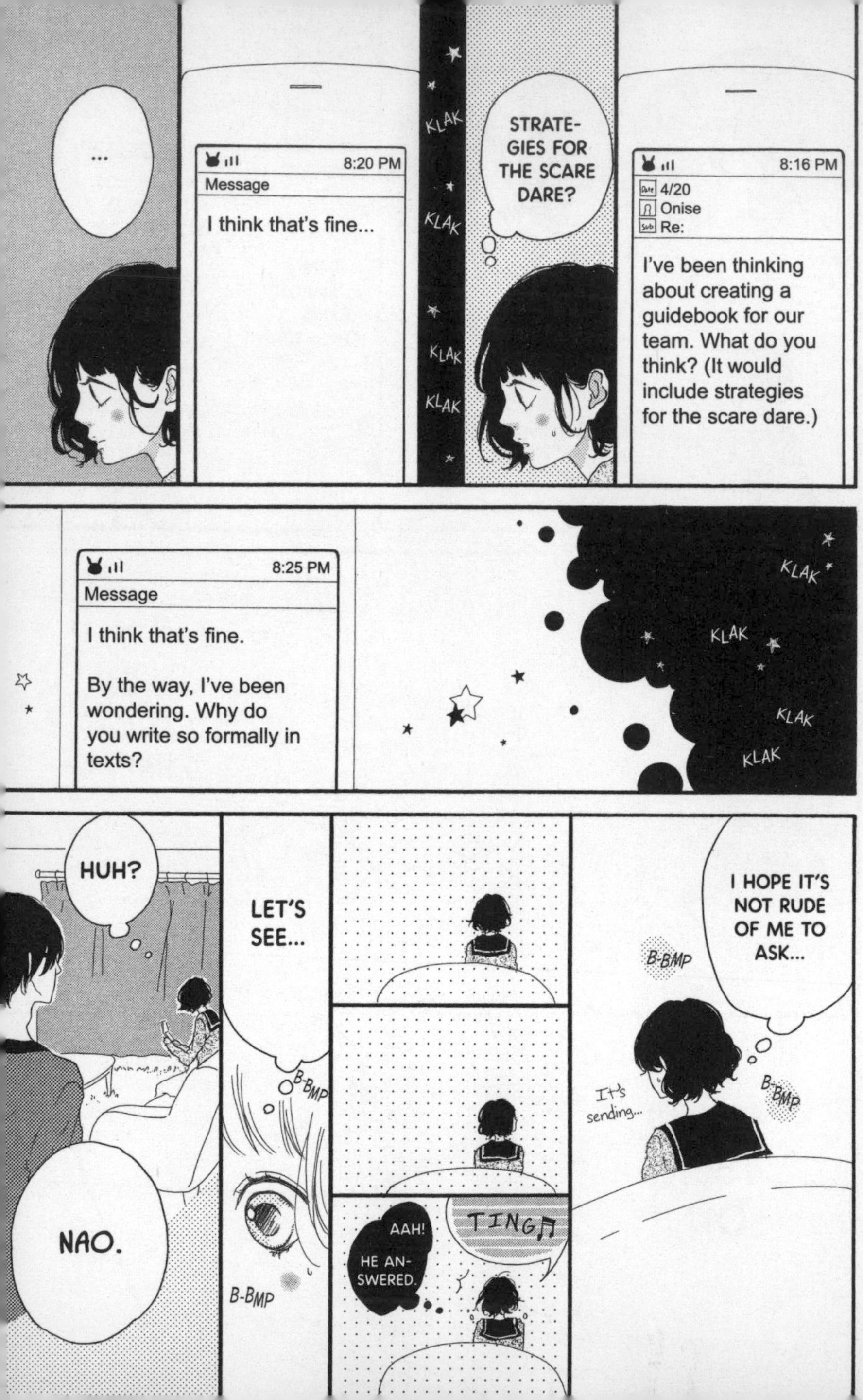
8:16 PM
4/20
Onise
Re:
I've been thinking about creating a guidebook for our team. What do you think? (It would include strategies for the scare dare.)
STRATE-GIES FOR THE SCARE DARE?
KLAK
KLAK
KLAK
KLAK
8:20 PM
Message
I think that's fine...
...
KLAK
KLAK
KLAK
KLAK
8:25 PM
Message
I think that's fine.
By the way, I've been wondering. Why do you write so formally in texts?
I HOPE IT'S NOT RUDE OF ME TO ASK...
B-BMP
It's sending...
B-BMP
TING
AAH! HE AN-SWERED.
LET'S SEE...
B-BMP
B-BMP
HUH?
NAO.

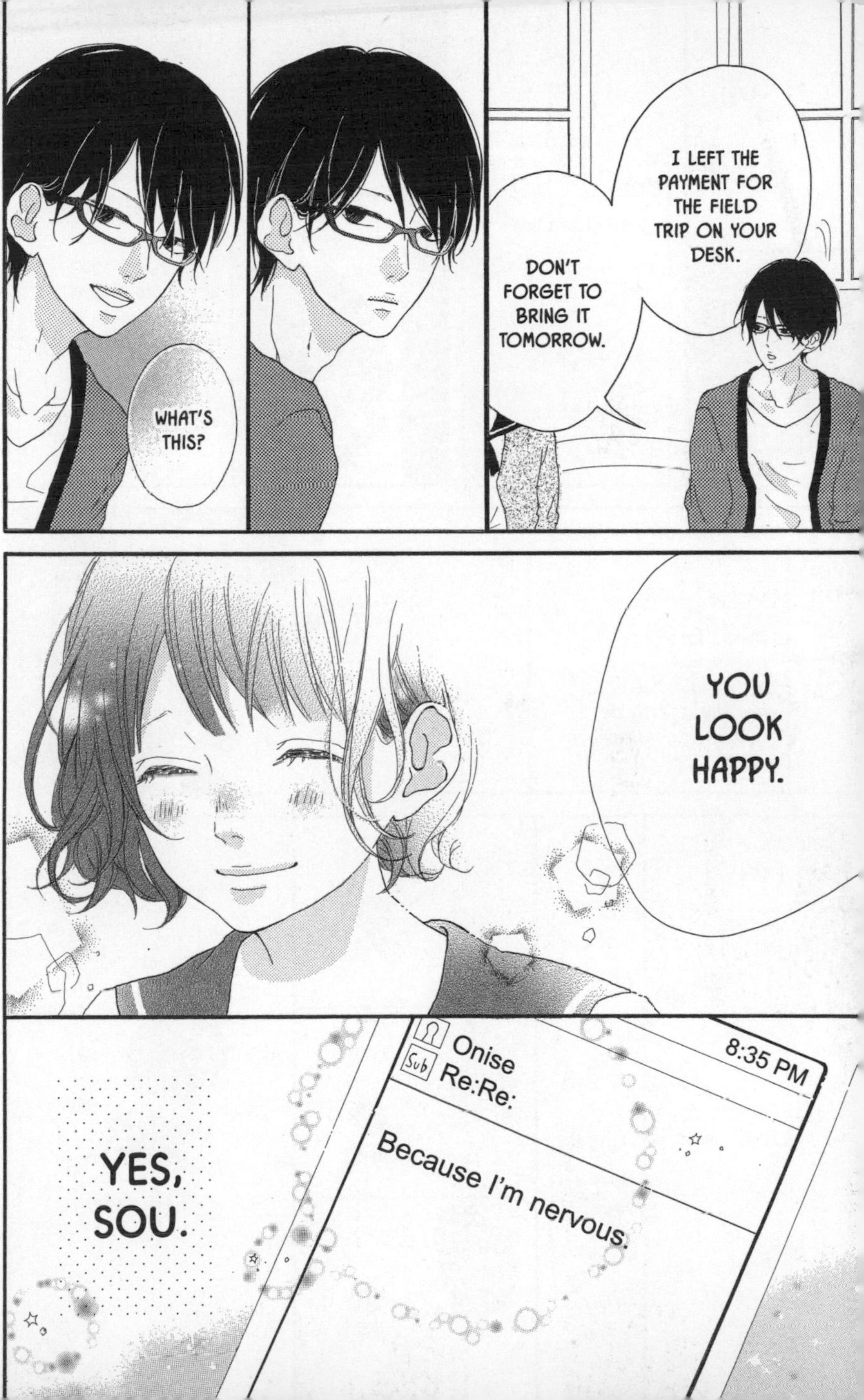
I LEFT THE PAYMENT FOR THE FIELD TRIP ON YOUR DESK.
DON'T FORGET TO BRING IT TOMORROW.
WHAT'S THIS?
YOU LOOK HAPPY.
Onise
Sub Re:Re:
8:35 PM
Because I'm nervous.
YES, SOU.

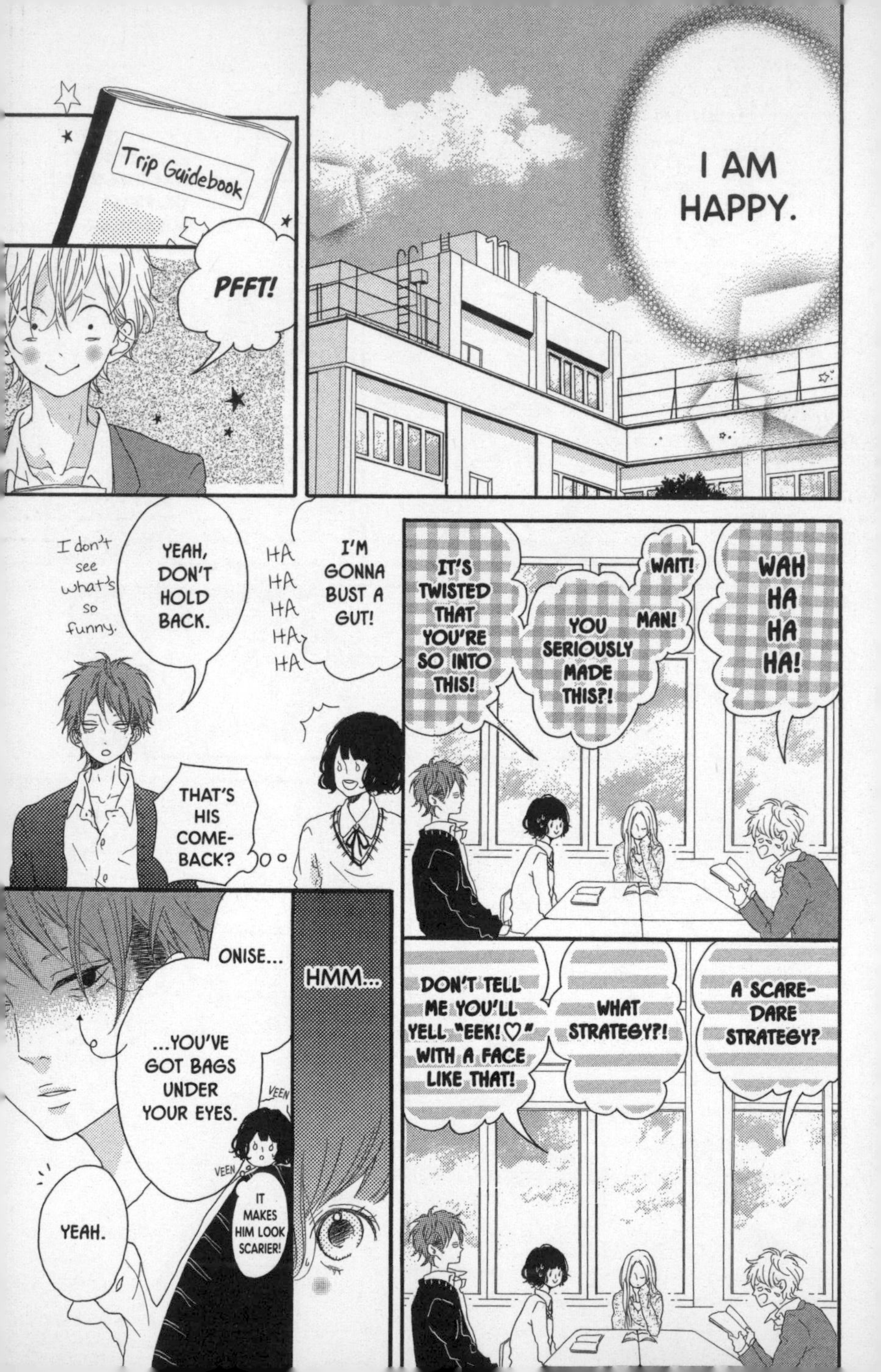
I AM HAPPY.
Trip Guidebook
PFFT!
WAH HA HA HA!
WAIT!
MAN!
YOU SERIOUSLY MADE THIS?!
IT'S TWISTED THAT YOU'RE SO INTO THIS!
I'M GONNA BUST A GUT!
HA HA HA HA HA
YEAH, DON'T HOLD BACK.
I don't see what's so funny.
THAT'S HIS COMEBACK?
A SCARE-DARE STRATEGY?
WHAT STRATEGY?!
DON'T TELL ME YOU'LL YELL "EEK!♡" WITH A FACE LIKE THAT!
HMM...
ONISE...
...YOU'VE GOT BAGS UNDER YOUR EYES.
VEEN
VEEN
IT MAKES HIM LOOK SCARIER!
YEAH.

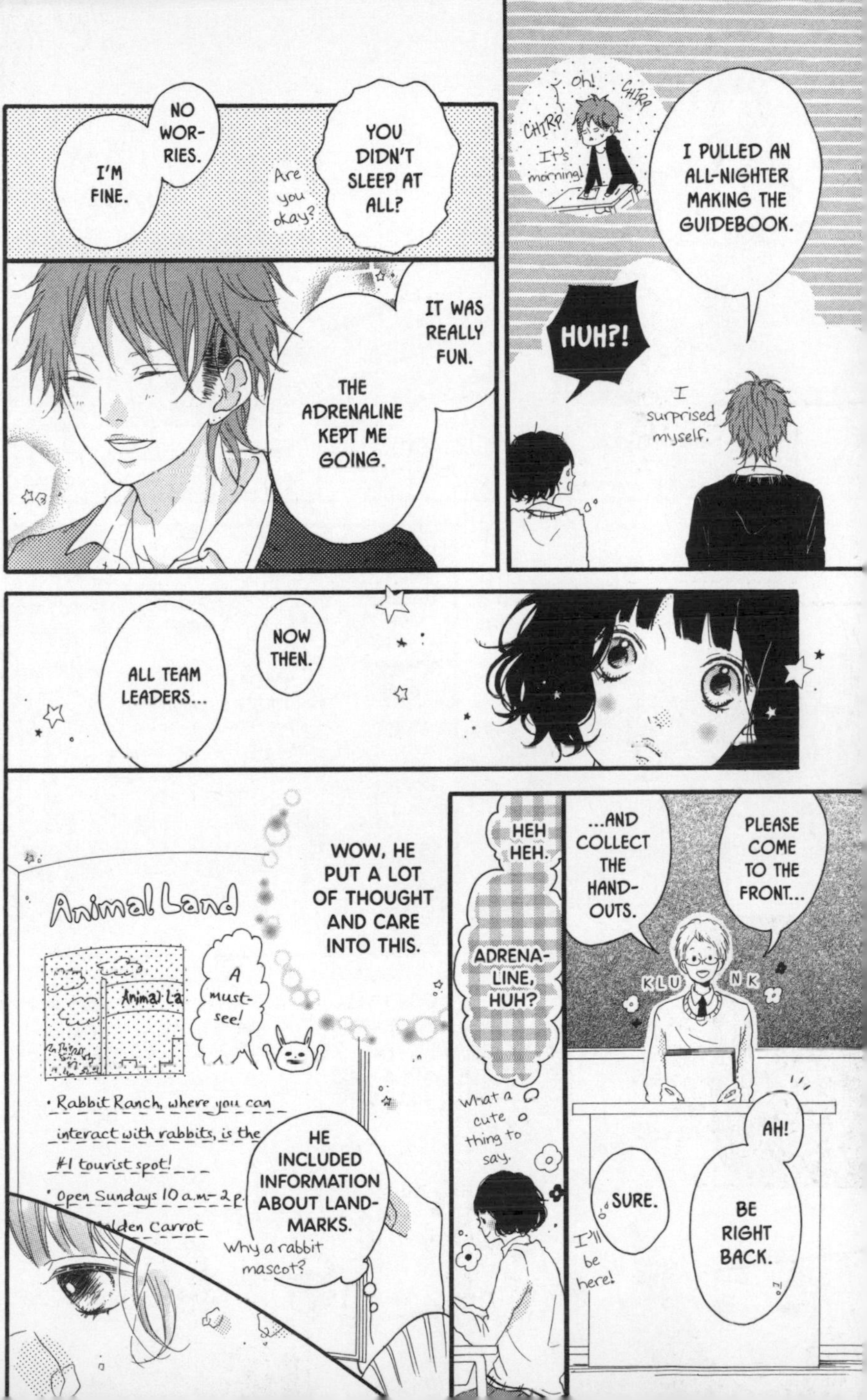

Oh!
CHIRP
CHIRP
It's morning!
I PULLED AN ALL-NIGHTER MAKING THE GUIDEBOOK.
HUH?!
I surprised myself.
YOU DIDN'T SLEEP AT ALL?
Are you okay?
NO WORRIES.
I'M FINE.
IT WAS REALLY FUN.
THE ADRENALINE KEPT ME GOING.
NOW THEN.
ALL TEAM LEADERS...
PLEASE COME TO THE FRONT...
...AND COLLECT THE HANDOUTS.
KLUNK
AH!
BE RIGHT BACK.
SURE.
I'll be here!
HEH HEH.
ADRENALINE, HUH?
What a cute thing to say.
WOW, HE PUT A LOT OF THOUGHT AND CARE INTO THIS.
Animal Land
Animal La
A must-see!
• Rabbit Ranch, where you can interact with rabbits, is the #1 tourist spot!
• Open Sundays 10 a.m.–2 p.
olden Carrot
HE INCLUDED INFORMATION ABOUT LANDMARKS.
Why a rabbit mascot?

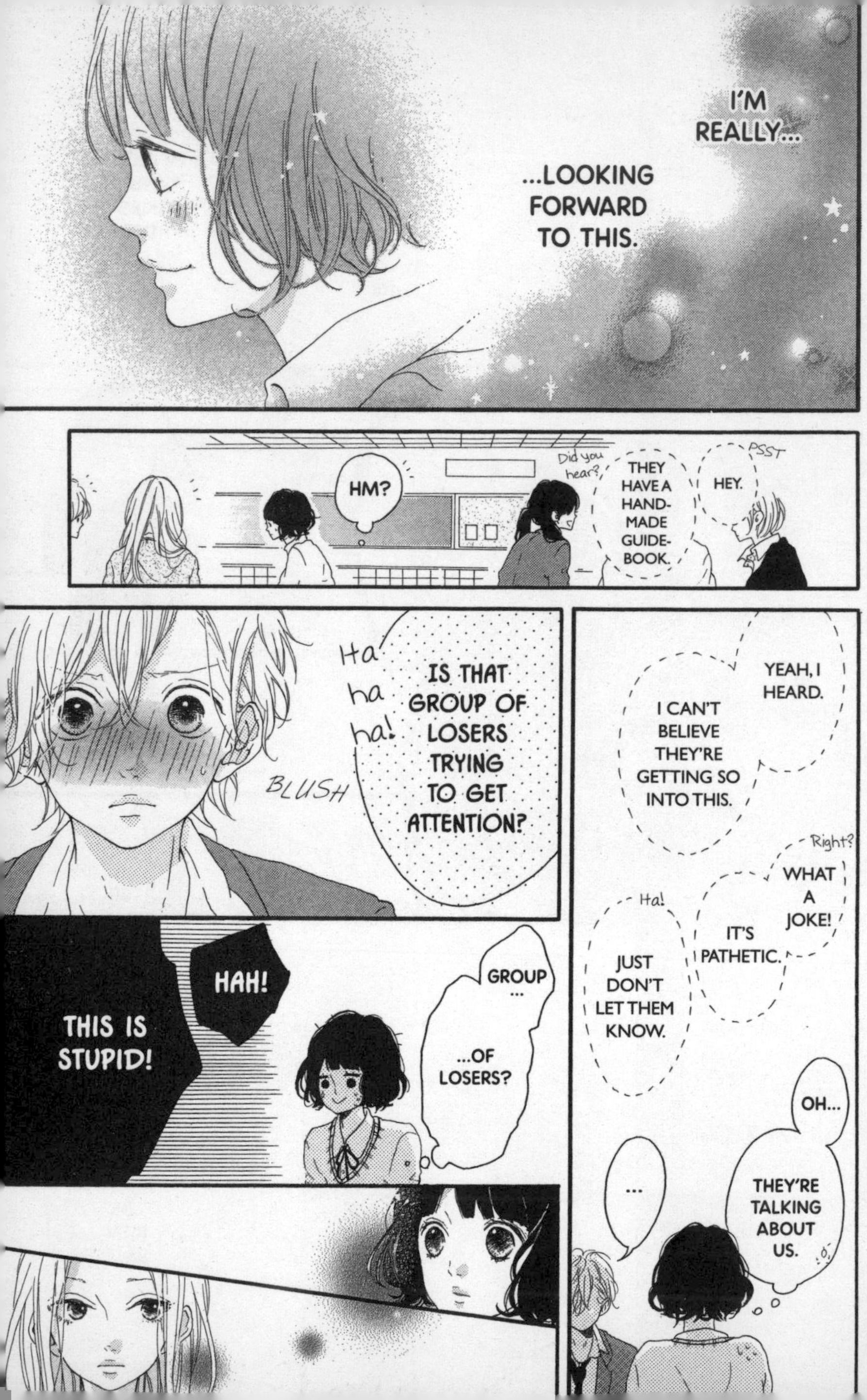
I'M REALLY...
...LOOKING FORWARD TO THIS.
PSST
HEY.
Did you hear?
THEY HAVE A HAND-MADE GUIDE-BOOK.
HM?
YEAH, I HEARD.
I CAN'T BELIEVE THEY'RE GETTING SO INTO THIS.
Right?
WHAT A JOKE!
IT'S PATHETIC.
Ha!
JUST DON'T LET THEM KNOW.
OH...
THEY'RE TALKING ABOUT US.
...
Ha ha ha!
IS THAT GROUP OF LOSERS TRYING TO GET ATTENTION?
BLUSH
GROUP...
...OF LOSERS?
HAH!
THIS IS STUPID!

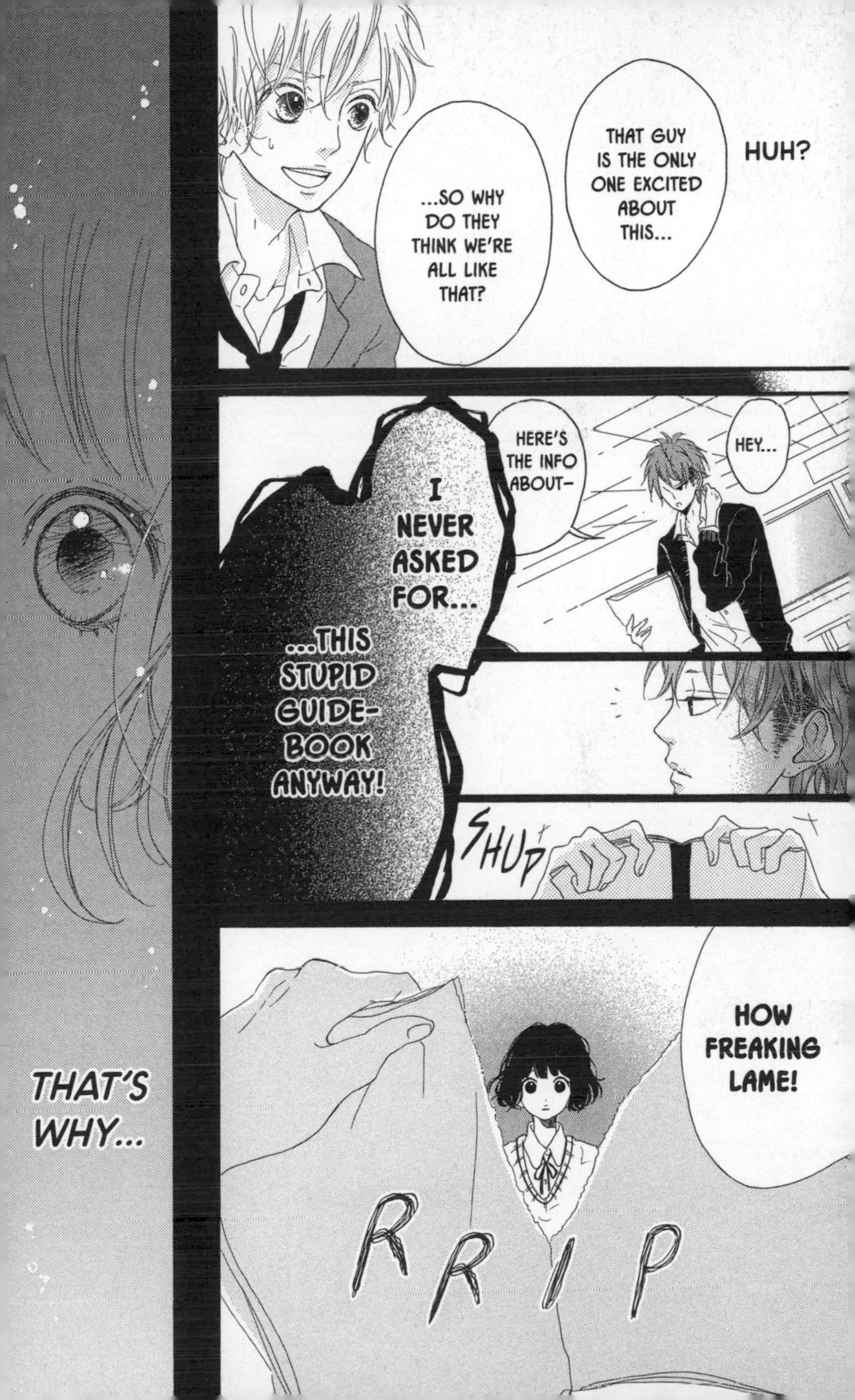
HUH?
THAT GUY IS THE ONLY ONE EXCITED ABOUT THIS...
...SO WHY DO THEY THINK WE'RE ALL LIKE THAT?
HEY...
HERE'S THE INFO ABOUT-
I NEVER ASKED FOR...
...THIS STUPID GUIDE-BOOK ANYWAY!
SHUP
HOW FREAKING LAME!
RRIP
THAT'S WHY...

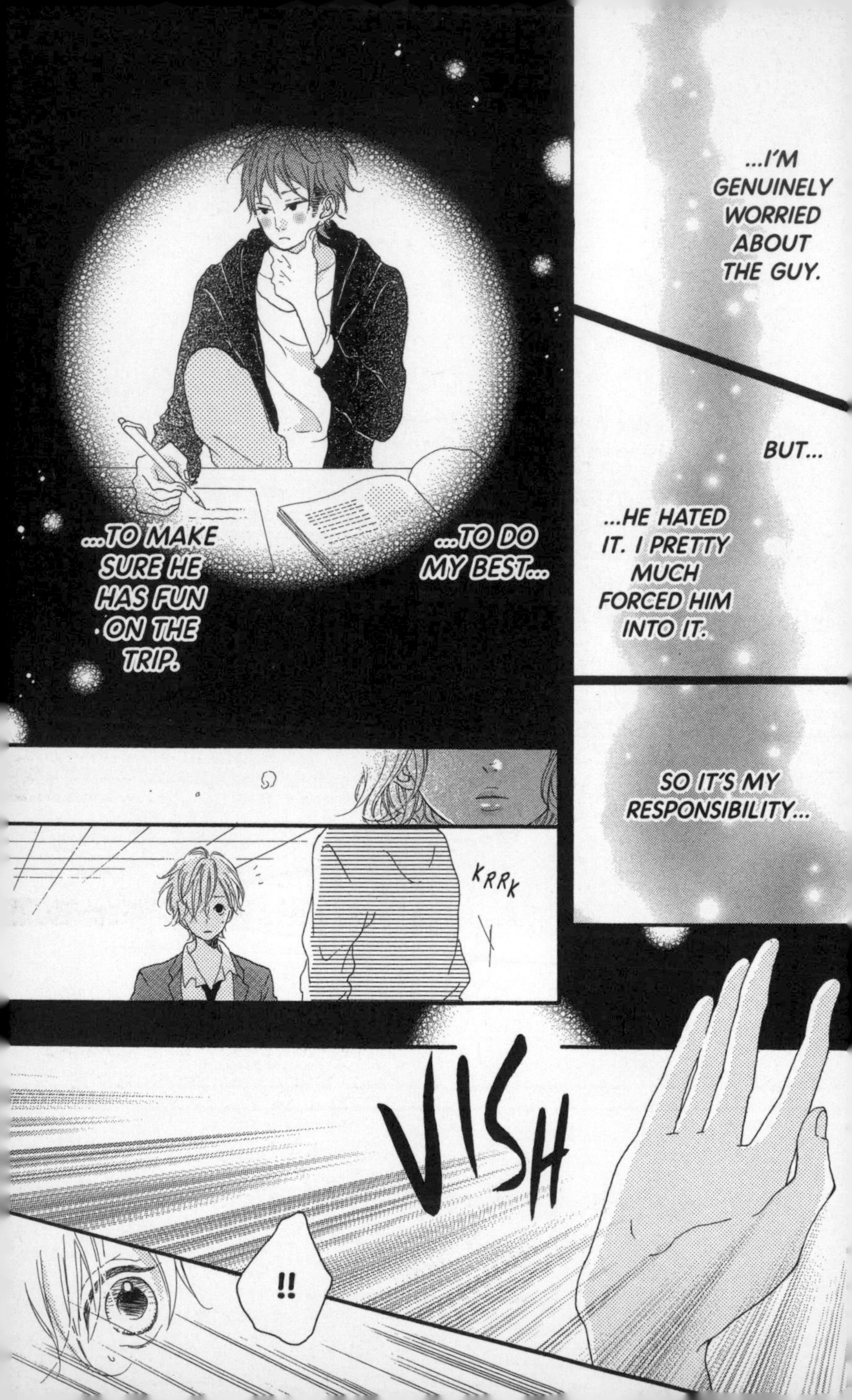
...I'M GENUINELY WORRIED ABOUT THE GUY.
BUT...
...HE HATED IT. I PRETTY MUCH FORCED HIM INTO IT.
SO IT'S MY RESPONSIBILITY...
...TO DO MY BEST...
...TO MAKE SURE HE HAS FUN ON THE TRIP.
KRRK
VISH
!!

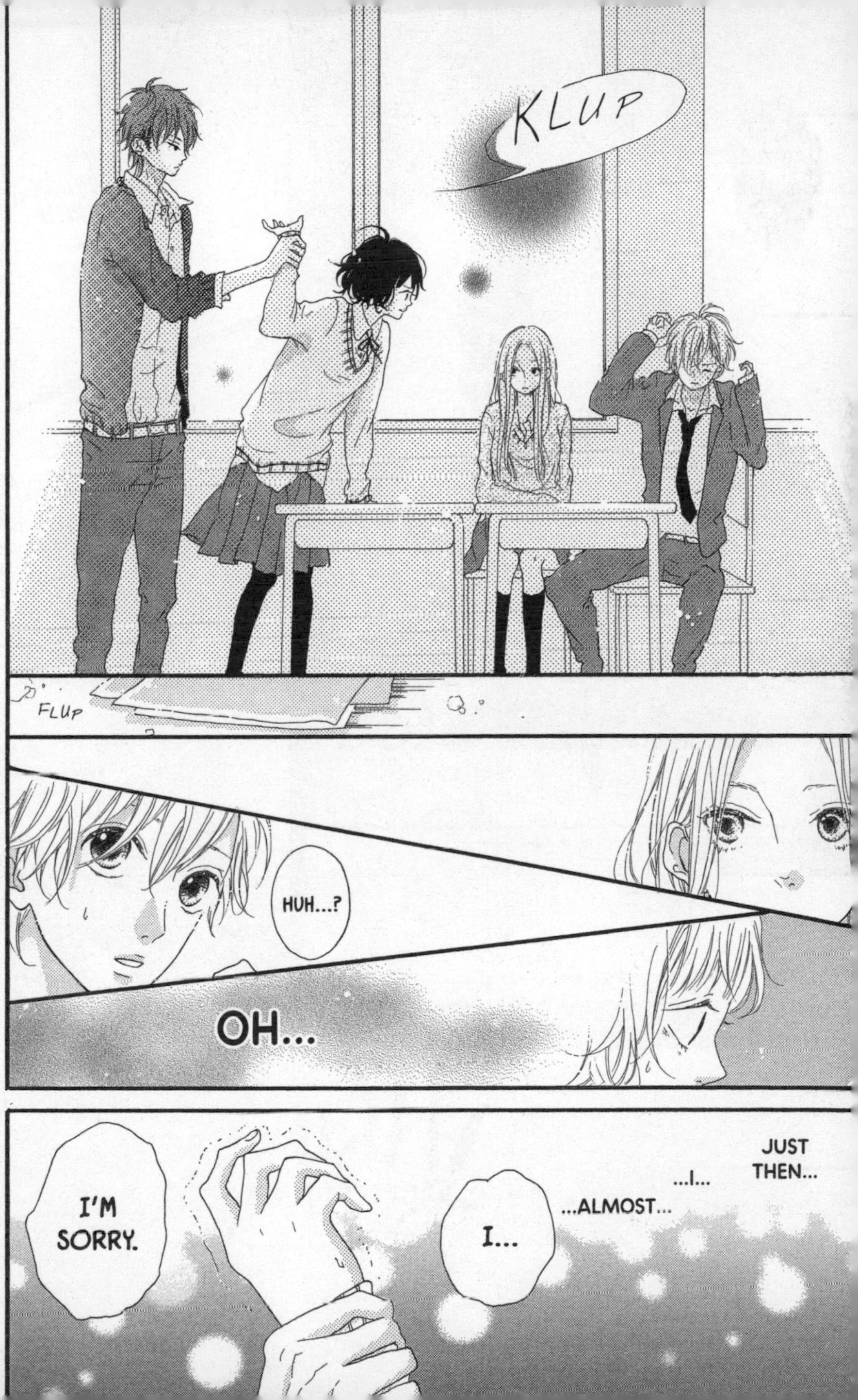
KLUP
FLUP
HUH...?
OH...
JUST THEN...
...I...
...ALMOST...
I...
I'M SORRY.

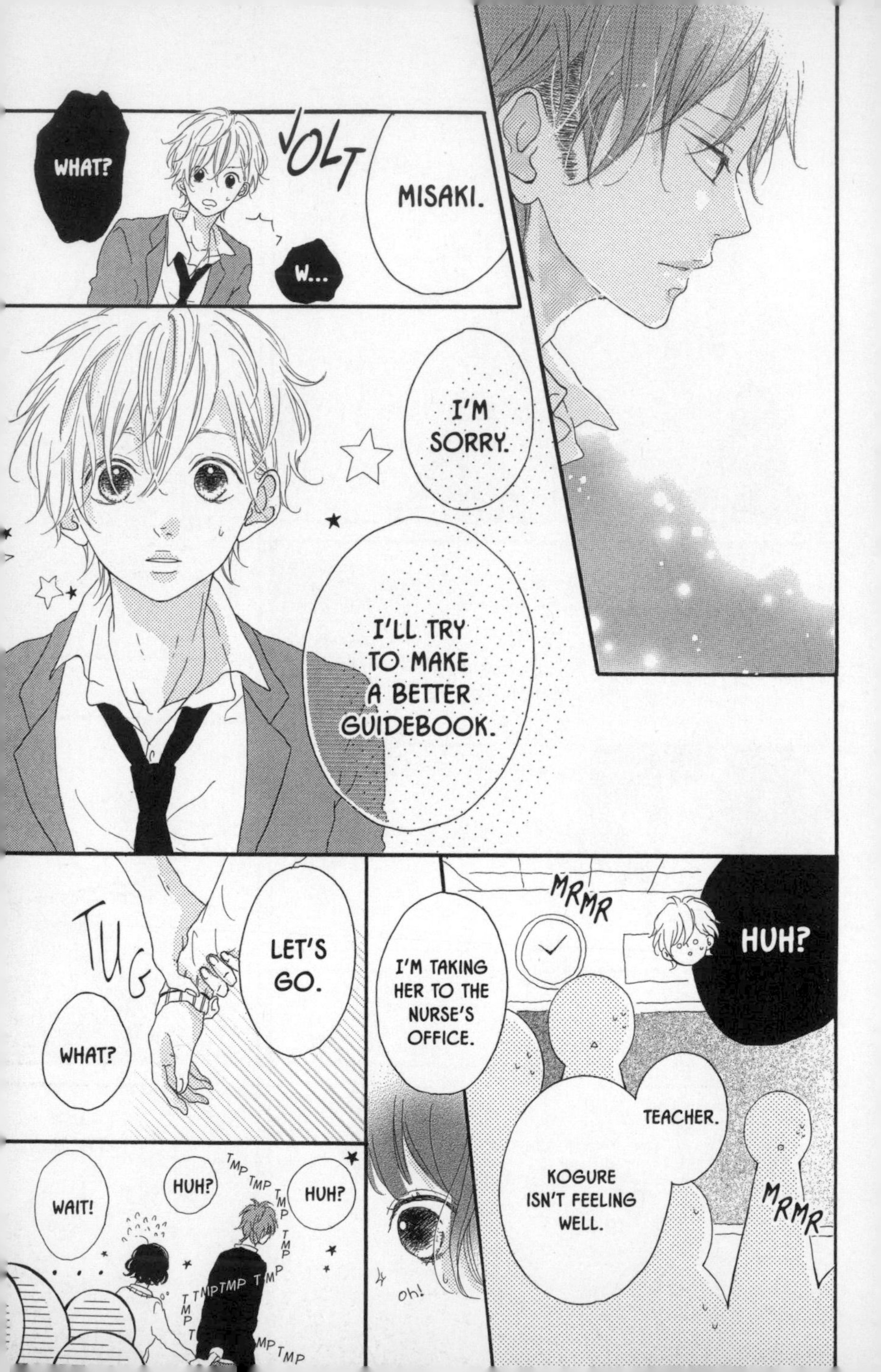
MISAKI.
VOLT
W...
WHAT?
I'M SORRY.
I'LL TRY TO MAKE A BETTER GUIDEBOOK.
HUH?
MRMR
I'M TAKING HER TO THE NURSE'S OFFICE.
TEACHER.
KOGURE ISN'T FEELING WELL.
MRMR
oh!
LET'S GO.
TUG
WHAT?
HUH?
TMP TMP TMP TMP
HUH?
WAIT!
TMP TMP TMP TMP TMP
TMP TMP

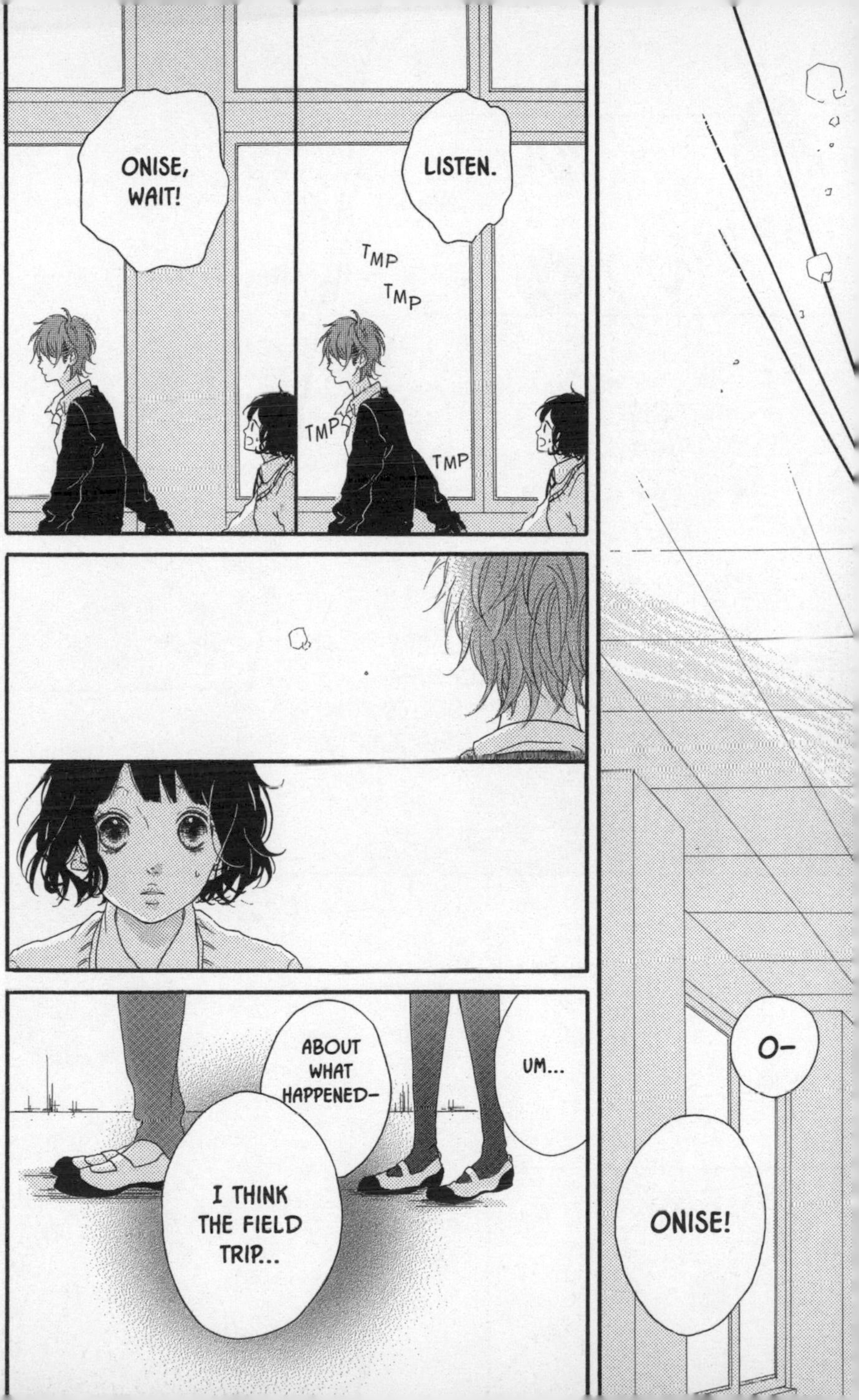
O-
ONISE!
LISTEN.
TMP
TMP
TMP
TMP
ONISE, WAIT!
UM...
ABOUT WHAT HAPPENED-
I THINK THE FIELD TRIP...

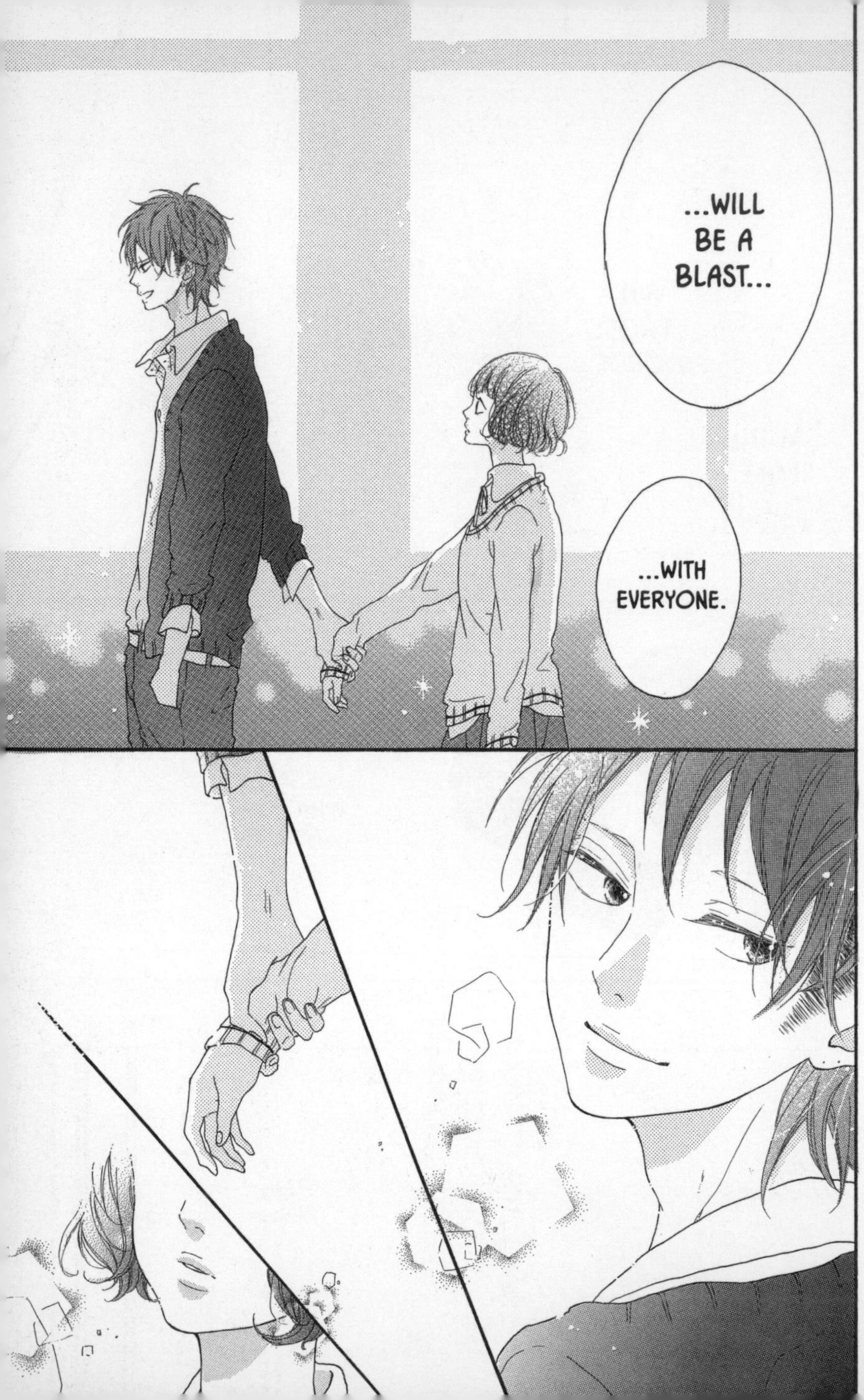
...WILL BE A BLAST...
...WITH EVERYONE.

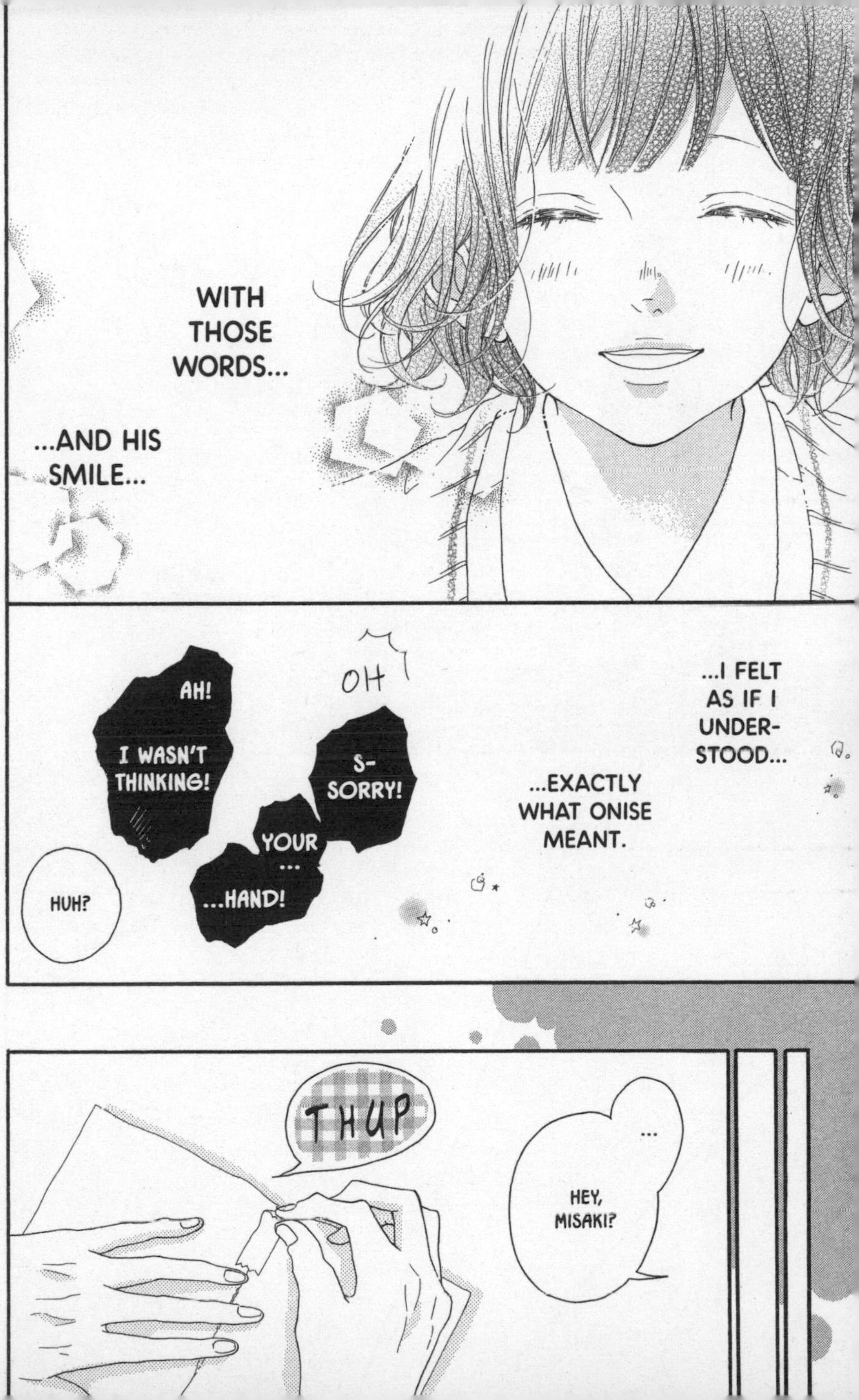
WITH THOSE WORDS...
...AND HIS SMILE...
...I FELT AS IF I UNDERSTOOD...
...EXACTLY WHAT ONISE MEANT.
OH
S-SORRY!
AH! I WASN'T THINKING!
YOUR... ...HAND!
HUH?
... HEY, MISAKI?
THUP

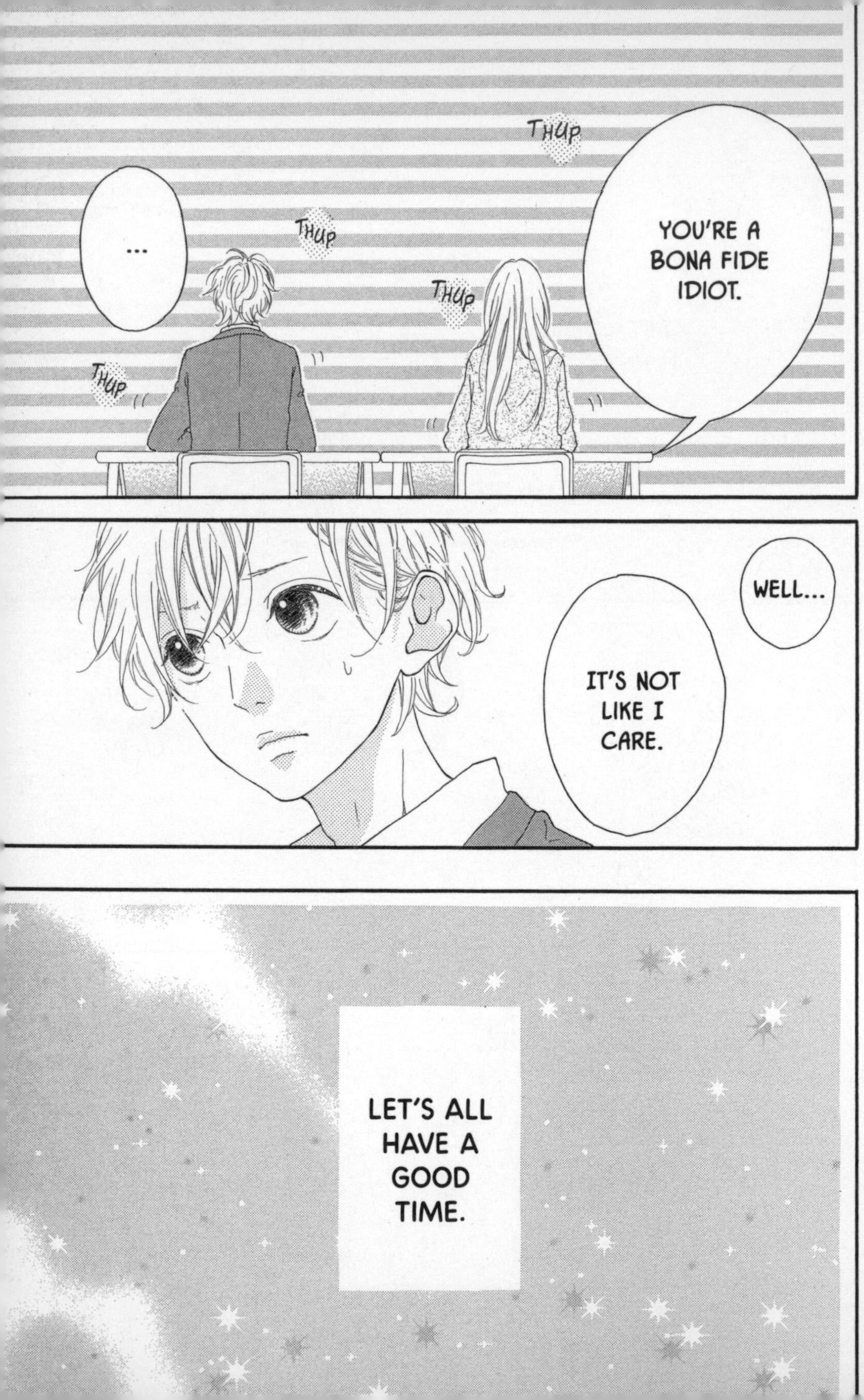
YOU'RE A BONA FIDE IDIOT.
THUP
THUP
THUP
...
THUP
WELL...
IT'S NOT LIKE I CARE.
LET'S ALL HAVE A GOOD TIME.

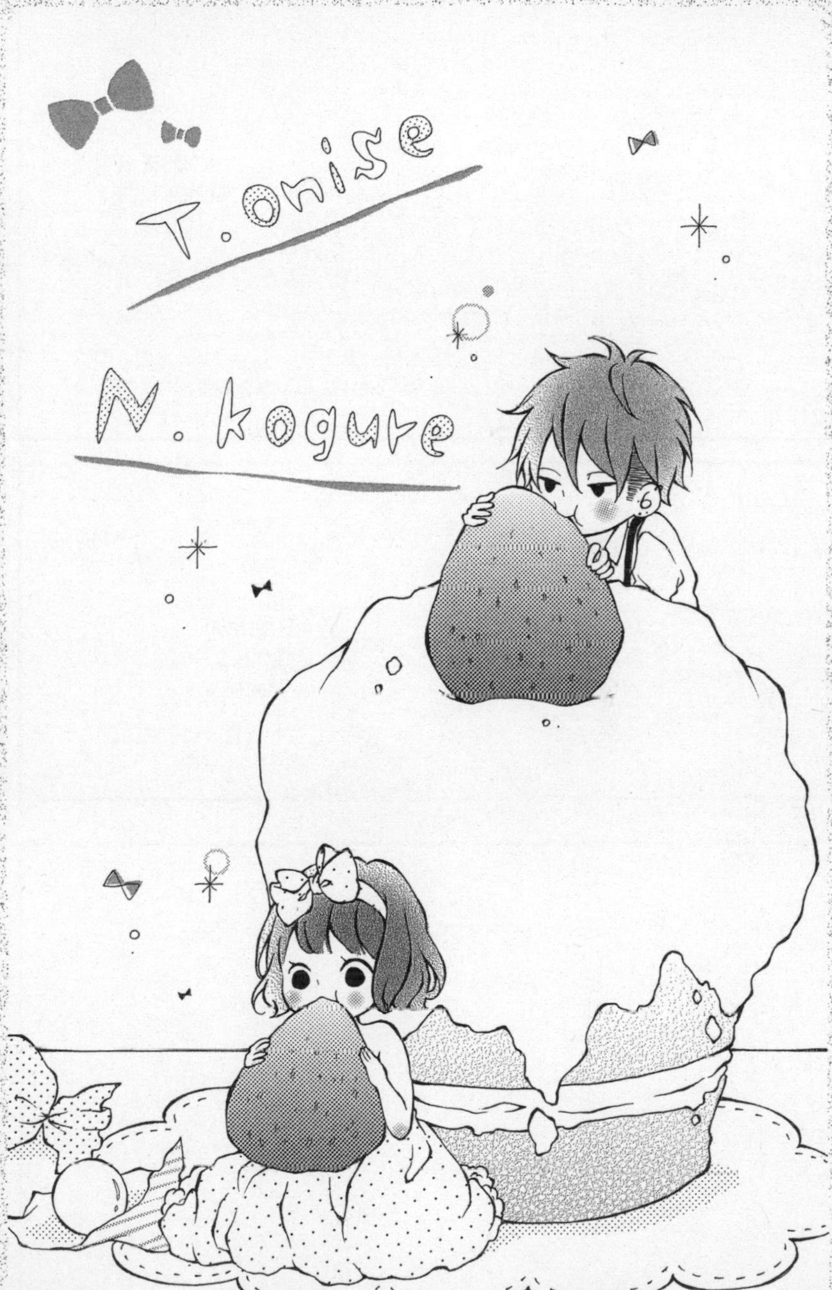
T. onise
N. kogure

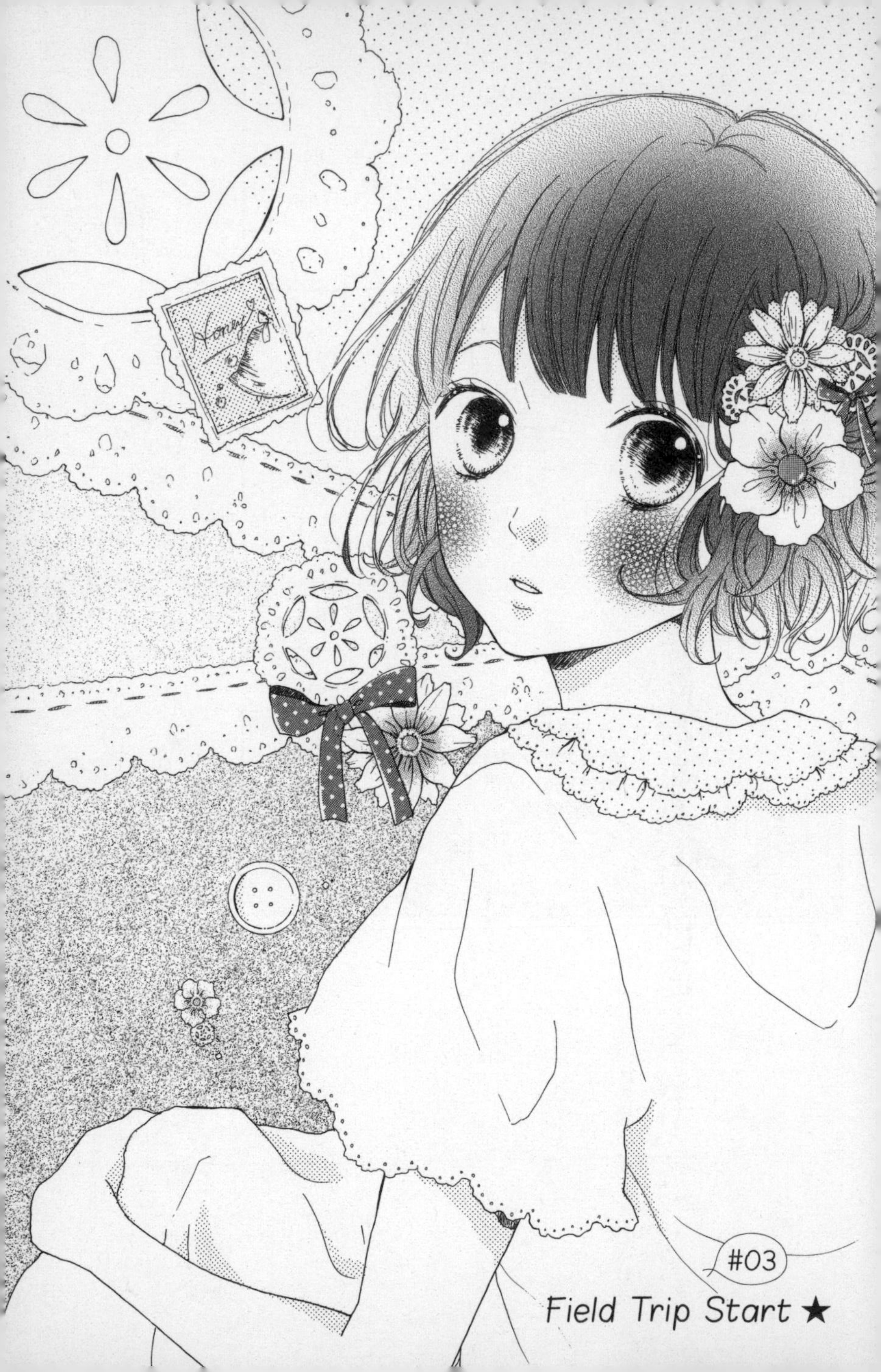
#03
Field Trip Start ★

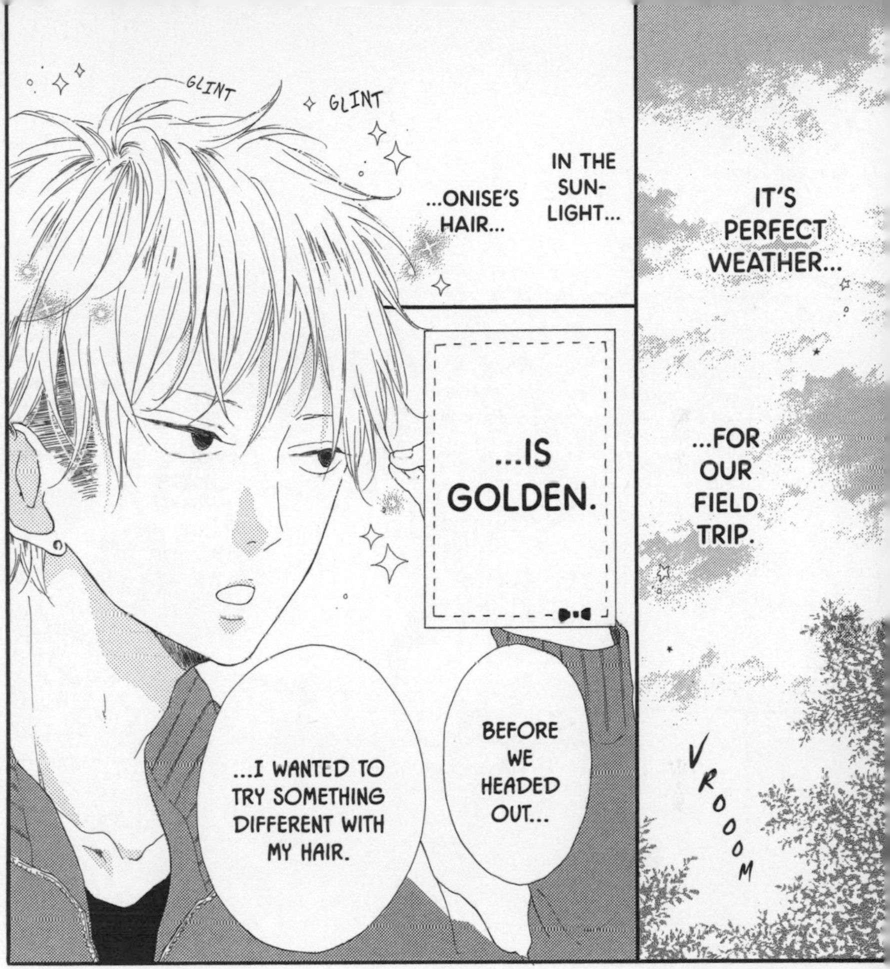
IT'S PERFECT WEATHER...
...FOR OUR FIELD TRIP.
VROOOM
IN THE SUN-LIGHT...
...ONISE'S HAIR...
GLINT
GLINT
...IS GOLDEN.
BEFORE WE HEADED OUT...
...I WANTED TO TRY SOMETHING DIFFERENT WITH MY HAIR.

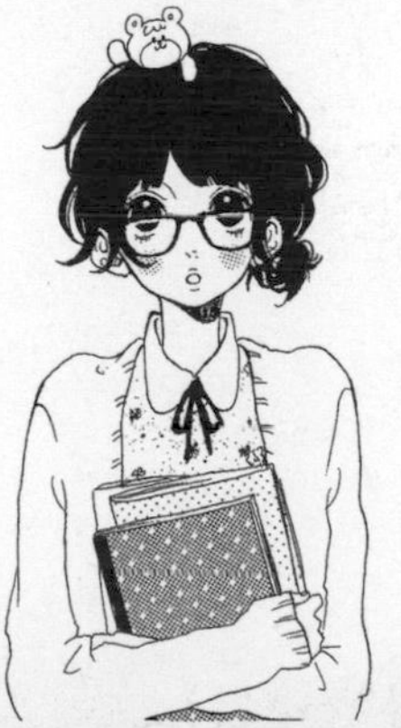

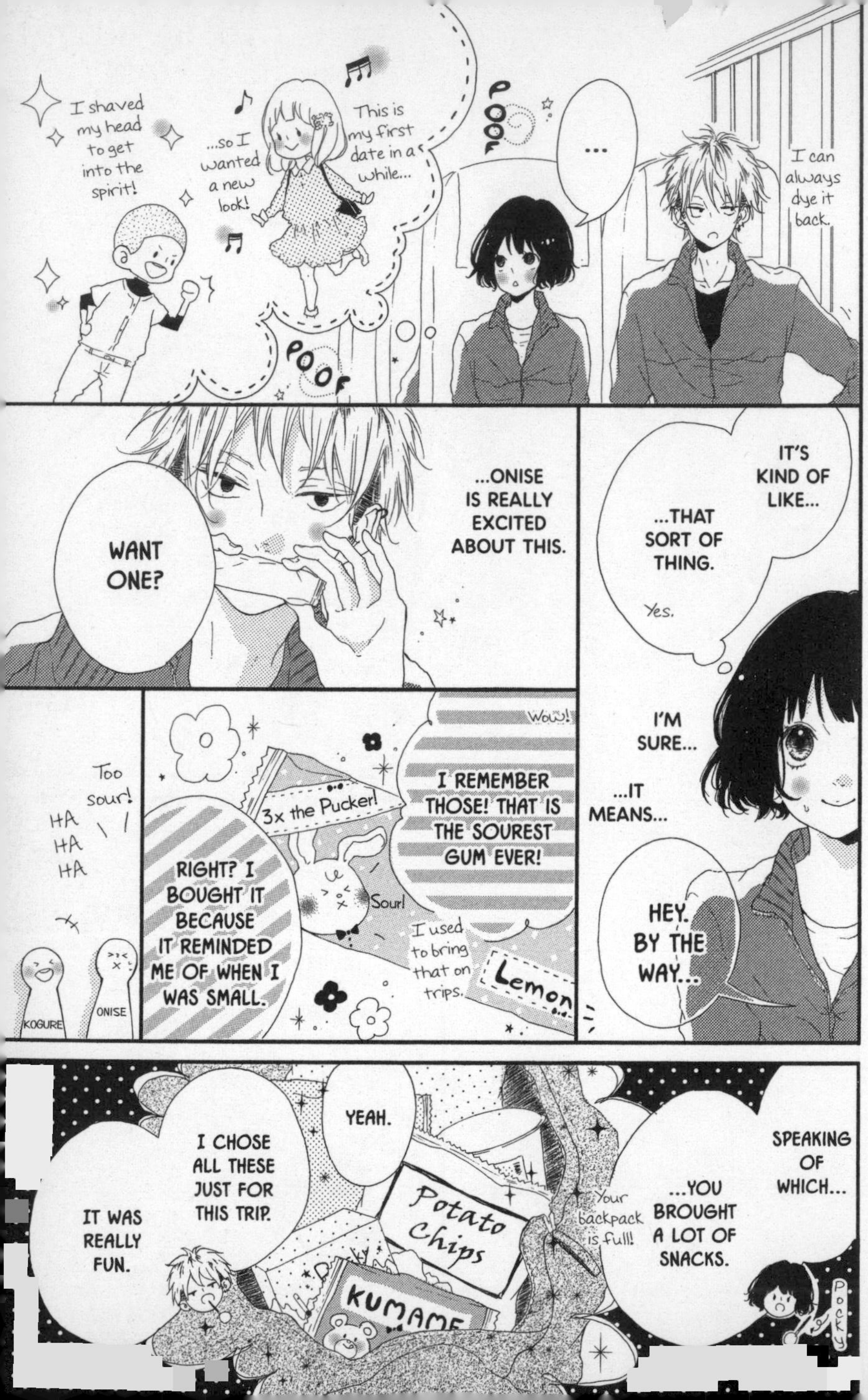
I can always dye it back.
...
POOF
This is my first date in a while...
...so I wanted a new look!
I shaved my head to get into the spirit!
POOF
IT'S KIND OF LIKE...
...THAT SORT OF THING.
Yes.
I'M SURE...
...IT MEANS...
HEY. BY THE WAY...
...ONISE IS REALLY EXCITED ABOUT THIS.
WANT ONE?
Wow!
I REMEMBER THOSE! THAT IS THE SOUREST GUM EVER!
3x the Pucker!
Sour!
I used to bring that on trips.
Lemon
RIGHT? I BOUGHT IT BECAUSE IT REMINDED ME OF WHEN I WAS SMALL.
Too sour!
HA HA HA
KOGURE
ONISE
SPEAKING OF WHICH...
...YOU BROUGHT A LOT OF SNACKS.
Your backpack is full!
Pocky
Potato Chips
KUMAME
YEAH.
I CHOSE ALL THESE JUST FOR THIS TRIP.
IT WAS REALLY FUN.

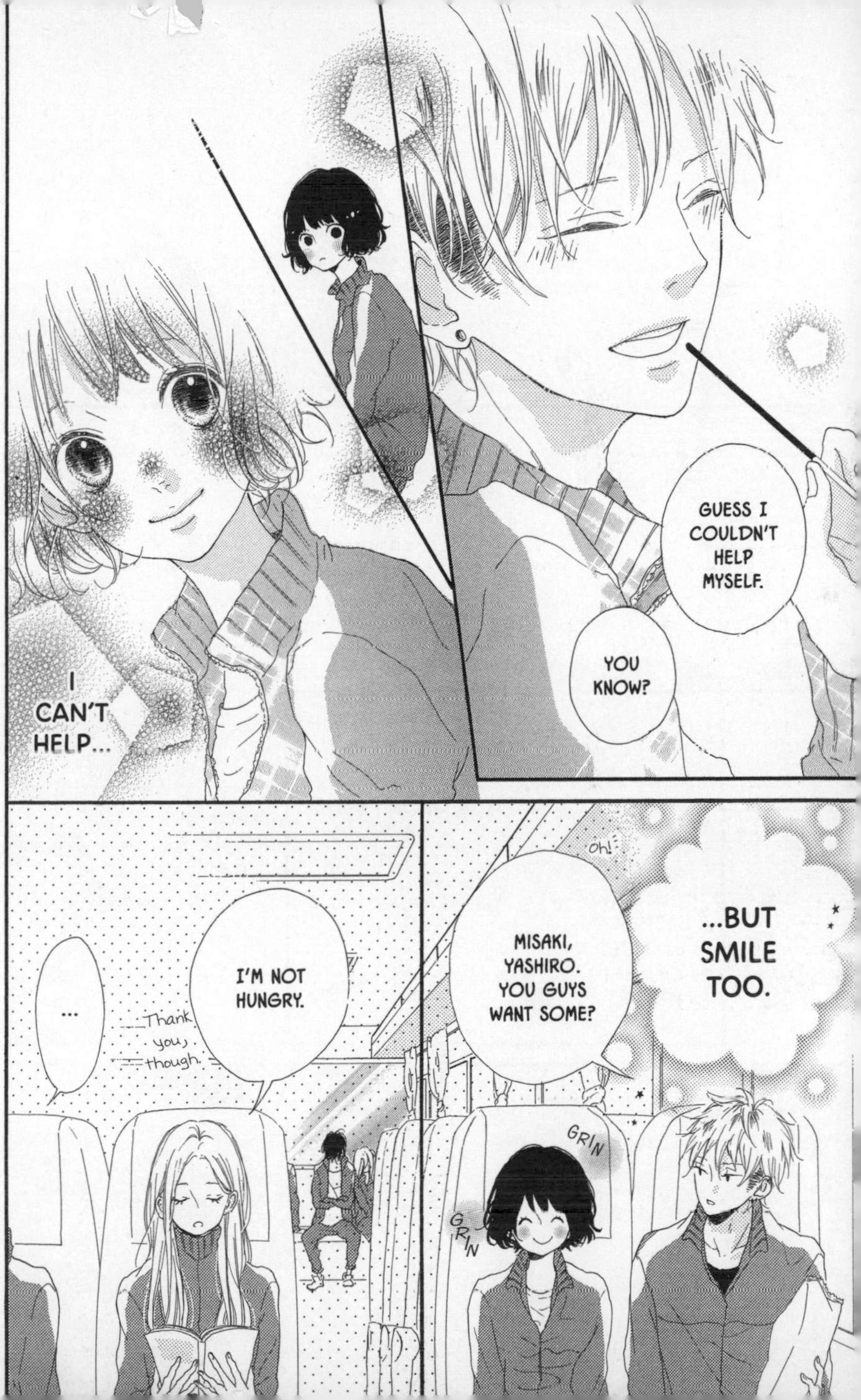
GUESS I COULDN'T HELP MYSELF.
YOU KNOW?
I CAN'T HELP...
...BUT SMILE TOO.
Oh!
MISAKI, YASHIRO. YOU GUYS WANT SOME?
GRIN
GRIN
I'M NOT HUNGRY.
Thank you, though.
...

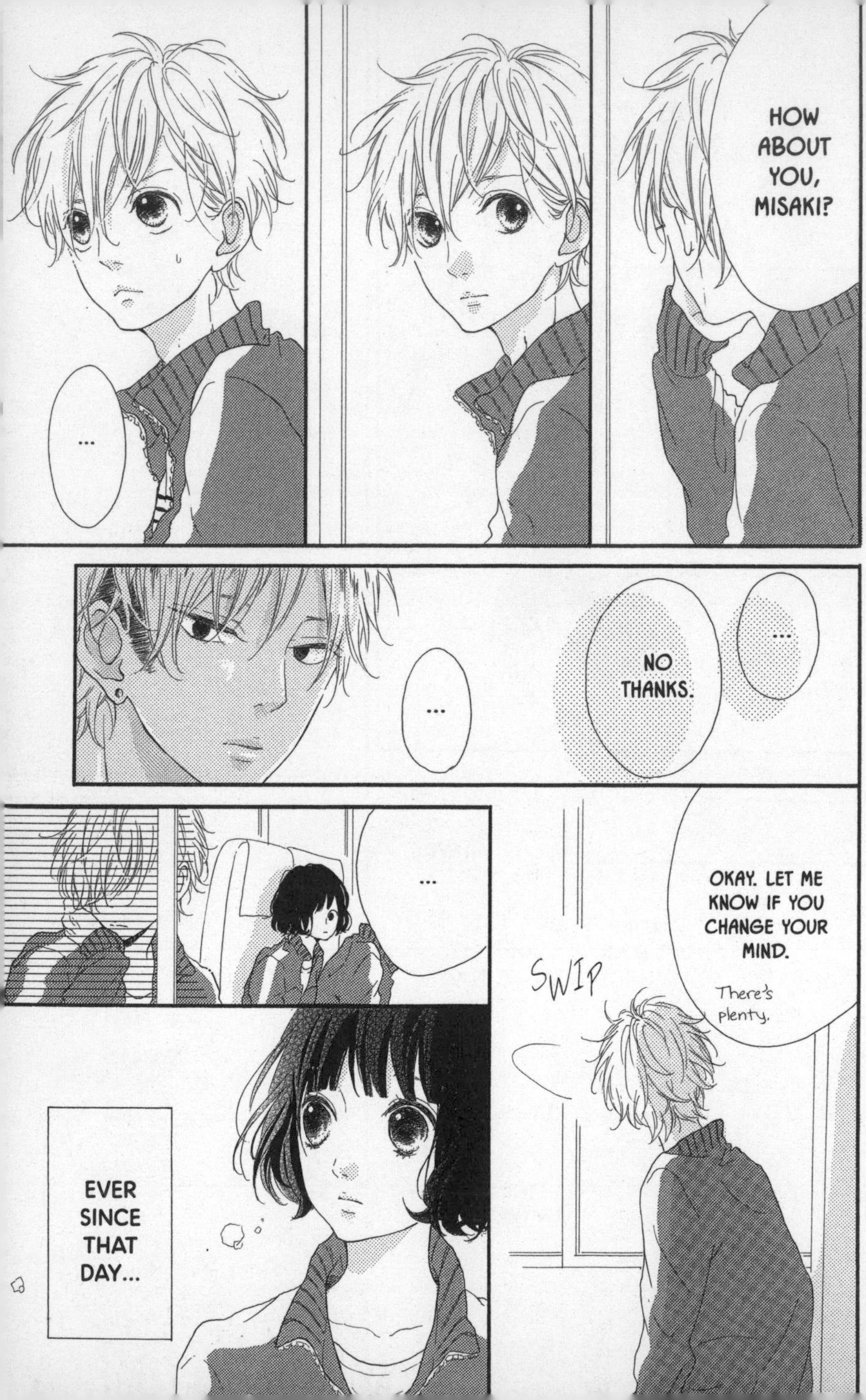
HOW ABOUT YOU, MISAKI?
...
...
NO THANKS.
...
OKAY. LET ME KNOW IF YOU CHANGE YOUR MIND.
There's plenty.
SWIP
...
EVER SINCE THAT DAY...

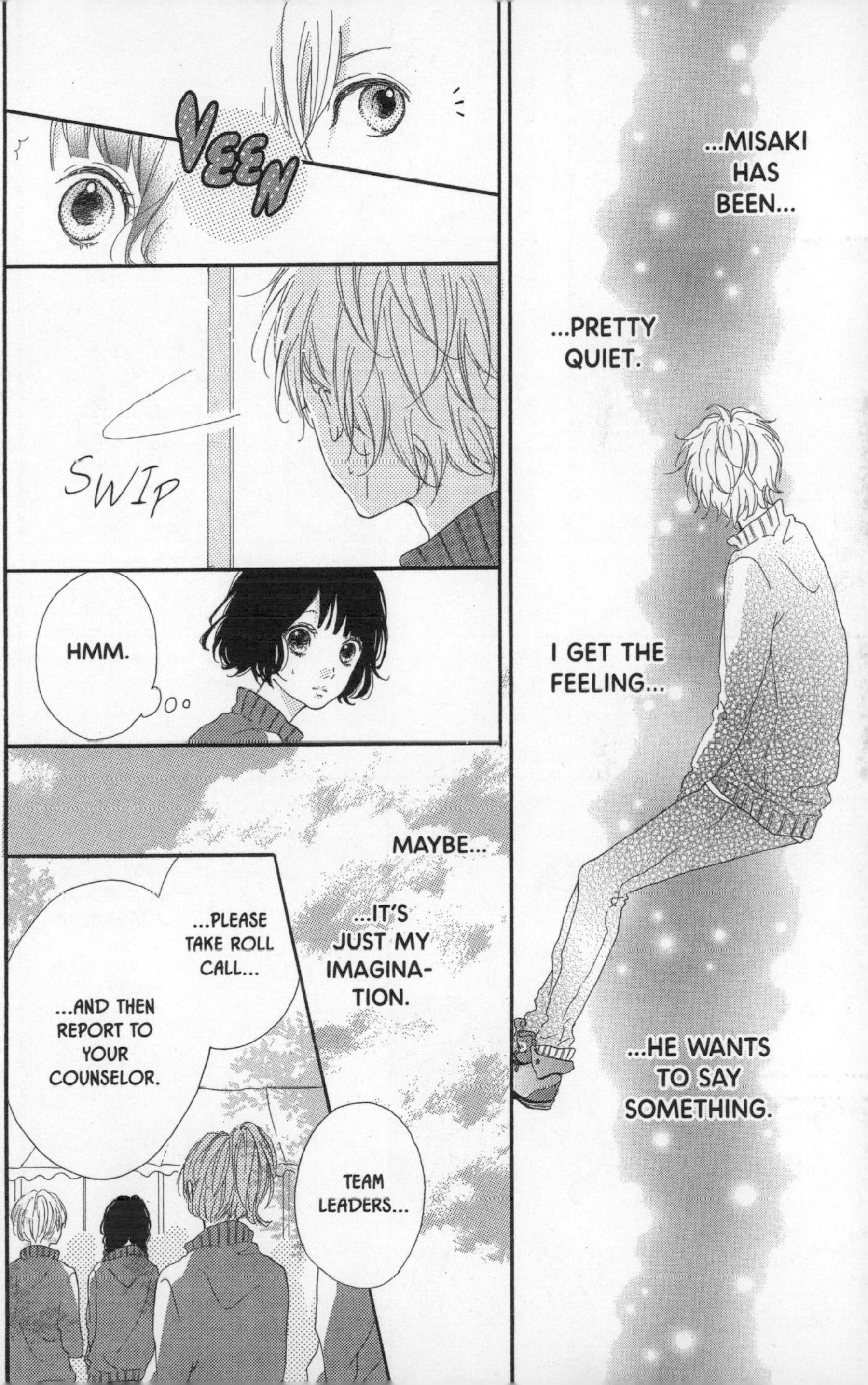
...MISAKI HAS BEEN...
...PRETTY QUIET.
I GET THE FEELING...
...HE WANTS TO SAY SOMETHING.
VEEN
SWIP
HMM.
MAYBE...
...IT'S JUST MY IMAGINATION.
TEAM LEADERS...
...PLEASE TAKE ROLL CALL...
...AND THEN REPORT TO YOUR COUNSELOR.

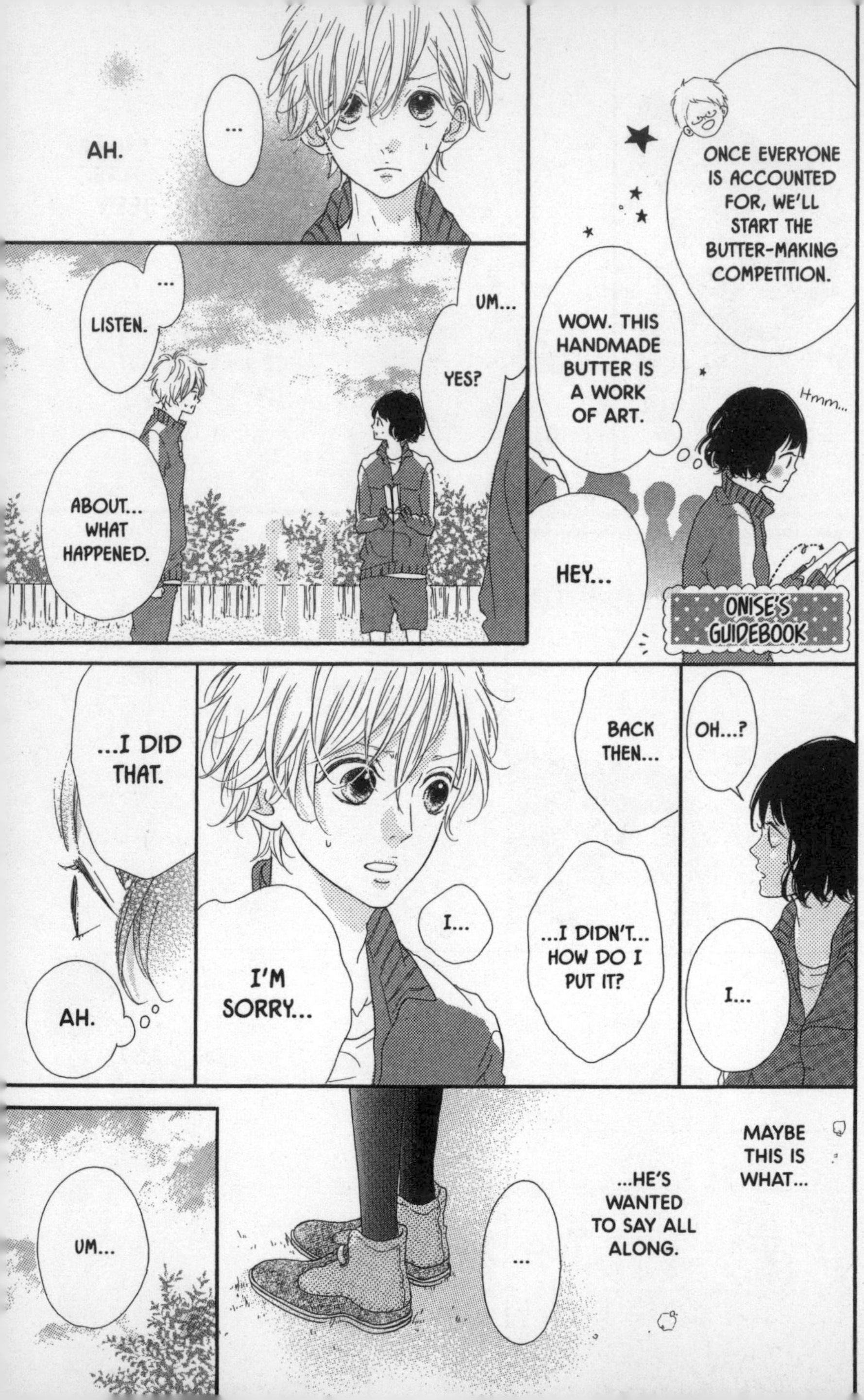
ONCE EVERYONE IS ACCOUNTED FOR, WE'LL START THE BUTTER-MAKING COMPETITION.
WOW. THIS HANDMADE BUTTER IS A WORK OF ART.
Hmm...
ONISE'S GUIDEBOOK
HEY...
...
AH.
UM...
YES?
...
LISTEN.
ABOUT... WHAT HAPPENED.
OH...?
I...
BACK THEN...
...I DIDN'T... HOW DO I PUT IT?
I...
I'M SORRY...
...I DID THAT.
AH.
MAYBE THIS IS WHAT...
...HE'S WANTED TO SAY ALL ALONG.
...
UM...

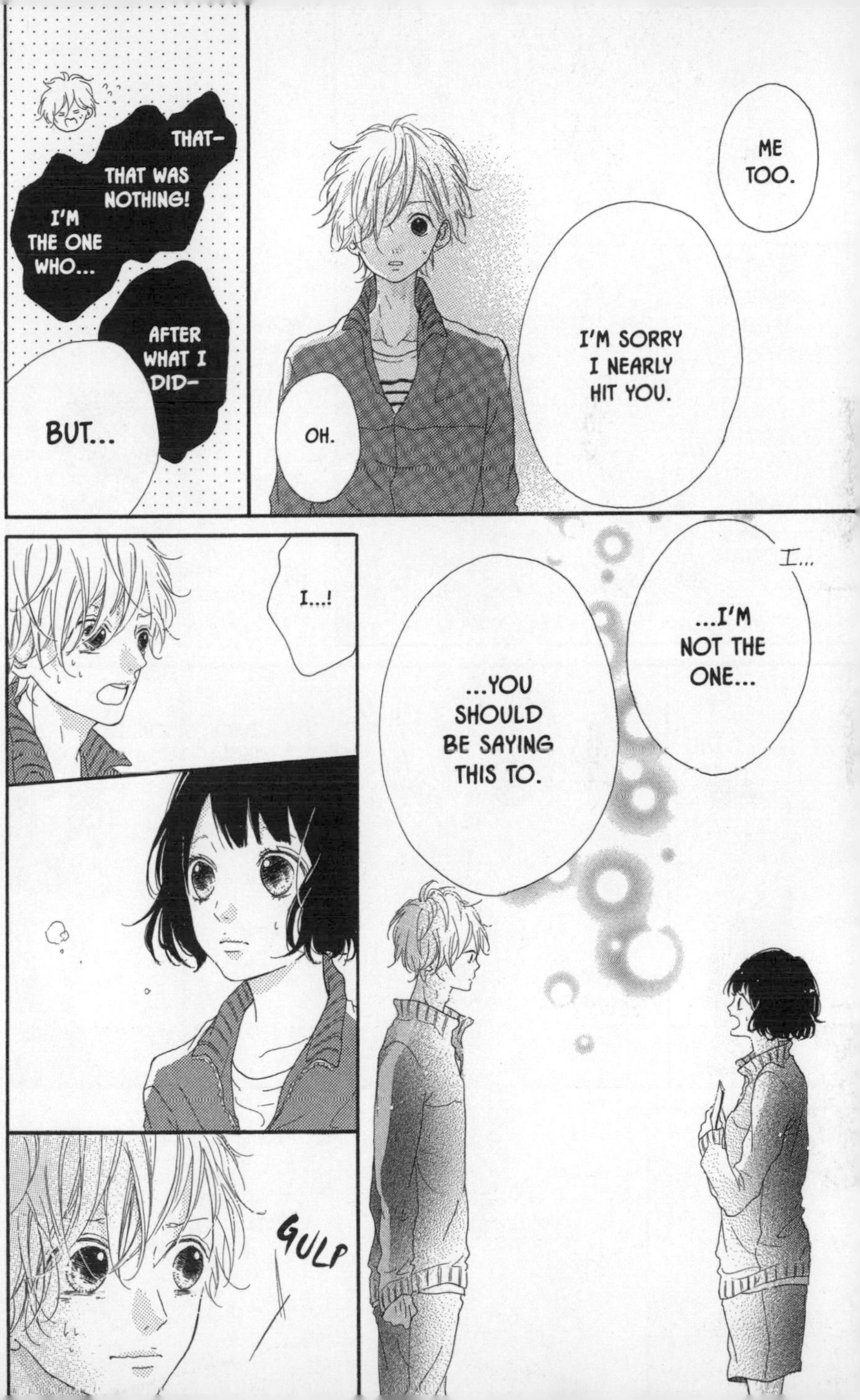
ME TOO.
I'M SORRY I NEARLY HIT YOU.
OH.
THAT- THAT WAS NOTHING!
I'M THE ONE WHO...
AFTER WHAT I DID-
BUT...
I...
...I'M NOT THE ONE...
...YOU SHOULD BE SAYING THIS TO.
I...!
GULP

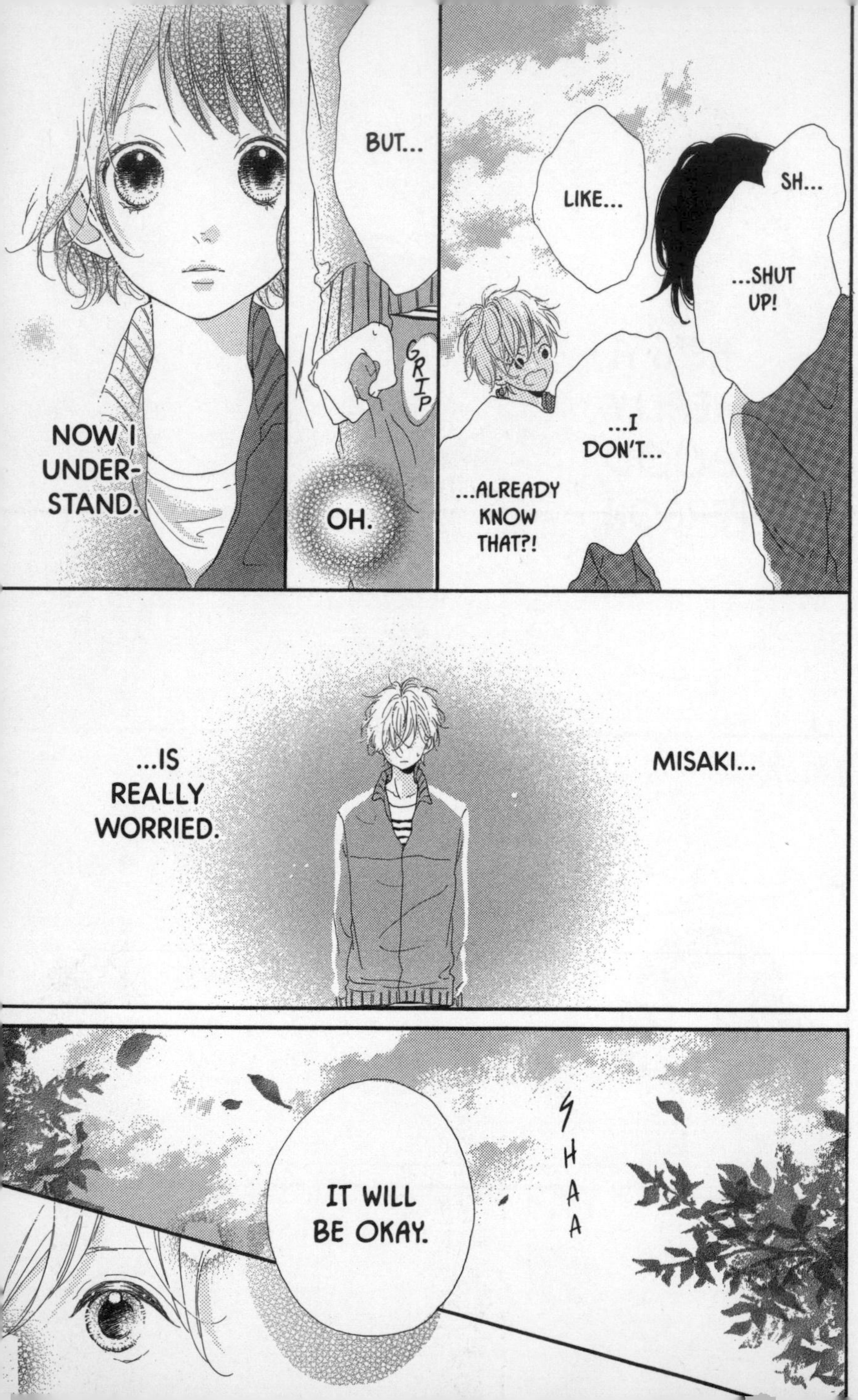
SH...
LIKE...
...SHUT UP!
...I DON'T...
...ALREADY KNOW THAT?!
BUT...
GRIP
OH.
NOW I UNDER-STAND.
MISAKI...
...IS REALLY WORRIED.
SHAA
IT WILL BE OKAY.

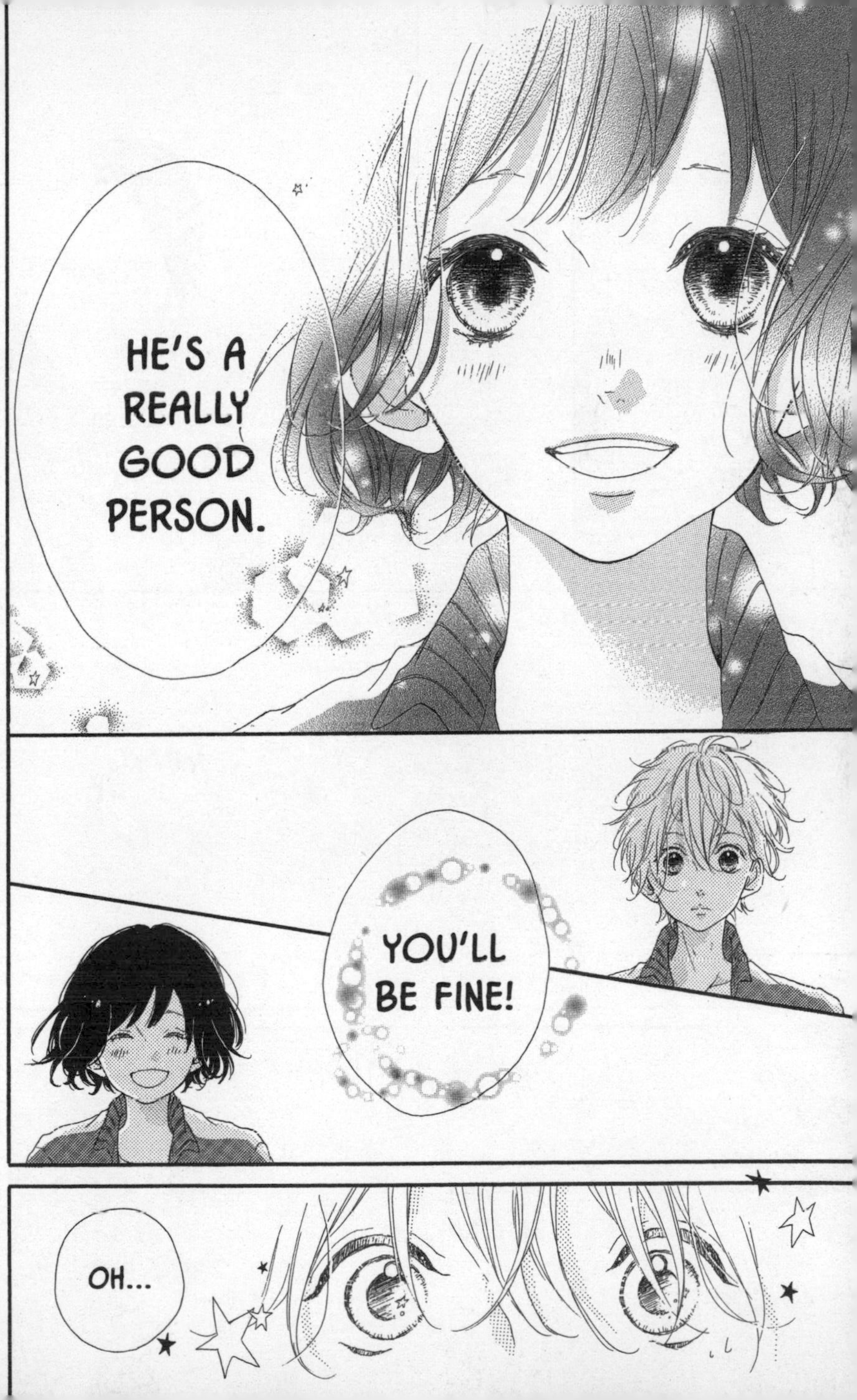
HE'S A REALLY GOOD PERSON.
YOU'LL BE FINE!
OH...

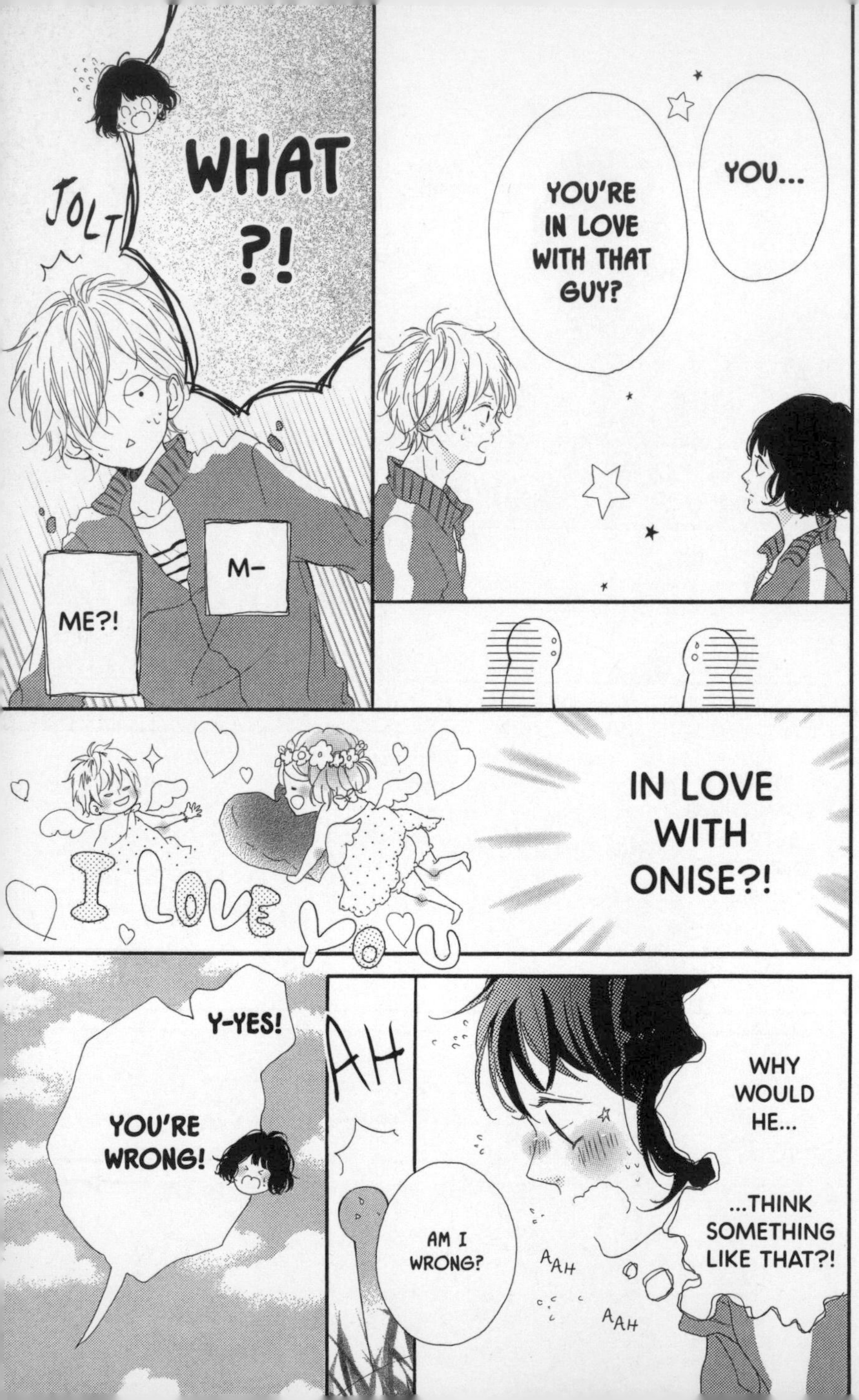
YOU...
YOU'RE IN LOVE WITH THAT GUY?
WHAT ?!
JOLT
M-
ME?!
IN LOVE WITH ONISE?!
I LOVE YOU
WHY WOULD HE...
...THINK SOMETHING LIKE THAT?!
AAH
AAH
AM I WRONG?
AH
Y-YES!
YOU'RE WRONG!

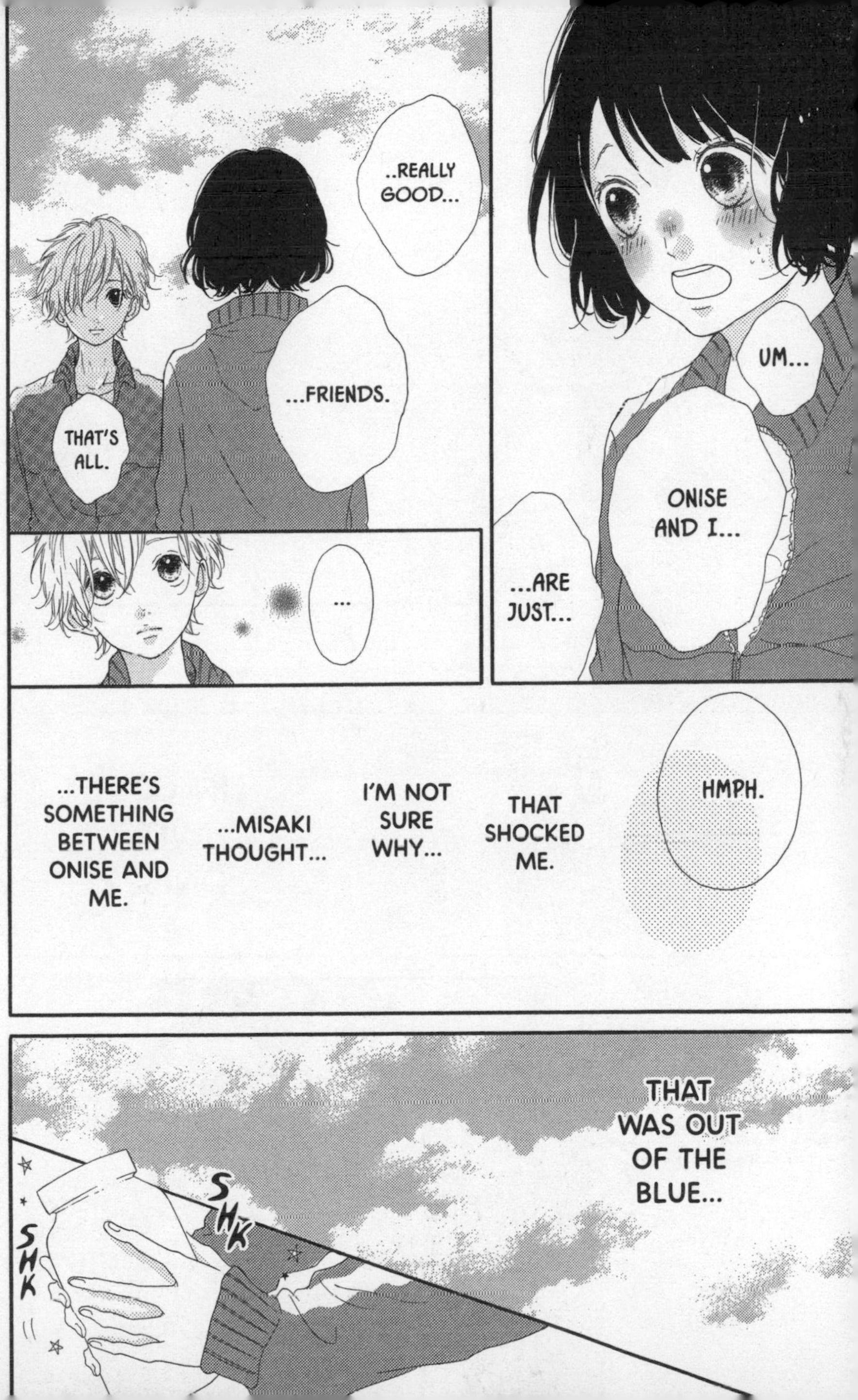
UM...
ONISE AND I...
...ARE JUST...
..REALLY GOOD...
...FRIENDS.
THAT'S ALL.
...
HMPH.
THAT SHOCKED ME.
I'M NOT SURE WHY...
...MISAKI THOUGHT...
...THERE'S SOMETHING BETWEEN ONISE AND ME.
THAT WAS OUT OF THE BLUE...
SHK
SHK

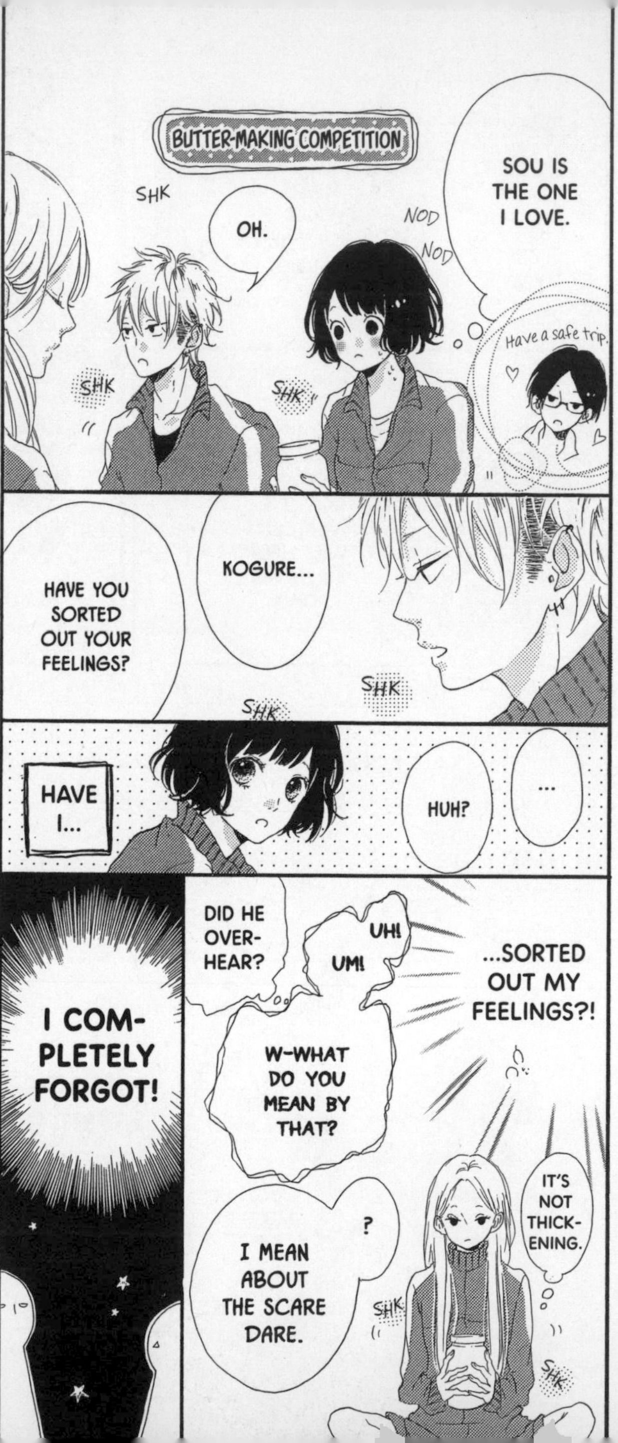
BUTTER-MAKING COMPETITION
SOU IS THE ONE I LOVE.
NOD
NOD
Have a safe trip.
OH.
SHK
SHK
SHK
KOGURE...
HAVE YOU SORTED OUT YOUR FEELINGS?
SHK
SHK
...
HUH?
HAVE I...
...SORTED OUT MY FEELINGS?!
UH!
UM!
DID HE OVER-HEAR?
W-WHAT DO YOU MEAN BY THAT?
IT'S NOT THICK-ENING.
?
I MEAN ABOUT THE SCARE DARE.
SHK
SHK
I COM-PLETELY FORGOT!

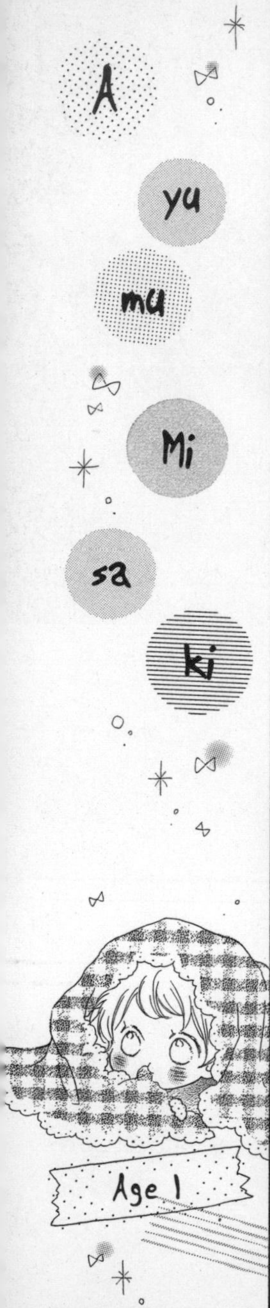
A yu mu Mi sa ki
Age 1

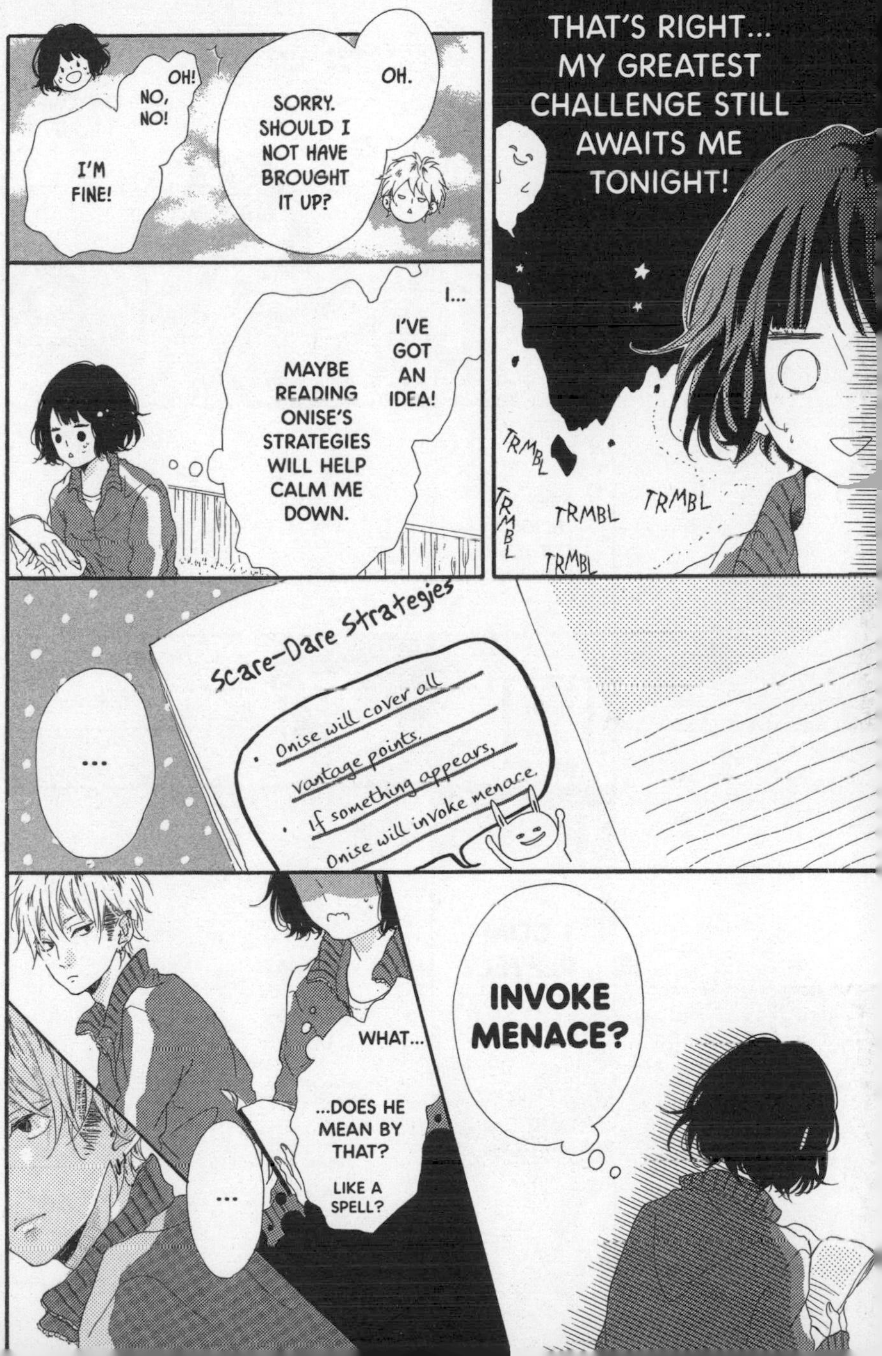
THAT'S RIGHT... MY GREATEST CHALLENGE STILL AWAITS ME TONIGHT!
TRMBL
TRMBL
TRMBL
TRMBL
TRMBL
OH.
SORRY. SHOULD I NOT HAVE BROUGHT IT UP?
OH! NO, NO!
I'M FINE!
I...
I'VE GOT AN IDEA!
MAYBE READING ONISE'S STRATEGIES WILL HELP CALM ME DOWN.
Scare-Dare Strategies
• Onise will cover all vantage points.
• If something appears, Onise will invoke menace.
...
INVOKE MENACE?
WHAT...
...DOES HE MEAN BY THAT?
LIKE A SPELL?
...

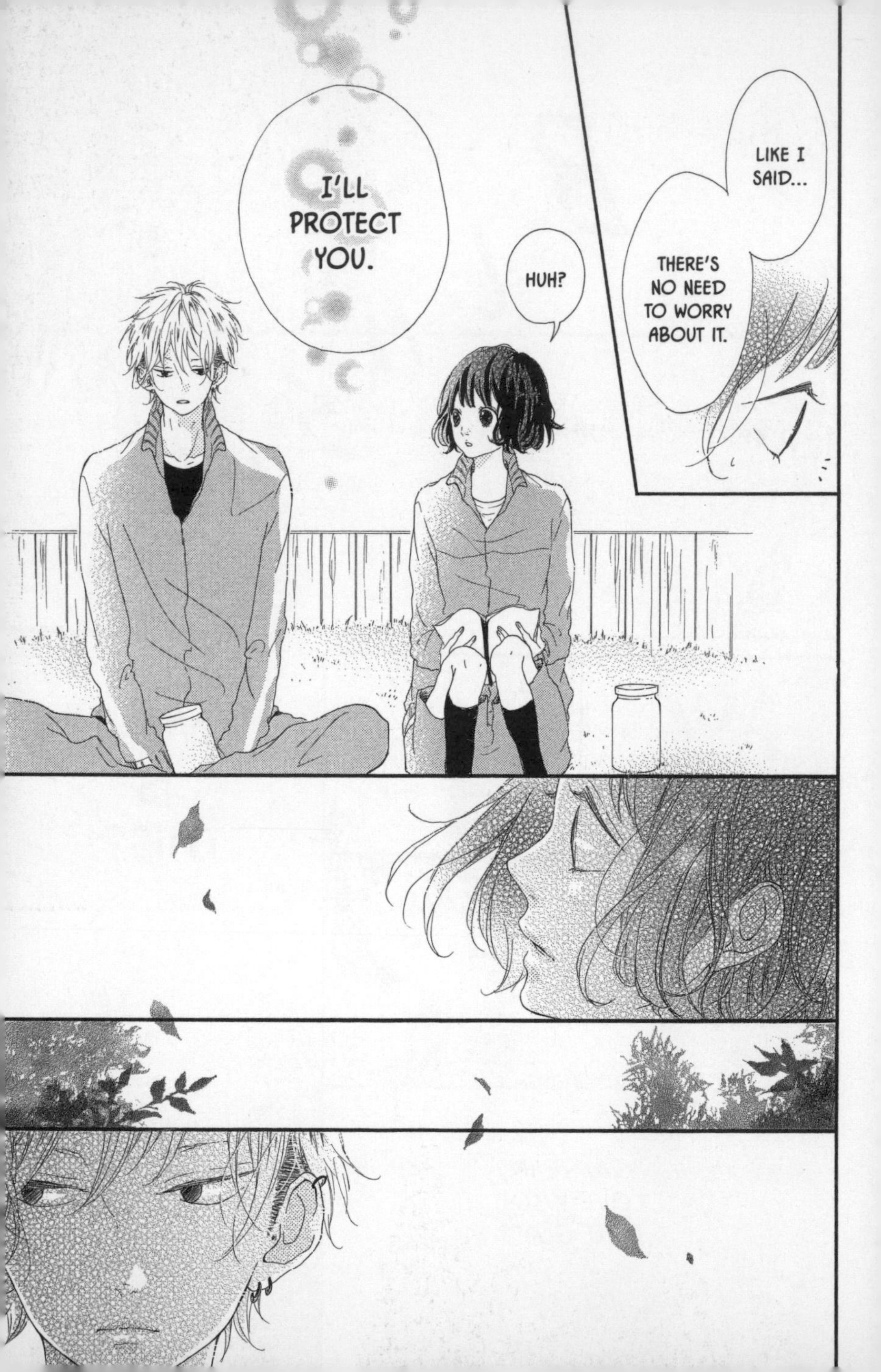
LIKE I SAID...
THERE'S NO NEED TO WORRY ABOUT IT.
I'LL PROTECT YOU.
HUH?

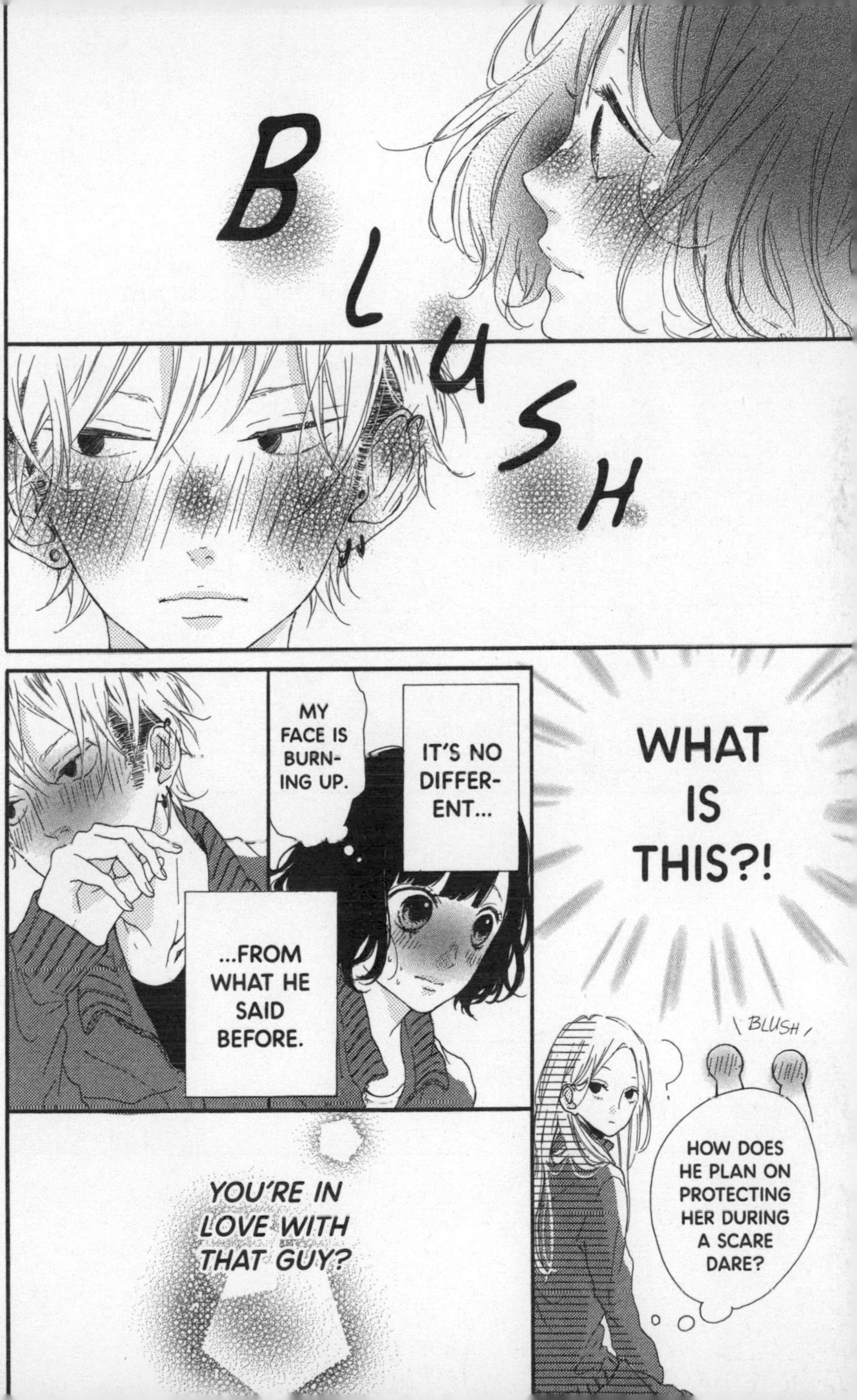
BLUSH
WHAT IS THIS?!
BLUSH
HOW DOES HE PLAN ON PROTECTING HER DURING A SCARE DARE?
IT'S NO DIFFERENT...
MY FACE IS BURNING UP.
...FROM WHAT HE SAID BEFORE.
YOU'RE IN LOVE WITH THAT GUY?

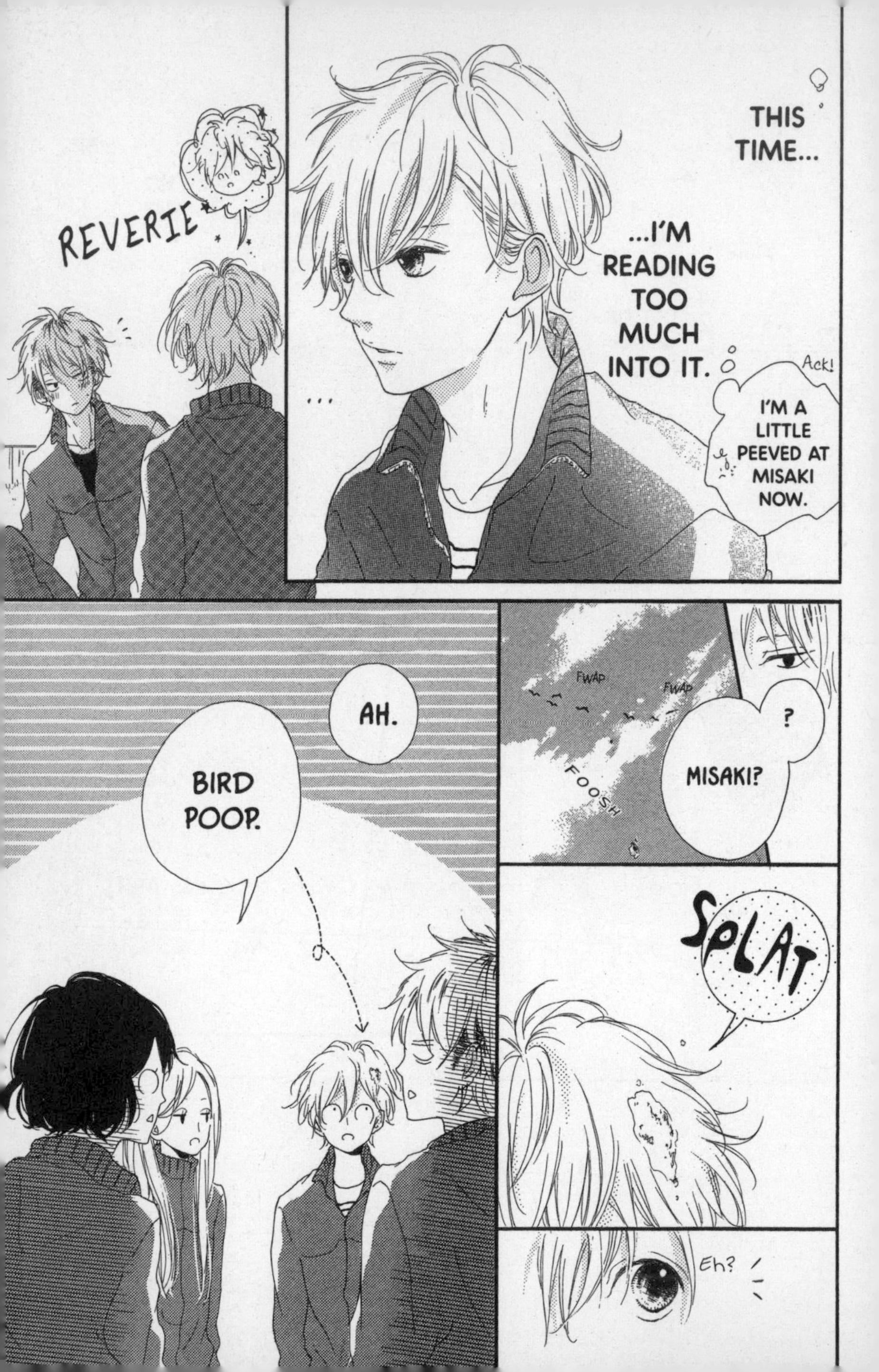
THIS TIME...
...I'M READING TOO MUCH INTO IT.
...
Ack!
I'M A LITTLE PEEVED AT MISAKI NOW.
REVERIE
FWAP
FWAP
FOOSH
?
MISAKI?
SPLAT
Eh?
AH.
BIRD POOP.

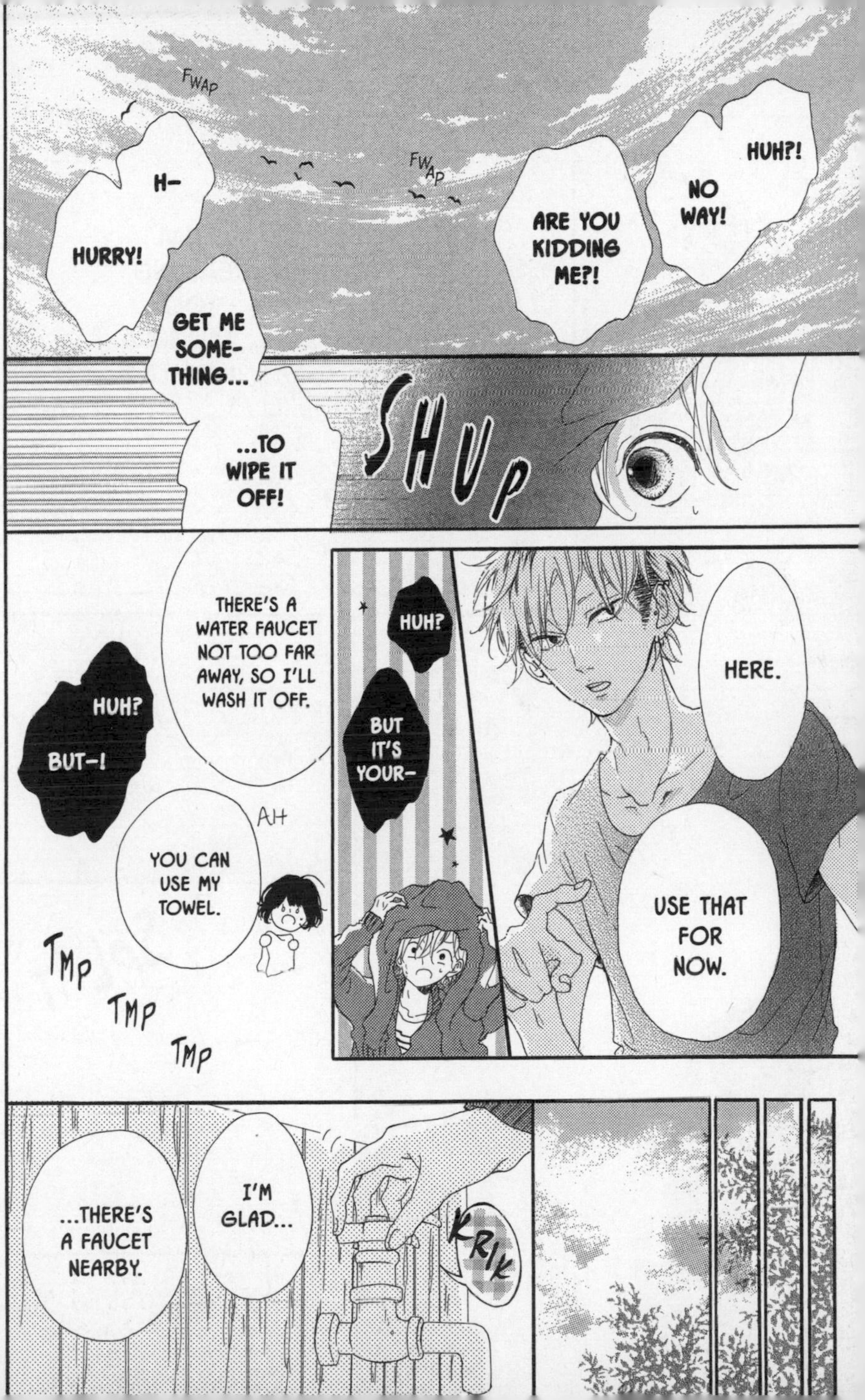
FWAP
FWAP
HUH?!
NO WAY!
ARE YOU KIDDING ME?!
H-
HURRY!
GET ME SOME-THING...
SHUP
...TO WIPE IT OFF!
HERE.
USE THAT FOR NOW.
HUH?
BUT IT'S YOUR-
THERE'S A WATER FAUCET NOT TOO FAR AWAY, SO I'LL WASH IT OFF.
HUH?
BUT-!
AH
YOU CAN USE MY TOWEL.
TMP
TMP
TMP
KRIK
I'M GLAD...
...THERE'S A FAUCET NEARBY.

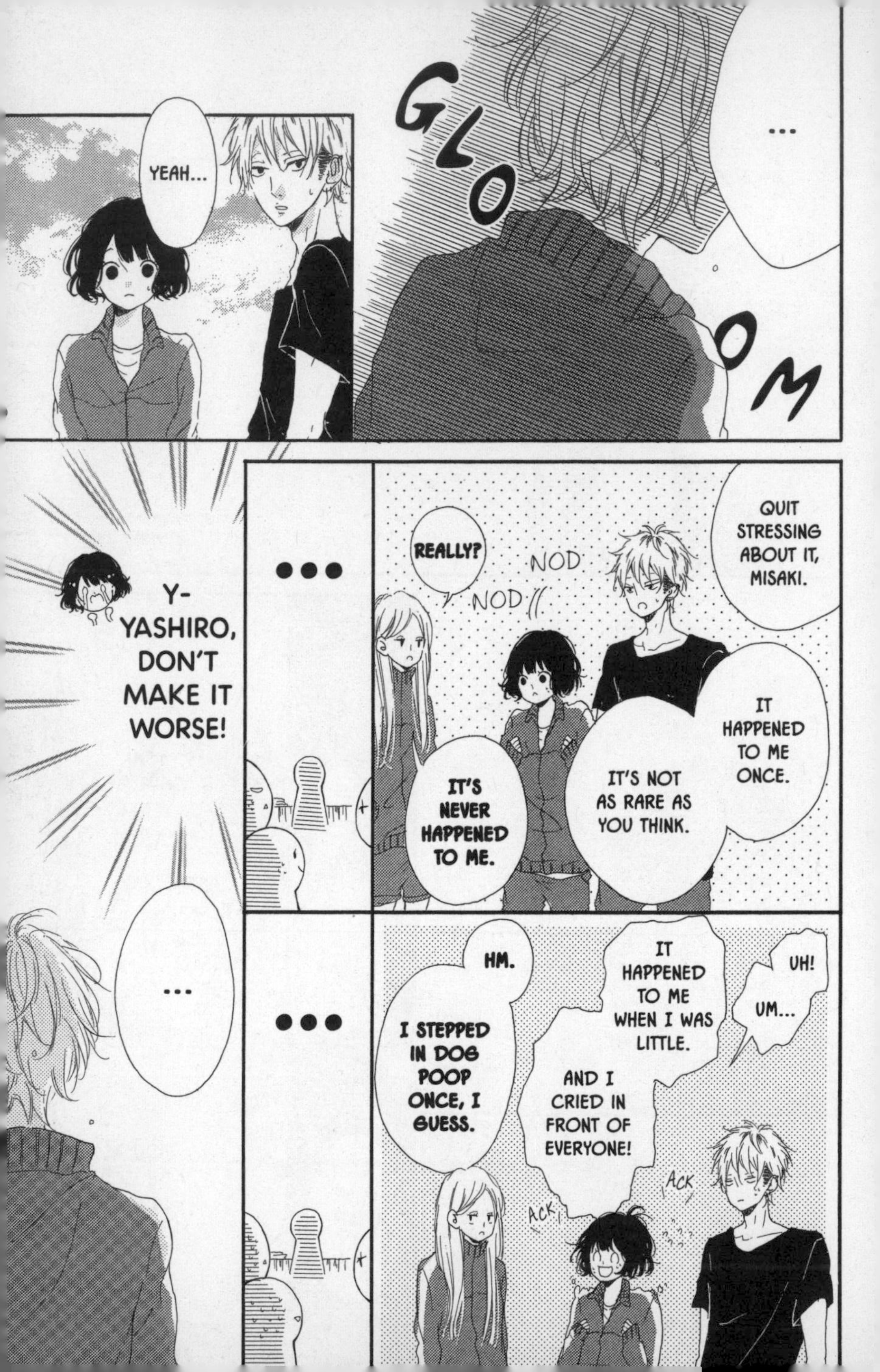

GLOOM
...
YEAH...
QUIT STRESSING ABOUT IT, MISAKI.
IT HAPPENED TO ME ONCE.
IT'S NOT AS RARE AS YOU THINK.
REALLY?
NOD NOD
IT'S NEVER HAPPENED TO ME.
•••
UH! UM...
IT HAPPENED TO ME WHEN I WAS LITTLE.
AND I CRIED IN FRONT OF EVERYONE!
HM.
I STEPPED IN DOG POOP ONCE, I GUESS.
ACK ACK
•••
Y-YASHIRO, DON'T MAKE IT WORSE!
...

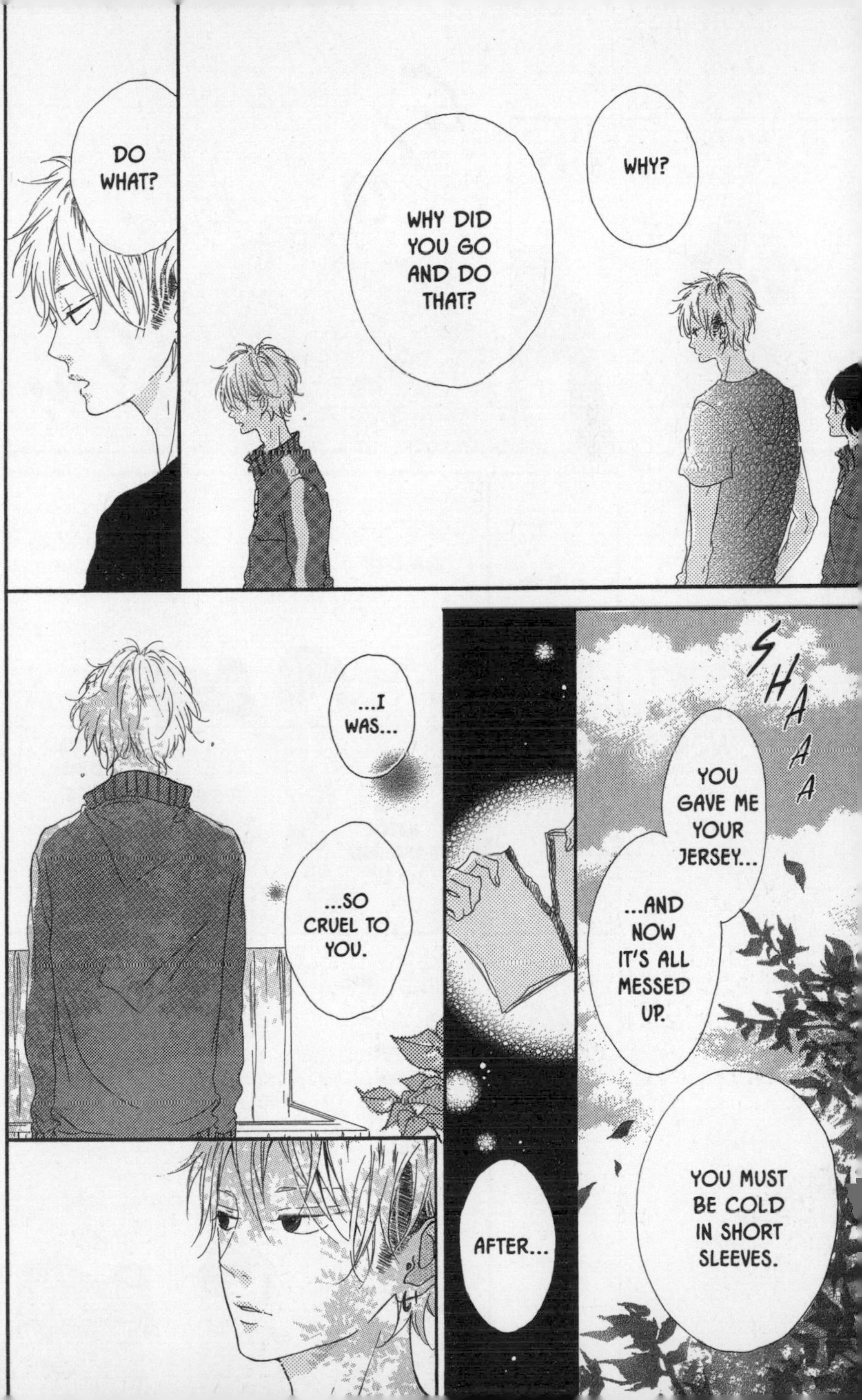
WHY?
WHY DID YOU GO AND DO THAT?
DO WHAT?
SHAAA
YOU GAVE ME YOUR JERSEY...
...AND NOW IT'S ALL MESSED UP.
YOU MUST BE COLD IN SHORT SLEEVES.
AFTER...
...I WAS...
...SO CRUEL TO YOU.

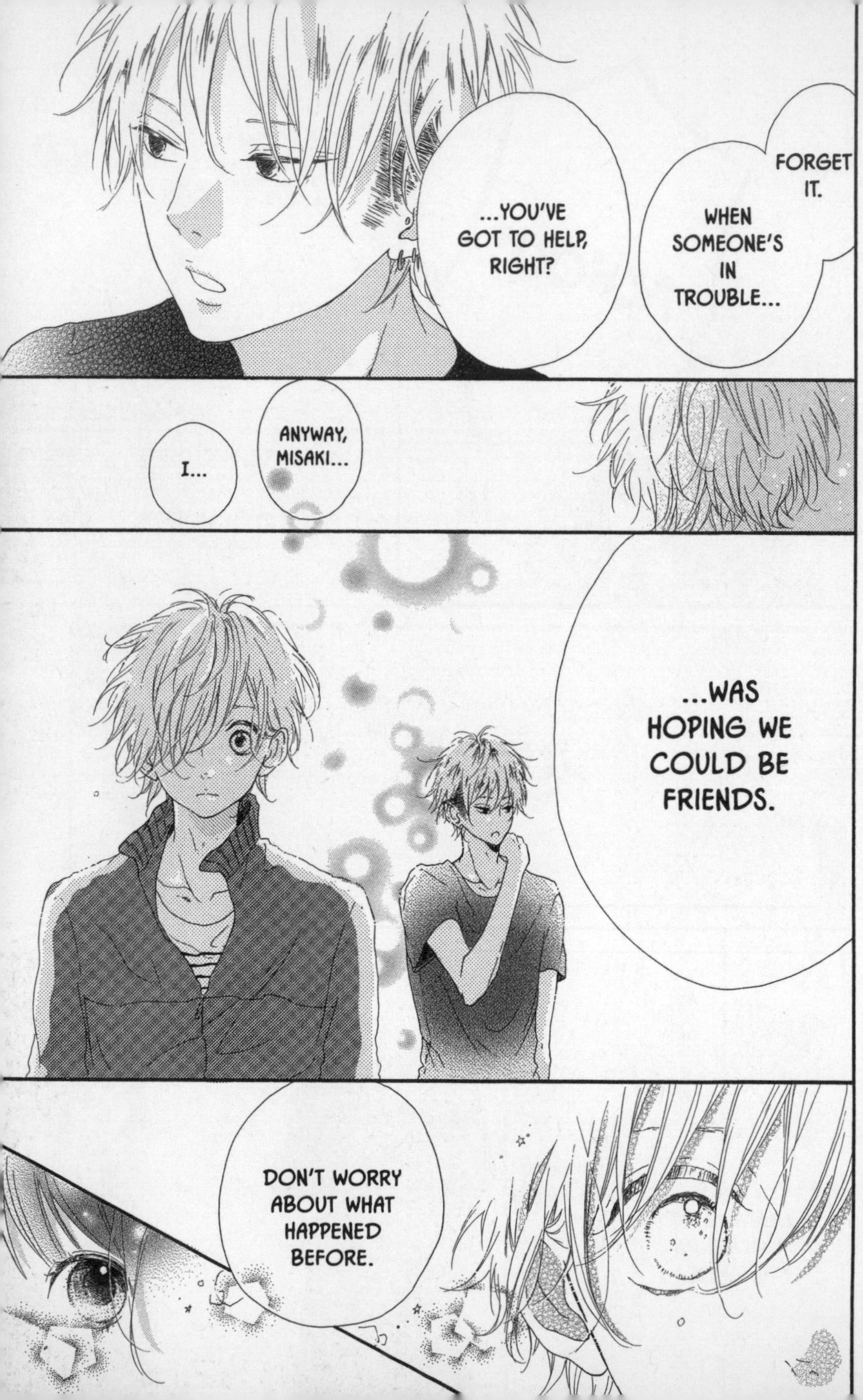
FORGET IT.
WHEN SOMEONE'S IN TROUBLE...
...YOU'VE GOT TO HELP, RIGHT?
ANYWAY, MISAKI...
I...
...WAS HOPING WE COULD BE FRIENDS.
DON'T WORRY ABOUT WHAT HAPPENED BEFORE.

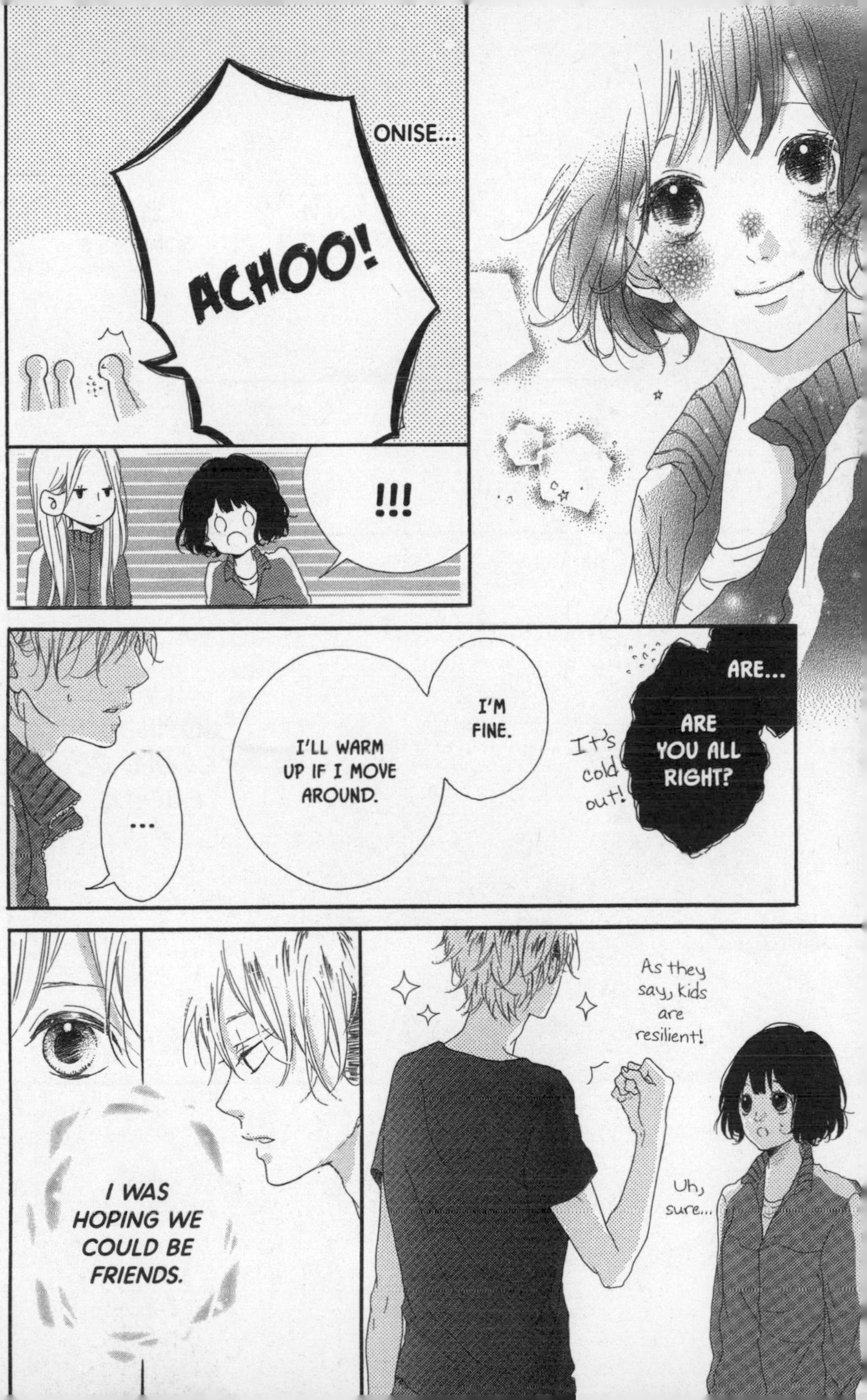
ONISE...
ACHOO!
!!!
ARE...
ARE YOU ALL RIGHT?
It's cold out!
I'M FINE.
I'LL WARM UP IF I MOVE AROUND.
...
As they say, kids are resilient!
Uh, sure...
I WAS HOPING WE COULD BE FRIENDS.

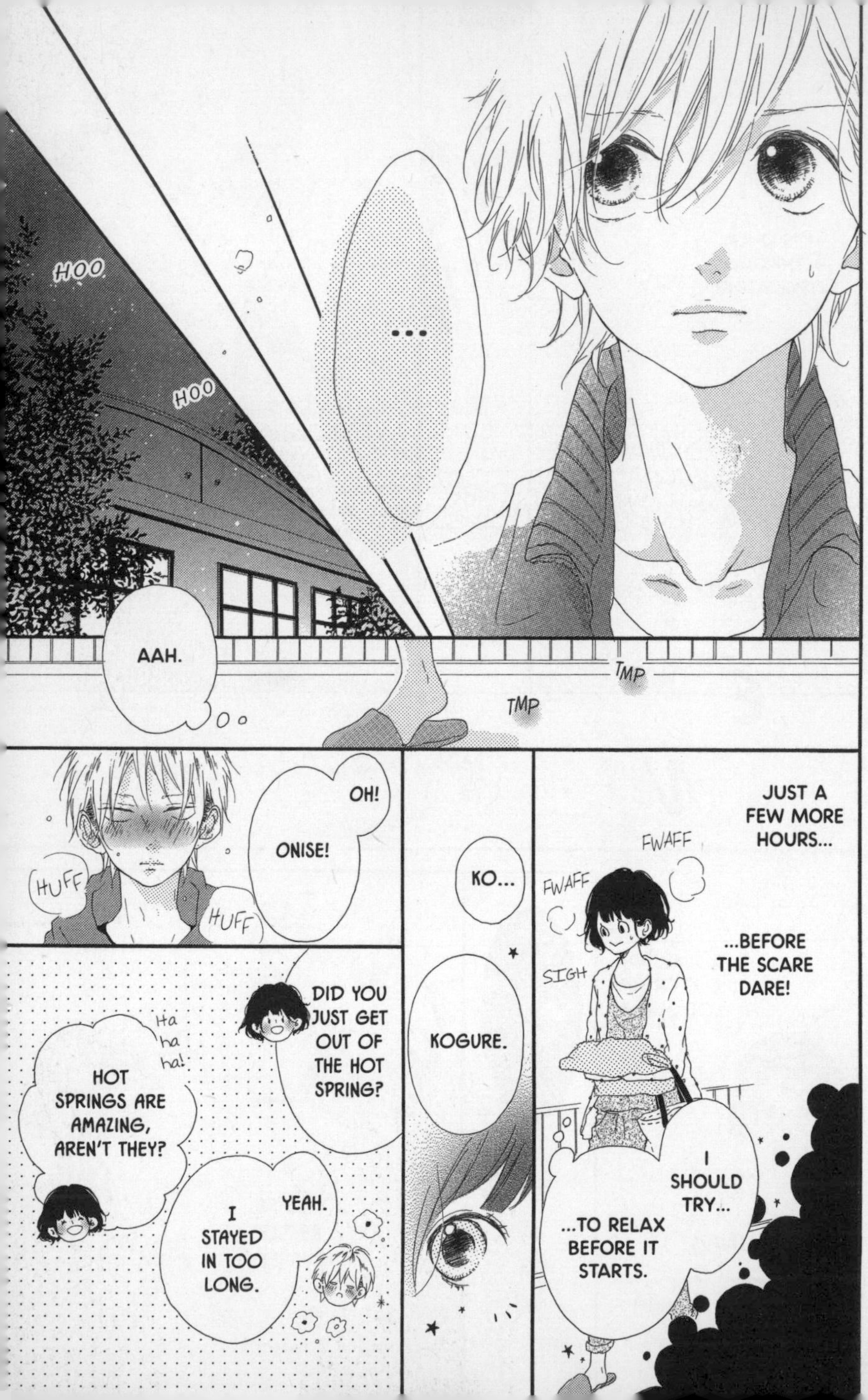
...
HOO
HOO
AAH.
TMP
TMP
JUST A FEW MORE HOURS...
FWAFF
FWAFF
SIGH
...BEFORE THE SCARE DARE!
I SHOULD TRY...
...TO RELAX BEFORE IT STARTS.
KO...
KOGURE.
OH!
ONISE!
HUFF
HUFF
DID YOU JUST GET OUT OF THE HOT SPRING?
Ha ha ha!
HOT SPRINGS ARE AMAZING, AREN'T THEY?
YEAH.
I STAYED IN TOO LONG.

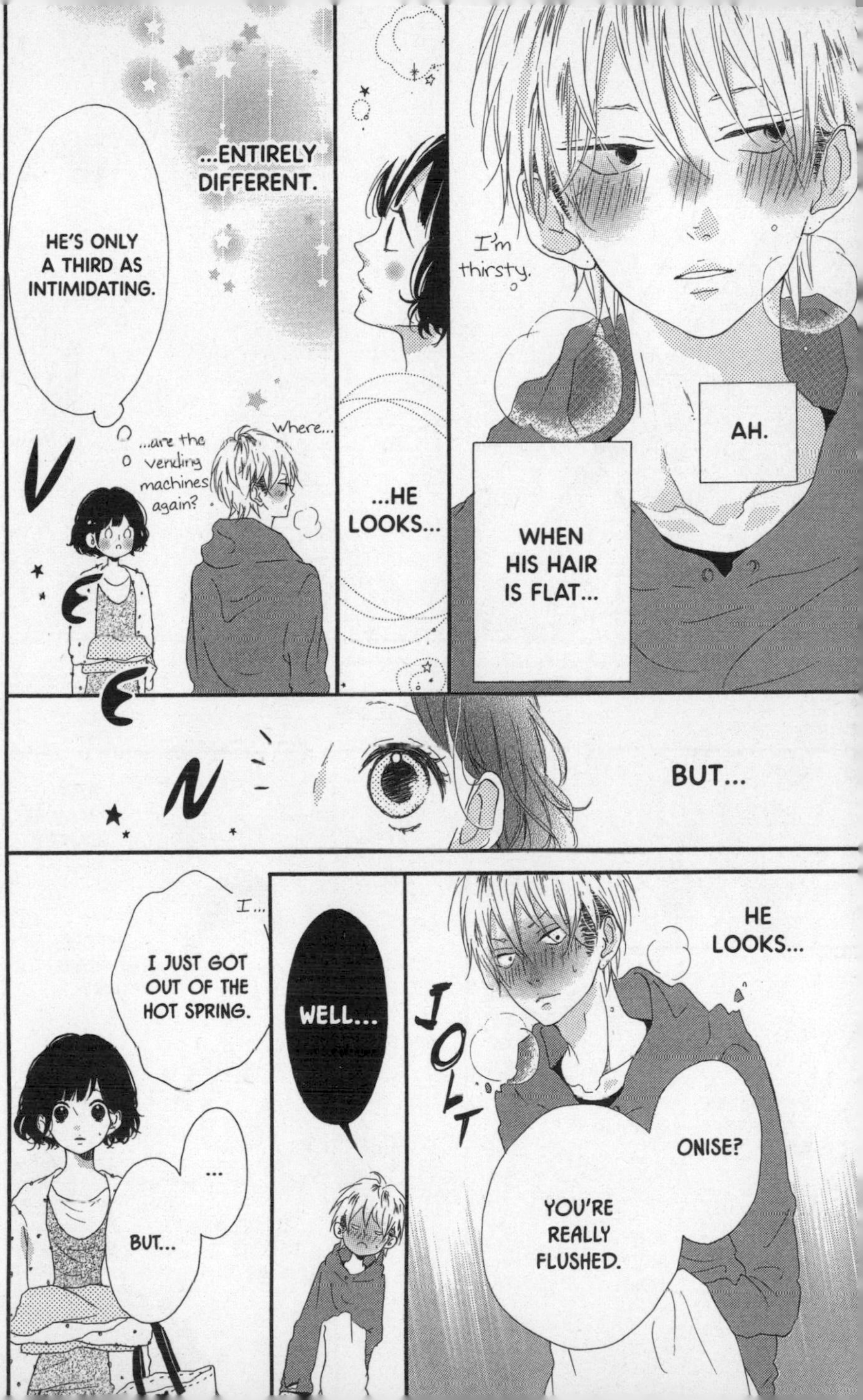
I'm thirsty.
AH.
WHEN HIS HAIR IS FLAT...
...HE LOOKS...
...ENTIRELY DIFFERENT.
HE'S ONLY A THIRD AS INTIMIDATING.
Where...
...are the vending machines again?
VEEN
BUT...
HE LOOKS...
JOLT
ONISE?
YOU'RE REALLY FLUSHED.
WELL...
I...
I JUST GOT OUT OF THE HOT SPRING.
...
BUT...

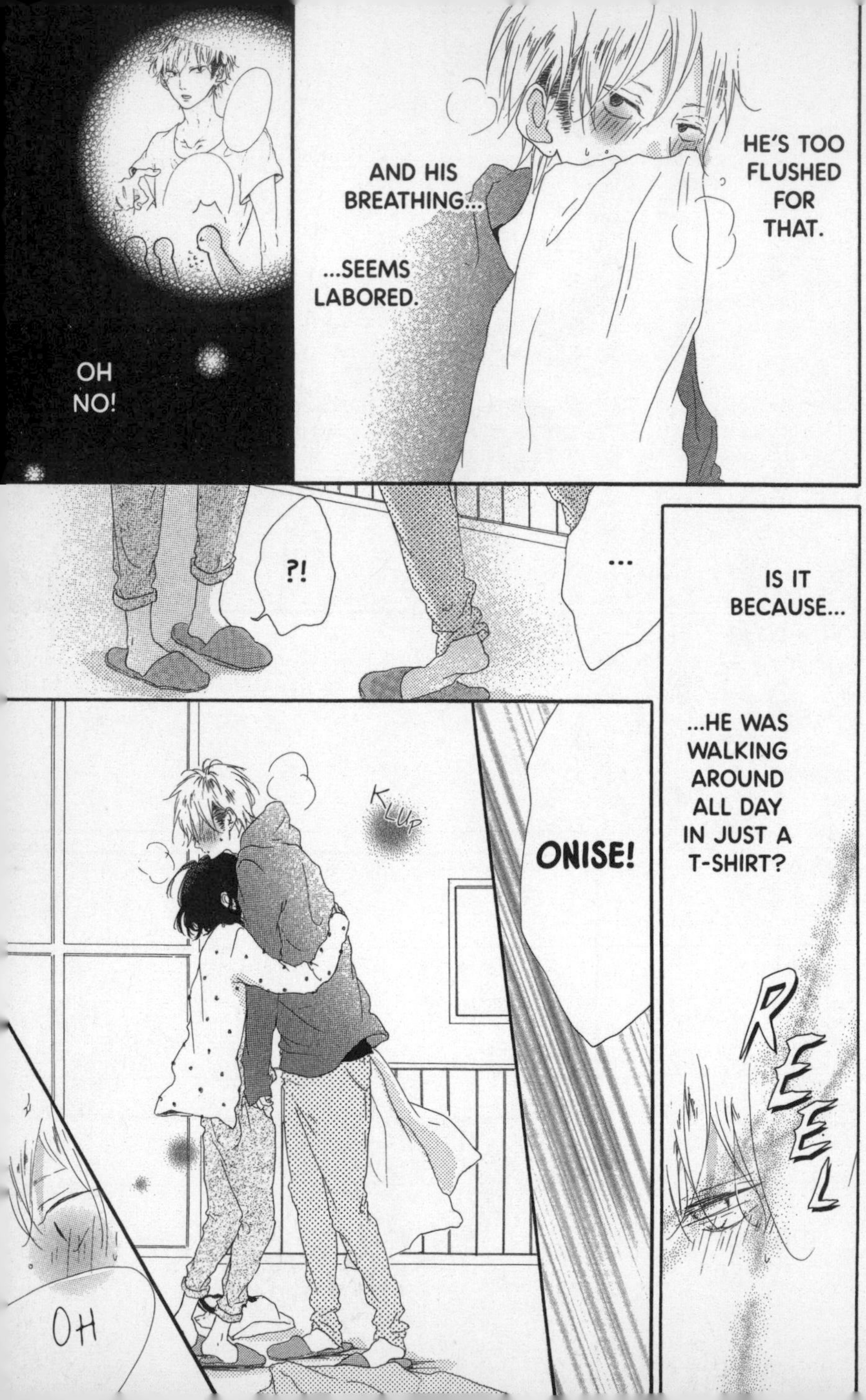
HE'S TOO FLUSHED FOR THAT.
AND HIS BREATHING...
...SEEMS LABORED.
OH NO!
IS IT BECAUSE...
...HE WAS WALKING AROUND ALL DAY IN JUST A T-SHIRT?
REEEL
...
?!
ONISE!
KLUP
OH

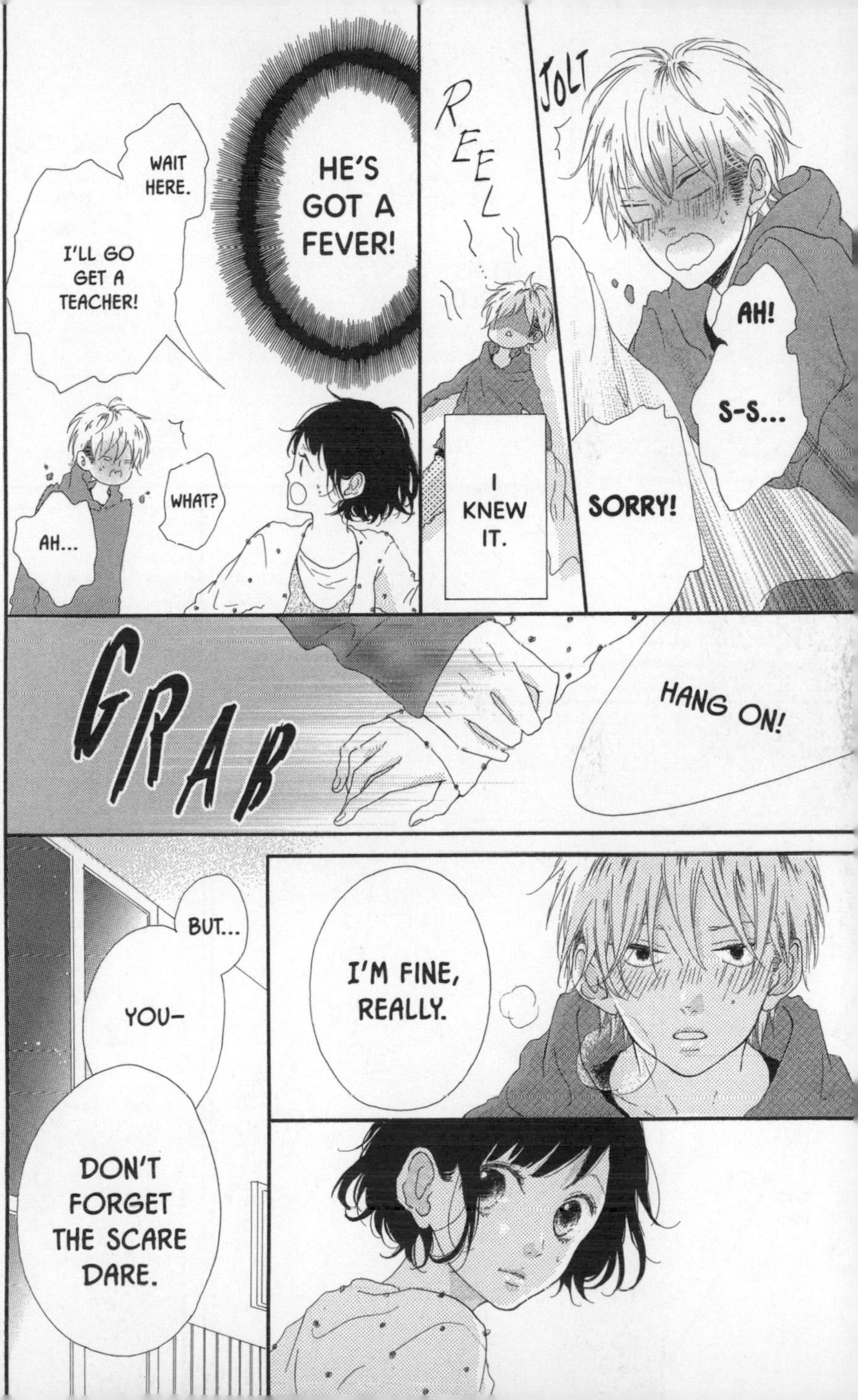
JOLT
AH!
S-S...
SORRY!
REEL
I KNEW IT.
HE'S GOT A FEVER!
WAIT HERE.
I'LL GO GET A TEACHER!
WHAT?
AH...
HANG ON!
GRAB
I'M FINE, REALLY.
BUT...
YOU–
DON'T FORGET THE SCARE DARE.

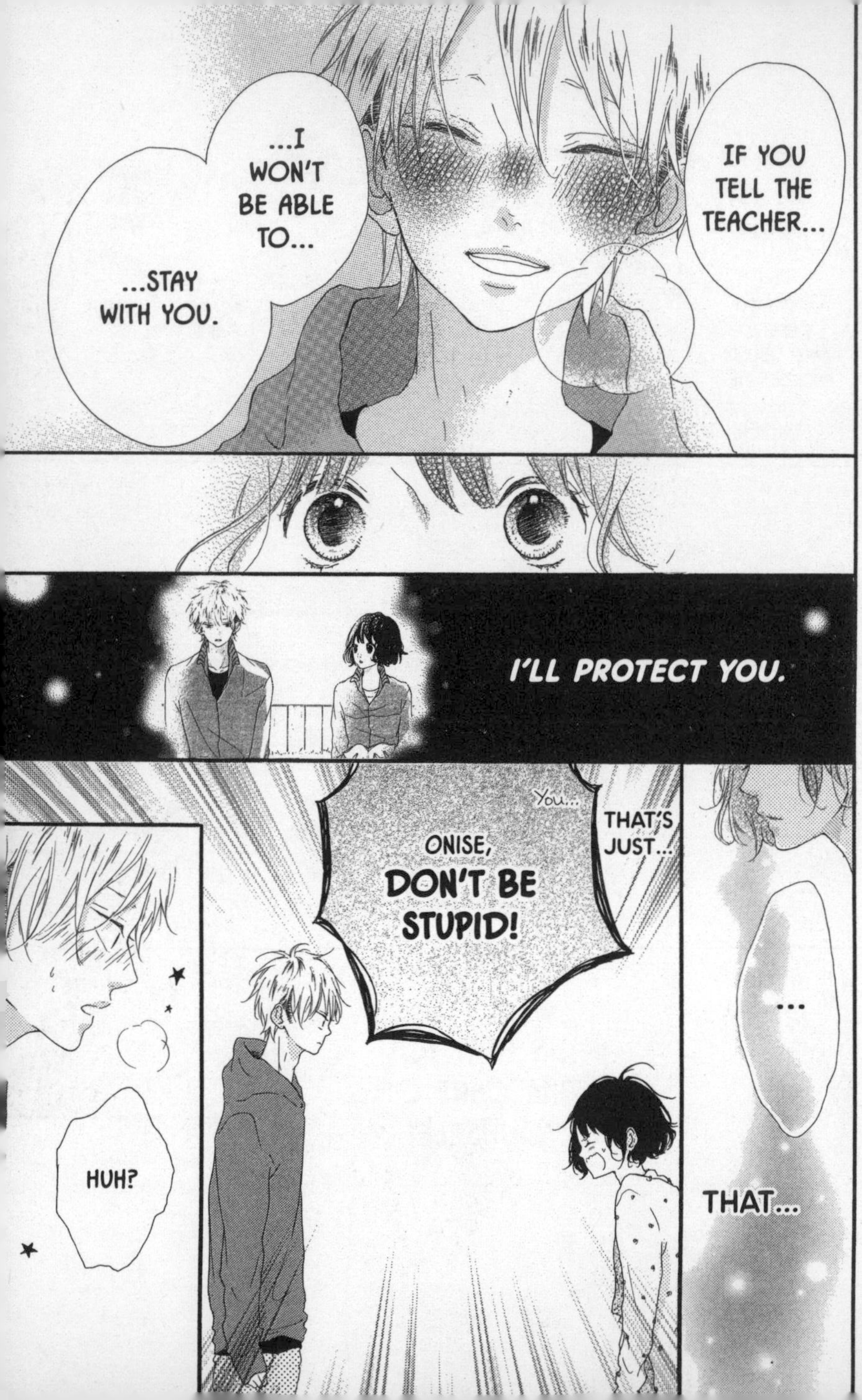
IF YOU TELL THE TEACHER...
...I WON'T BE ABLE TO...
...STAY WITH YOU.
I'LL PROTECT YOU.
...
THAT...
THAT'S JUST...
You...
ONISE, DON'T BE STUPID!
HUH?

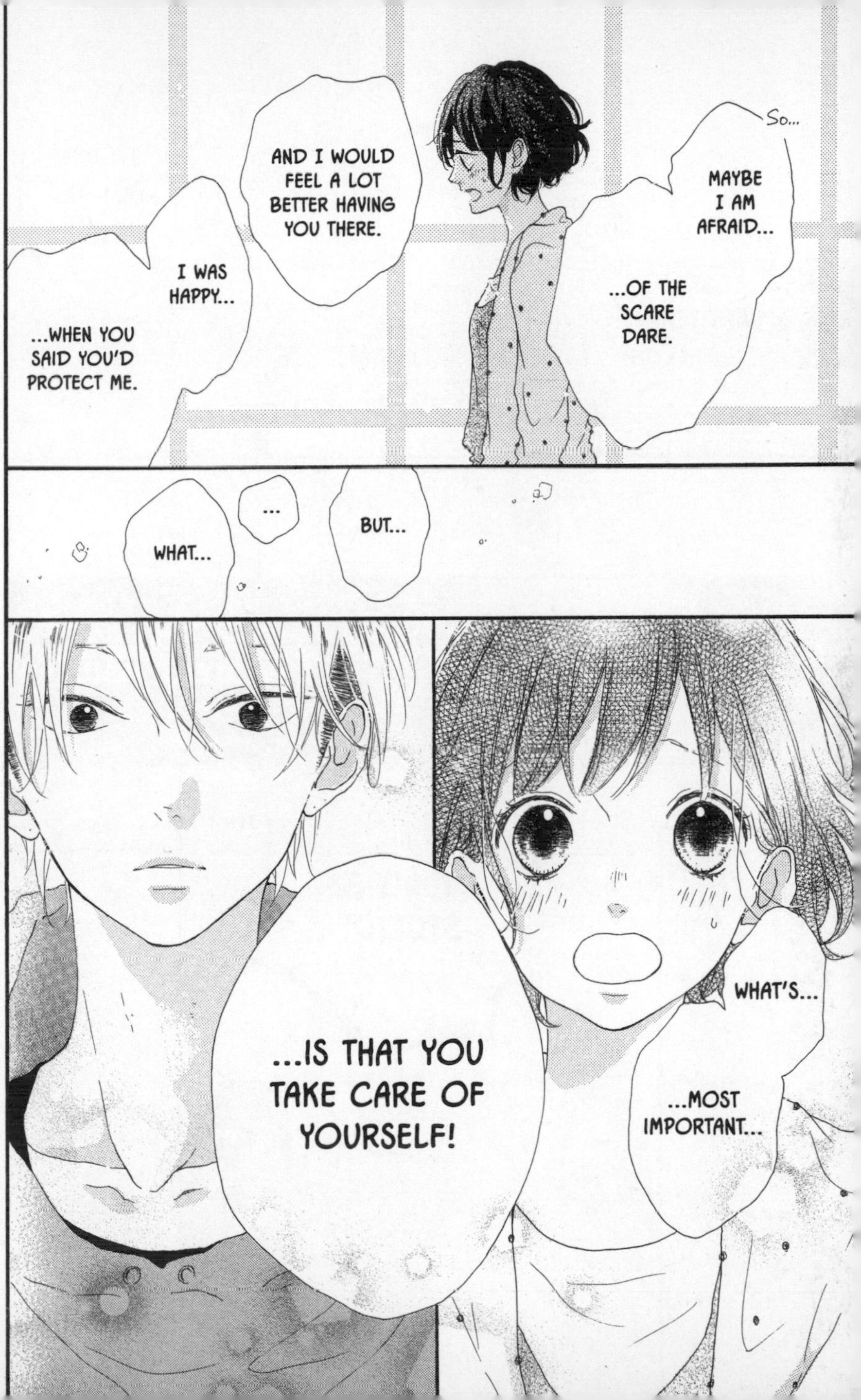
So...
MAYBE I AM AFRAID...
...OF THE SCARE DARE.
I WAS HAPPY...
...WHEN YOU SAID YOU'D PROTECT ME.
AND I WOULD FEEL A LOT BETTER HAVING YOU THERE.
BUT...
...
WHAT...
WHAT'S...
...MOST IMPORTANT...
...IS THAT YOU TAKE CARE OF YOURSELF!

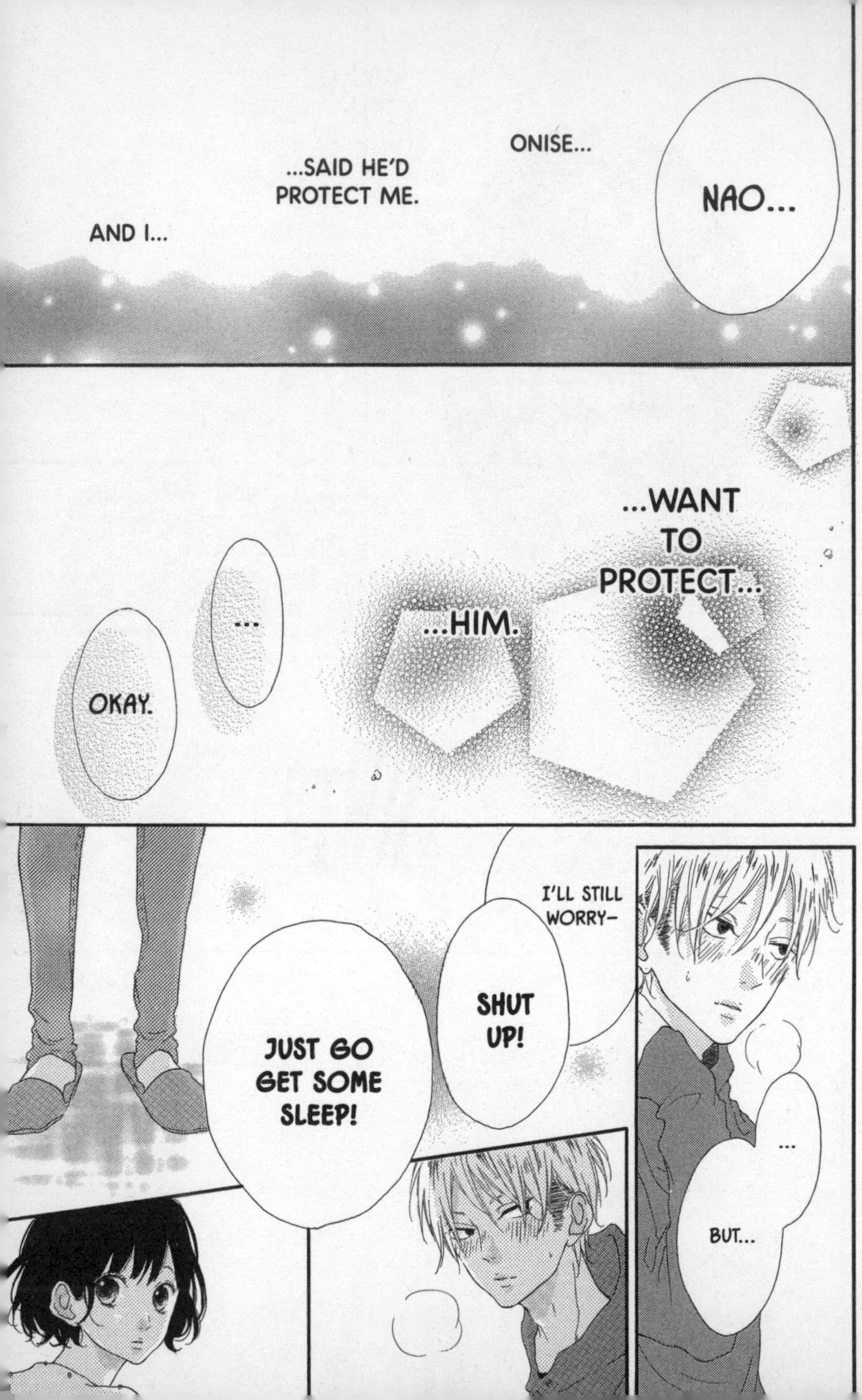
NAO...
ONISE...
...SAID HE'D PROTECT ME.
AND I...
...WANT TO PROTECT...
...HIM.
...
OKAY.
...
BUT...
I'LL STILL WORRY—
SHUT UP!
JUST GO GET SOME SLEEP!

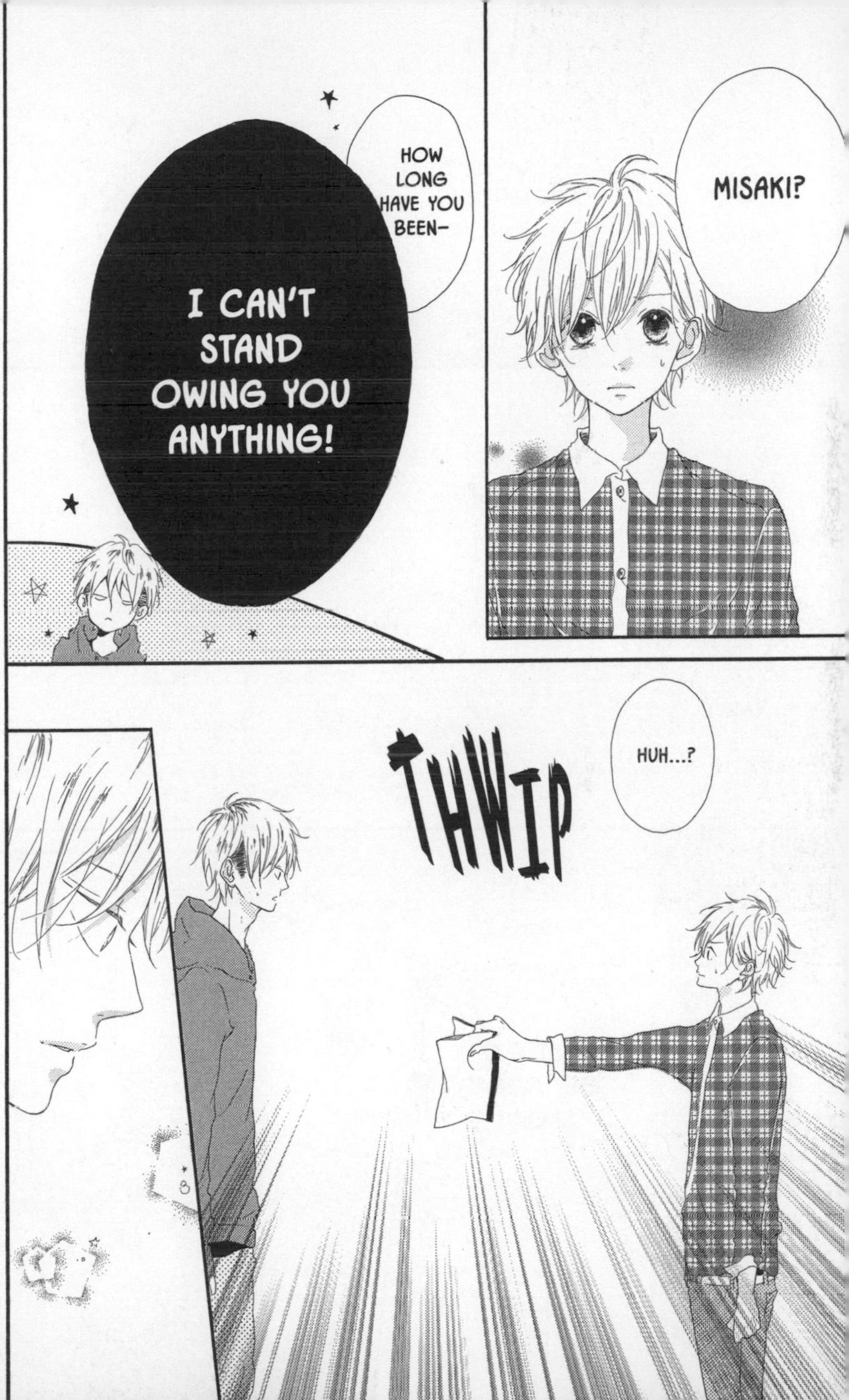
MISAKI?
HOW LONG HAVE YOU BEEN—
I CAN'T STAND OWING YOU ANYTHING!
HUH...?
THWIP

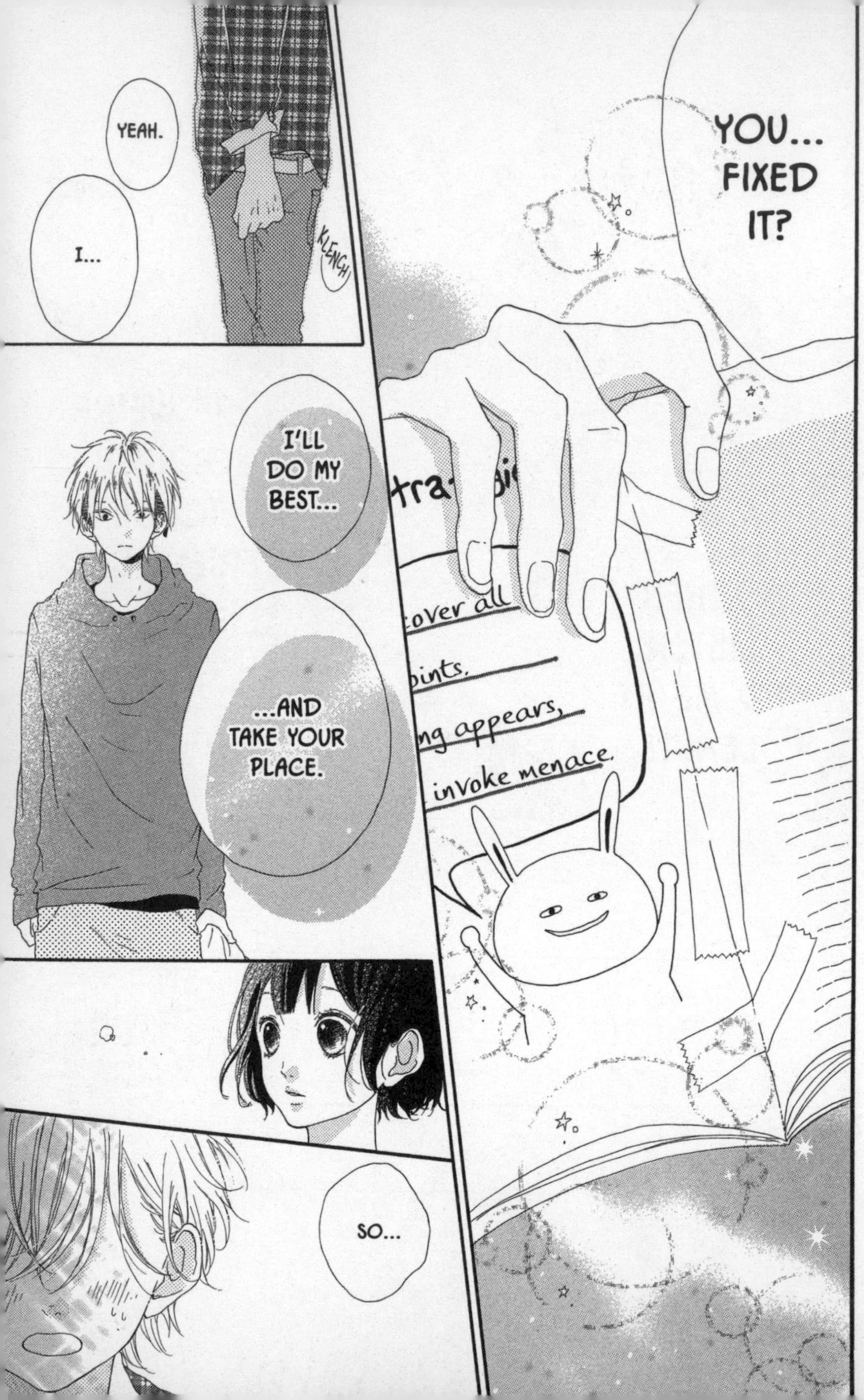
YOU... FIXED IT?
YEAH.
I...
KLENCH
I'LL DO MY BEST...
...AND TAKE YOUR PLACE.
SO...

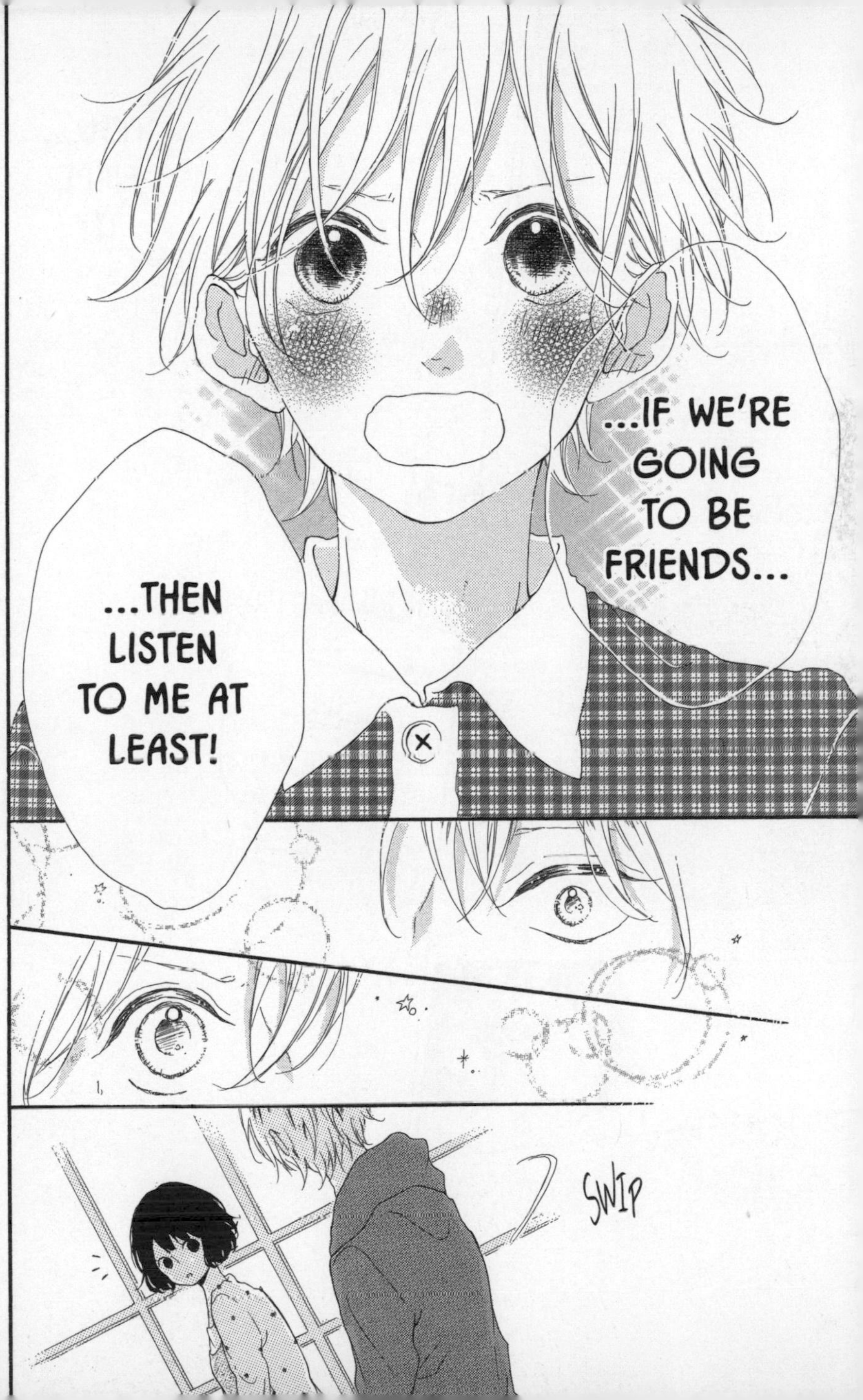
...IF WE'RE GOING TO BE FRIENDS...
...THEN LISTEN TO ME AT LEAST!
SWIP

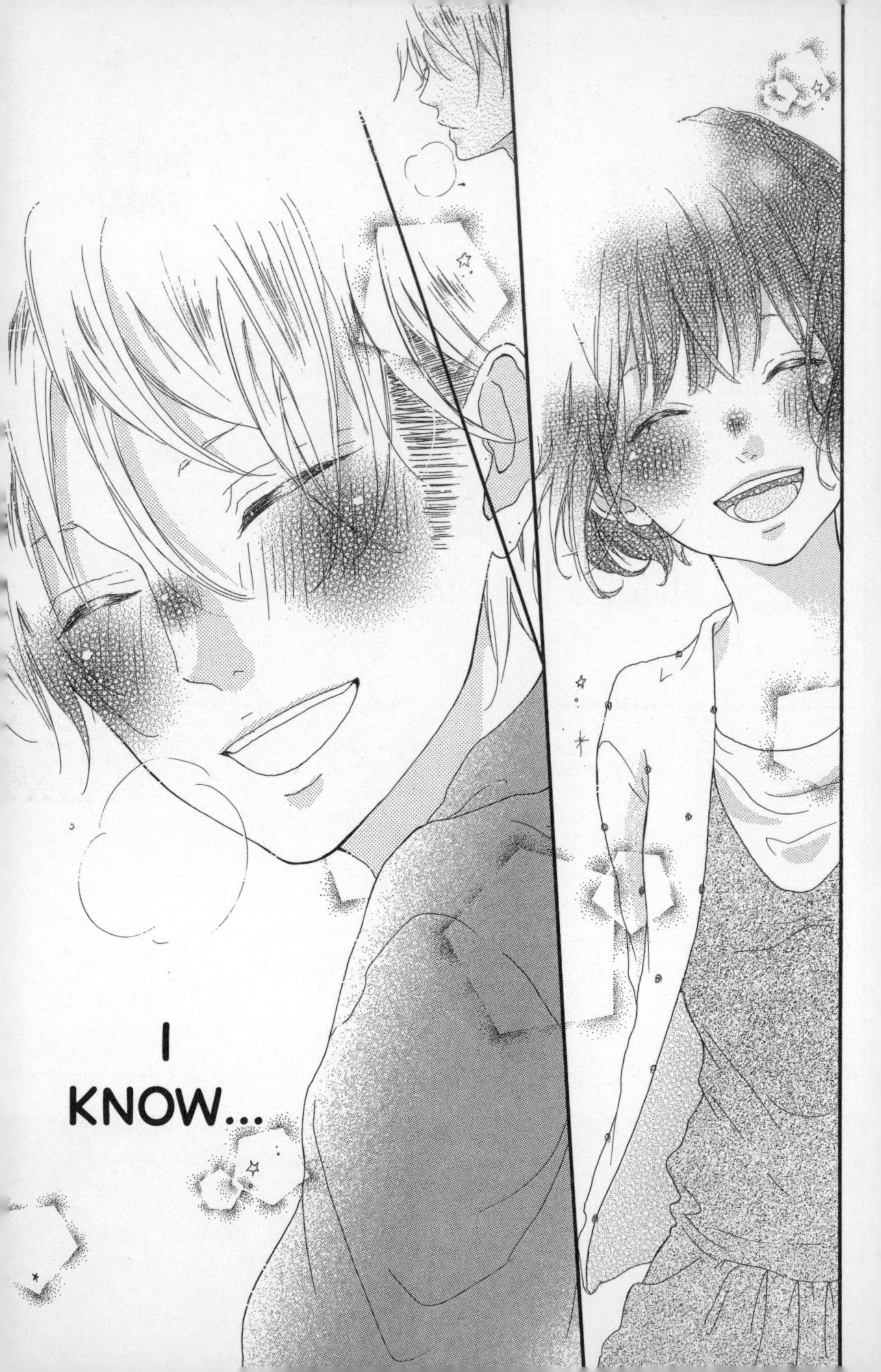
I KNOW...

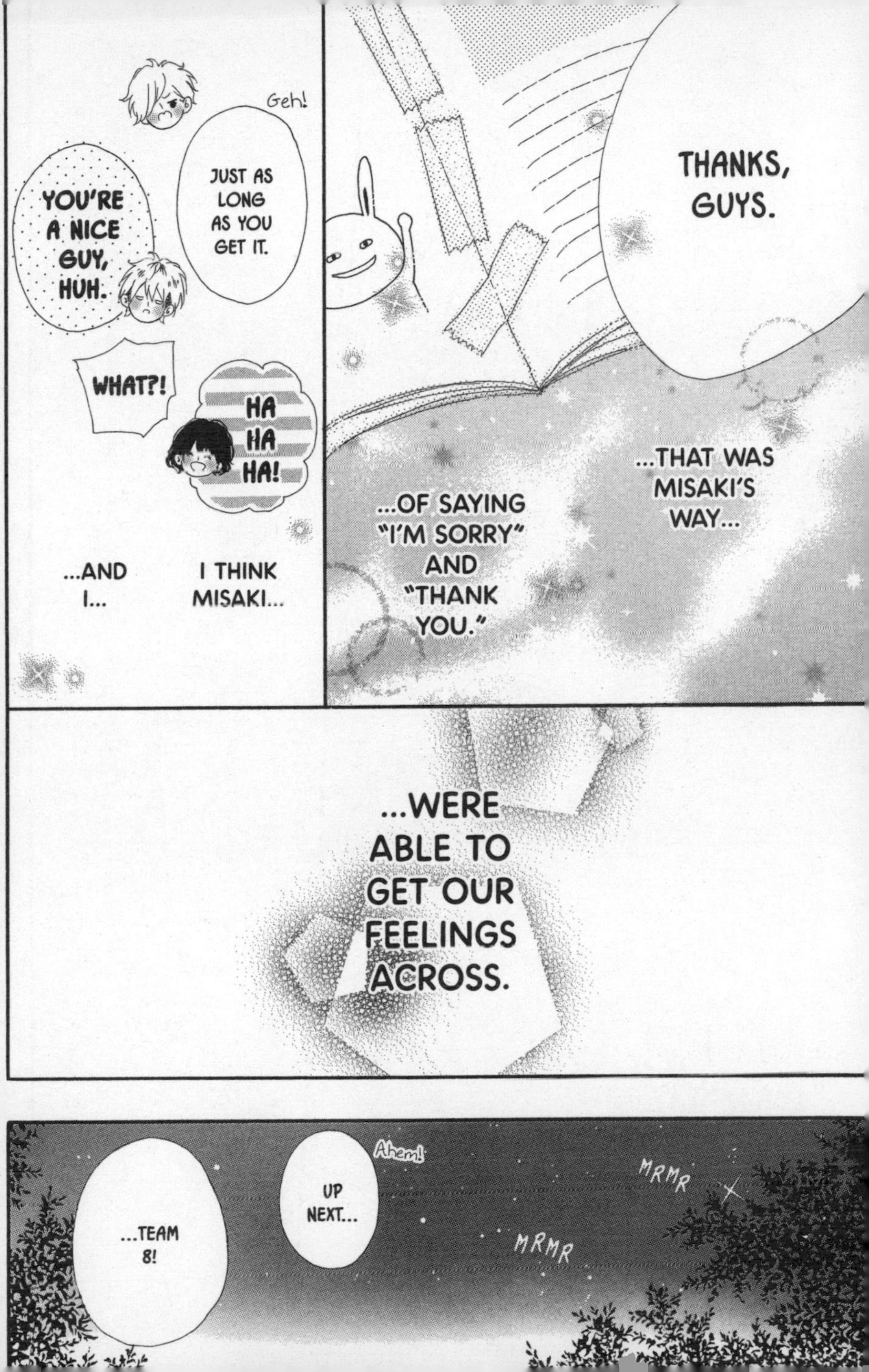
THANKS, GUYS.
...THAT WAS MISAKI'S WAY...
...OF SAYING "I'M SORRY" AND "THANK YOU."
Geh!
JUST AS LONG AS YOU GET IT.
YOU'RE A NICE GUY, HUH.
WHAT?!
HA HA HA!
I THINK MISAKI...
...AND I...
...WERE ABLE TO GET OUR FEELINGS ACROSS.
Ahem!
UP NEXT...
MRMR
MRMR
...TEAM 8!

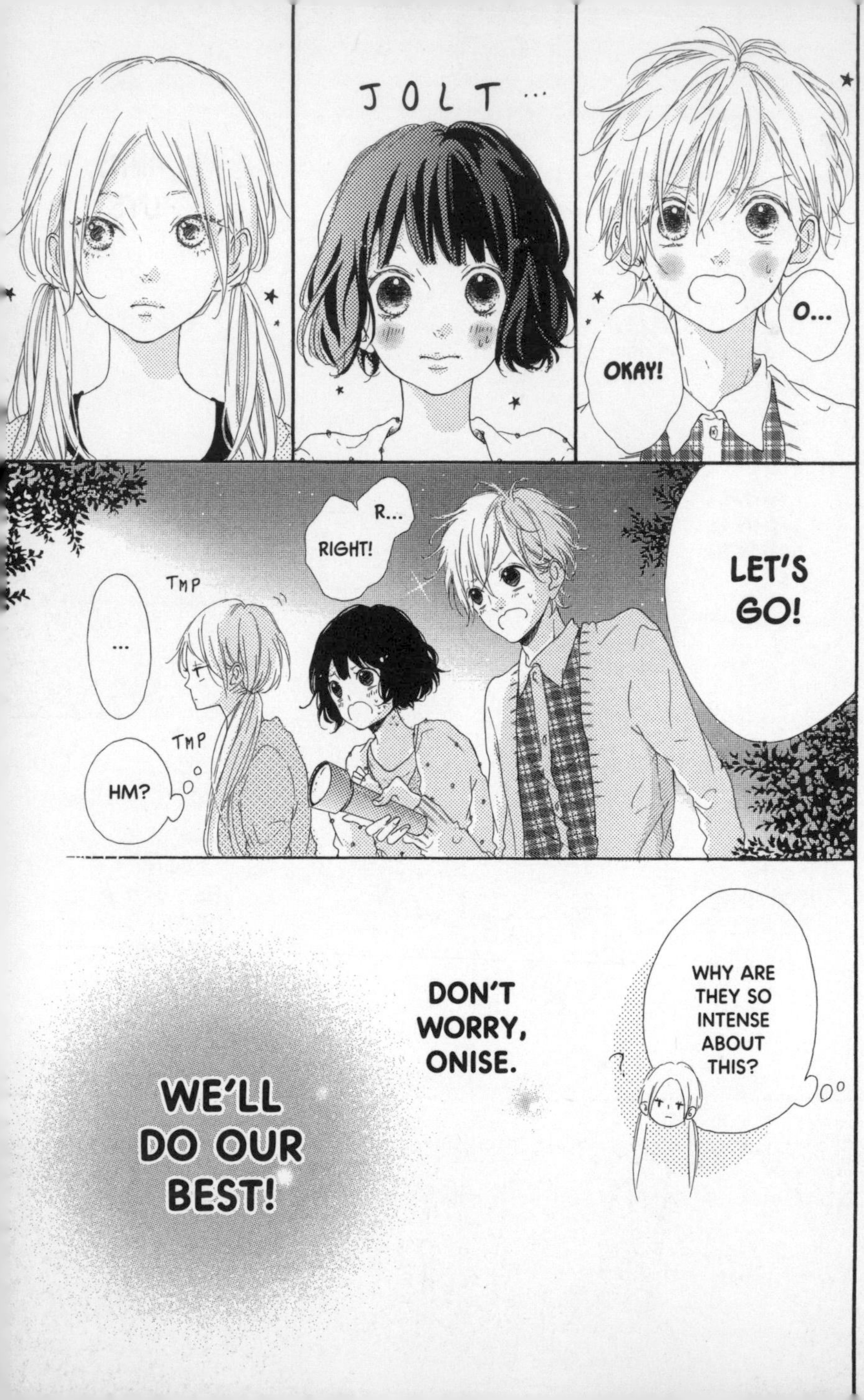
O...
OKAY!
JOLT...
LET'S GO!
R... RIGHT!
TMP
...
TMP
HM?
WHY ARE THEY SO INTENSE ABOUT THIS?
DON'T WORRY, ONISE.
WE'LL DO OUR BEST!

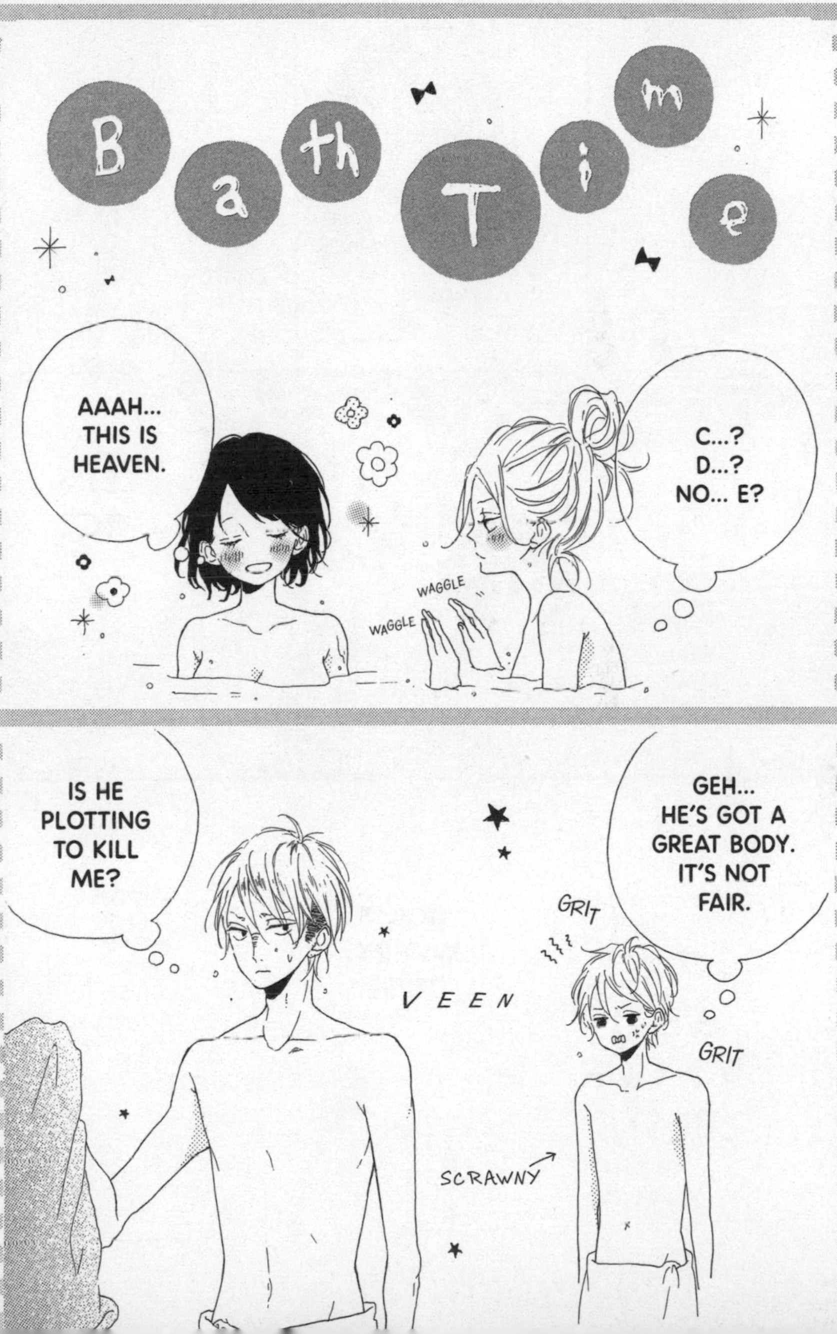
Bath Time
C...? D...? NO... E?
WAGGLE WAGGLE
AAAH... THIS IS HEAVEN.
GEH... HE'S GOT A GREAT BODY. IT'S NOT FAIR.
GRIT GRIT
SCRAWNY
VEEN
IS HE PLOTTING TO KILL ME?

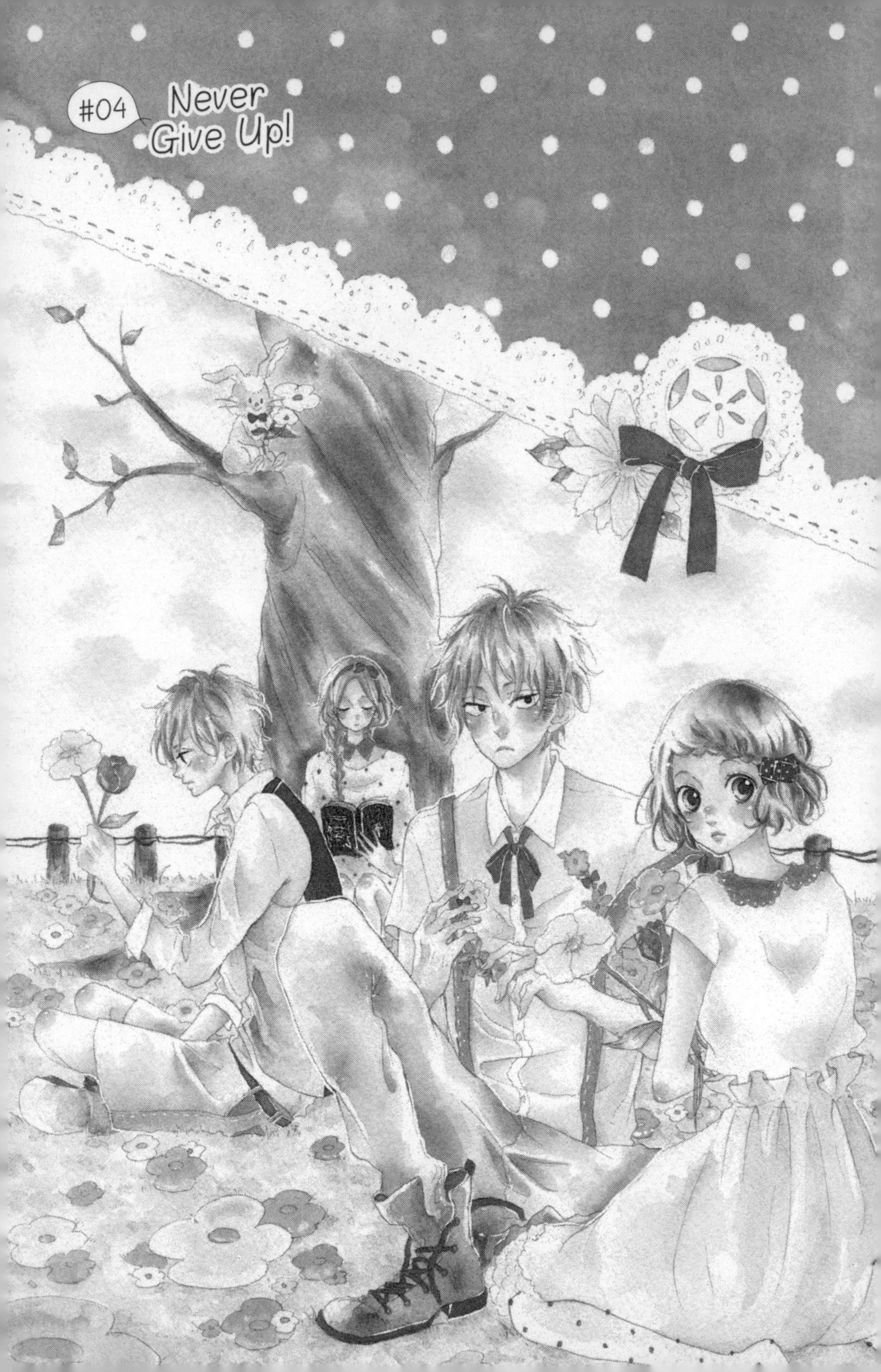
#04
Never Give Up!

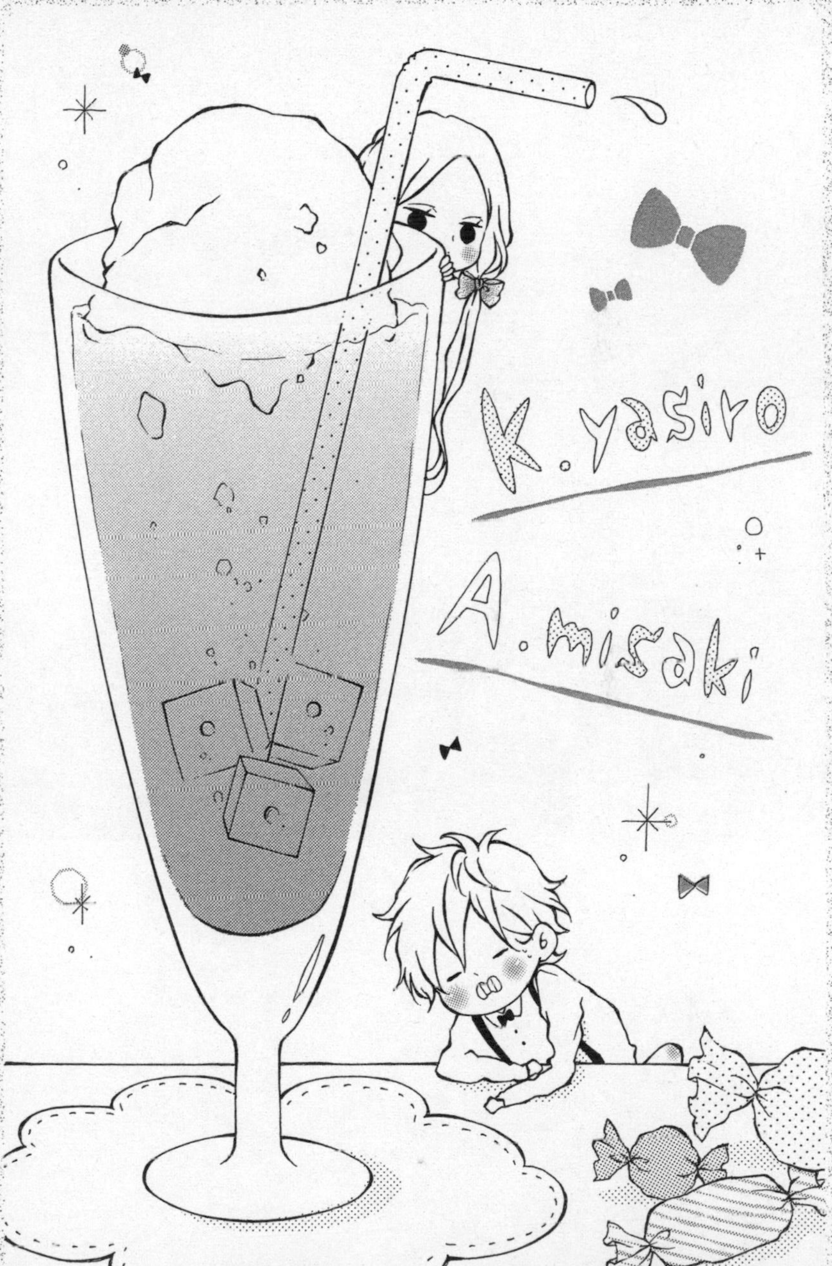
K. yasiro
A. misaki

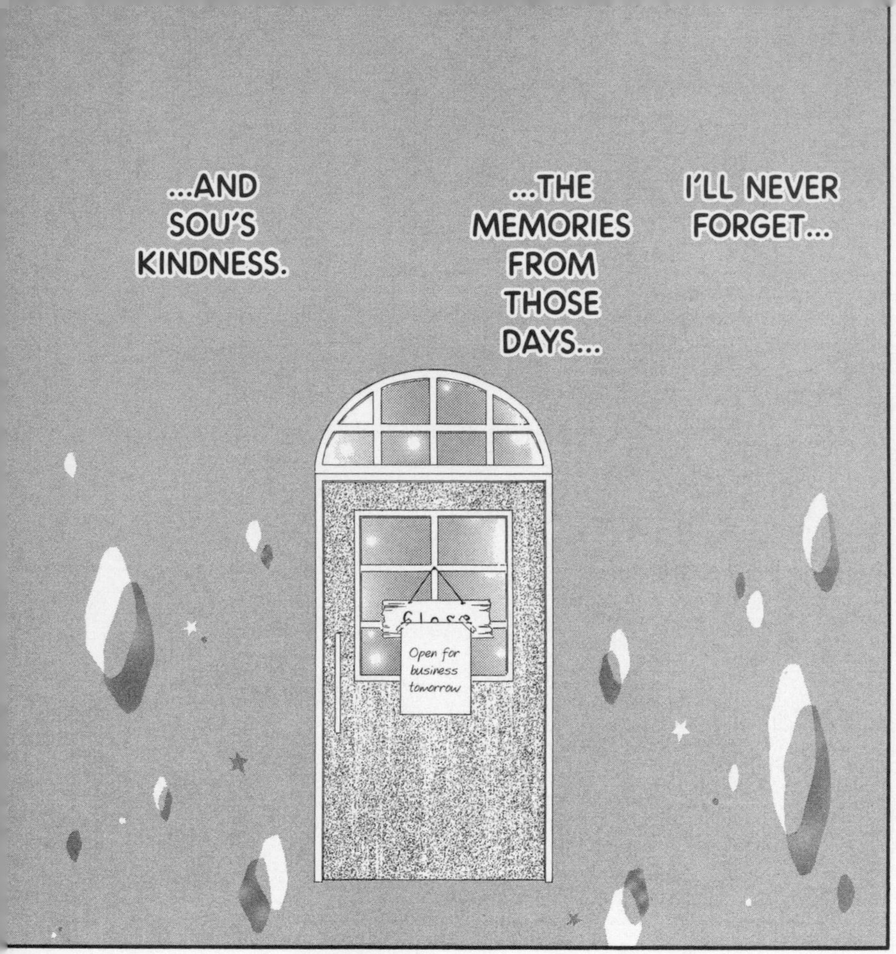
I'LL NEVER FORGET...
...THE MEMORIES FROM THOSE DAYS...
...AND SOU'S KINDNESS.
Open for business tomorrow

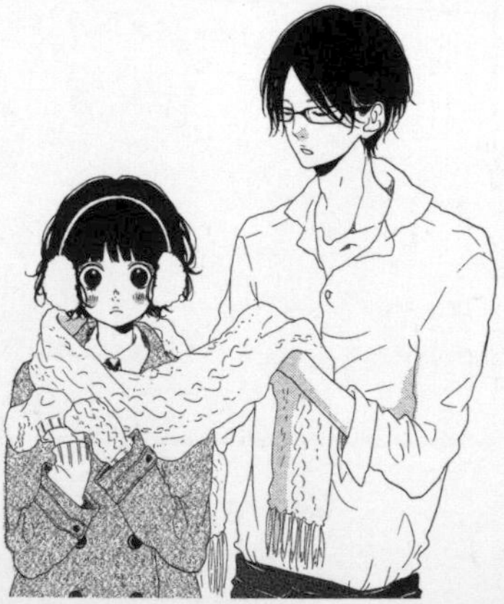

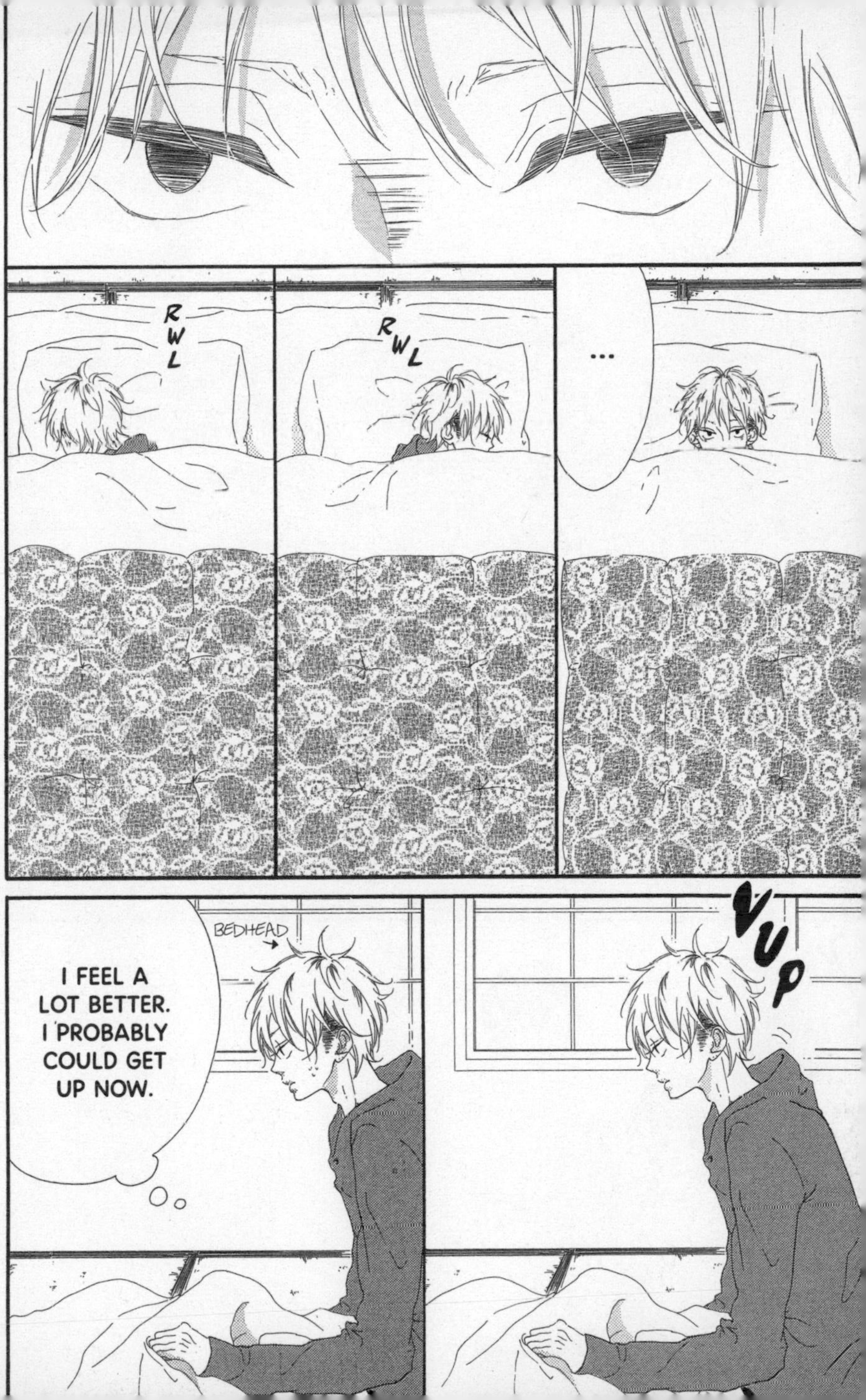
...
RWL
RWL
VUP
BEDHEAD
I FEEL A LOT BETTER. I PROBABLY COULD GET UP NOW.

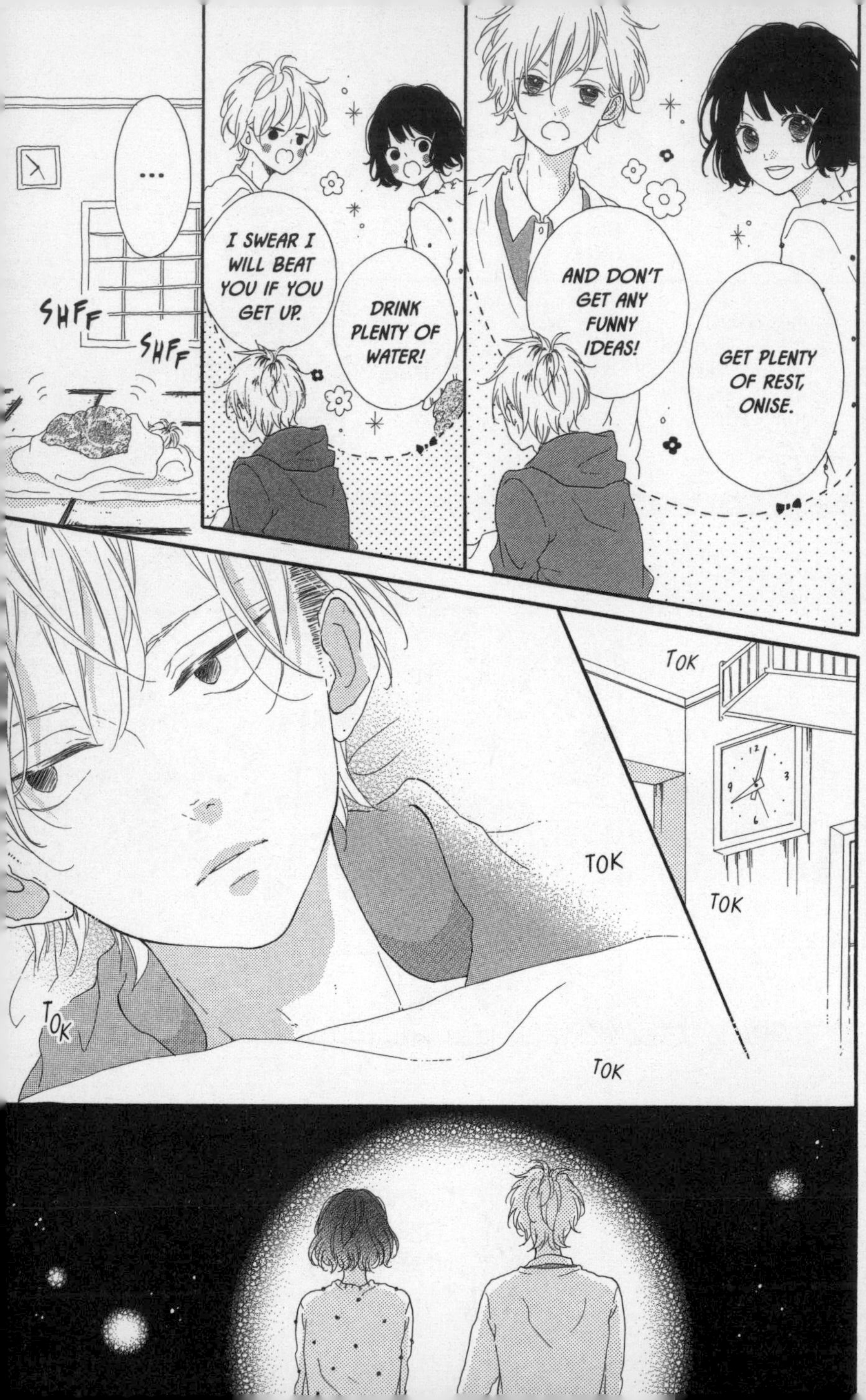
GET PLENTY OF REST, ONISE.
AND DON'T GET ANY FUNNY IDEAS!
DRINK PLENTY OF WATER!
I SWEAR I WILL BEAT YOU IF YOU GET UP.
...
SHFF
SHFF
TOK
TOK
TOK
TOK
TOK

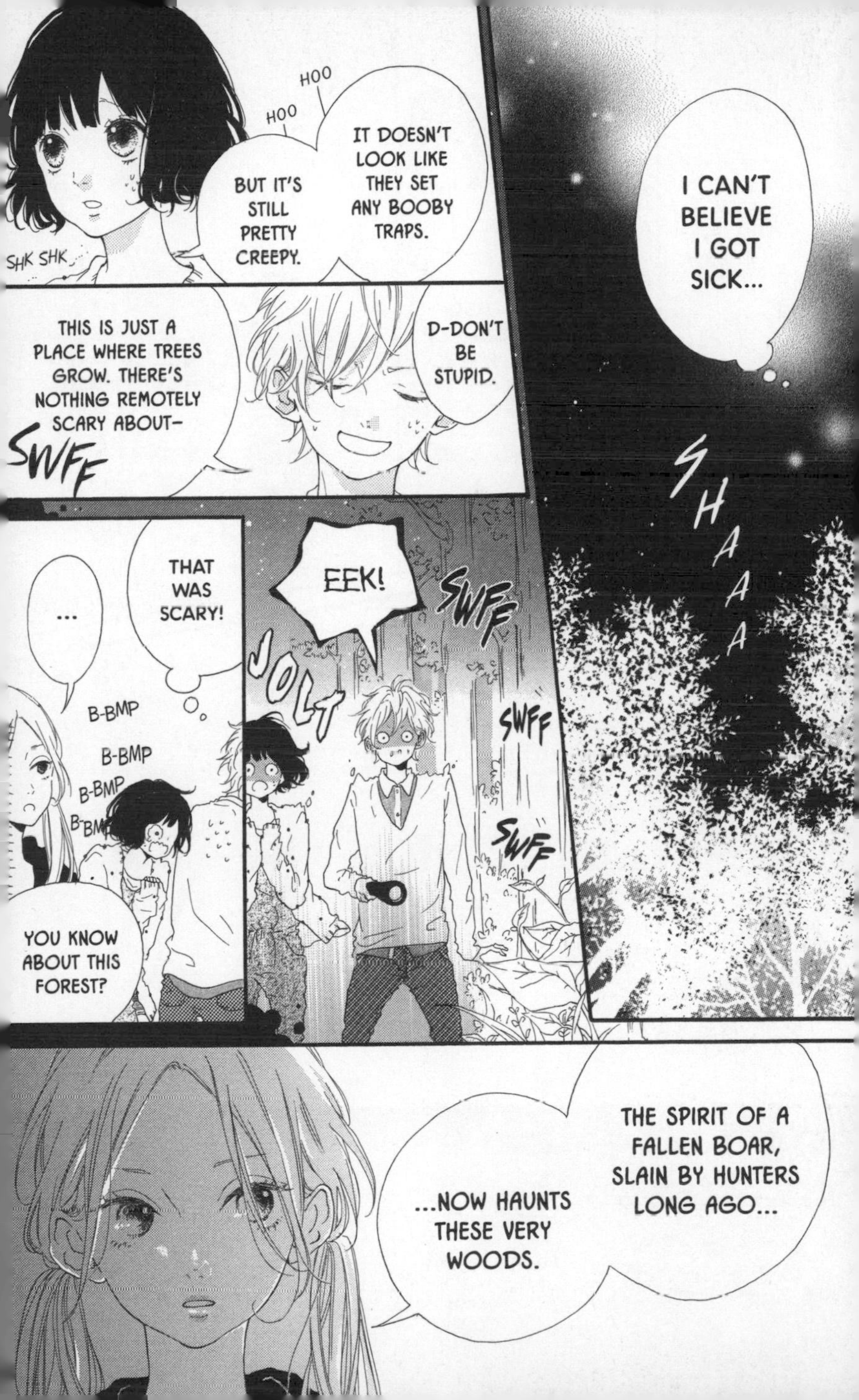
I CAN'T BELIEVE I GOT SICK...
SHAAAA
HOO
HOO
IT DOESN'T LOOK LIKE THEY SET ANY BOOBY TRAPS.
BUT IT'S STILL PRETTY CREEPY.
SHK SHK
D-DON'T BE STUPID.
THIS IS JUST A PLACE WHERE TREES GROW. THERE'S NOTHING REMOTELY SCARY ABOUT–
SWFF
EEK!
SWFF
JOLT
SWFF
SWFF
THAT WAS SCARY!
...
B-BMP
B-BMP
B-BMP
B-BMP
YOU KNOW ABOUT THIS FOREST?
THE SPIRIT OF A FALLEN BOAR, SLAIN BY HUNTERS LONG AGO...
...NOW HAUNTS THESE VERY WOODS.

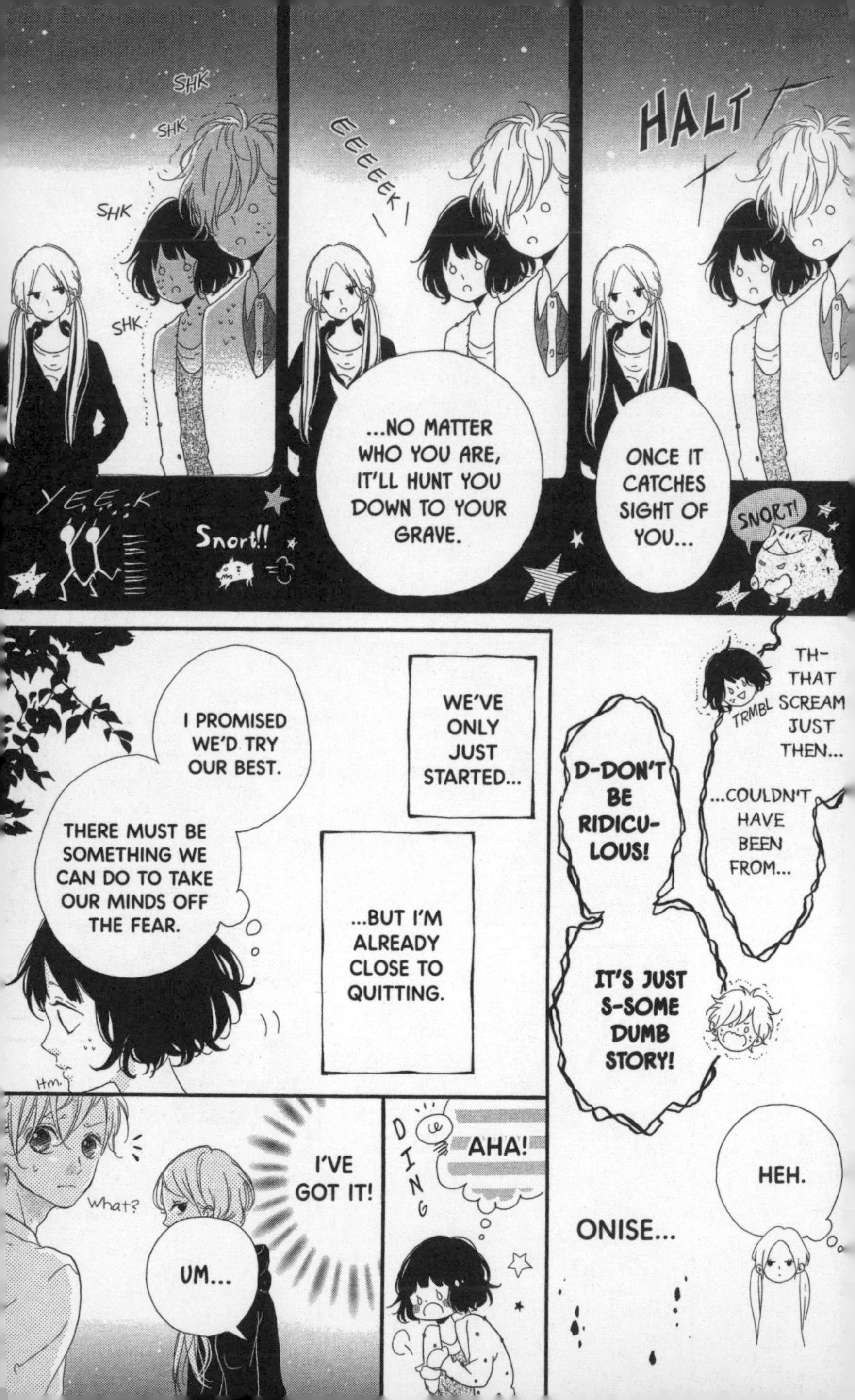
HALT
ONCE IT CATCHES SIGHT OF YOU...
SNORT!
EEEEEEK
...NO MATTER WHO YOU ARE, IT'LL HUNT YOU DOWN TO YOUR GRAVE.
Snort!!
SHK
SHK
SHK
SHK
YEE..K
TH-THAT SCREAM JUST THEN...
TRMBL
...COULDN'T HAVE BEEN FROM...
D-DON'T BE RIDICULOUS!
IT'S JUST S-SOME DUMB STORY!
HEH.
ONISE...
WE'VE ONLY JUST STARTED...
...BUT I'M ALREADY CLOSE TO QUITTING.
I PROMISED WE'D TRY OUR BEST.
THERE MUST BE SOMETHING WE CAN DO TO TAKE OUR MINDS OFF THE FEAR.
Hm.
DING
AHA!
I'VE GOT IT!
What?
UM...

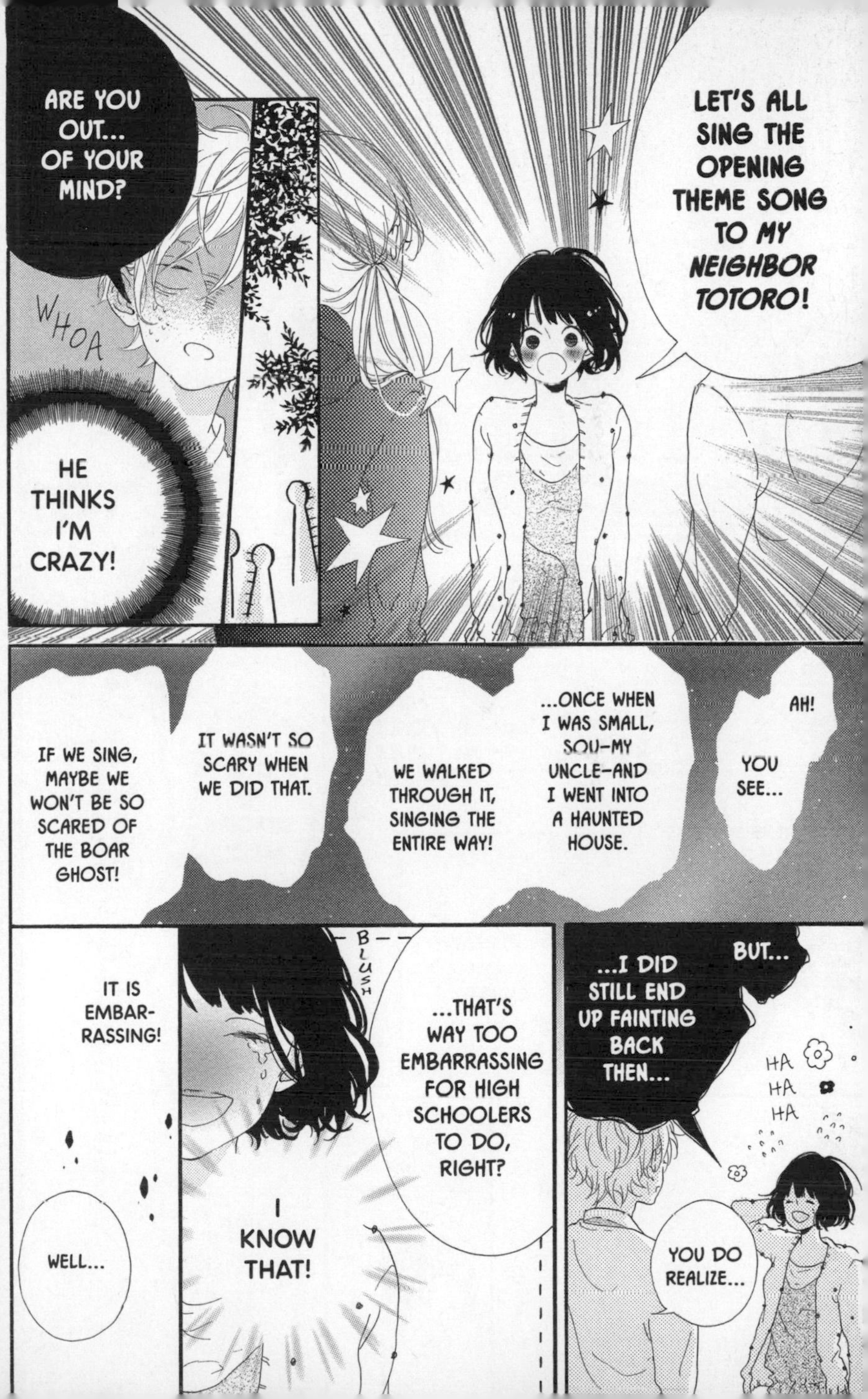

LET'S ALL SING THE OPENING THEME SONG TO MY NEIGHBOR TOTORO!
ARE YOU OUT... OF YOUR MIND?
WHOA
HE THINKS I'M CRAZY!
AH!
YOU SEE...
...ONCE WHEN I WAS SMALL, SOU—MY UNCLE—AND I WENT INTO A HAUNTED HOUSE.
WE WALKED THROUGH IT, SINGING THE ENTIRE WAY!
IT WASN'T SO SCARY WHEN WE DID THAT.
IF WE SING, MAYBE WE WON'T BE SO SCARED OF THE BOAR GHOST!
BUT...
...I DID STILL END UP FAINTING BACK THEN...
HA HA HA
YOU DO REALIZE...
B——
BLUSH
...THAT'S WAY TOO EMBARRASSING FOR HIGH SCHOOLERS TO DO, RIGHT?
I KNOW THAT!
IT IS EMBARRASSING!
WELL...

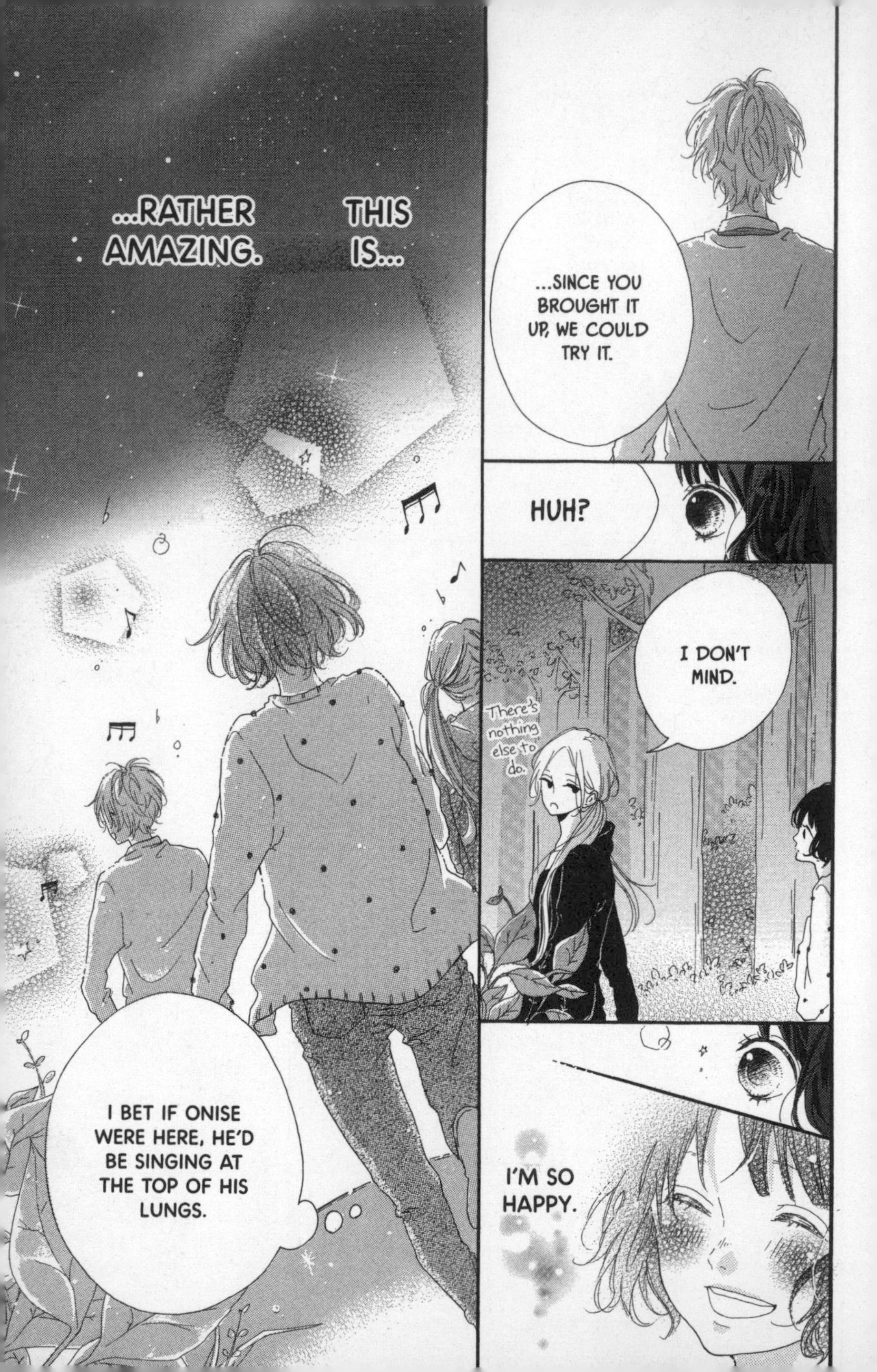
...SINCE YOU BROUGHT IT UP, WE COULD TRY IT.
HUH?
I DON'T MIND.
There's nothing else to do.
I'M SO HAPPY.
THIS IS...
...RATHER AMAZING.
I BET IF ONISE WERE HERE, HE'D BE SINGING AT THE TOP OF HIS LUNGS.

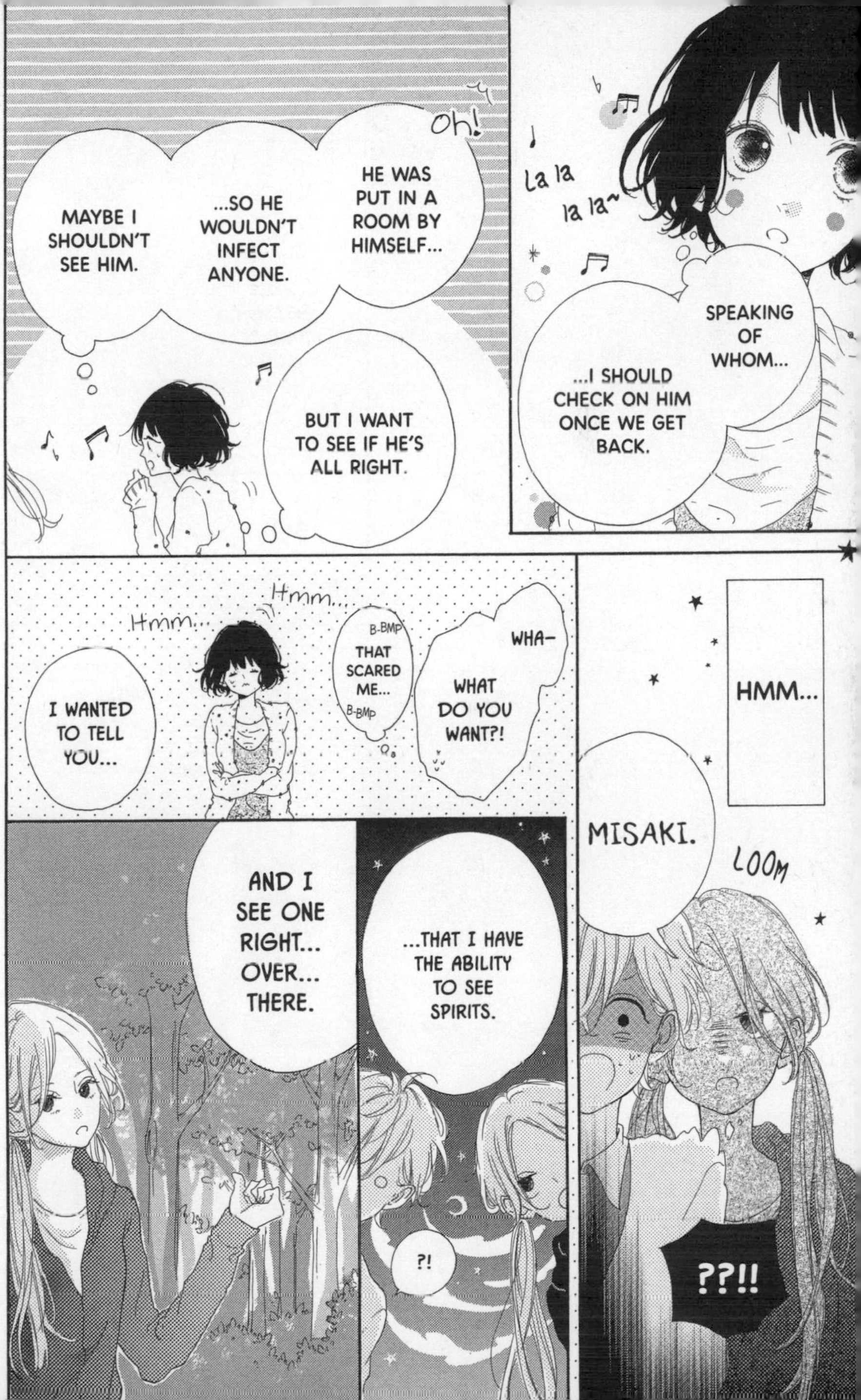
La la
la la~
SPEAKING OF WHOM...
...I SHOULD CHECK ON HIM ONCE WE GET BACK.
Oh!
HE WAS PUT IN A ROOM BY HIMSELF...
...SO HE WOULDN'T INFECT ANYONE.
MAYBE I SHOULDN'T SEE HIM.
BUT I WANT TO SEE IF HE'S ALL RIGHT.
HMM...
MISAKI.
LOOM
??!!
Hmm...
WHA-
WHAT DO YOU WANT?!
B-BMP
THAT SCARED ME...
B-BMP
Hmm...
I WANTED TO TELL YOU...
...THAT I HAVE THE ABILITY TO SEE SPIRITS.
?!
AND I SEE ONE RIGHT... OVER... THERE.

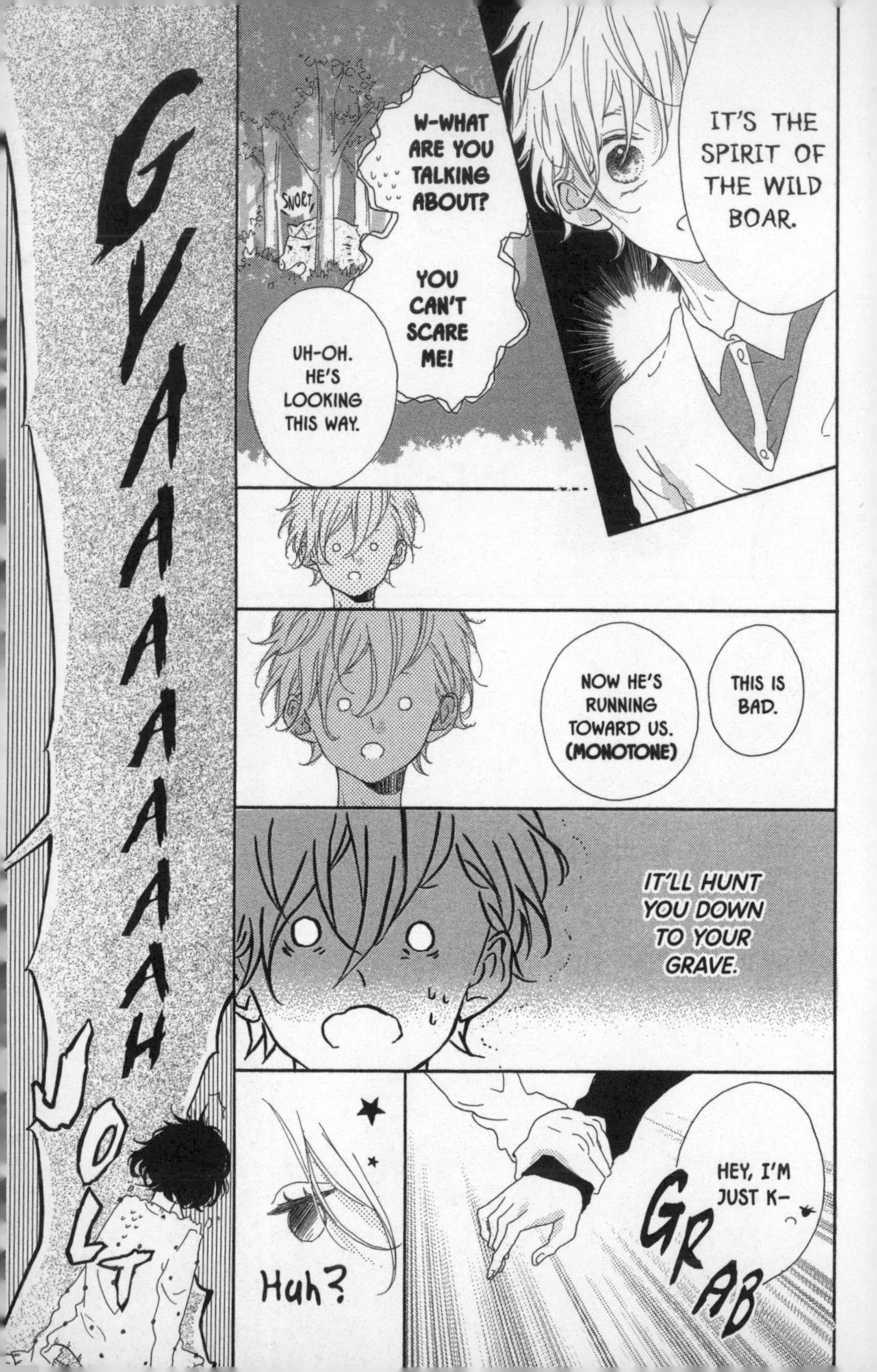
IT'S THE SPIRIT OF THE WILD BOAR.
W-WHAT ARE YOU TALKING ABOUT?
YOU CAN'T SCARE ME!
SNORT
UH-OH. HE'S LOOKING THIS WAY.
THIS IS BAD.
NOW HE'S RUNNING TOWARD US. (MONOTONE)
IT'LL HUNT YOU DOWN TO YOUR GRAVE.
HEY, I'M JUST K-
GRAB
Huh?
GYAAAAAAAH
JOLT

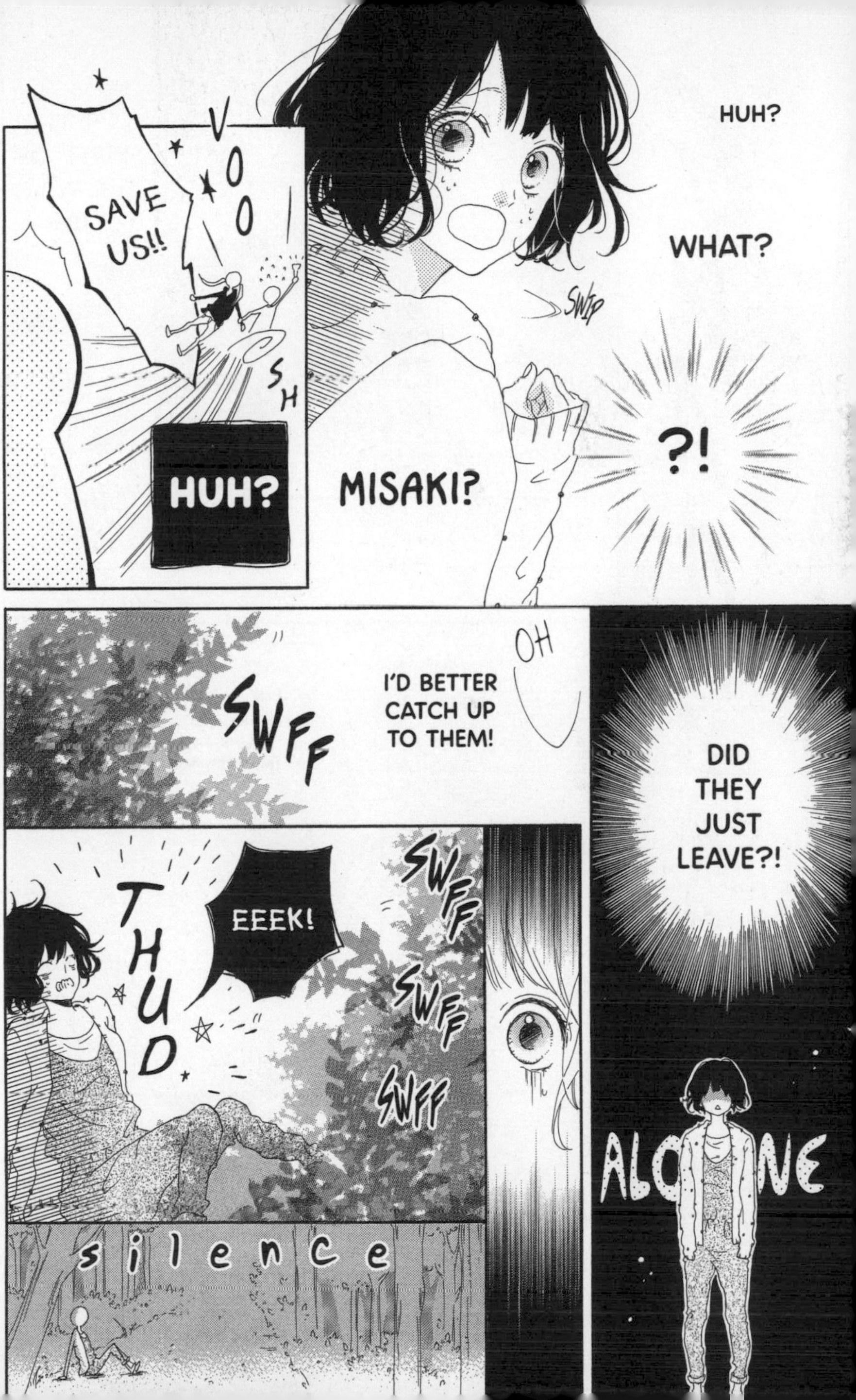
HUH?
WHAT?
SWIP
?!
MISAKI?
VOOO
SAVE US!!
SH
HUH?
DID THEY JUST LEAVE?!
ALONE
OH
I'D BETTER CATCH UP TO THEM!
SWFF
SWFF
SWFF
SWFF
EEEK!
THUD
silence

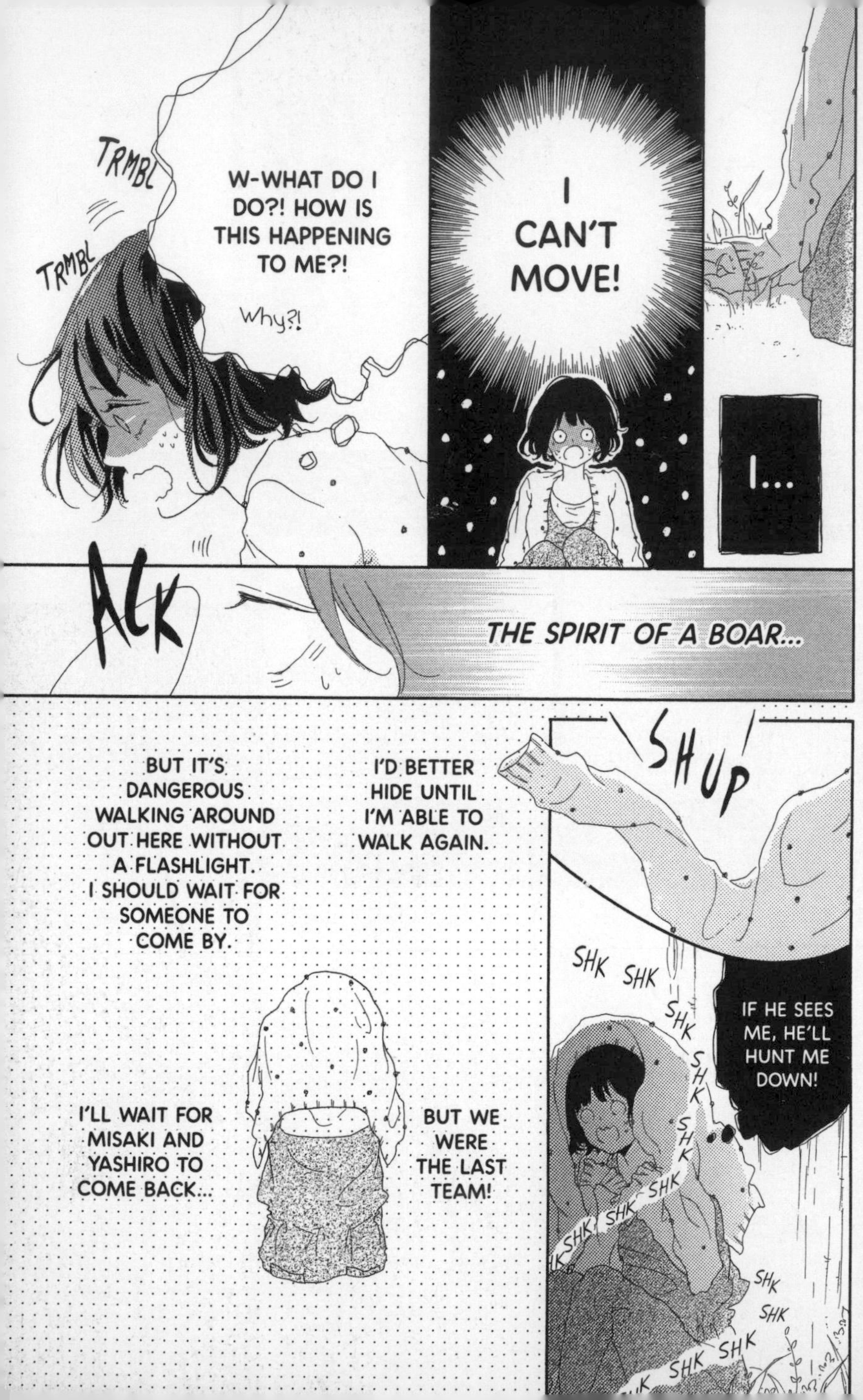
I...
I CAN'T MOVE!
TRMBL
TRMBL
W-WHAT DO I DO?! HOW IS THIS HAPPENING TO ME?!
Why?!
THE SPIRIT OF A BOAR...
ACK
SHUP
SHK SHK
SHK
SHK
SHK
SHK
SHK
IF HE SEES ME, HE'LL HUNT ME DOWN!
SHK SHK SHK
SHK
SHK
SHK SHK
SHK
I'D BETTER HIDE UNTIL I'M ABLE TO WALK AGAIN.
BUT IT'S DANGEROUS WALKING AROUND OUT HERE WITHOUT A FLASHLIGHT. I SHOULD WAIT FOR SOMEONE TO COME BY.
BUT WE WERE THE LAST TEAM!
I'LL WAIT FOR MISAKI AND YASHIRO TO COME BACK...

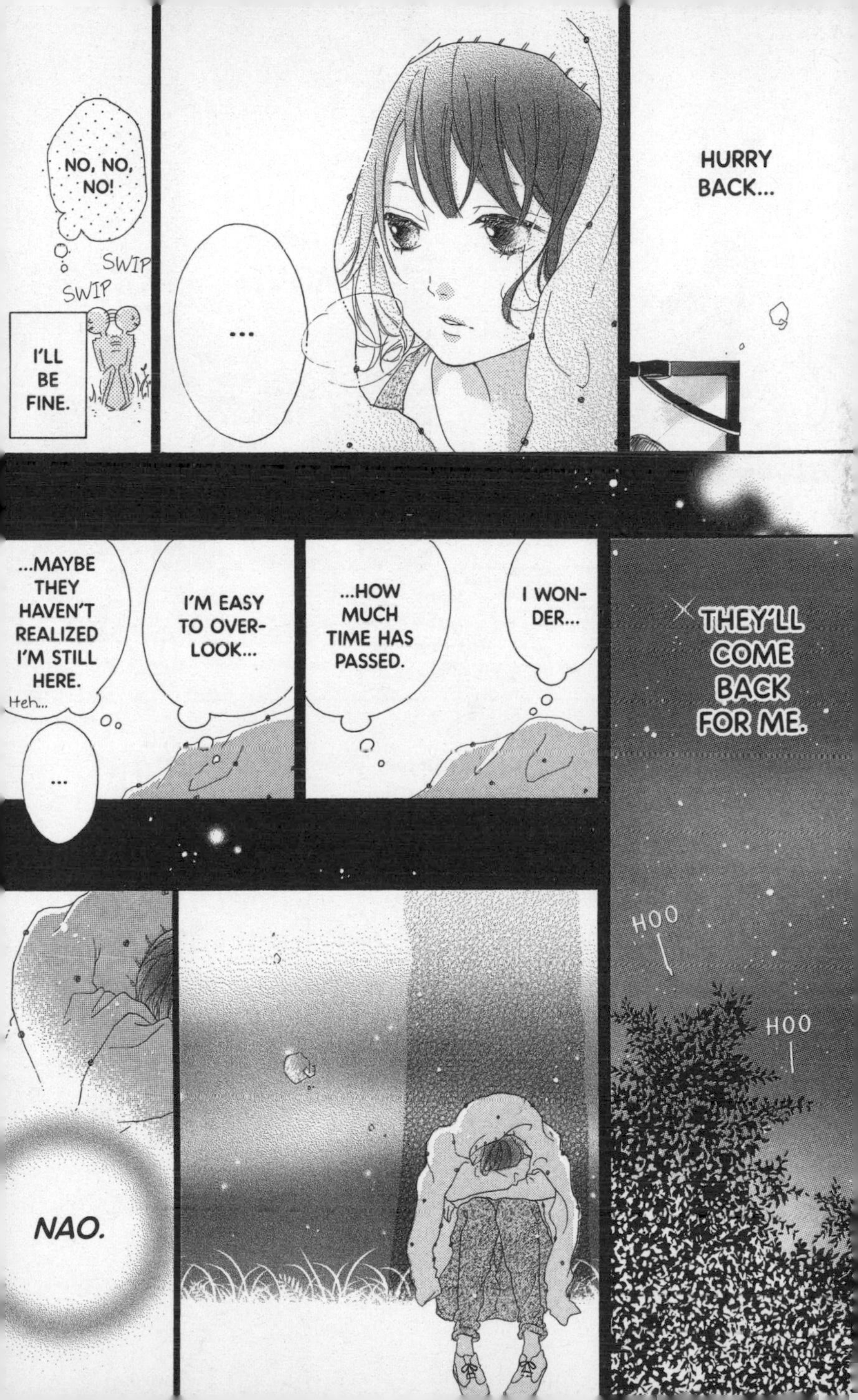
HURRY BACK...
...
NO, NO, NO!
SWIP
SWIP
I'LL BE FINE.
THEY'LL COME BACK FOR ME.
HOO
HOO
I WON-DER...
...HOW MUCH TIME HAS PASSED.
I'M EASY TO OVER-LOOK...
...MAYBE THEY HAVEN'T REALIZED I'M STILL HERE.
Heh...
...
NAO.

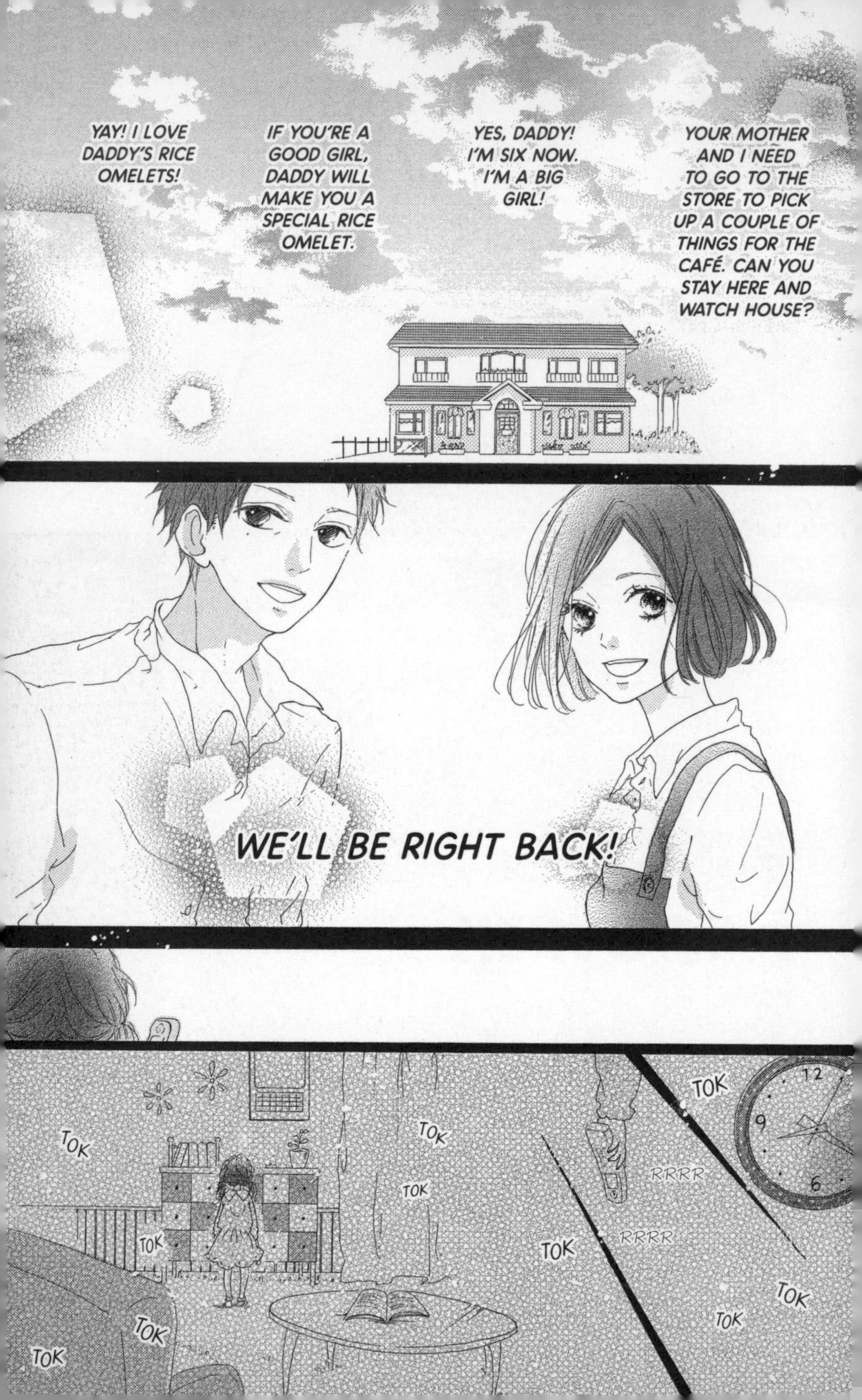
YOUR MOTHER AND I NEED TO GO TO THE STORE TO PICK UP A COUPLE OF THINGS FOR THE CAFÉ. CAN YOU STAY HERE AND WATCH HOUSE?
YES, DADDY! I'M SIX NOW. I'M A BIG GIRL!
IF YOU'RE A GOOD GIRL, DADDY WILL MAKE YOU A SPECIAL RICE OMELET.
YAY! I LOVE DADDY'S RICE OMELETS!
WE'LL BE RIGHT BACK!
12
9
6
TOK
RRRR
RRRR
TOK
TOK
TOK
TOK
TOK
TOK
TOK
TOK
TOK

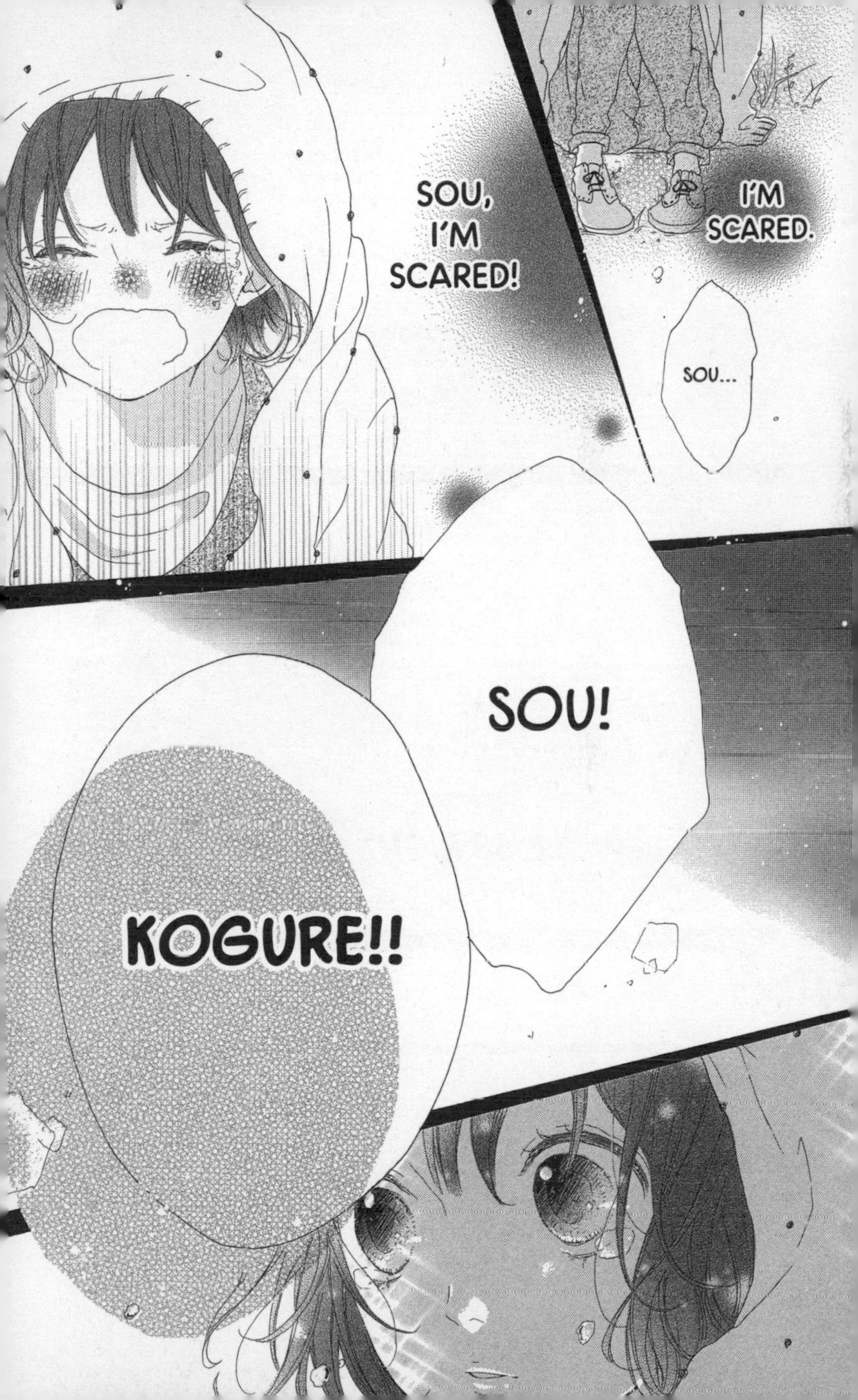
I'M SCARED.
SOU...
SOU, I'M SCARED!
SOU!
KOGURE!!

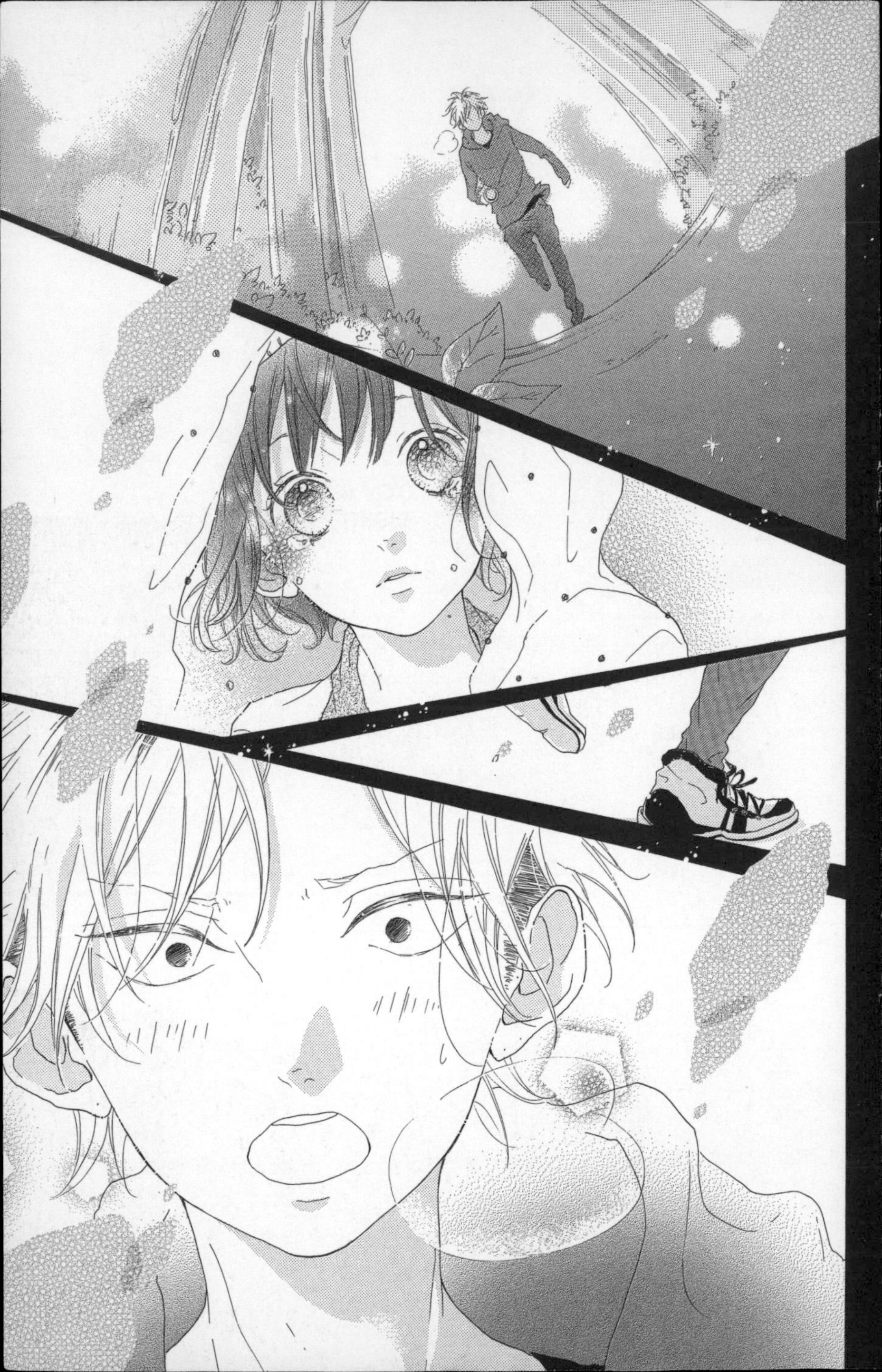

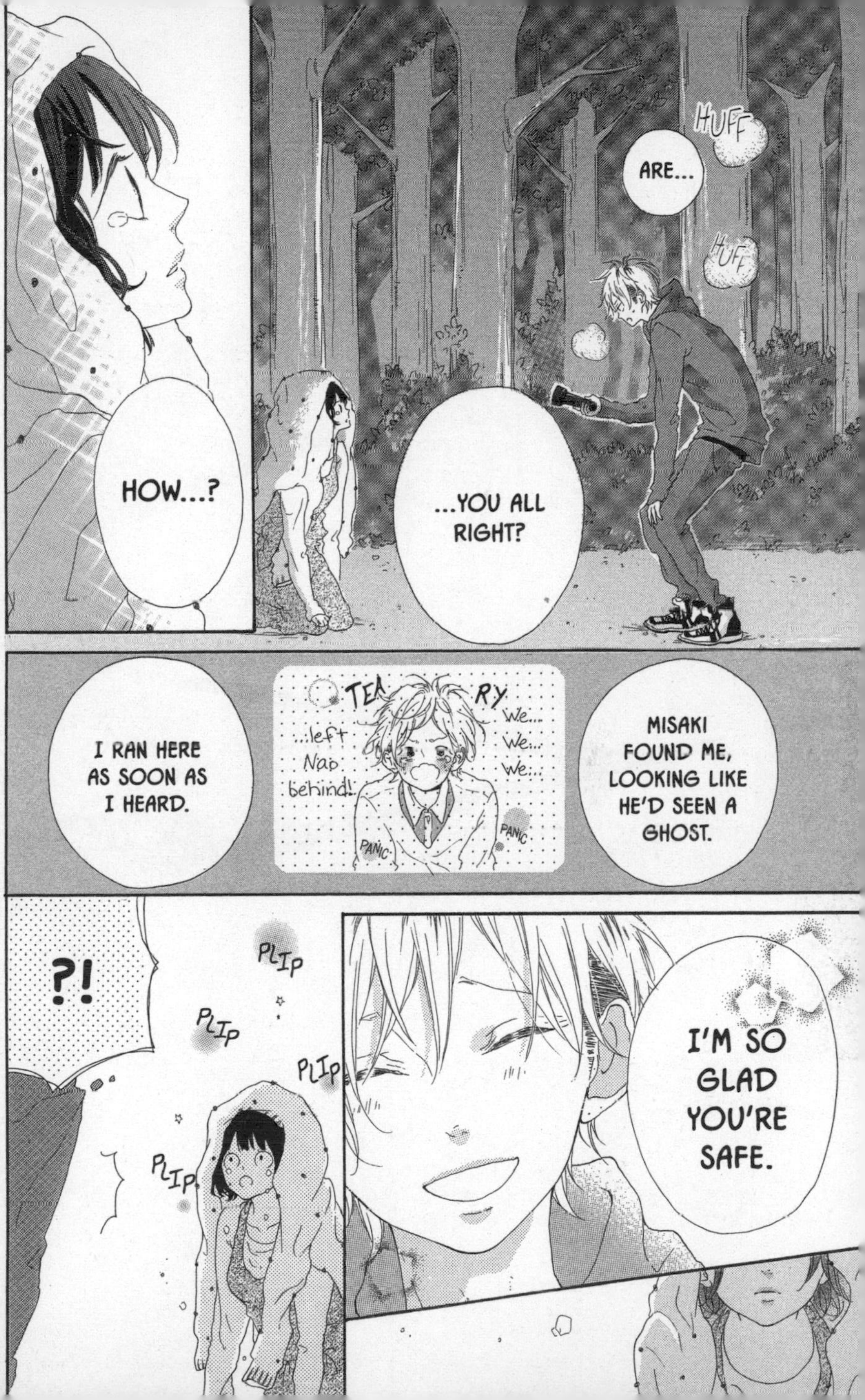
HUFF
ARE...
HUFF
...YOU ALL RIGHT?
HOW...?
MISAKI FOUND ME, LOOKING LIKE HE'D SEEN A GHOST.
TEA RY
We... We... We...
...left Nao behind!
PANIC
PANIC
I RAN HERE AS SOON AS I HEARD.
I'M SO GLAD YOU'RE SAFE.
PLIP
PLIP
PLIP
PLIP
?!

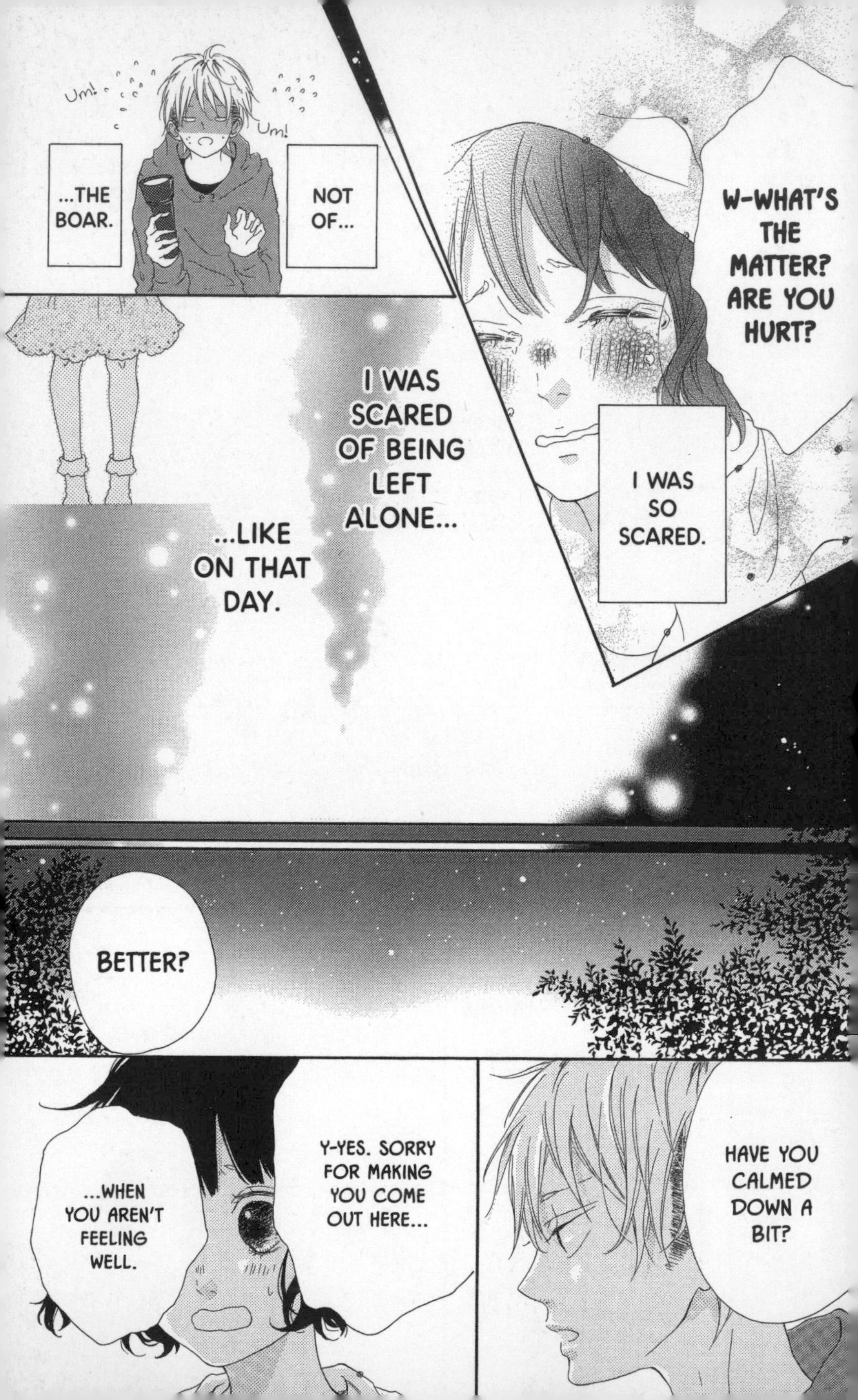
W-WHAT'S THE MATTER? ARE YOU HURT?
I WAS SO SCARED.
Um!
Um!
NOT OF...
...THE BOAR.
I WAS SCARED OF BEING LEFT ALONE...
...LIKE ON THAT DAY.
BETTER?
HAVE YOU CALMED DOWN A BIT?
Y-YES. SORRY FOR MAKING YOU COME OUT HERE...
...WHEN YOU AREN'T FEELING WELL.

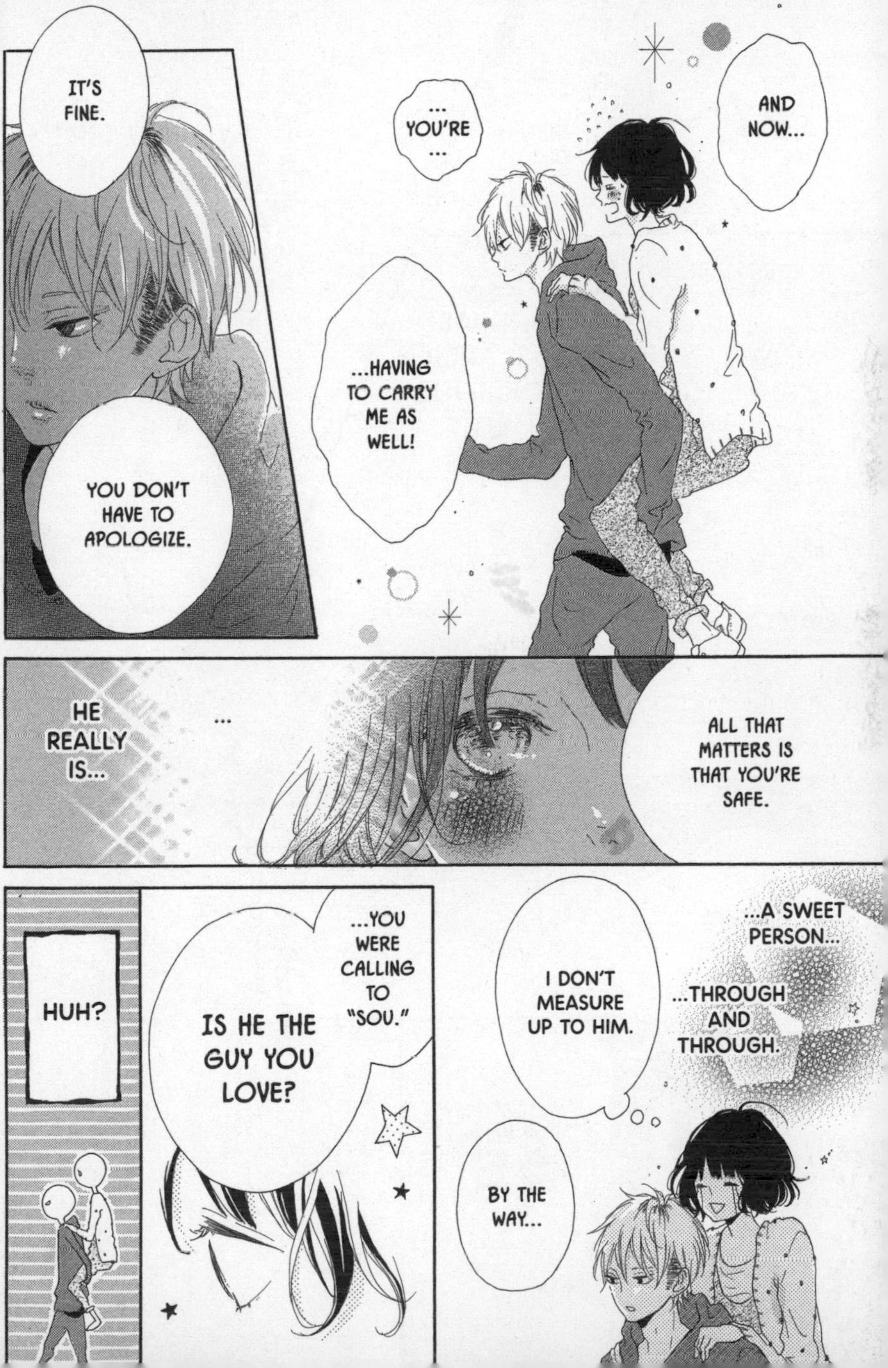
AND NOW...
... YOU'RE ...
...HAVING TO CARRY ME AS WELL!
IT'S FINE.
YOU DON'T HAVE TO APOLOGIZE.
ALL THAT MATTERS IS THAT YOU'RE SAFE.
...
HE REALLY IS...
...A SWEET PERSON...
...THROUGH AND THROUGH.
I DON'T MEASURE UP TO HIM.
BY THE WAY...
...YOU WERE CALLING TO "SOU."
IS HE THE GUY YOU LOVE?
HUH?

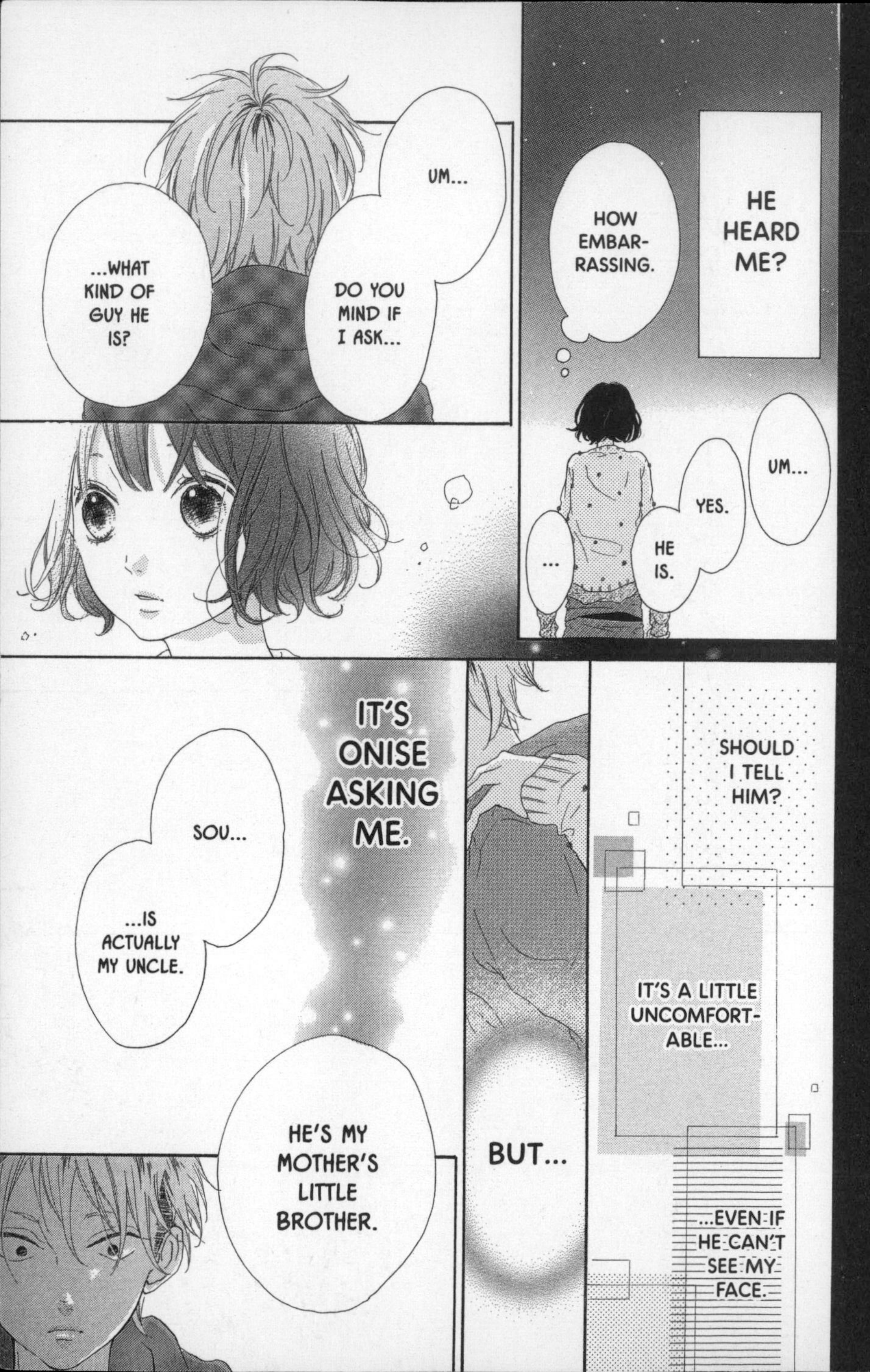
HE HEARD ME?
HOW EMBARRASSING.
UM...
YES.
HE IS.
...
UM...
DO YOU MIND IF I ASK...
...WHAT KIND OF GUY HE IS?
SHOULD I TELL HIM?
IT'S A LITTLE UNCOMFORTABLE...
...EVEN IF HE CAN'T SEE MY FACE.
BUT...
IT'S ONISE ASKING ME.
SOU...
...IS ACTUALLY MY UNCLE.
HE'S MY MOTHER'S LITTLE BROTHER.

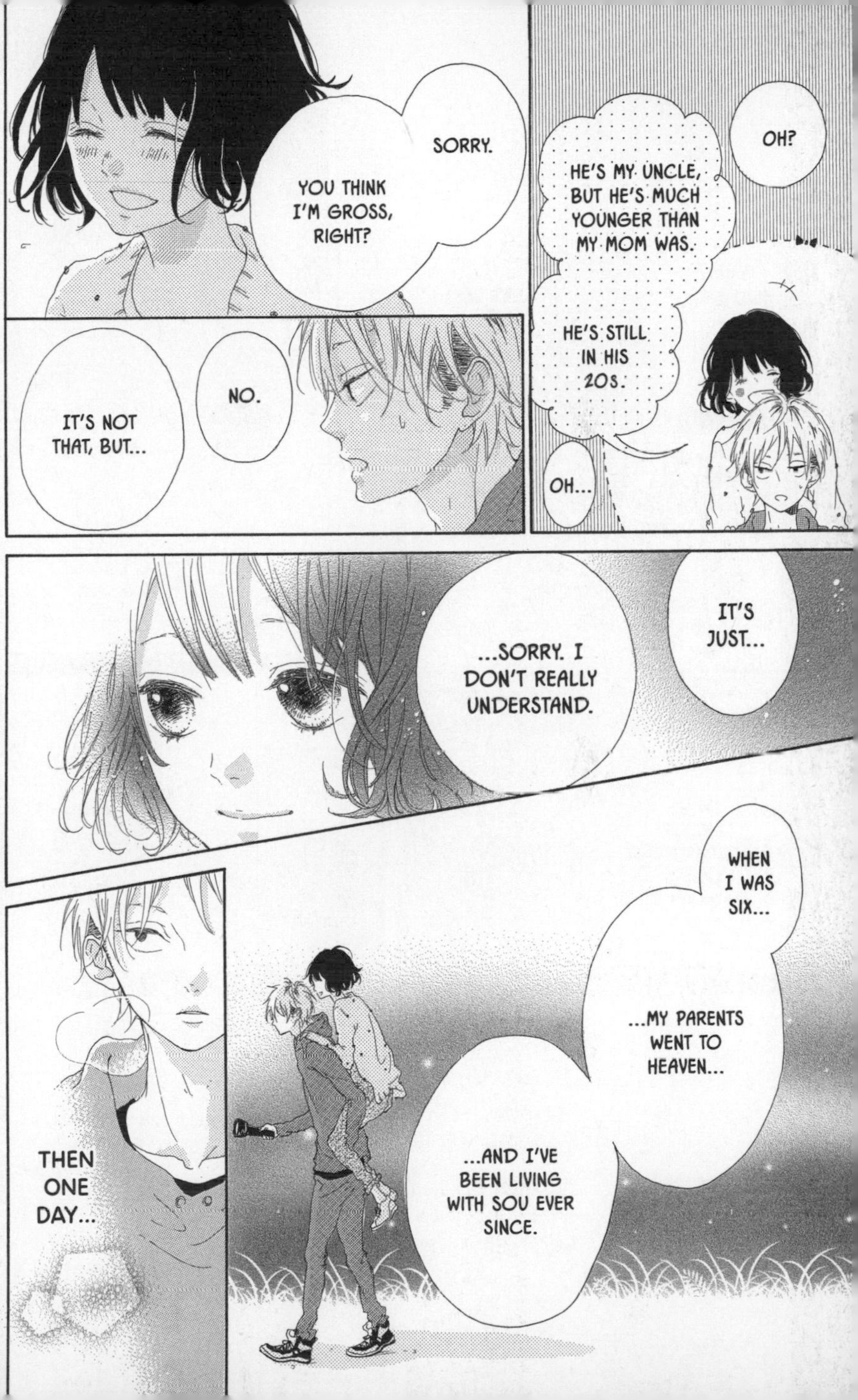
OH?
HE'S MY UNCLE, BUT HE'S MUCH YOUNGER THAN MY MOM WAS.
HE'S STILL IN HIS 20S.
OH...
SORRY.
YOU THINK I'M GROSS, RIGHT?
NO.
IT'S NOT THAT, BUT...
IT'S JUST...
...SORRY. I DON'T REALLY UNDERSTAND.
WHEN I WAS SIX...
...MY PARENTS WENT TO HEAVEN...
...AND I'VE BEEN LIVING WITH SOU EVER SINCE.
THEN ONE DAY...

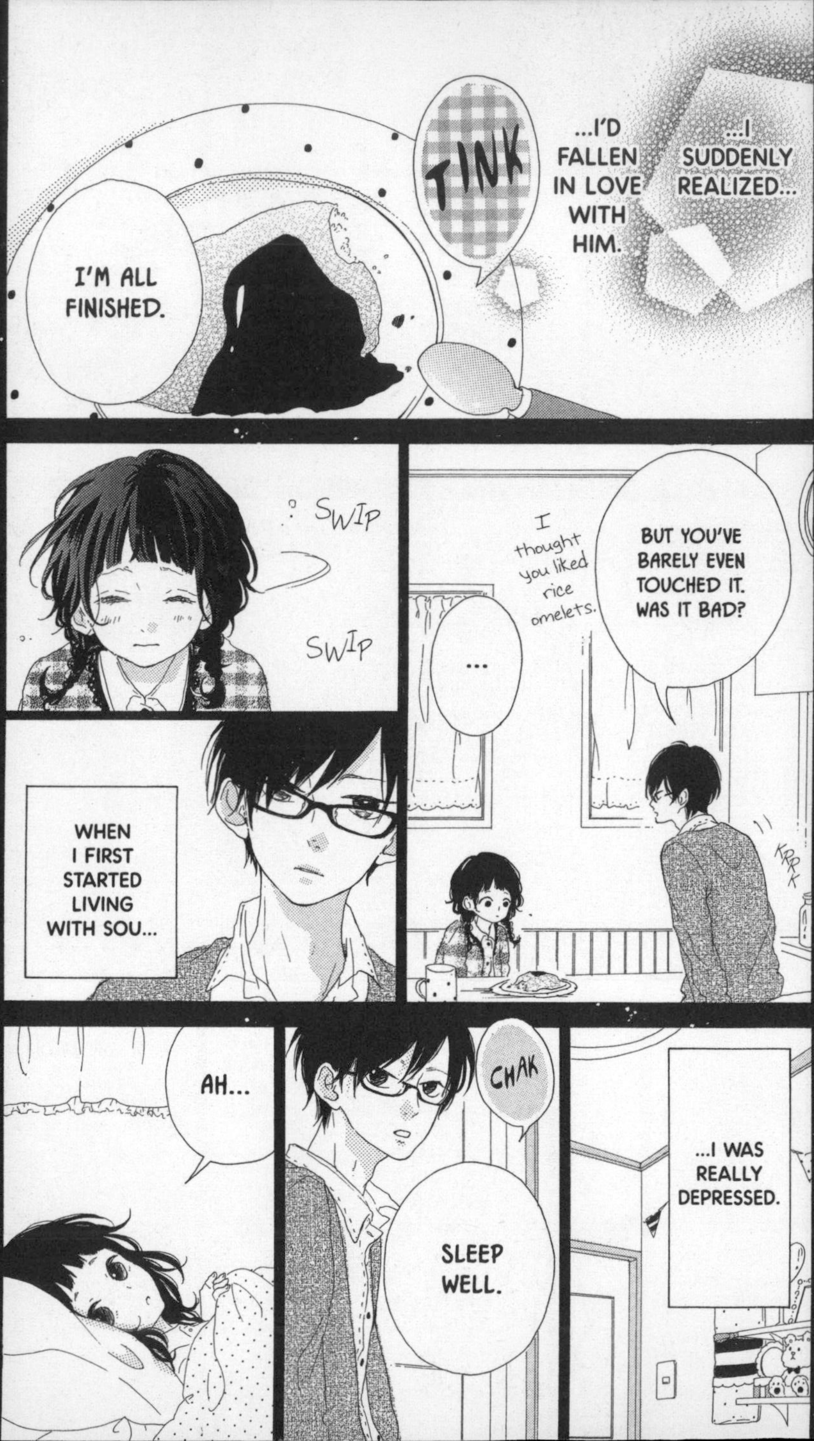
...I SUDDENLY REALIZED...
...I'D FALLEN IN LOVE WITH HIM.
TINK
I'M ALL FINISHED.
BUT YOU'VE BARELY EVEN TOUCHED IT. WAS IT BAD?
I thought you liked rice omelets.
...
KRRK
SWIP
SWIP
WHEN I FIRST STARTED LIVING WITH SOU...
...I WAS REALLY DEPRESSED.
CHAK
SLEEP WELL.
AH...

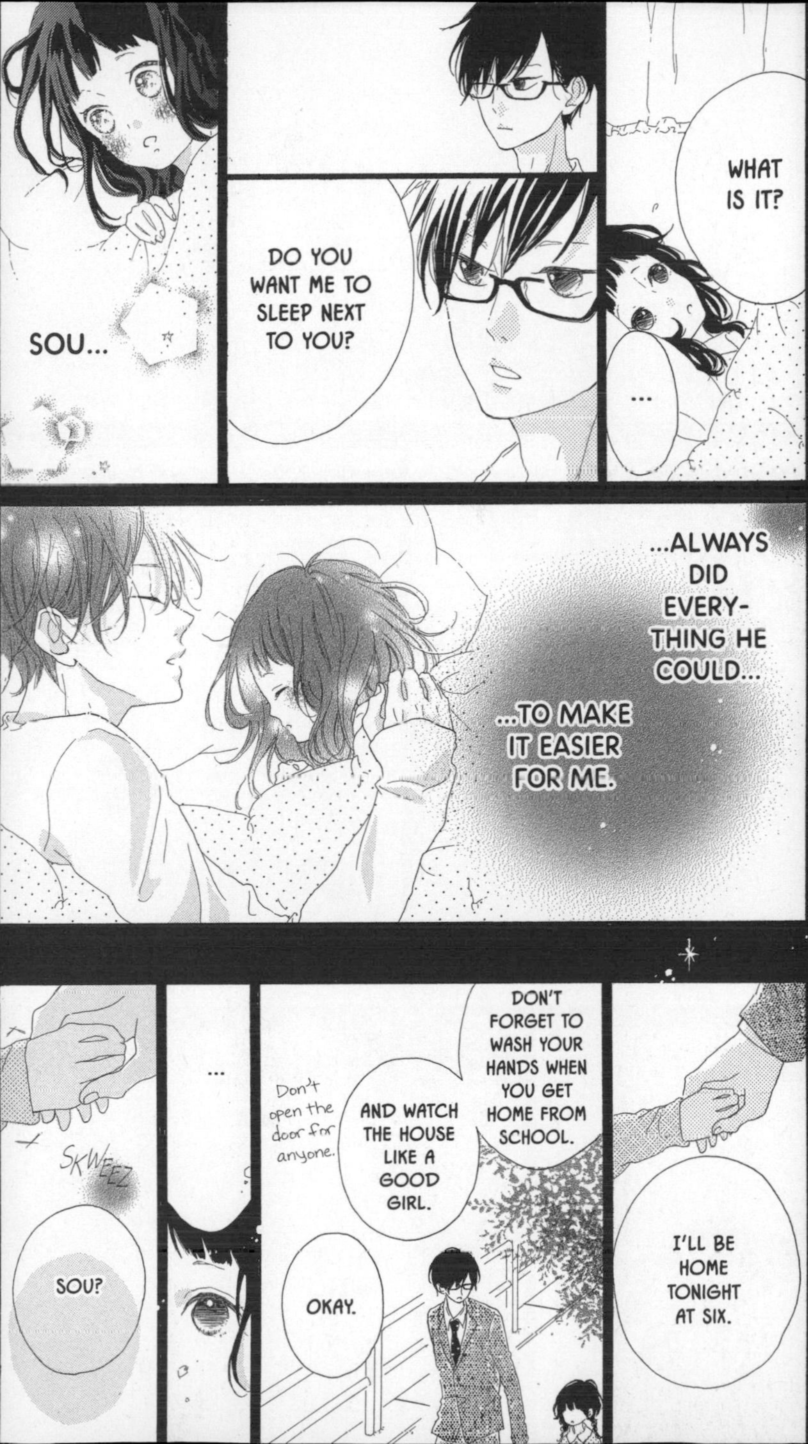
WHAT IS IT?
...
DO YOU WANT ME TO SLEEP NEXT TO YOU?
SOU...
...ALWAYS DID EVERY-THING HE COULD...
...TO MAKE IT EASIER FOR ME.
I'LL BE HOME TONIGHT AT SIX.
DON'T FORGET TO WASH YOUR HANDS WHEN YOU GET HOME FROM SCHOOL.
AND WATCH THE HOUSE LIKE A GOOD GIRL.
Don't open the door for anyone.
OKAY.
...
SKWEEZ
SOU?

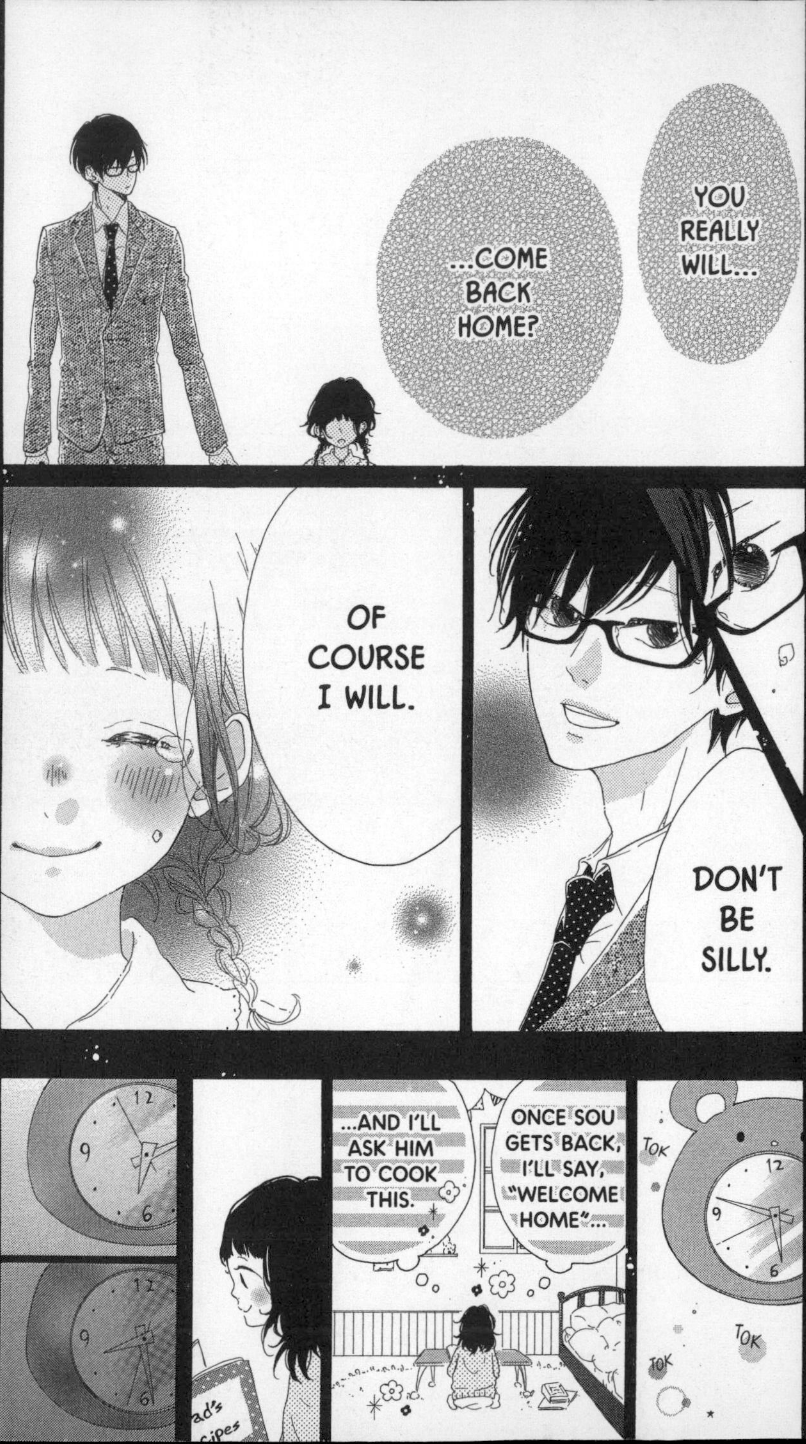
YOU REALLY WILL...
...COME BACK HOME?
DON'T BE SILLY.
OF COURSE I WILL.
TOK
TOK
TOK
ONCE SOU GETS BACK, I'LL SAY, "WELCOME HOME"...
...AND I'LL ASK HIM TO COOK THIS.

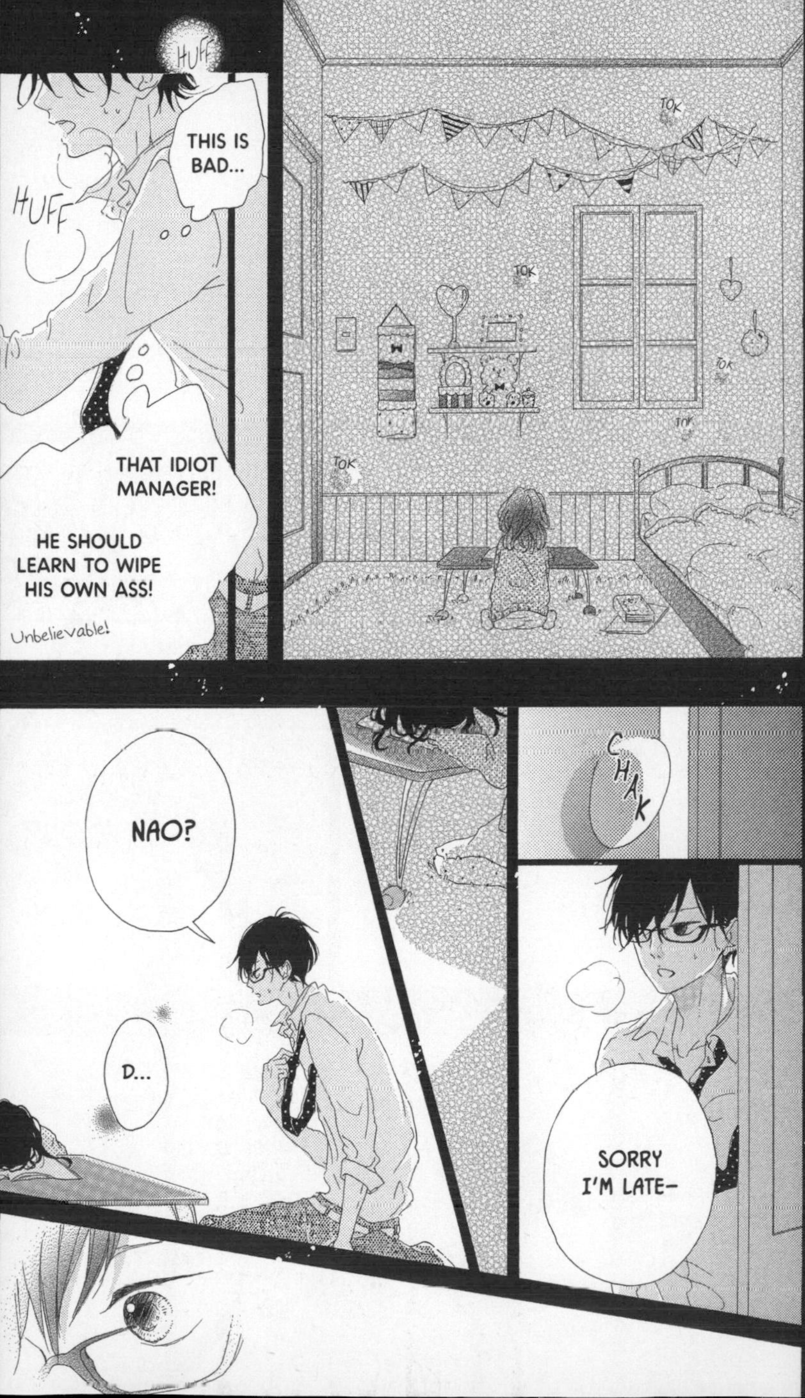
TOK
TOK
TOK
TOK
TOK
HUFF
THIS IS BAD...
HUFF
THAT IDIOT MANAGER!
HE SHOULD LEARN TO WIPE HIS OWN ASS!
Unbelievable!
CHAK
SORRY I'M LATE-
NAO?
D...

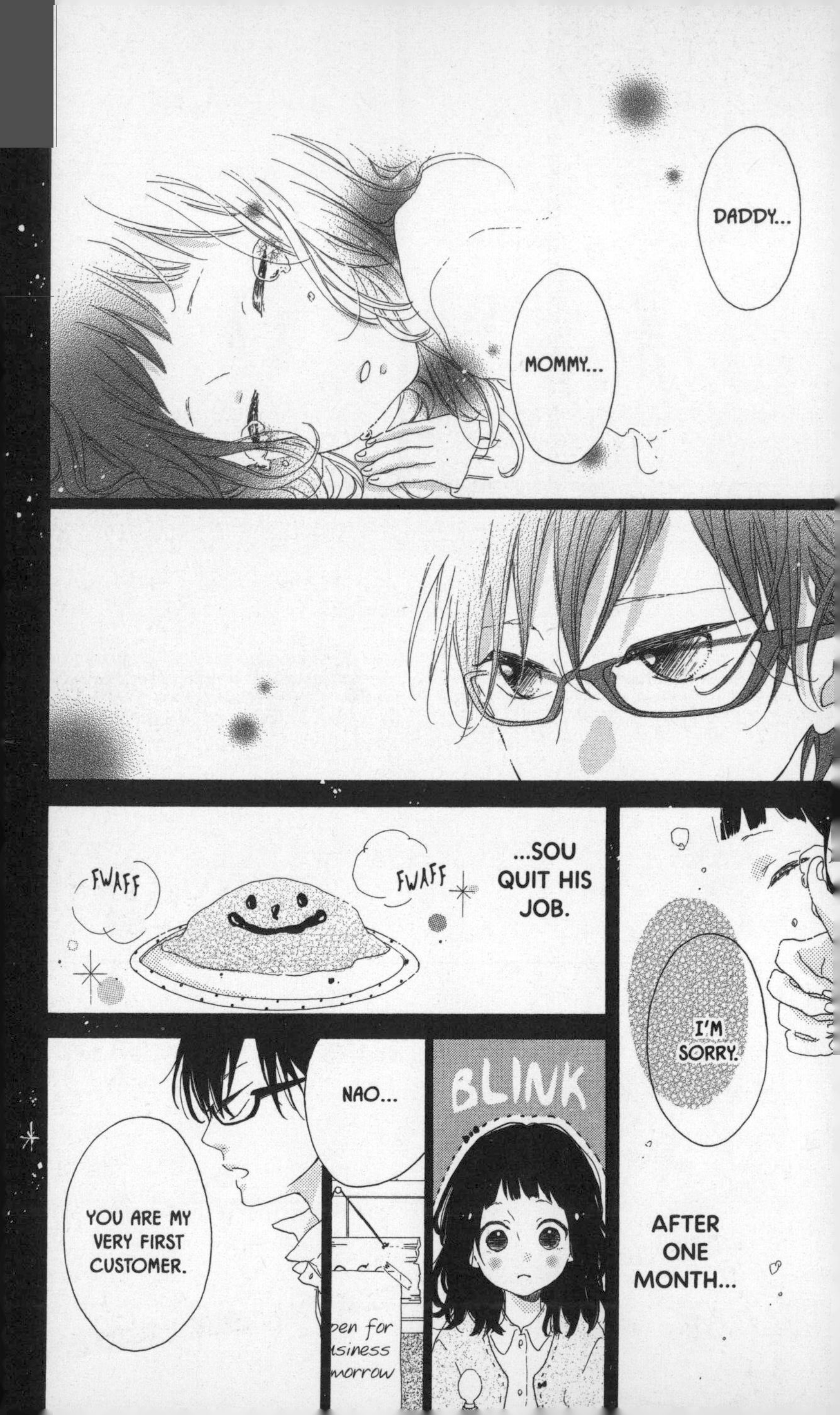
DADDY...
MOMMY...
I'M SORRY.
AFTER ONE MONTH...
...SOU QUIT HIS JOB.
FWAFF
FWAFF
BLINK
NAO...
YOU ARE MY VERY FIRST CUSTOMER.
pen for
usiness
morrow

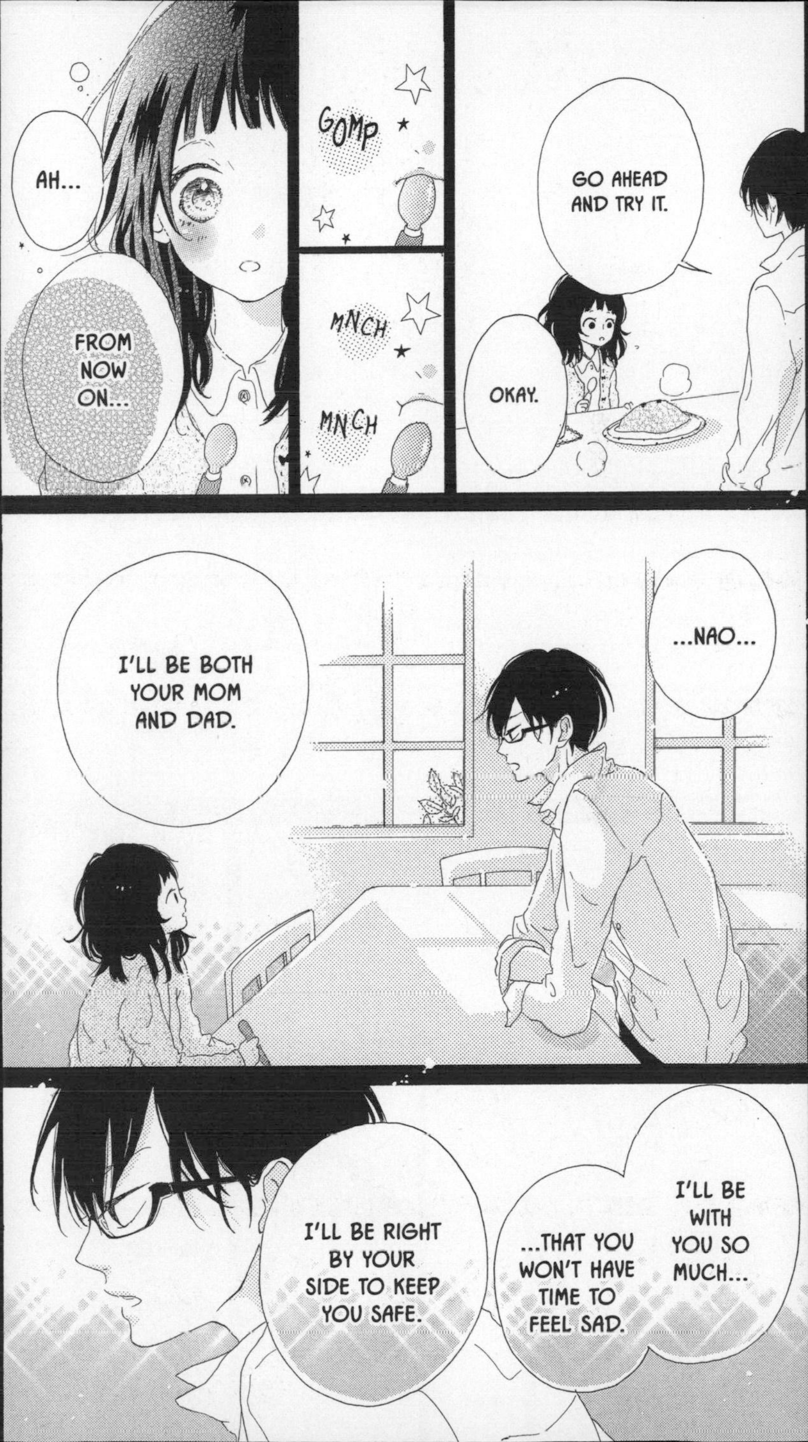
GO AHEAD AND TRY IT.
OKAY.
GOMP
MNCH
MNCH
AH...
FROM NOW ON...
...NAO...
I'LL BE BOTH YOUR MOM AND DAD.
I'LL BE WITH YOU SO MUCH...
...THAT YOU WON'T HAVE TIME TO FEEL SAD.
I'LL BE RIGHT BY YOUR SIDE TO KEEP YOU SAFE.

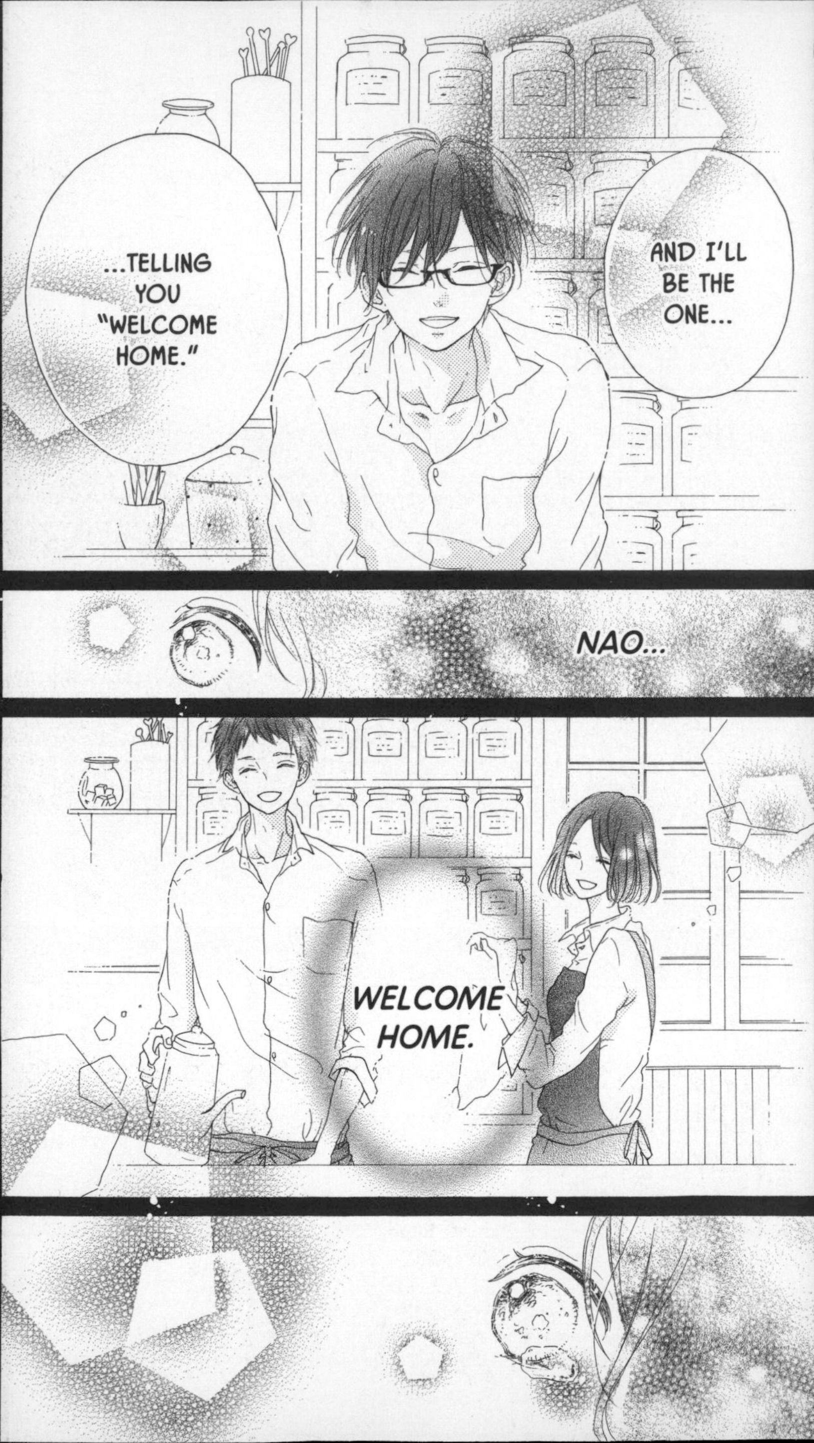
AND I'LL BE THE ONE...
...TELLING YOU "WELCOME HOME."
NAO...
WELCOME HOME.

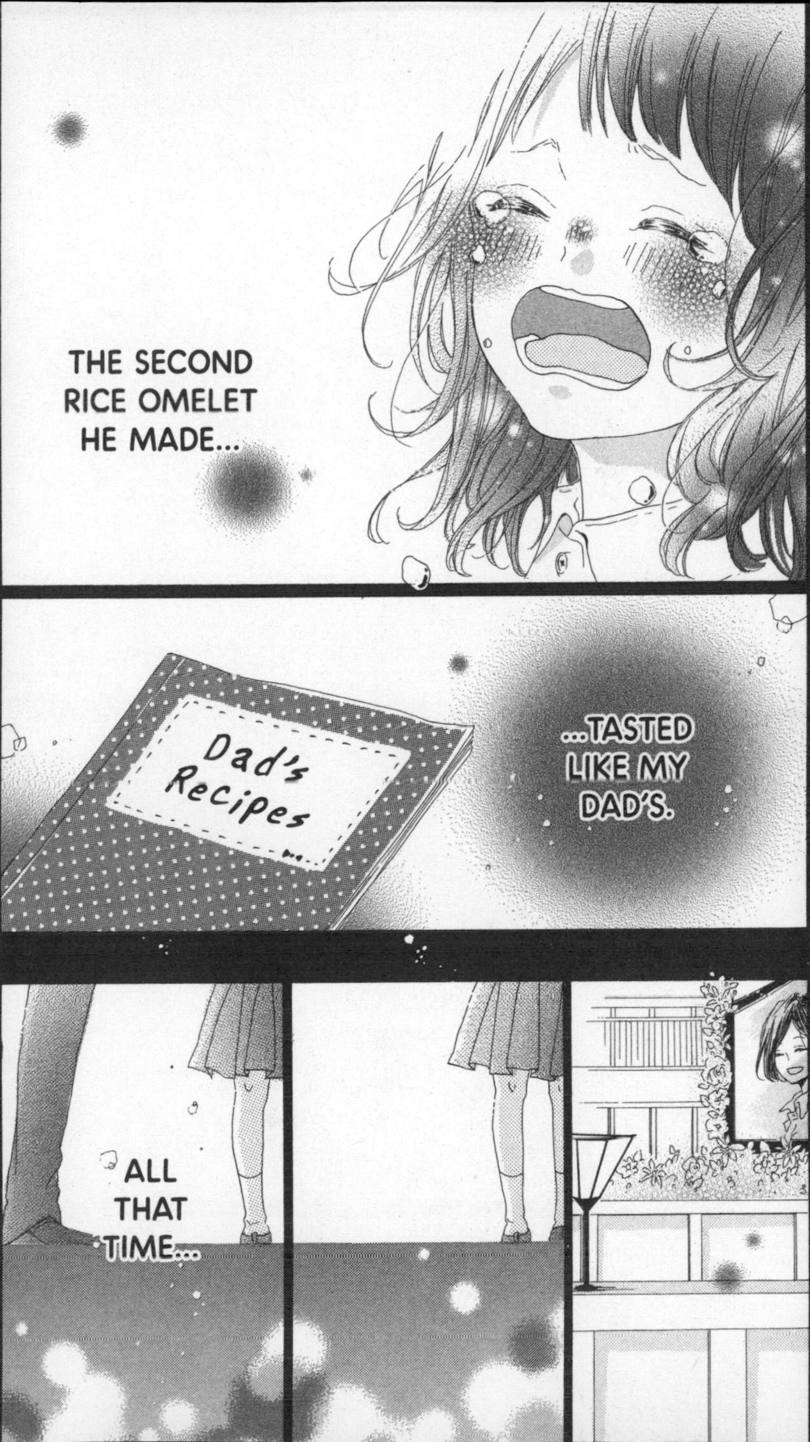
THE SECOND RICE OMELET HE MADE...
...TASTED LIKE MY DAD'S.
Dad's Recipes
ALL THAT TIME...

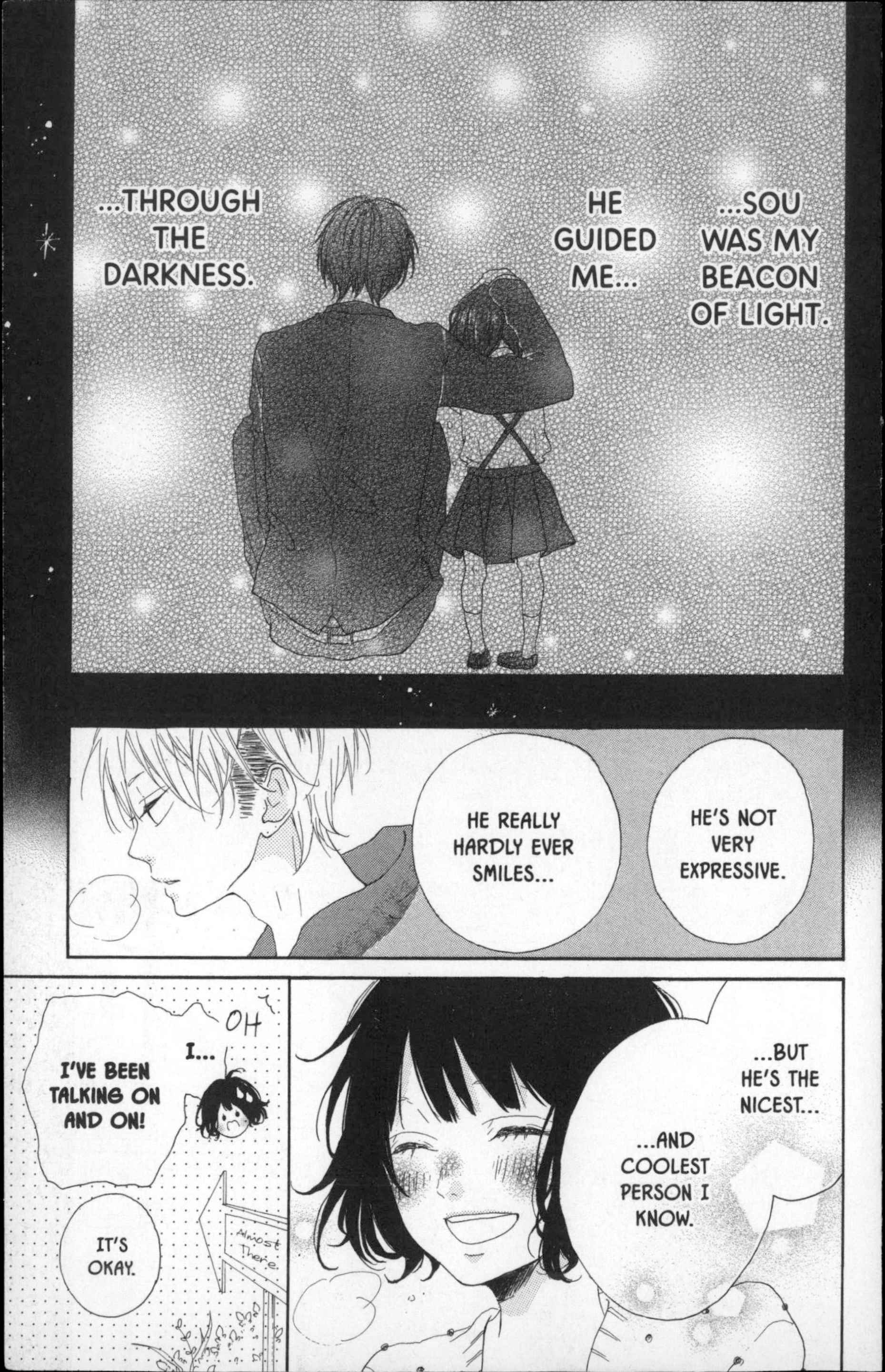
...SOU WAS MY BEACON OF LIGHT.
HE GUIDED ME...
...THROUGH THE DARKNESS.
HE'S NOT VERY EXPRESSIVE.
HE REALLY HARDLY EVER SMILES...
...BUT HE'S THE NICEST...
...AND COOLEST PERSON I KNOW.
OH
I...
I'VE BEEN TALKING ON AND ON!
Almost There.
IT'S OKAY.

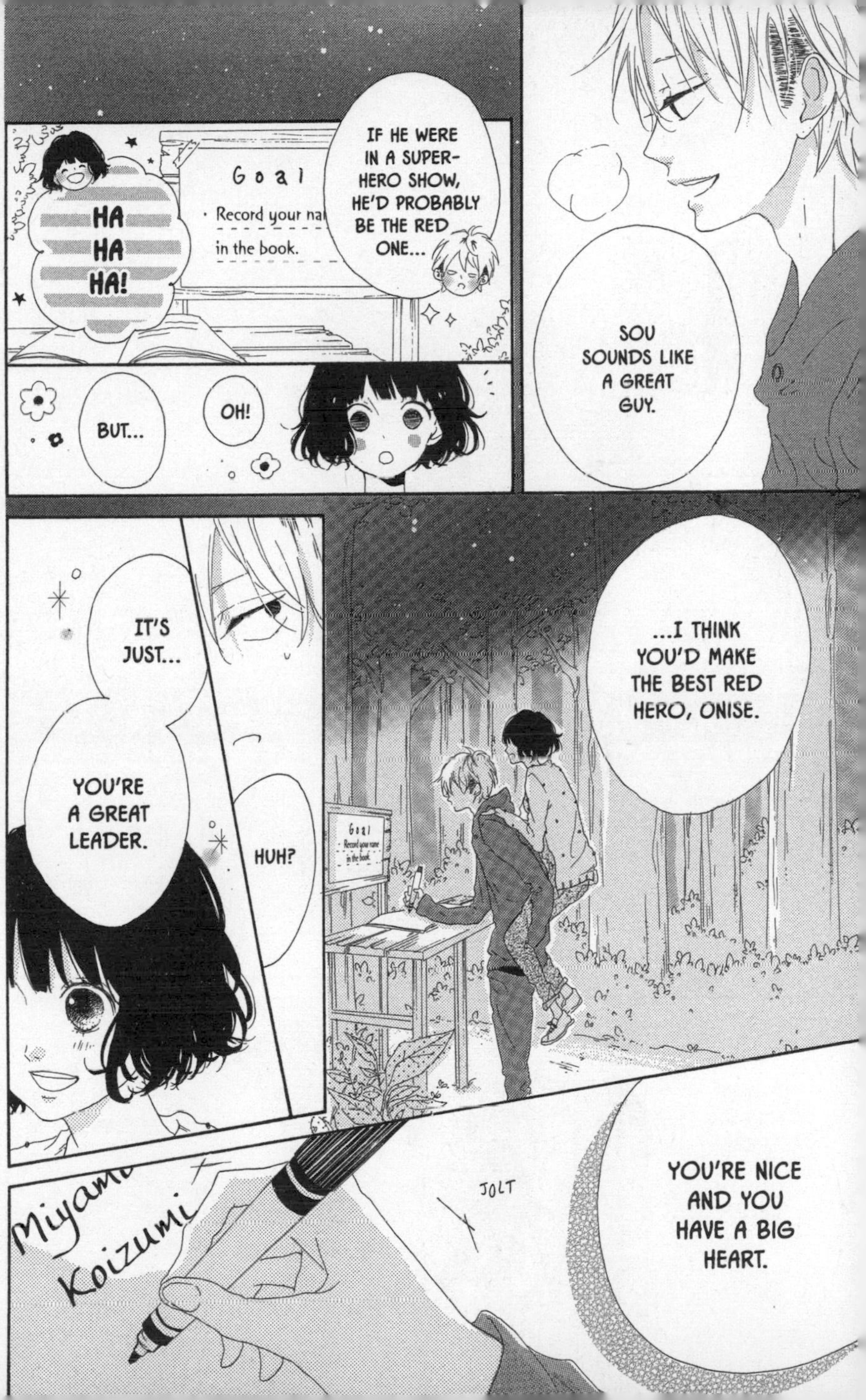
SOU SOUNDS LIKE A GREAT GUY.
IF HE WERE IN A SUPER-HERO SHOW, HE'D PROBABLY BE THE RED ONE...
Goal
· Record your na
in the book.
HA HA HA!
OH!
BUT...
...I THINK YOU'D MAKE THE BEST RED HERO, ONISE.
Goal
Record your name in the book.
HUH?
IT'S JUST...
YOU'RE A GREAT LEADER.
YOU'RE NICE AND YOU HAVE A BIG HEART.
JOLT
Miyam
Koizumi

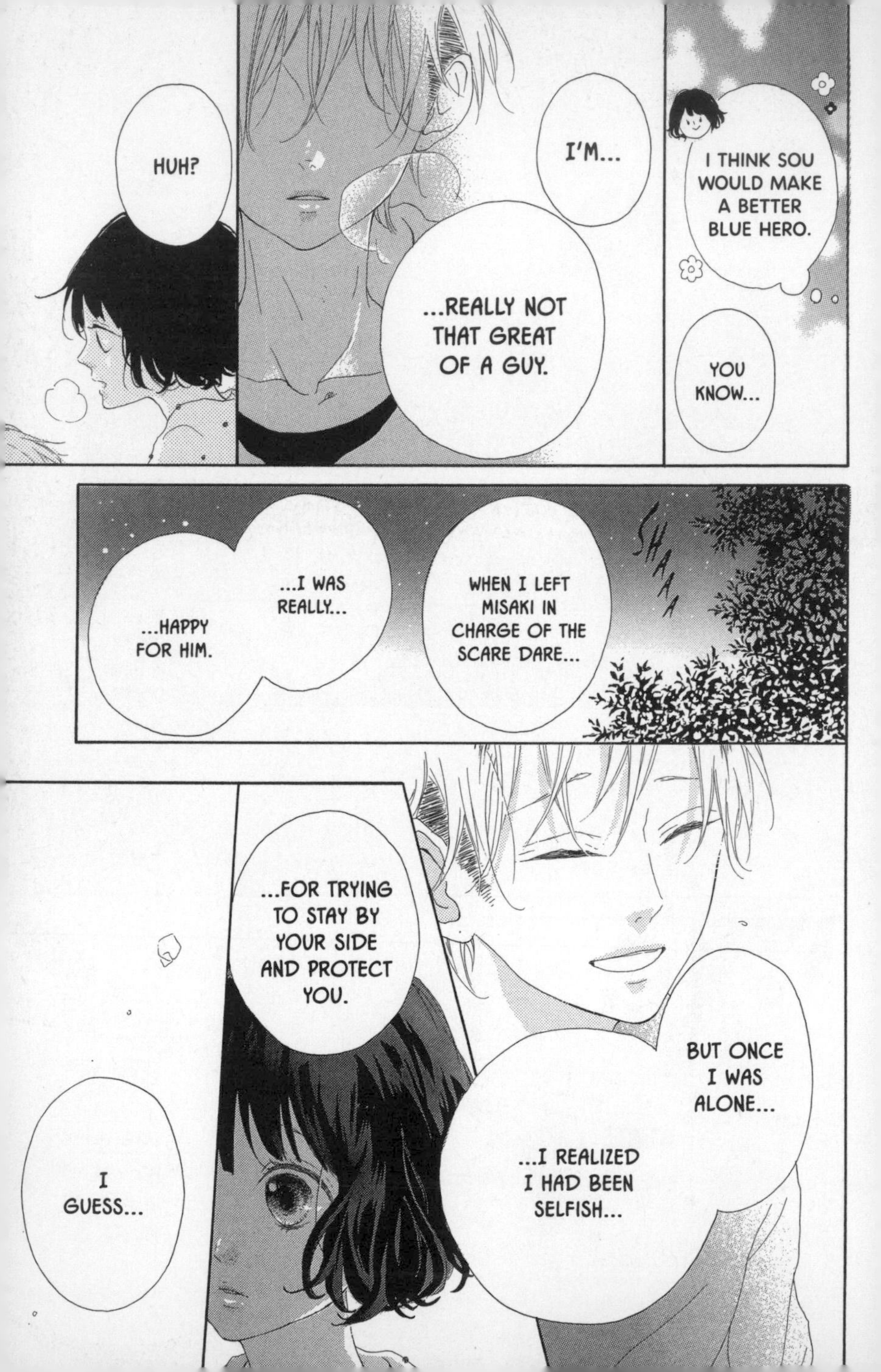
I THINK SOU WOULD MAKE A BETTER BLUE HERO.
YOU KNOW...
I'M...
...REALLY NOT THAT GREAT OF A GUY.
HUH?
SHAAA
WHEN I LEFT MISAKI IN CHARGE OF THE SCARE DARE...
...I WAS REALLY...
...HAPPY FOR HIM.
BUT ONCE I WAS ALONE...
...I REALIZED I HAD BEEN SELFISH...
...FOR TRYING TO STAY BY YOUR SIDE AND PROTECT YOU.
I GUESS...

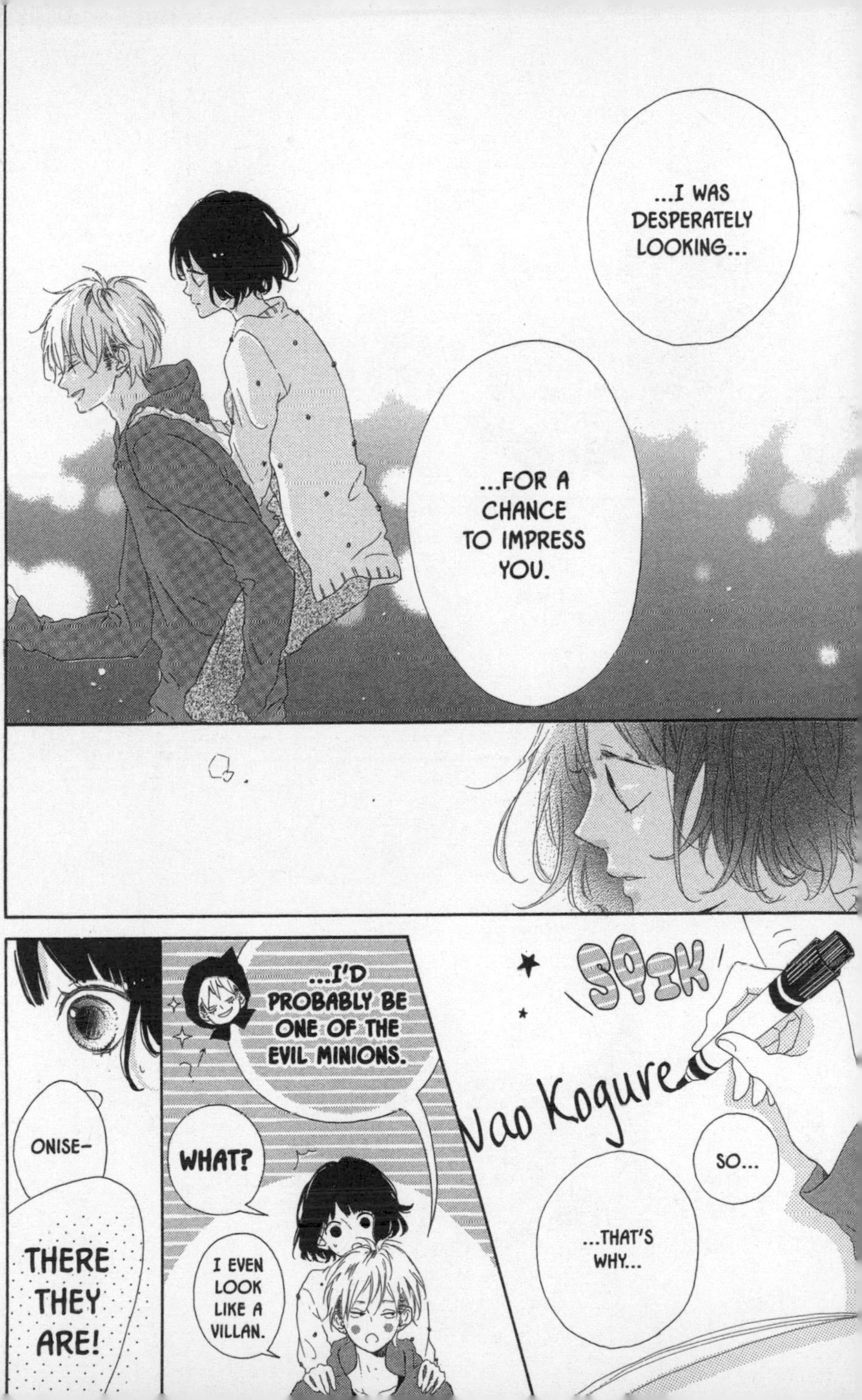
...I WAS DESPERATELY LOOKING...
...FOR A CHANCE TO IMPRESS YOU.
SQIK
Nao Kogure
SO...
...THAT'S WHY...
...I'D PROBABLY BE ONE OF THE EVIL MINIONS.
WHAT?
I EVEN LOOK LIKE A VILLAN.
ONISE-
THERE THEY ARE!

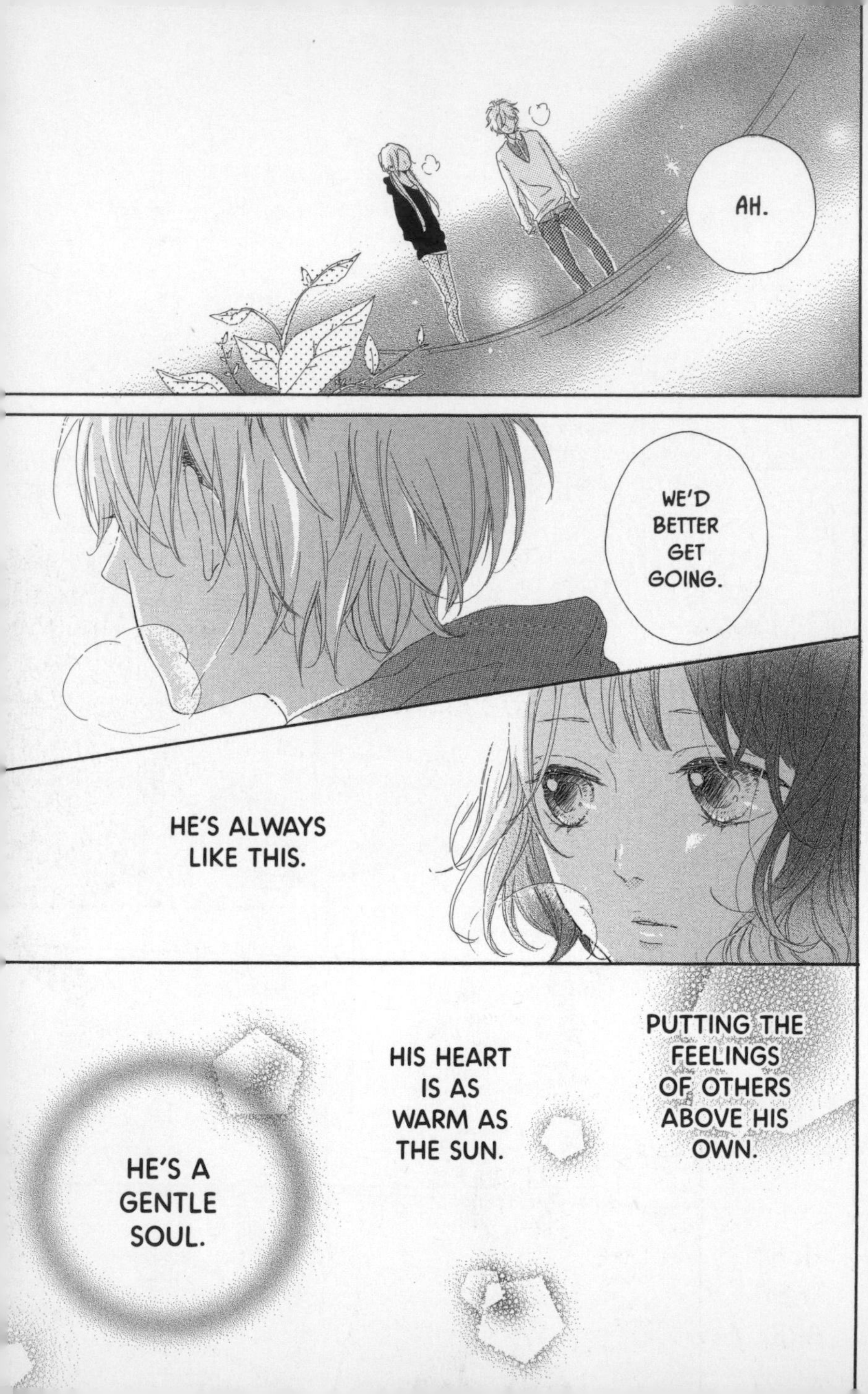
AH.
WE'D BETTER GET GOING.
HE'S ALWAYS LIKE THIS.
PUTTING THE FEELINGS OF OTHERS ABOVE HIS OWN.
HIS HEART IS AS WARM AS THE SUN.
HE'S A GENTLE SOUL.

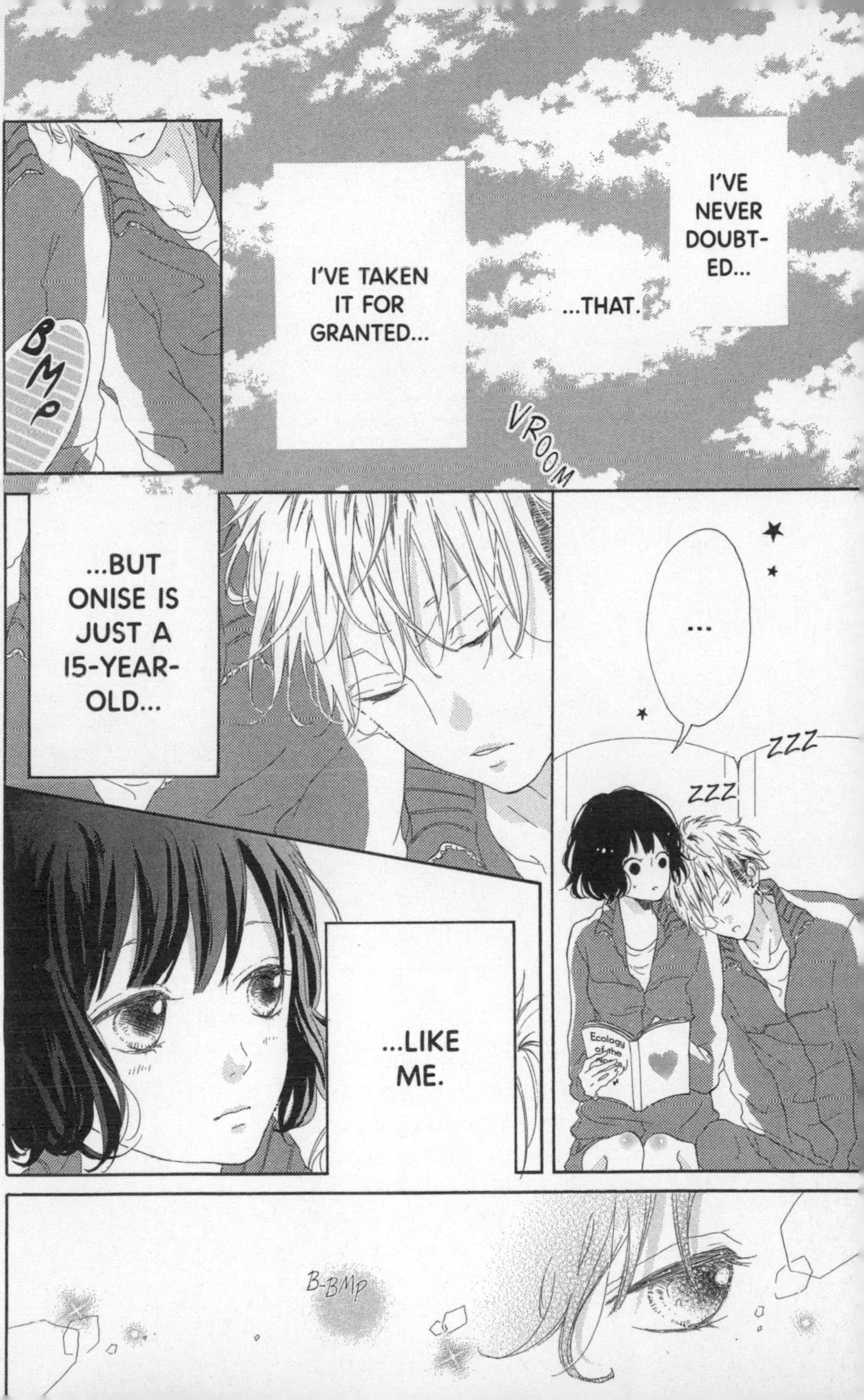
I'VE NEVER DOUBTED...
...THAT.
I'VE TAKEN IT FOR GRANTED...
VROOM
BMP
...
ZZZ
ZZZ
Ecology of the
...BUT ONISE IS JUST A 15-YEAR-OLD...
...LIKE ME.
B-BMP

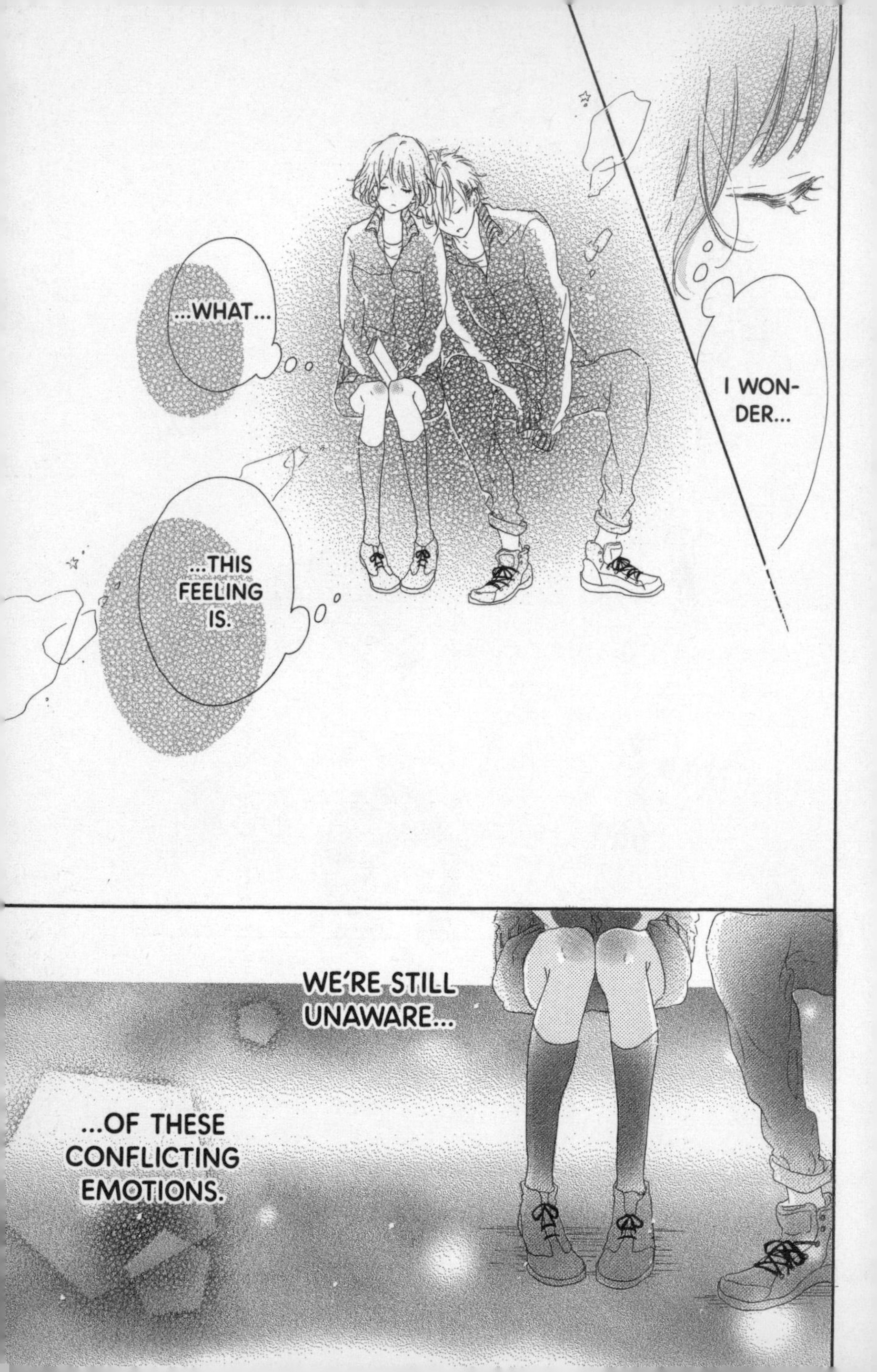
I WON-
DER...
...WHAT...
...THIS FEELING IS.
WE'RE STILL UNAWARE...
...OF THESE CONFLICTING EMOTIONS.

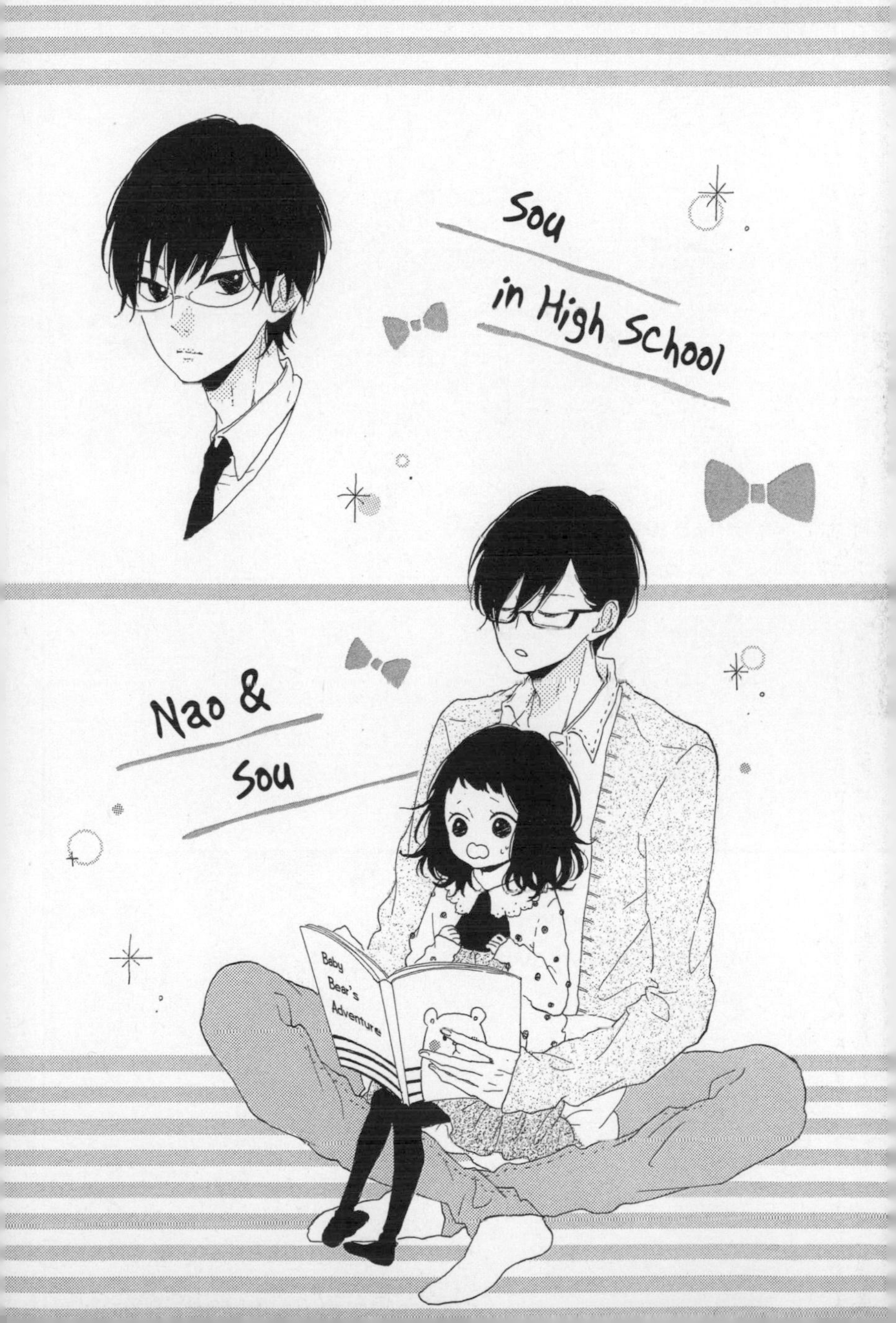
Sou
in High School
Nao &
Sou
Baby Bear's Adventure

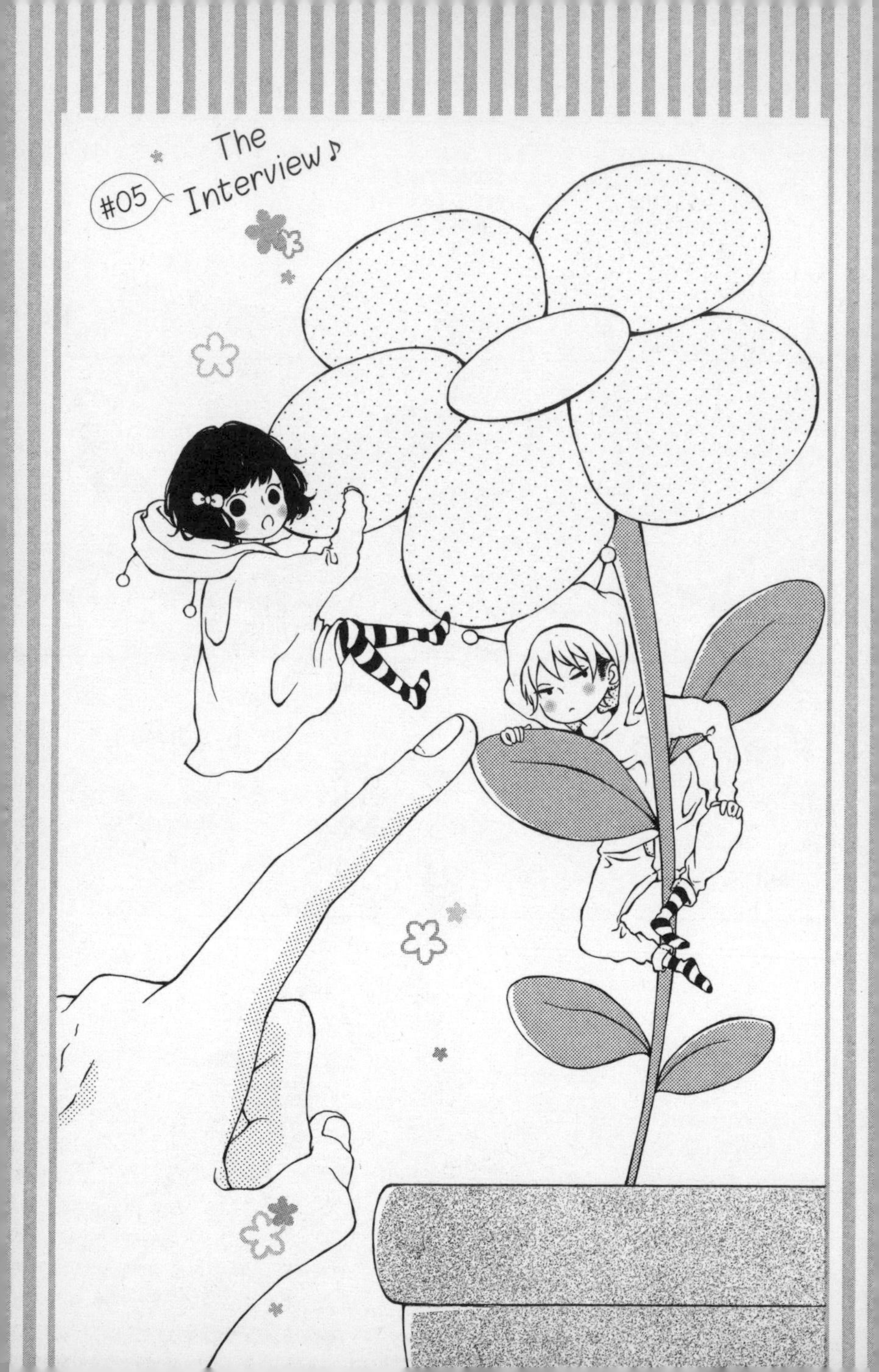
#05
The Interview♪

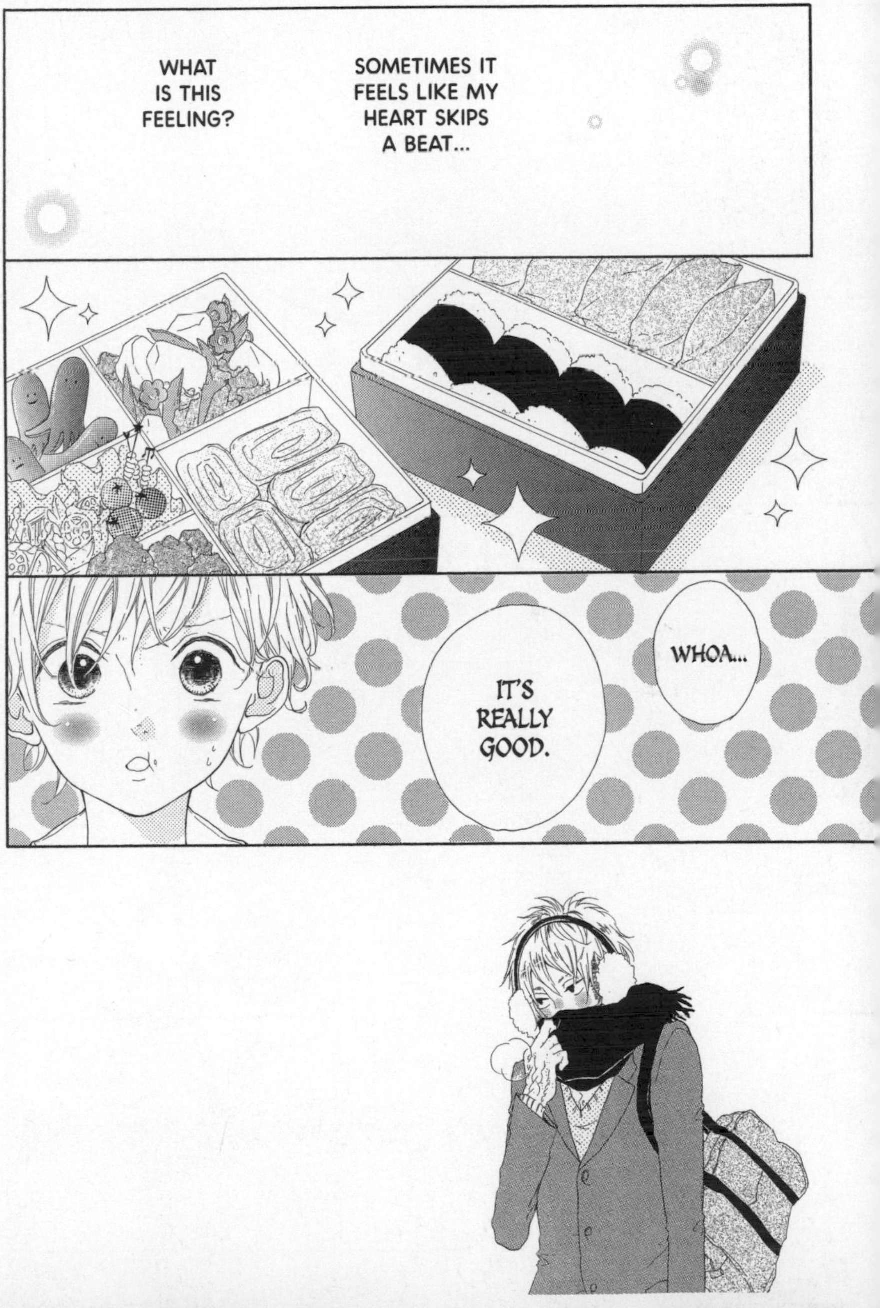
SOMETIMES IT FEELS LIKE MY HEART SKIPS A BEAT...
WHAT IS THIS FEELING?
WHOA...
IT'S REALLY GOOD.

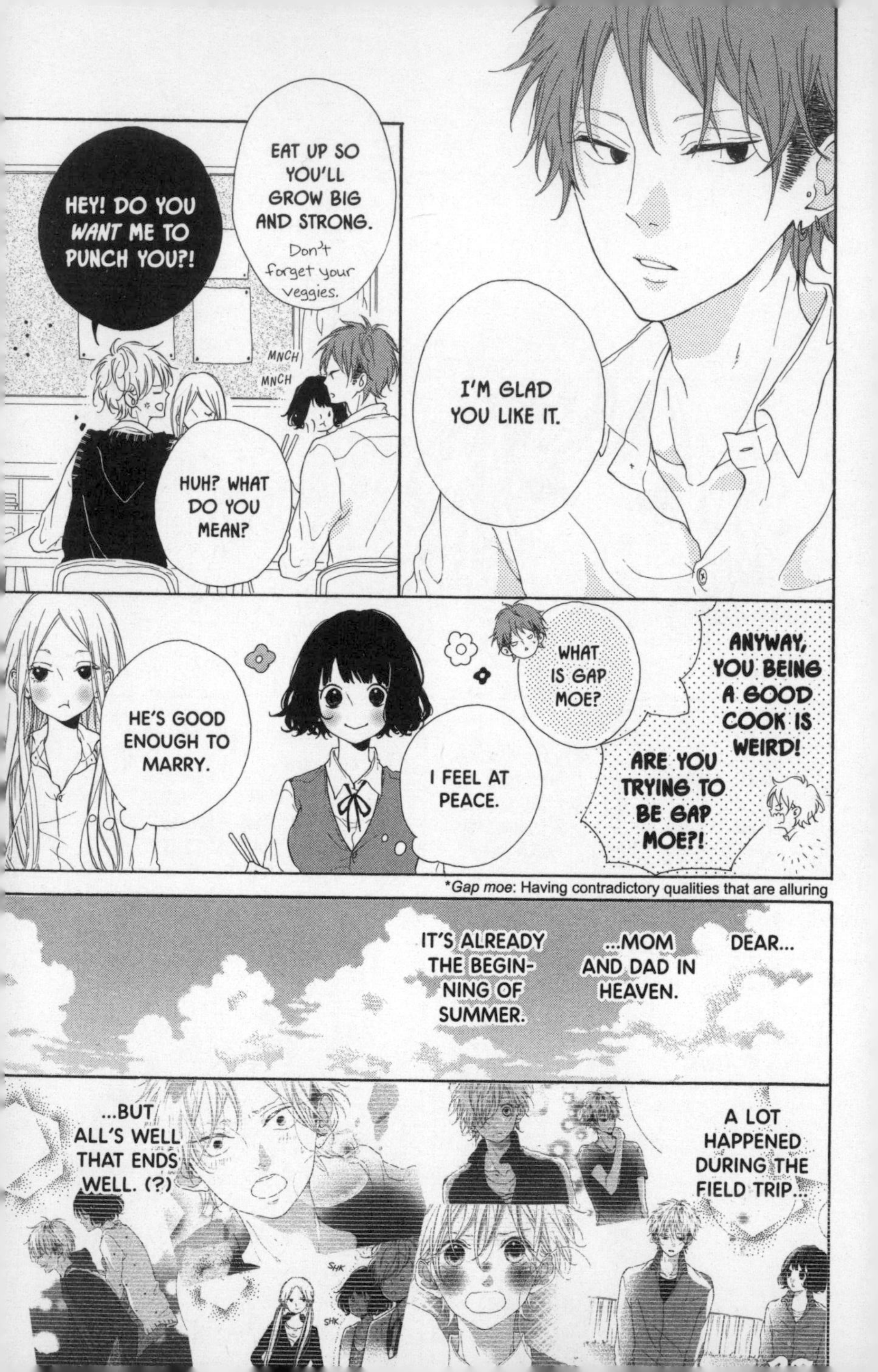
I'M GLAD YOU LIKE IT.
EAT UP SO YOU'LL GROW BIG AND STRONG.
Don't forget your veggies.
HEY! DO YOU WANT ME TO PUNCH YOU?!
MNCH
MNCH
HUH? WHAT DO YOU MEAN?
ANYWAY, YOU BEING A GOOD COOK IS WEIRD!
ARE YOU TRYING TO BE GAP MOE?!
WHAT IS GAP MOE?
I FEEL AT PEACE.
HE'S GOOD ENOUGH TO MARRY.
DEAR...
...MOM AND DAD IN HEAVEN.
IT'S ALREADY THE BEGIN-NING OF SUMMER.
A LOT HAPPENED DURING THE FIELD TRIP...
SHK
SHK
...BUT ALL'S WELL THAT ENDS WELL. (?)

**Gap moe*: Having contradictory qualities that are alluring

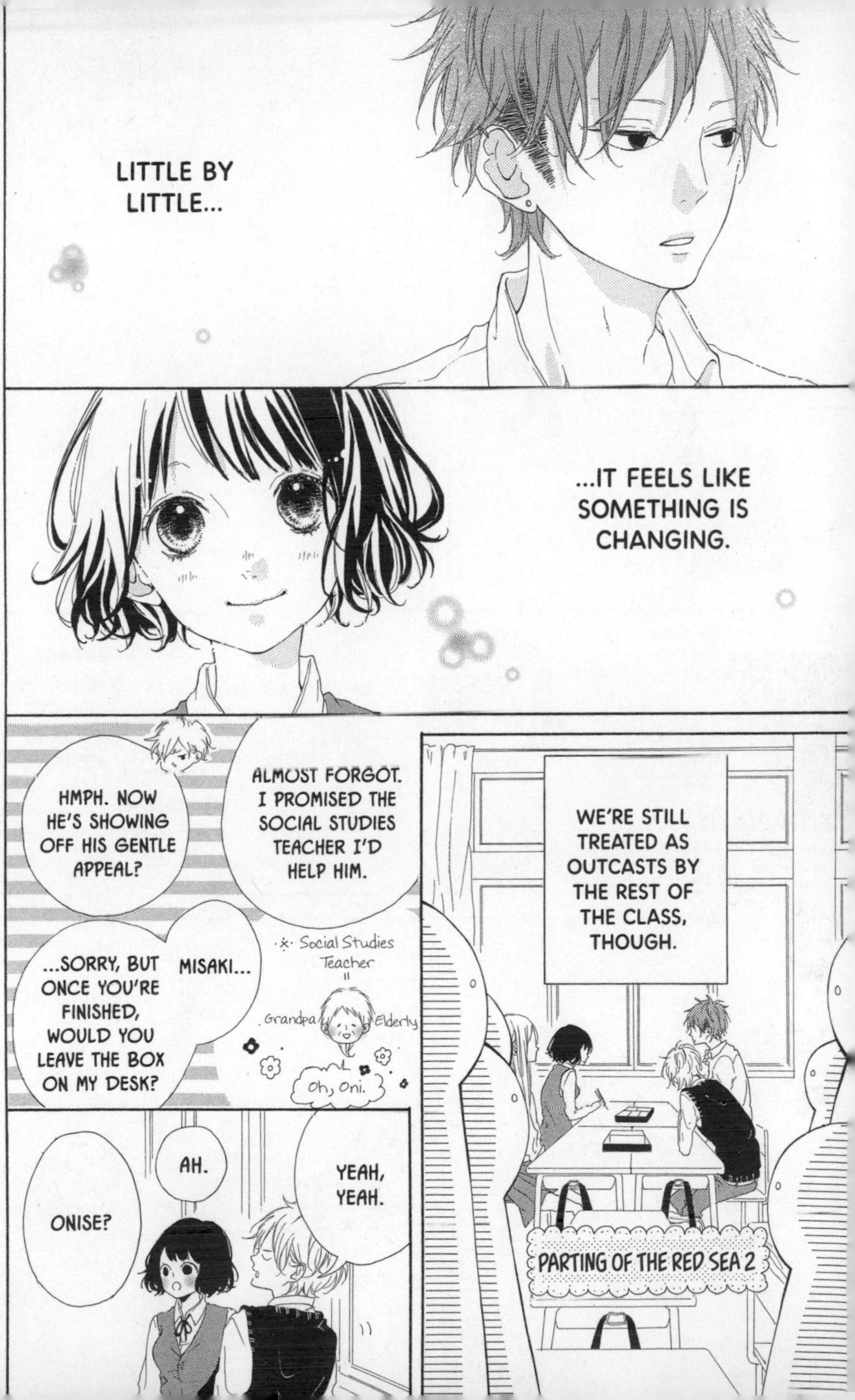

LITTLE BY LITTLE...
...IT FEELS LIKE SOMETHING IS CHANGING.
WE'RE STILL TREATED AS OUTCASTS BY THE REST OF THE CLASS, THOUGH.
PARTING OF THE RED SEA 2
ALMOST FORGOT. I PROMISED THE SOCIAL STUDIES TEACHER I'D HELP HIM.
HMPH. NOW HE'S SHOWING OFF HIS GENTLE APPEAL?
MISAKI...
...SORRY, BUT ONCE YOU'RE FINISHED, WOULD YOU LEAVE THE BOX ON MY DESK?
※ Social Studies Teacher
=
Grandpa
Elderly
Oh, Oni.
YEAH, YEAH.
AH.
ONISE?

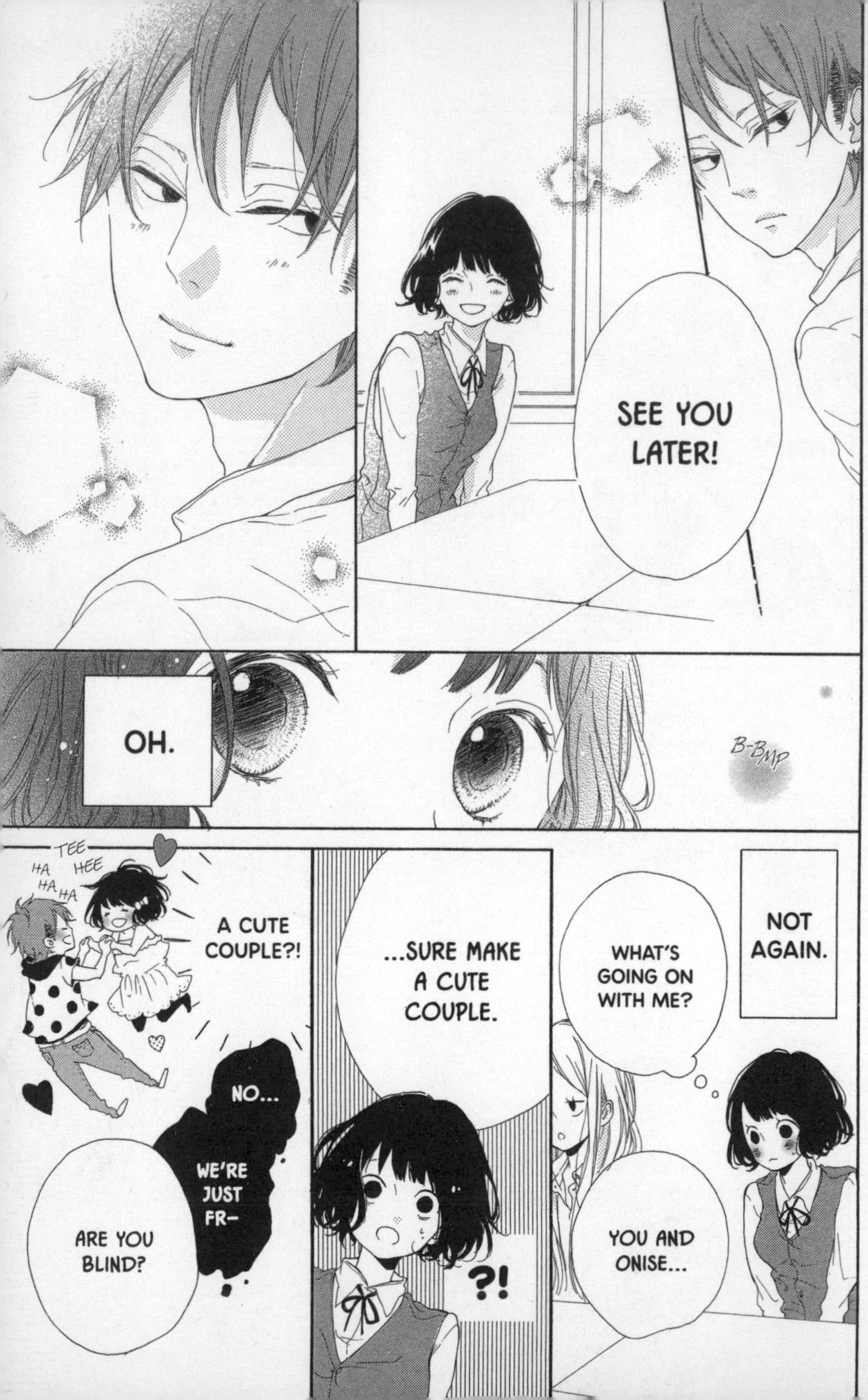
SEE YOU LATER!
B-BMP
OH.
NOT AGAIN.
WHAT'S GOING ON WITH ME?
YOU AND ONISE...
...SURE MAKE A CUTE COUPLE.
?!
A CUTE COUPLE?!
TEE HEE
HA HA HA
NO...
WE'RE JUST FR-
ARE YOU BLIND?

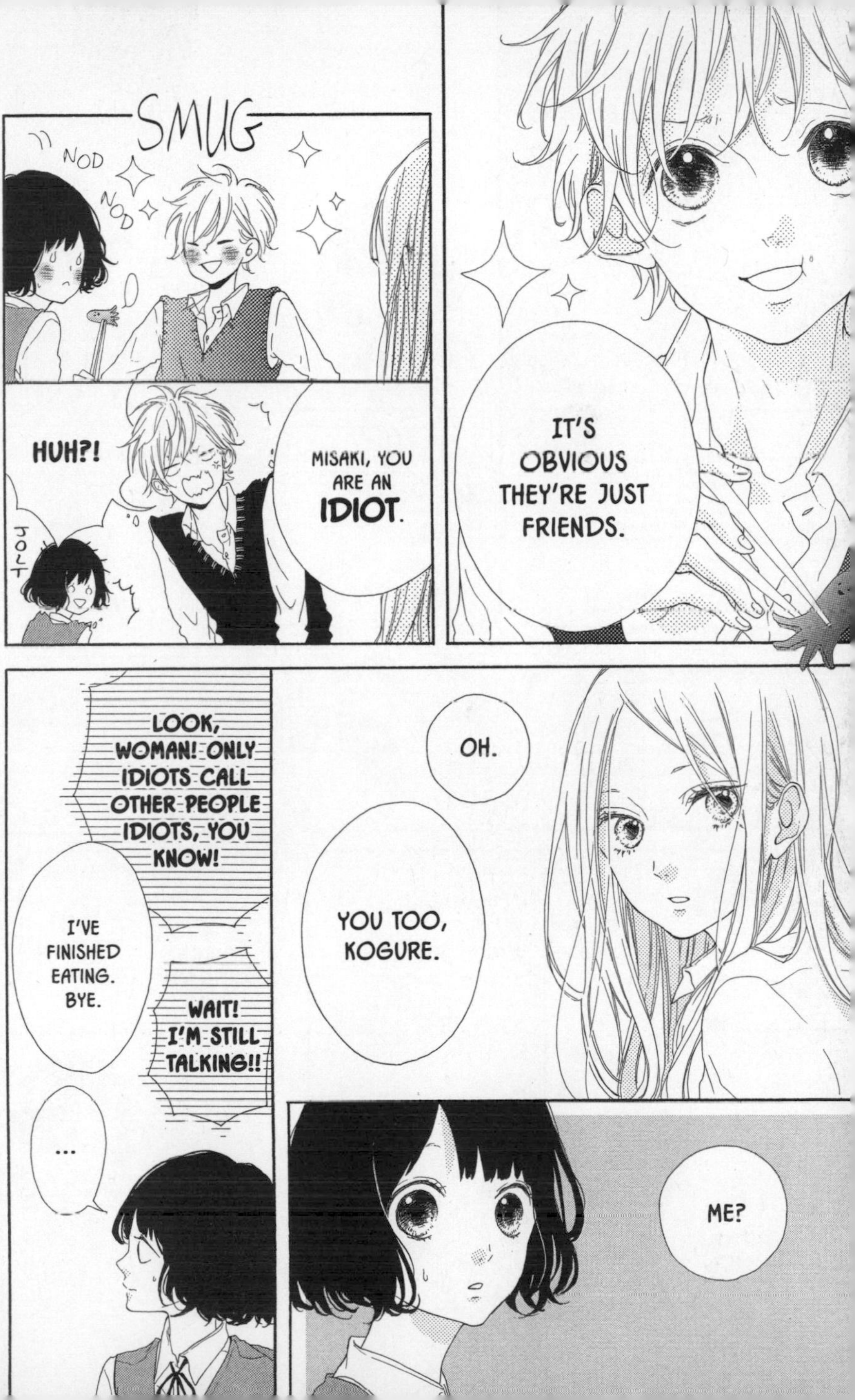
IT'S OBVIOUS THEY'RE JUST FRIENDS.
SMUG
NOD
NOD
MISAKI, YOU ARE AN IDIOT.
HUH?!
JOLT
OH.
YOU TOO, KOGURE.
ME?
LOOK, WOMAN! ONLY IDIOTS CALL OTHER PEOPLE IDIOTS, YOU KNOW!
I'VE FINISHED EATING. BYE.
WAIT! I'M STILL TALKING!!
...

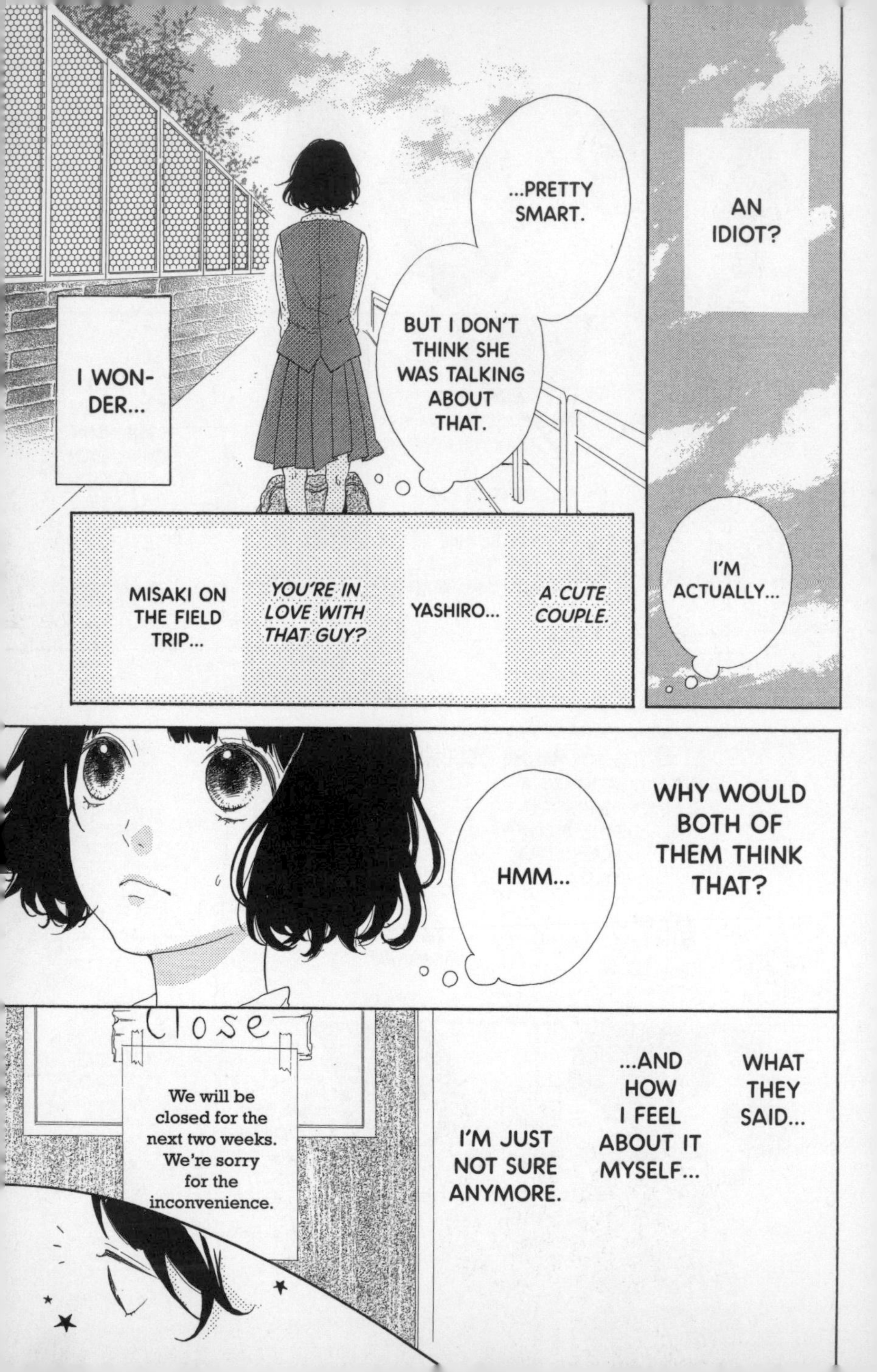
AN IDIOT?
I'M ACTUALLY...
...PRETTY SMART.
BUT I DON'T THINK SHE WAS TALKING ABOUT THAT.
I WONDER...
A CUTE COUPLE.
YASHIRO...
YOU'RE IN LOVE WITH THAT GUY?
MISAKI ON THE FIELD TRIP...
WHY WOULD BOTH OF THEM THINK THAT?
HMM...
WHAT THEY SAID...
...AND HOW I FEEL ABOUT IT MYSELF...
I'M JUST NOT SURE ANYMORE.
Close
We will be closed for the next two weeks. We're sorry for the inconvenience.

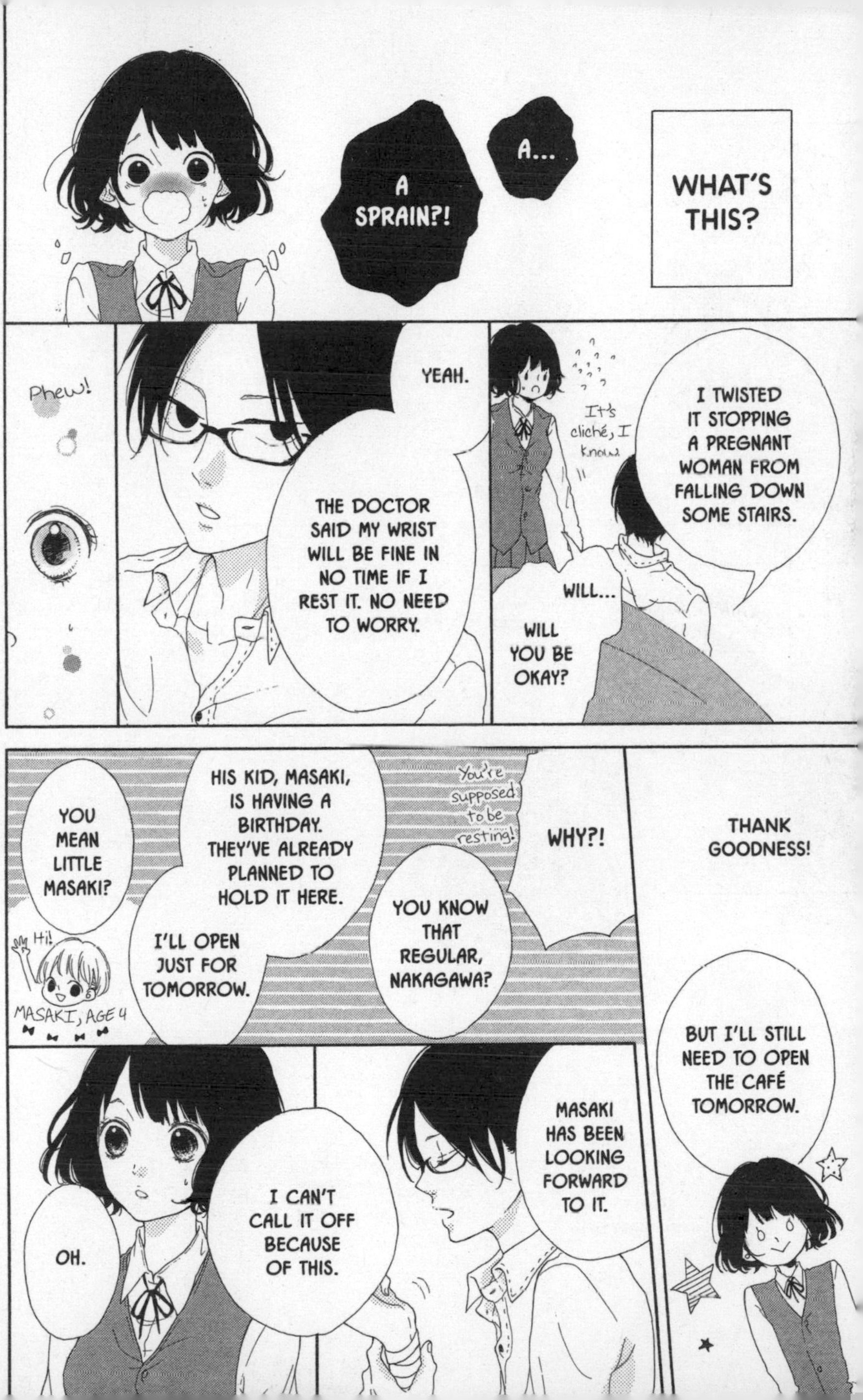
WHAT'S THIS?
A...
A SPRAIN?!
I TWISTED IT STOPPING A PREGNANT WOMAN FROM FALLING DOWN SOME STAIRS.
It's cliché, I know
WILL...
WILL YOU BE OKAY?
YEAH.
THE DOCTOR SAID MY WRIST WILL BE FINE IN NO TIME IF I REST IT. NO NEED TO WORRY.
Phew!
THANK GOODNESS!
BUT I'LL STILL NEED TO OPEN THE CAFÉ TOMORROW.
WHY?!
You're supposed to be resting!
YOU KNOW THAT REGULAR, NAKAGAWA?
HIS KID, MASAKI, IS HAVING A BIRTHDAY. THEY'VE ALREADY PLANNED TO HOLD IT HERE.
YOU MEAN LITTLE MASAKI?
Hi!
MASAKI, AGE 4
I'LL OPEN JUST FOR TOMORROW.
MASAKI HAS BEEN LOOKING FORWARD TO IT.
I CAN'T CALL IT OFF BECAUSE OF THIS.
OH.

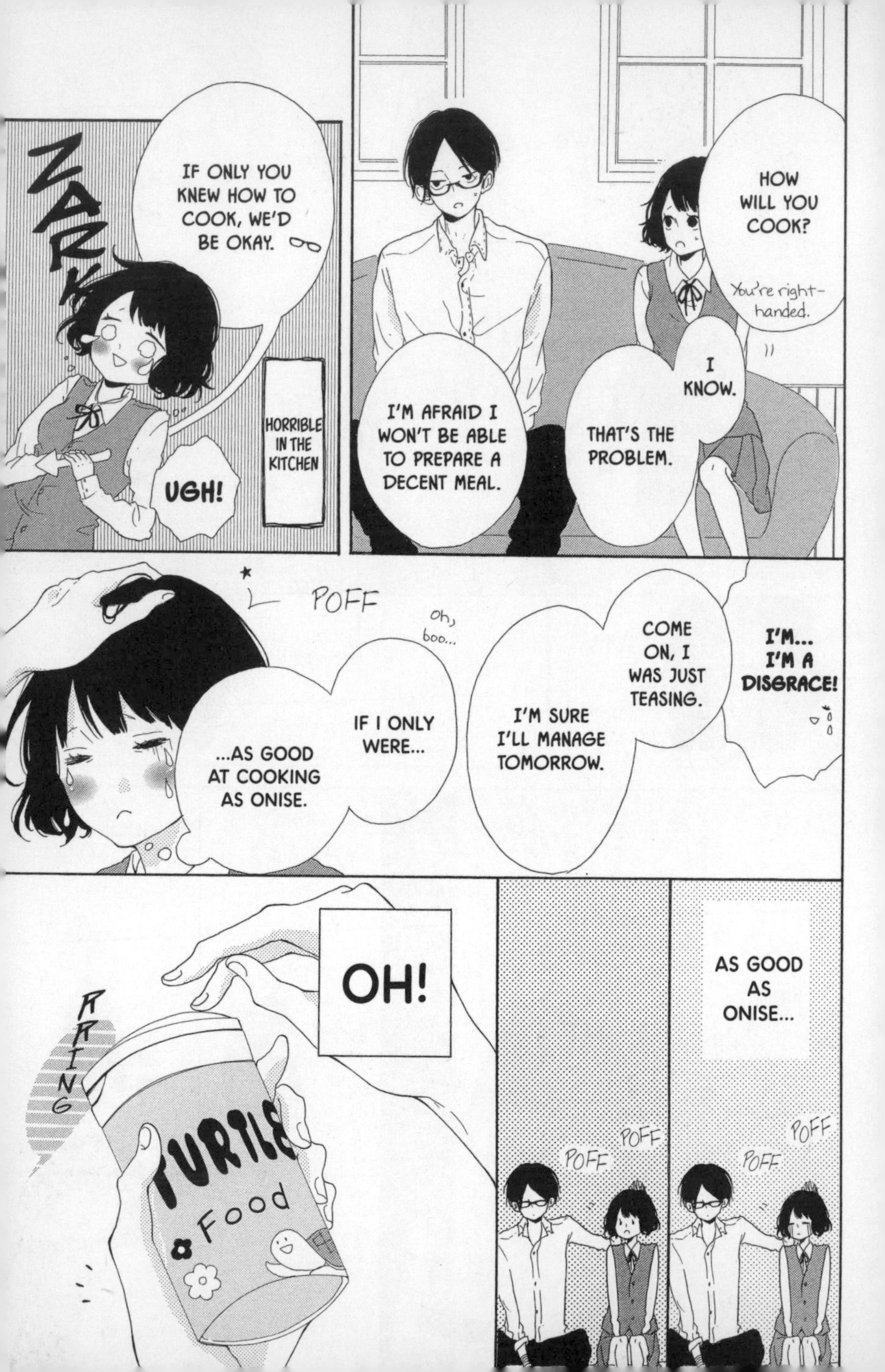
HOW WILL YOU COOK?
You're right-handed.
I KNOW.
THAT'S THE PROBLEM.
I'M AFRAID I WON'T BE ABLE TO PREPARE A DECENT MEAL.
IF ONLY YOU KNEW HOW TO COOK, WE'D BE OKAY.
ZARK
HORRIBLE IN THE KITCHEN
UGH!
I'M... I'M A DISGRACE!
COME ON, I WAS JUST TEASING.
I'M SURE I'LL MANAGE TOMORROW.
Oh, boo...
IF I ONLY WERE...
...AS GOOD AT COOKING AS ONISE.
POFF
AS GOOD AS ONISE...
POFF
POFF
POFF
POFF
OH!
RRING
TURTLE
Food

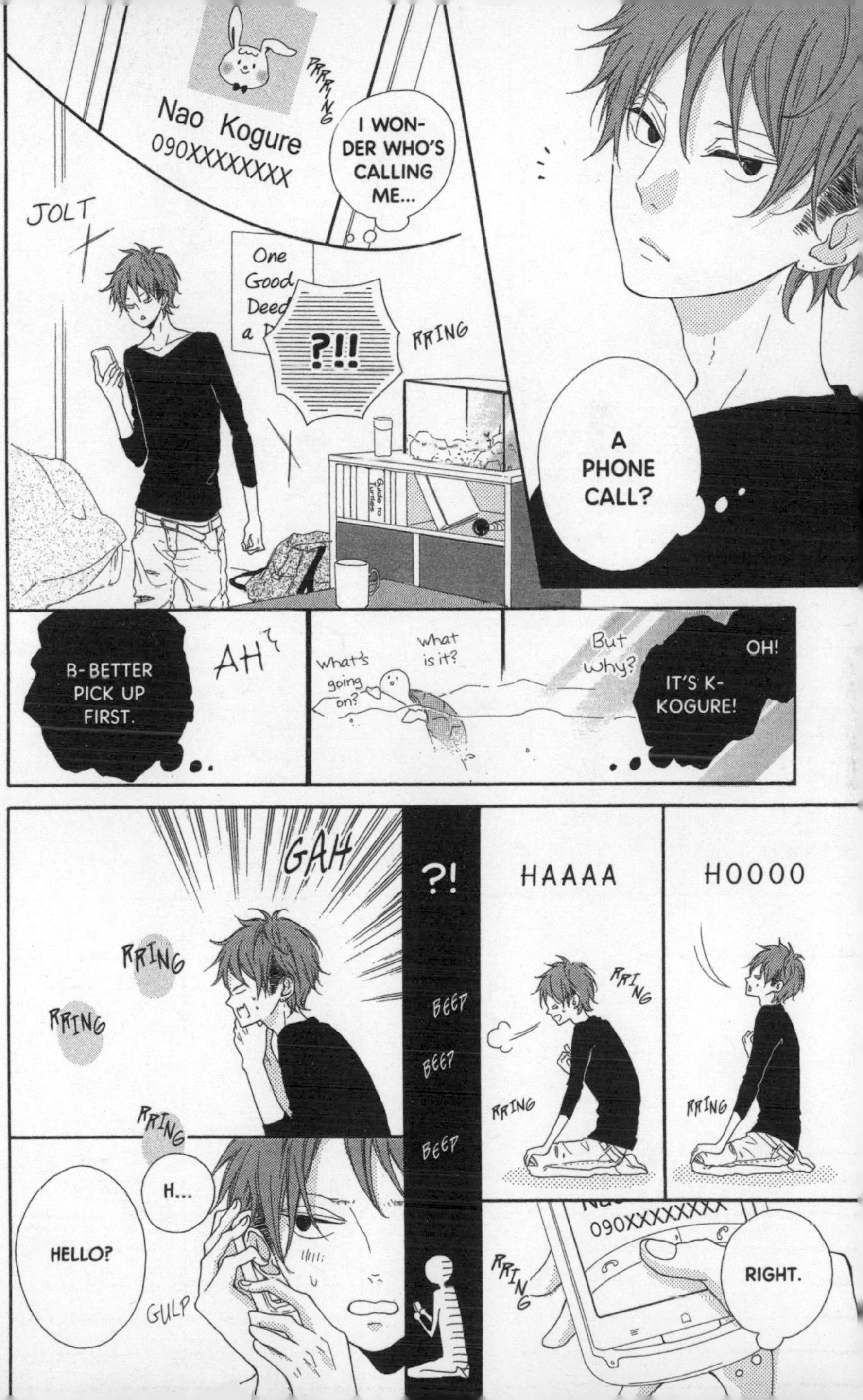
A PHONE CALL?
Nao Kogure
090XXXXXXXX
RRRING
I WONDER WHO'S CALLING ME...
JOLT
One Good Deed a D
?!!
RRING
Guide to Turtles
OH!
IT'S K-KOGURE!
But why?
What is it?
What's going on?
AH
B-BETTER PICK UP FIRST.
HOOOO
RRING
HAAAA
RRING
090XXXXXXXX
RRING
RIGHT.
?!
BEEP
BEEP
BEEP
GAH
RRING
RRING
RRING
H...
HELLO?
GULP

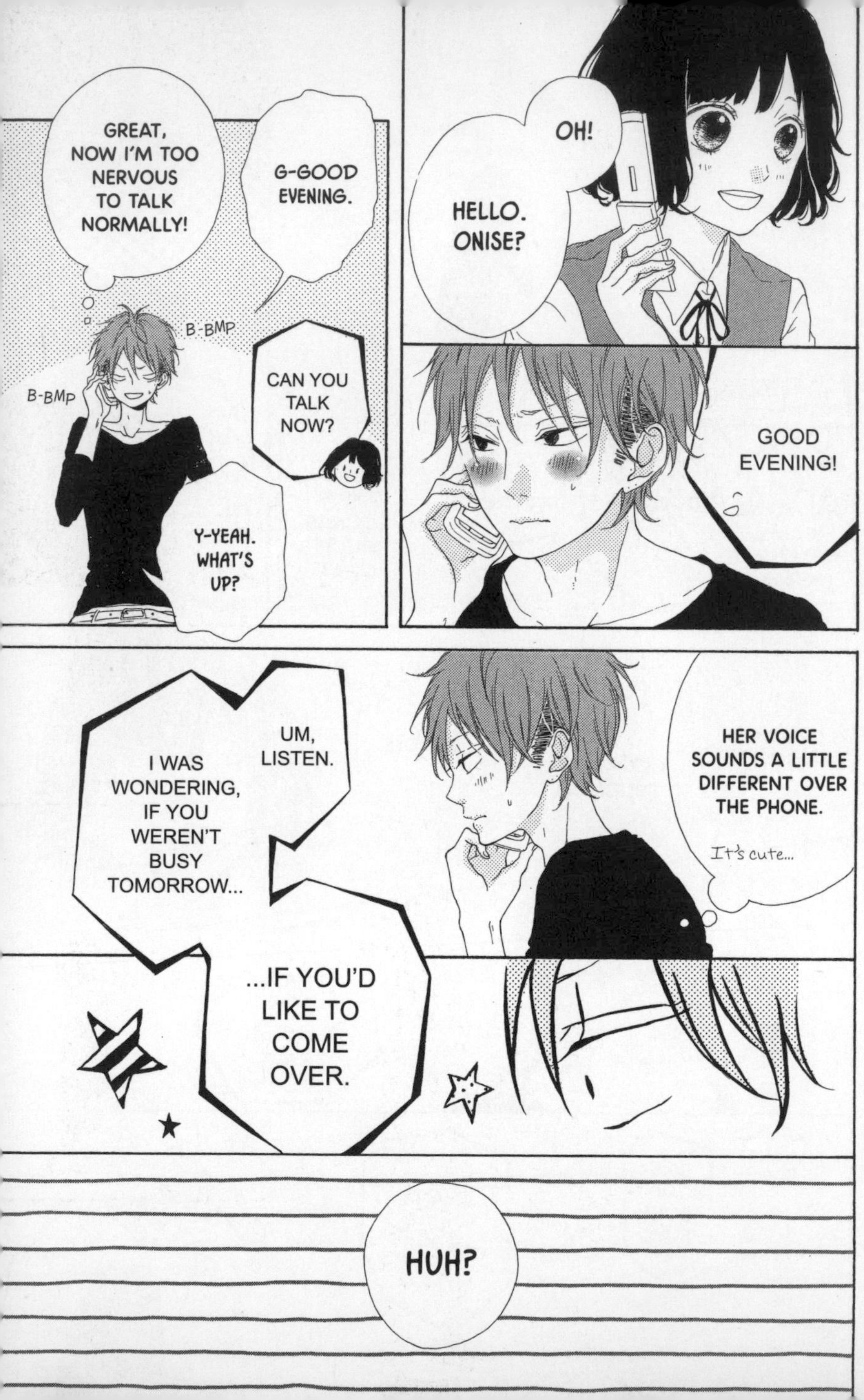
OH!
HELLO. ONISE?
GOOD EVENING!
G-GOOD EVENING.
GREAT, NOW I'M TOO NERVOUS TO TALK NORMALLY!
B-BMP
B-BMP
CAN YOU TALK NOW?
Y-YEAH. WHAT'S UP?
HER VOICE SOUNDS A LITTLE DIFFERENT OVER THE PHONE.
It's cute...
UM, LISTEN.
I WAS WONDERING, IF YOU WEREN'T BUSY TOMORROW...
...IF YOU'D LIKE TO COME OVER.
HUH?

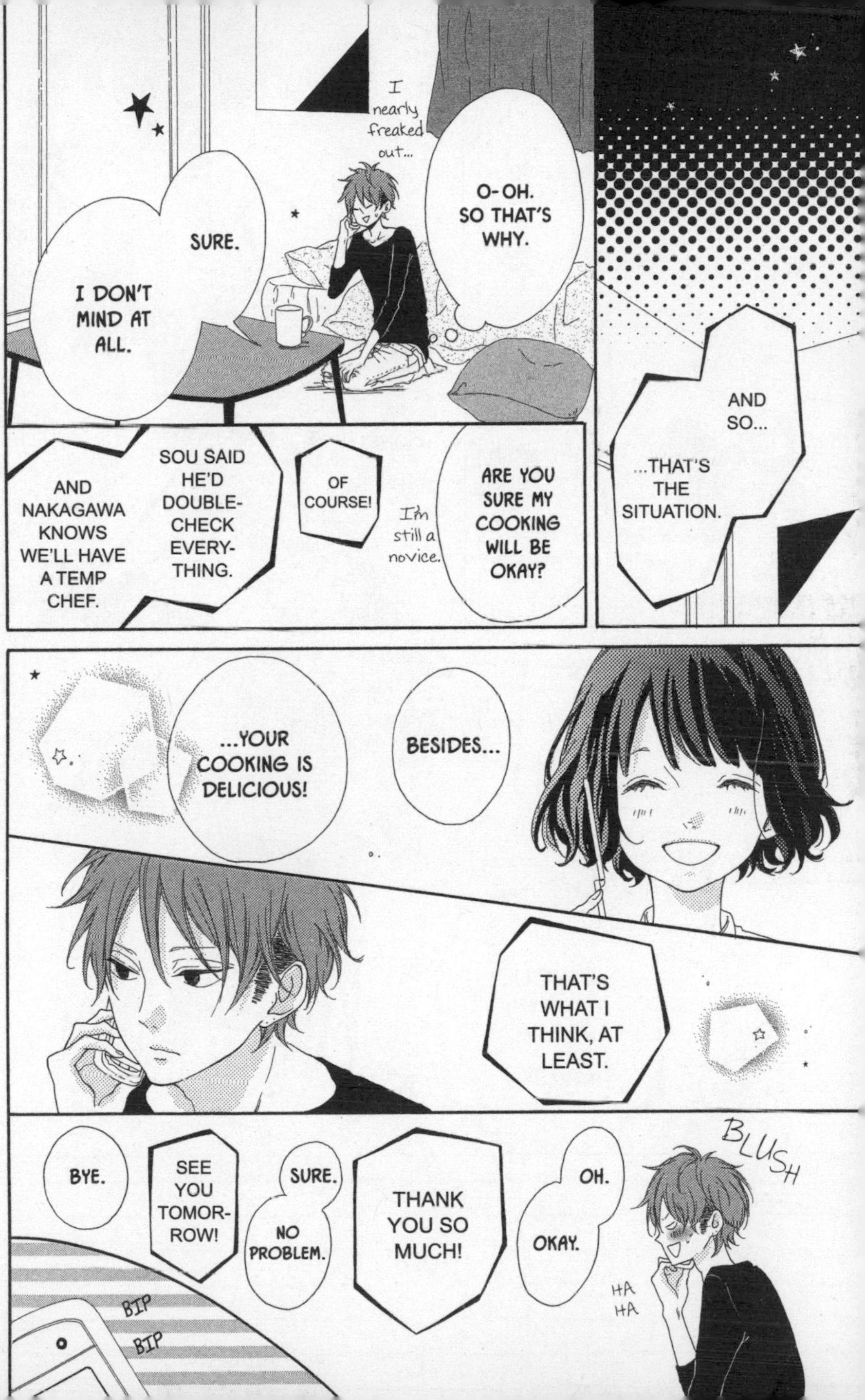
AND SO...
...THAT'S THE SITUATION.
I nearly freaked out...
O-OH. SO THAT'S WHY.
SURE.
I DON'T MIND AT ALL.
ARE YOU SURE MY COOKING WILL BE OKAY?
I'm still a novice.
OF COURSE!
SOU SAID HE'D DOUBLE-CHECK EVERYTHING.
AND NAKAGAWA KNOWS WE'LL HAVE A TEMP CHEF.
BESIDES...
...YOUR COOKING IS DELICIOUS!
THAT'S WHAT I THINK, AT LEAST.
BLUSH
OH.
OKAY.
HA HA
THANK YOU SO MUCH!
SURE.
NO PROBLEM.
SEE YOU TOMORROW!
BYE.
BIP
BIP

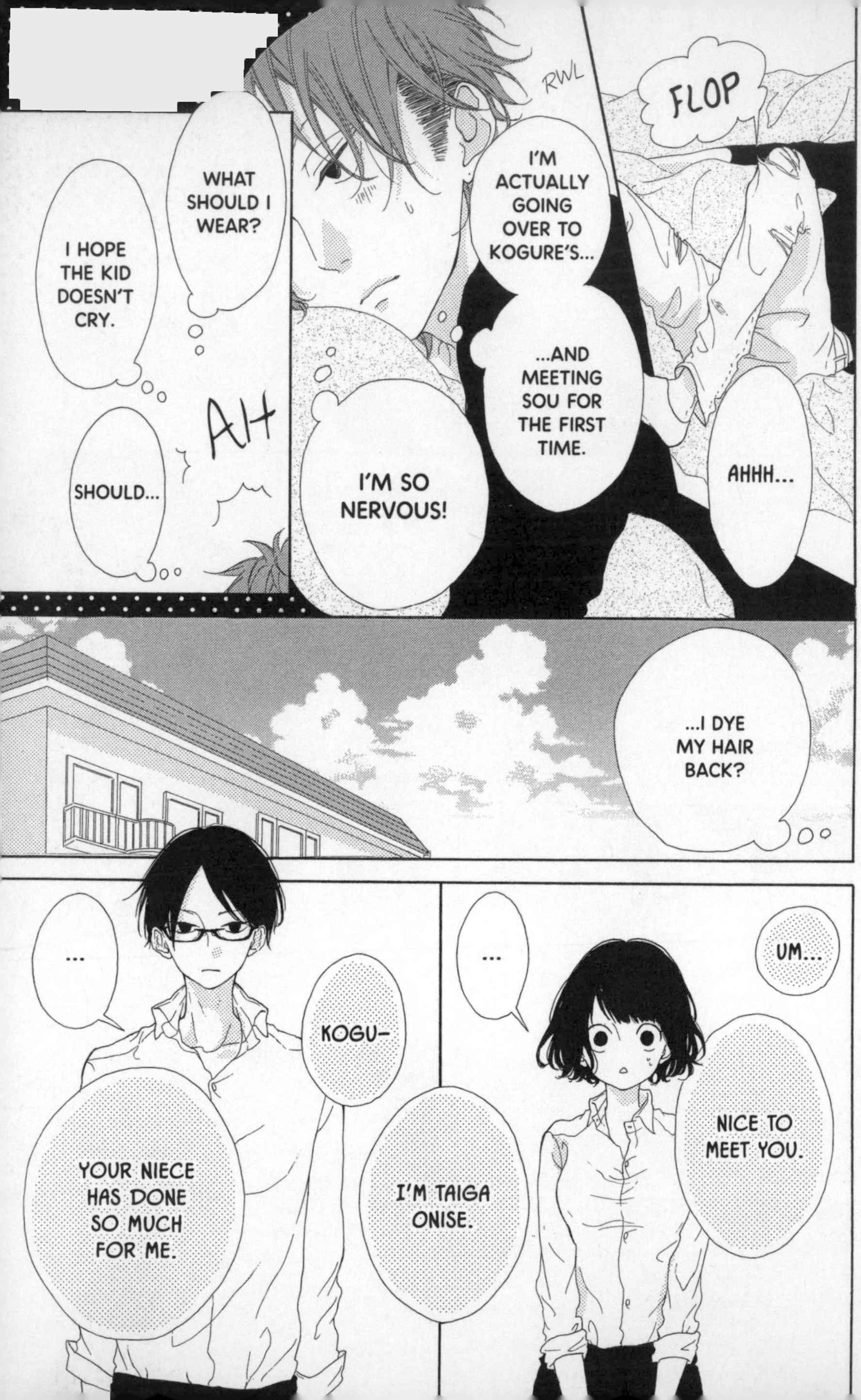
FLOP
AHHH...
RWL
I'M ACTUALLY GOING OVER TO KOGURE'S...
...AND MEETING SOU FOR THE FIRST TIME.
I'M SO NERVOUS!
WHAT SHOULD I WEAR?
I HOPE THE KID DOESN'T CRY.
AH
SHOULD...
...I DYE MY HAIR BACK?
UM...
...
NICE TO MEET YOU.
I'M TAIGA ONISE.
KOGU-
...
YOUR NIECE HAS DONE SO MUCH FOR ME.

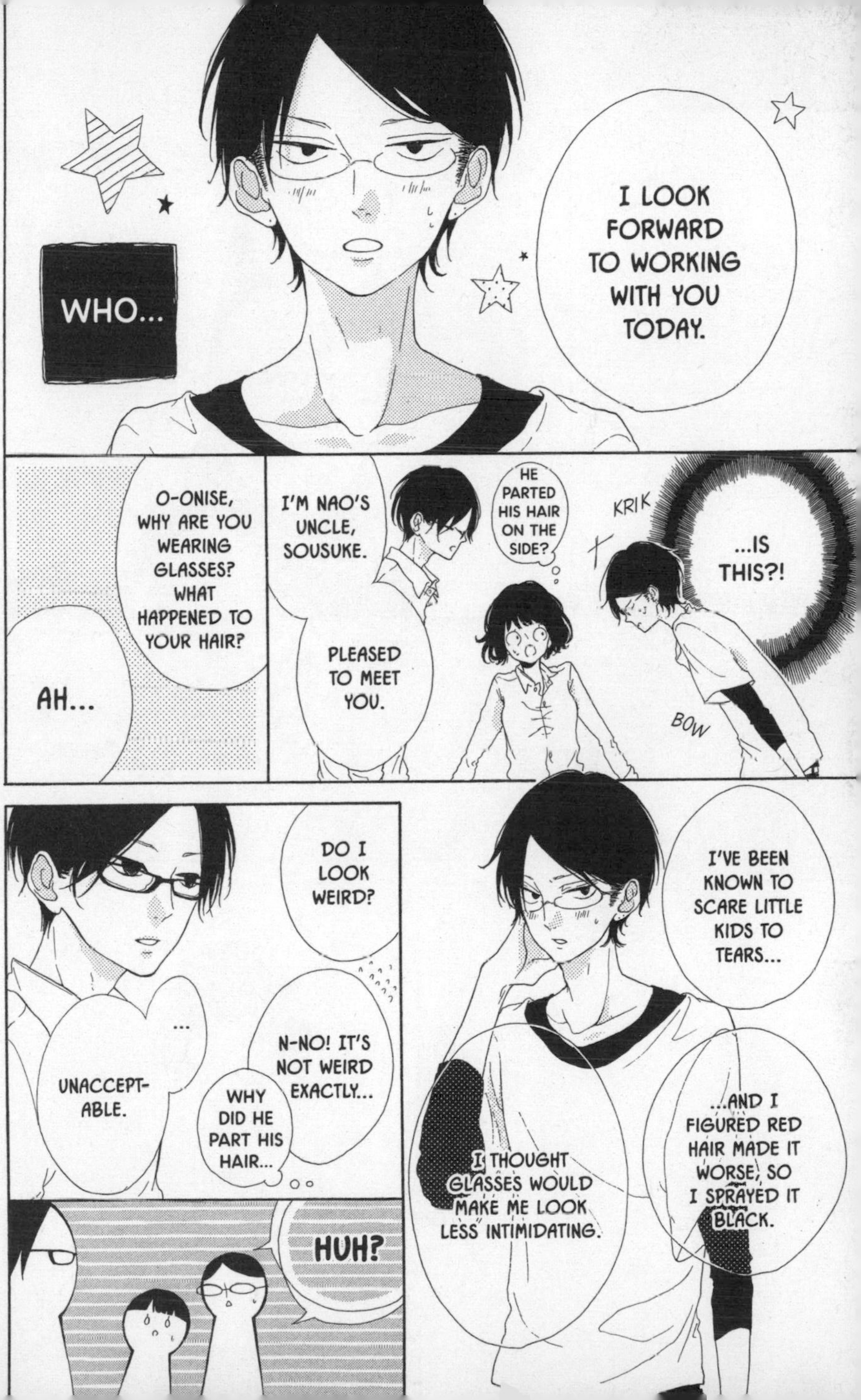
I LOOK FORWARD TO WORKING WITH YOU TODAY.
WHO...
...IS THIS?!
KRIK
HE PARTED HIS HAIR ON THE SIDE?
BOW
I'M NAO'S UNCLE, SOUSUKE.
PLEASED TO MEET YOU.
O-ONISE, WHY ARE YOU WEARING GLASSES? WHAT HAPPENED TO YOUR HAIR?
AH...
I'VE BEEN KNOWN TO SCARE LITTLE KIDS TO TEARS...
I THOUGHT GLASSES WOULD MAKE ME LOOK LESS INTIMIDATING.
...AND I FIGURED RED HAIR MADE IT WORSE, SO I SPRAYED IT BLACK.
DO I LOOK WEIRD?
N-NO! IT'S NOT WEIRD EXACTLY...
...
UNACCEPT-ABLE.
WHY DID HE PART HIS HAIR...
HUH?

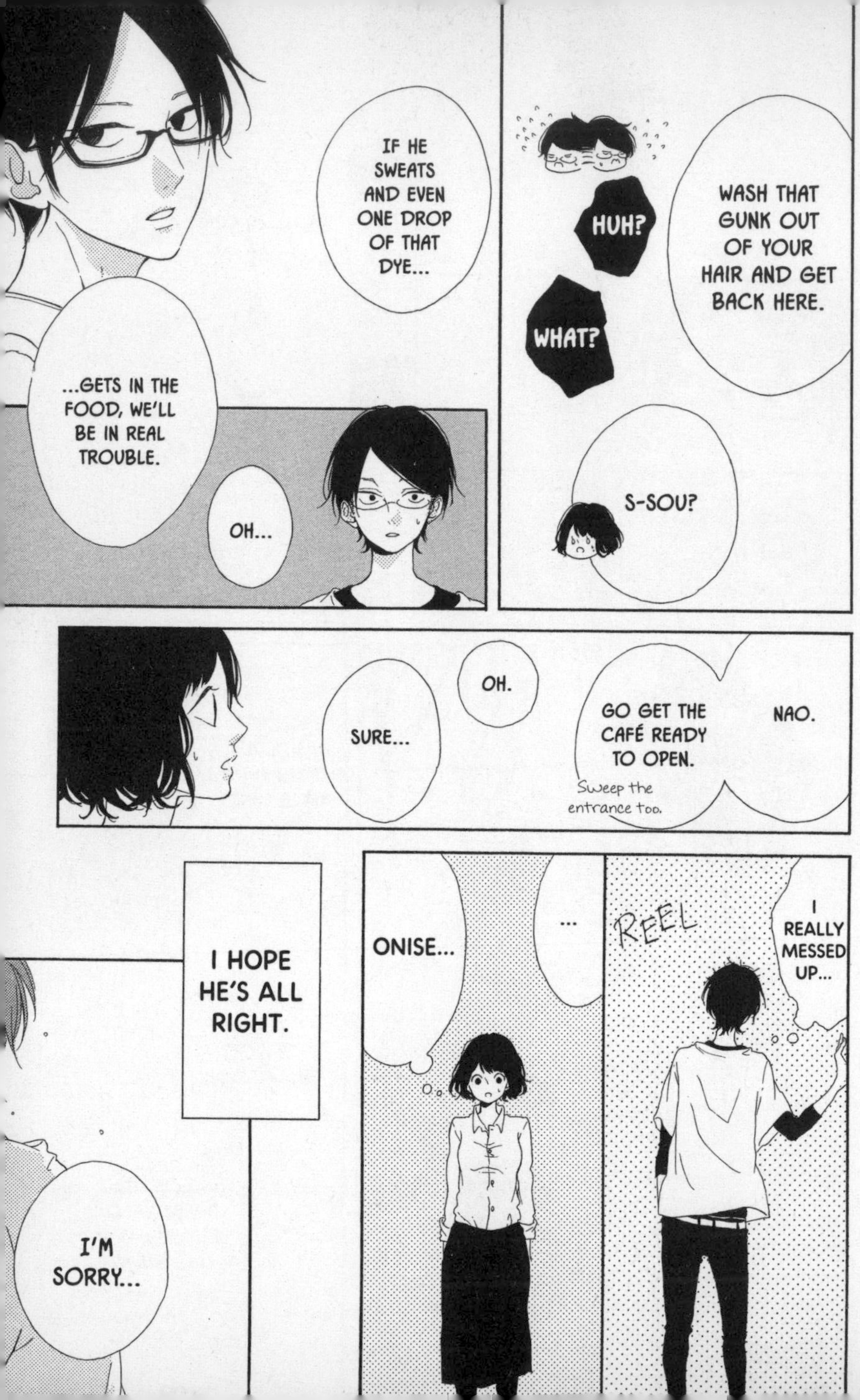
WASH THAT GUNK OUT OF YOUR HAIR AND GET BACK HERE.
HUH?
WHAT?
S-SOU?
IF HE SWEATS AND EVEN ONE DROP OF THAT DYE...
...GETS IN THE FOOD, WE'LL BE IN REAL TROUBLE.
OH...
NAO.
GO GET THE CAFÉ READY TO OPEN.
Sweep the entrance too.
OH.
SURE...
I REALLY MESSED UP...
REEL
...
ONISE...
I HOPE HE'S ALL RIGHT.
I'M SORRY...

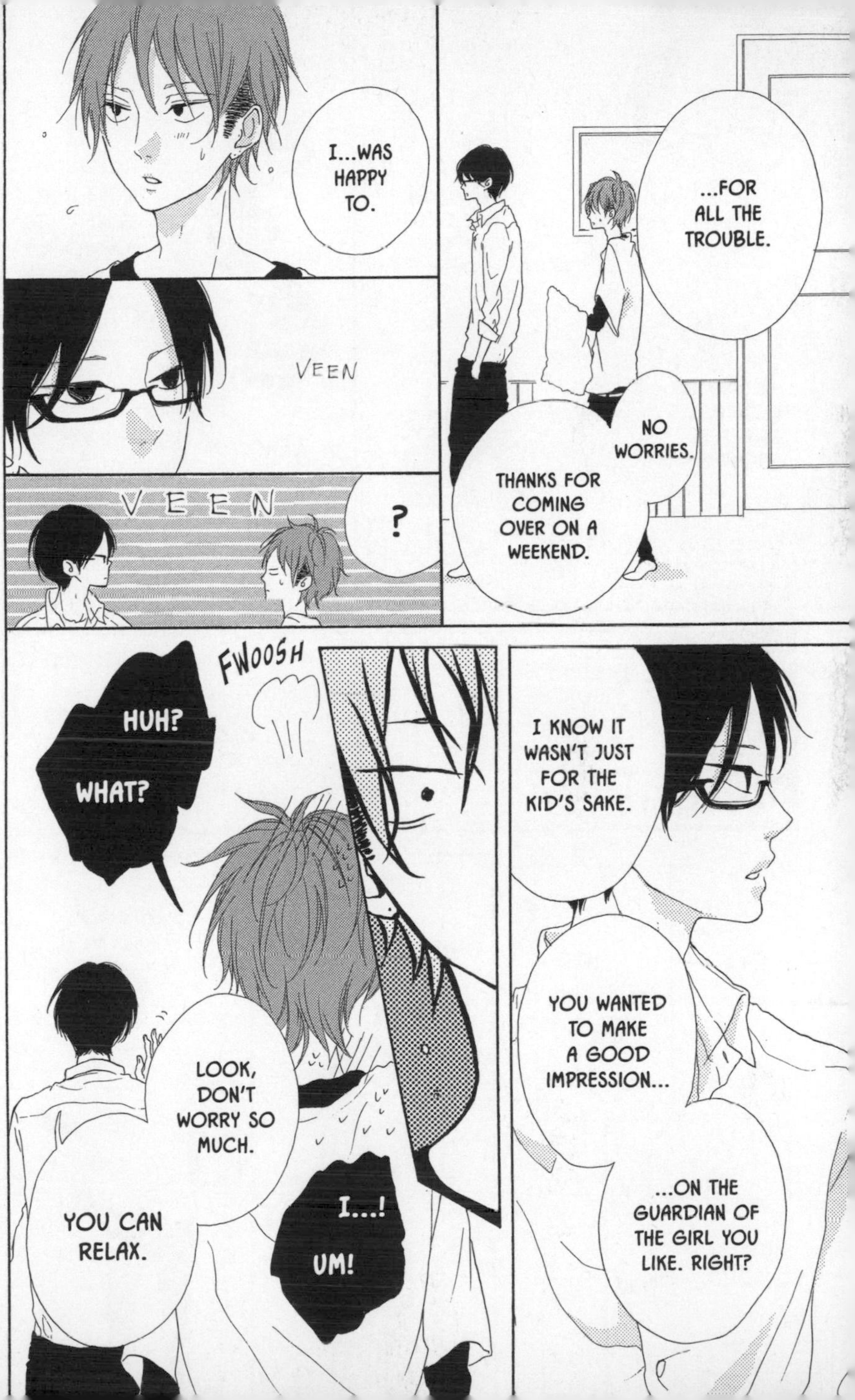
...FOR ALL THE TROUBLE.
NO WORRIES.
THANKS FOR COMING OVER ON A WEEKEND.
I...WAS HAPPY TO.
VEEN
V E E N
?
I KNOW IT WASN'T JUST FOR THE KID'S SAKE.
YOU WANTED TO MAKE A GOOD IMPRESSION...
...ON THE GUARDIAN OF THE GIRL YOU LIKE. RIGHT?
FWOOSH
HUH?
WHAT?
LOOK, DON'T WORRY SO MUCH.
I...!
UM!
YOU CAN RELAX.

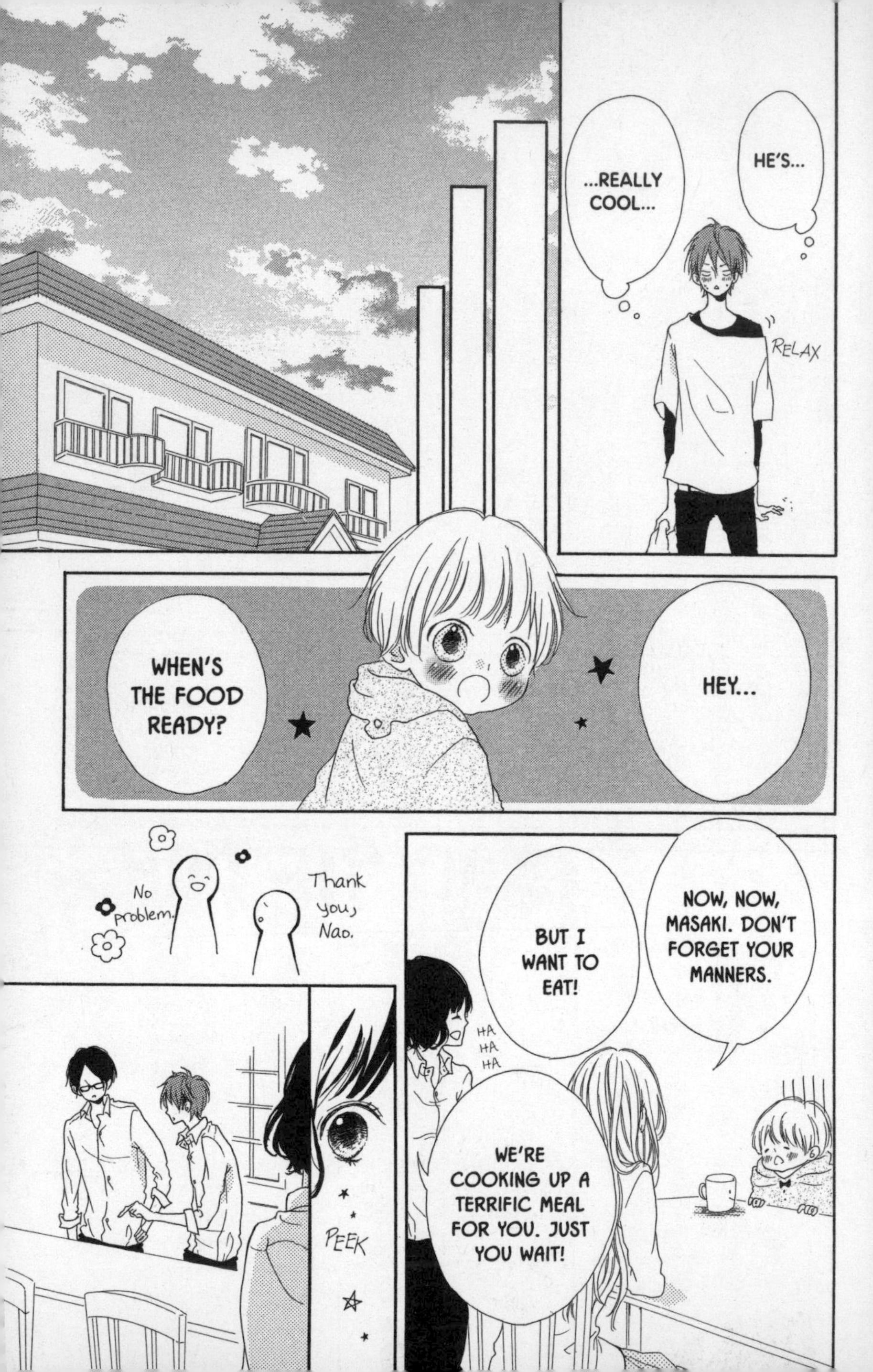
HE'S...
...REALLY COOL...
RELAX
HEY...
WHEN'S THE FOOD READY?
NOW, NOW, MASAKI. DON'T FORGET YOUR MANNERS.
BUT I WANT TO EAT!
HA HA HA
WE'RE COOKING UP A TERRIFIC MEAL FOR YOU. JUST YOU WAIT!
Thank you, Nao.
No problem.
PEEK

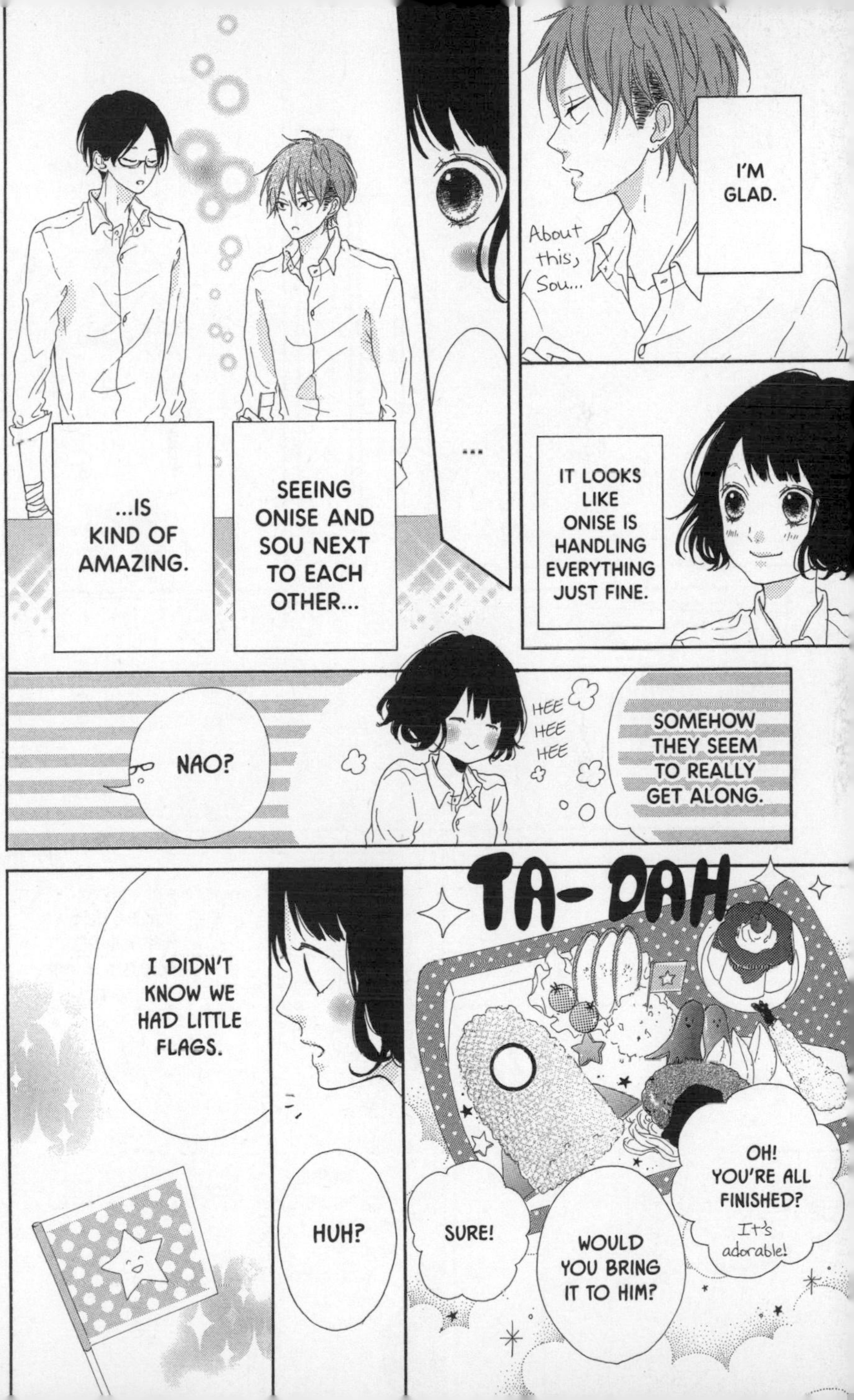
I'M GLAD.
About this, Sou...
IT LOOKS LIKE ONISE IS HANDLING EVERYTHING JUST FINE.
...
SEEING ONISE AND SOU NEXT TO EACH OTHER...
...IS KIND OF AMAZING.
SOMEHOW THEY SEEM TO REALLY GET ALONG.
HEE HEE HEE
NAO?
TA-DAH
OH! YOU'RE ALL FINISHED?
It's adorable!
WOULD YOU BRING IT TO HIM?
SURE!
HUH?
I DIDN'T KNOW WE HAD LITTLE FLAGS.

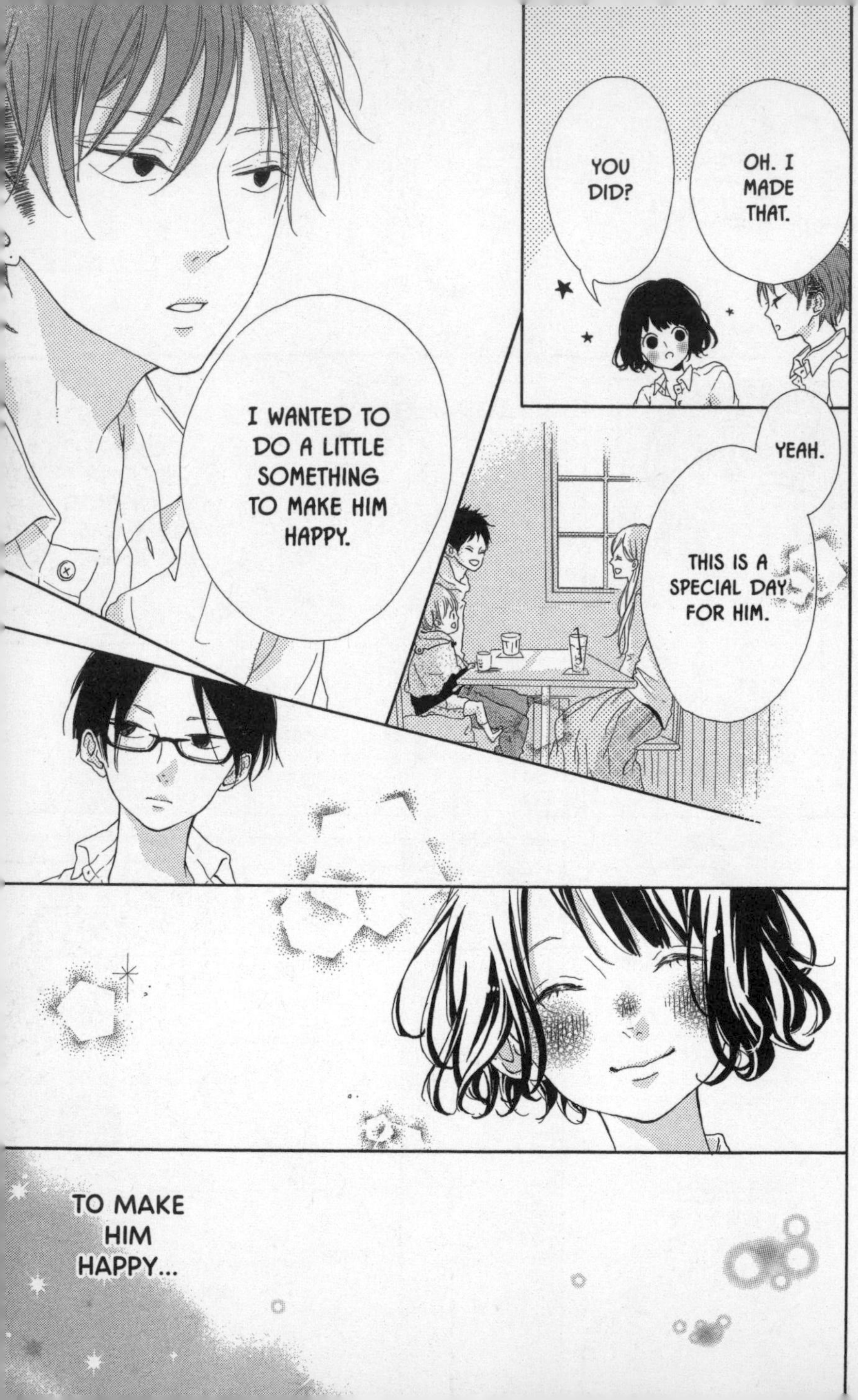
OH. I MADE THAT.
YOU DID?
YEAH.
THIS IS A SPECIAL DAY FOR HIM.
I WANTED TO DO A LITTLE SOMETHING TO MAKE HIM HAPPY.
TO MAKE HIM HAPPY...

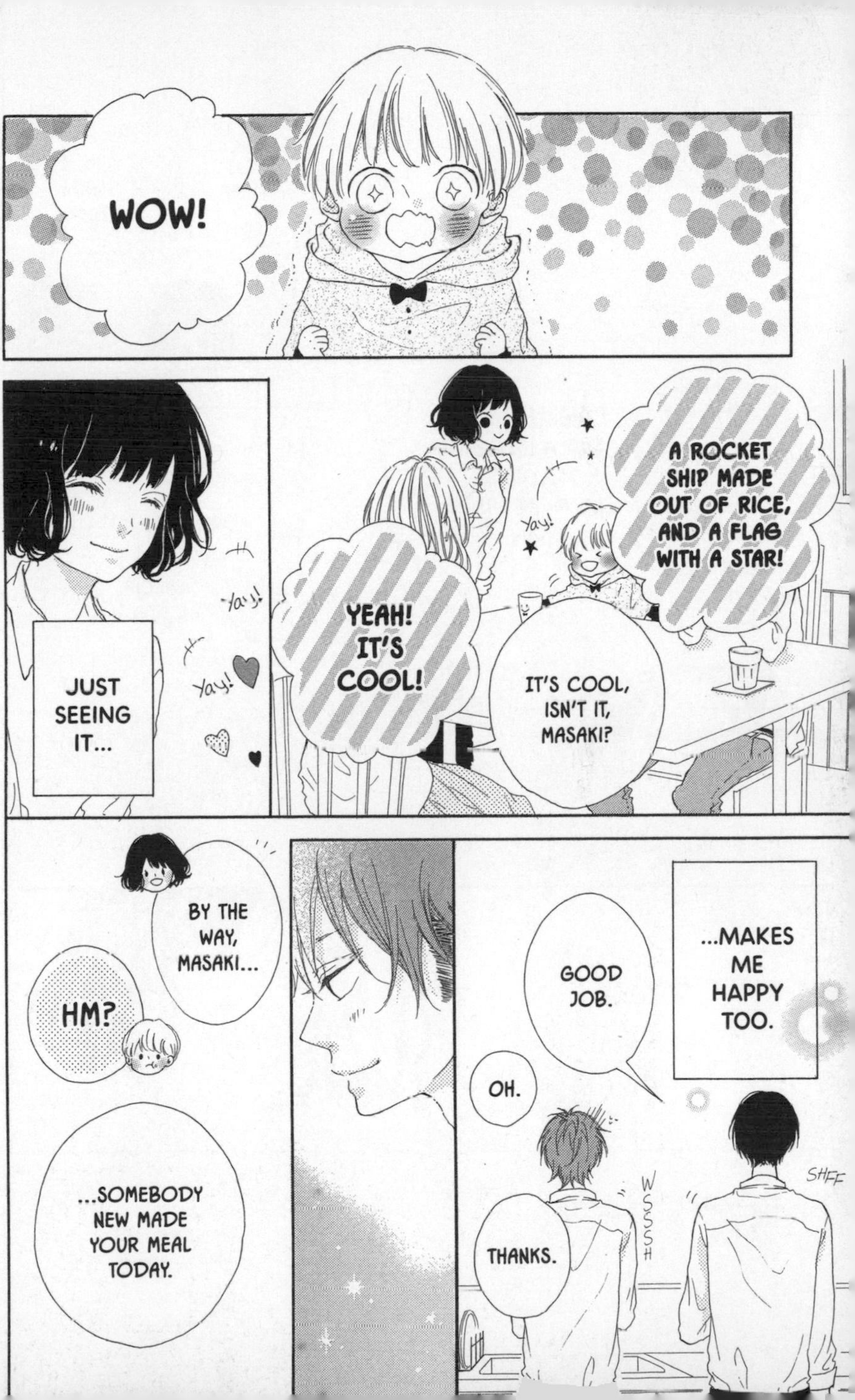
WOW!
A ROCKET SHIP MADE OUT OF RICE, AND A FLAG WITH A STAR!
Yay!
IT'S COOL, ISN'T IT, MASAKI?
YEAH! IT'S COOL!
Yay!
Yay!
JUST SEEING IT...
...MAKES ME HAPPY TOO.
GOOD JOB.
OH.
SHFF
WSSSH
THANKS.
BY THE WAY, MASAKI...
HM?
...SOMEBODY NEW MADE YOUR MEAL TODAY.

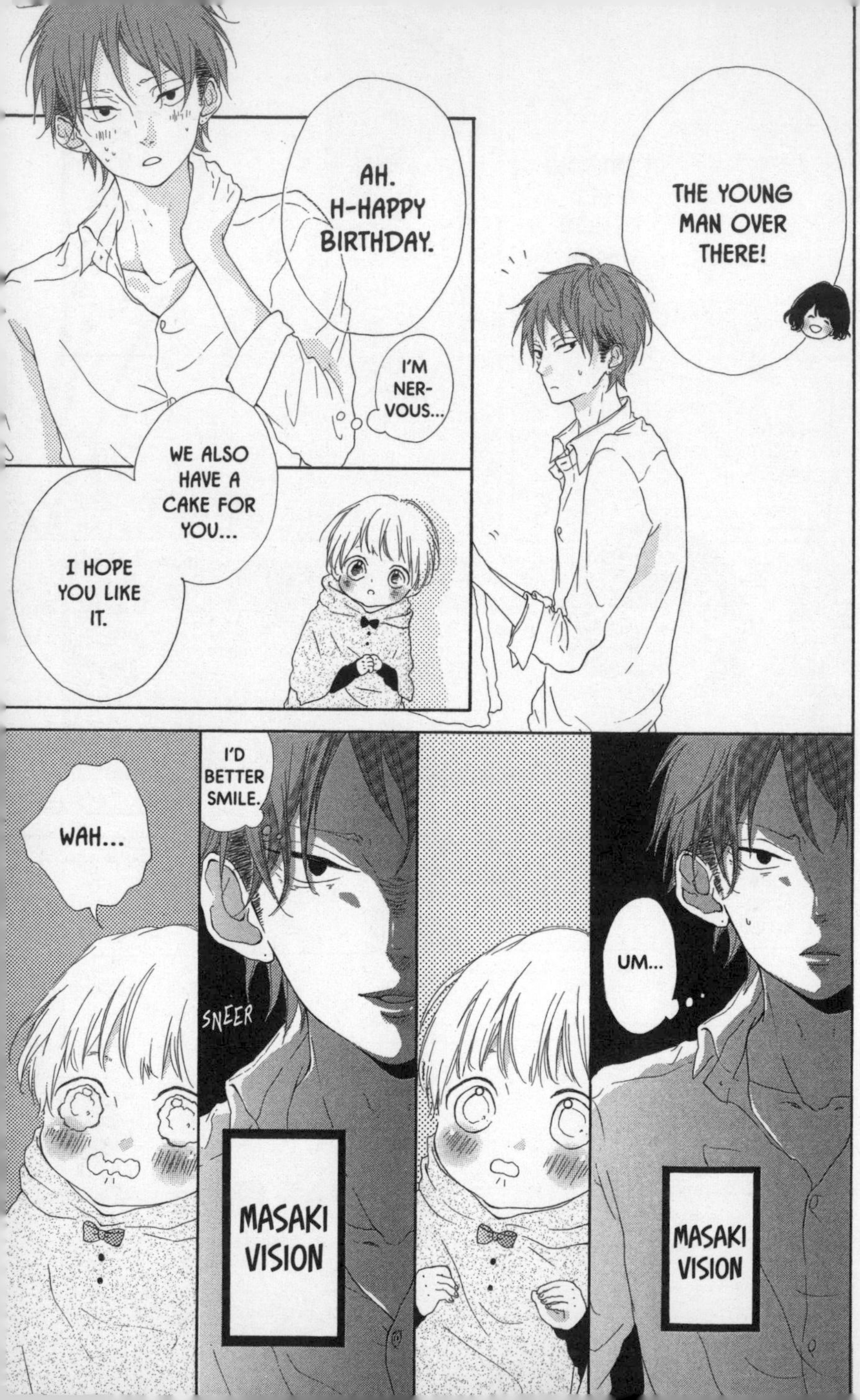
THE YOUNG MAN OVER THERE!
AH. H-HAPPY BIRTHDAY.
I'M NER-VOUS...
WE ALSO HAVE A CAKE FOR YOU...
I HOPE YOU LIKE IT.
UM...
MASAKI VISION
I'D BETTER SMILE.
SNEER
MASAKI VISION
WAH...

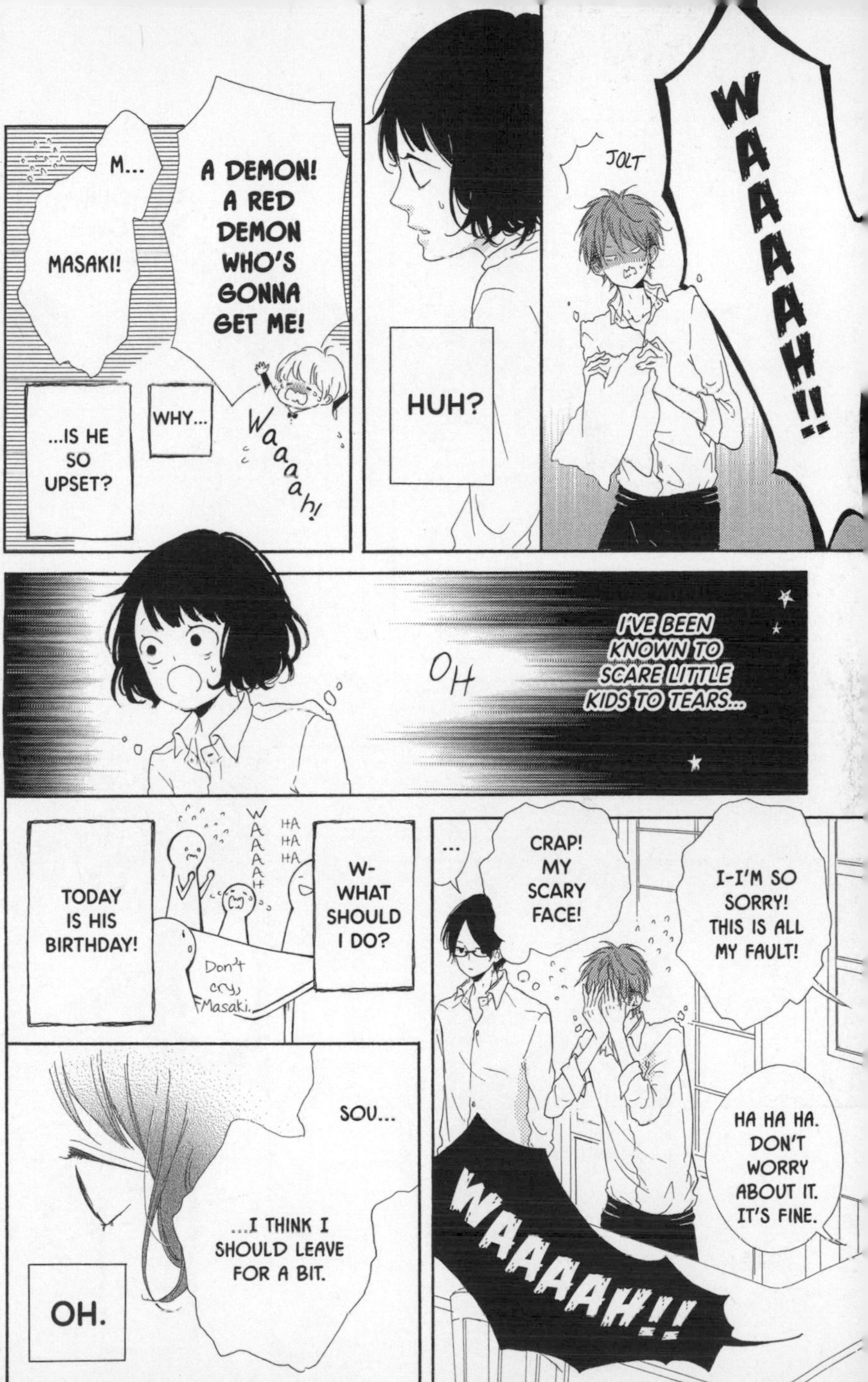
WAAAAH!!
JOLT
HUH?
A DEMON! A RED DEMON WHO'S GONNA GET ME!
M... MASAKI!
WHY...
...IS HE SO UPSET?
Waaaah!
I'VE BEEN KNOWN TO SCARE LITTLE KIDS TO TEARS...
OH
I-I'M SO SORRY! THIS IS ALL MY FAULT!
CRAP! MY SCARY FACE!
...
HA HA HA. DON'T WORRY ABOUT IT. IT'S FINE.
WAAAAAH!!
W- WHAT SHOULD I DO?
WAAAAAH
HA HA HA
TODAY IS HIS BIRTHDAY!
Don't cry, Masaki.
SOU...
...I THINK I SHOULD LEAVE FOR A BIT.
OH.

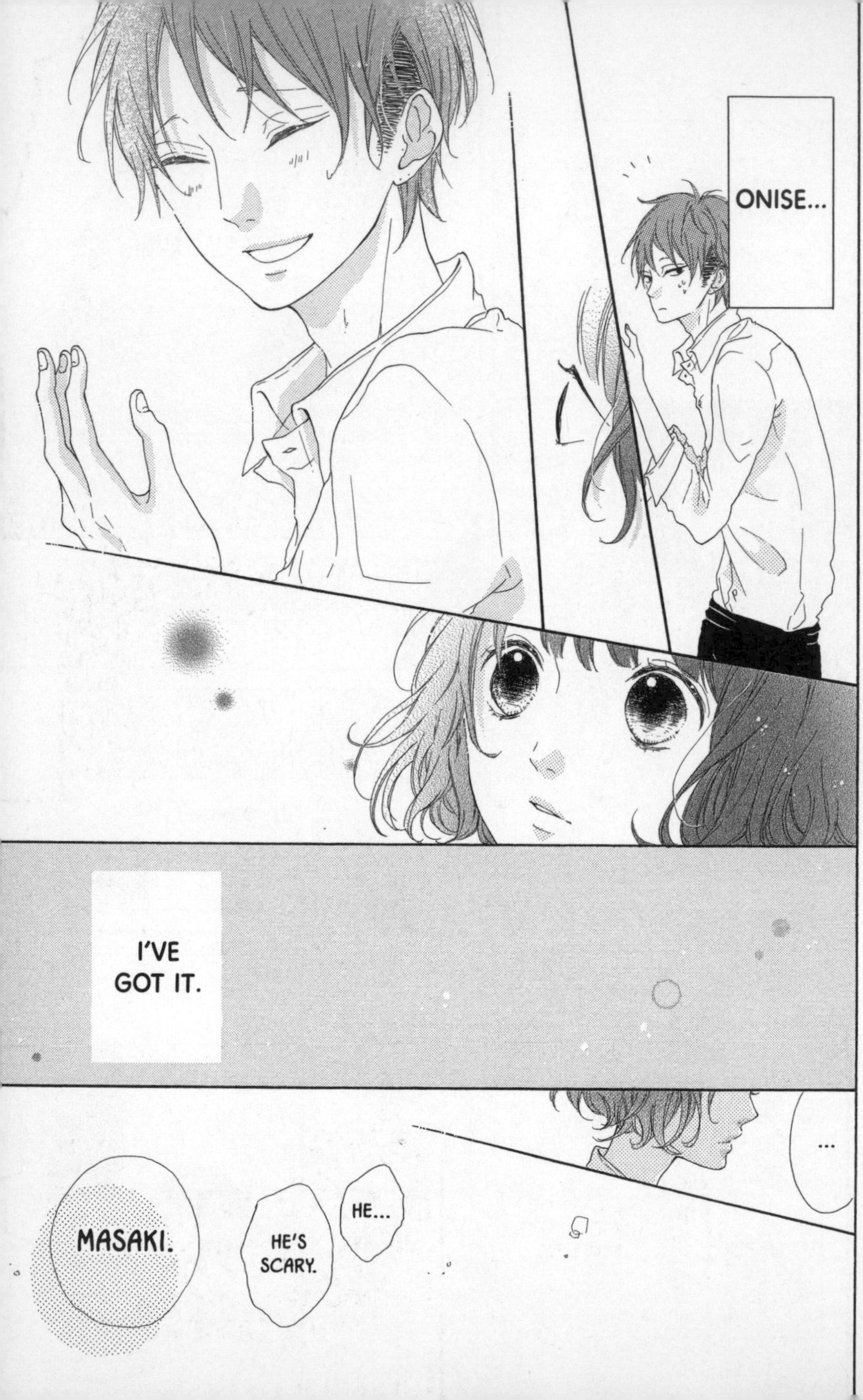
ONISE...
I'VE GOT IT.
...
HE...
HE'S SCARY.
MASAKI.

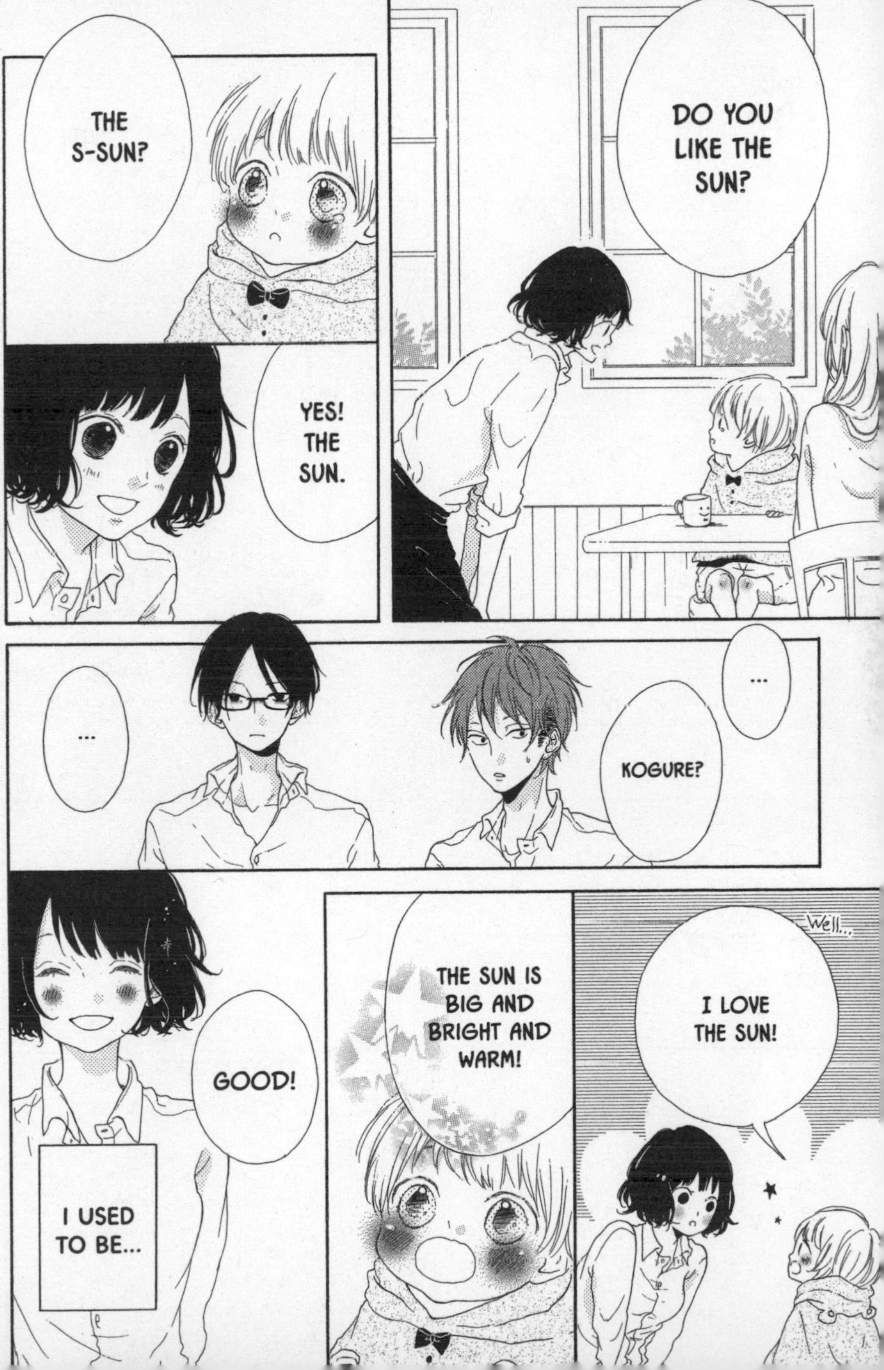
DO YOU LIKE THE SUN?
THE S-SUN?
YES! THE SUN.
...
KOGURE?
...
Well...
I LOVE THE SUN!
THE SUN IS BIG AND BRIGHT AND WARM!
GOOD!
I USED TO BE...

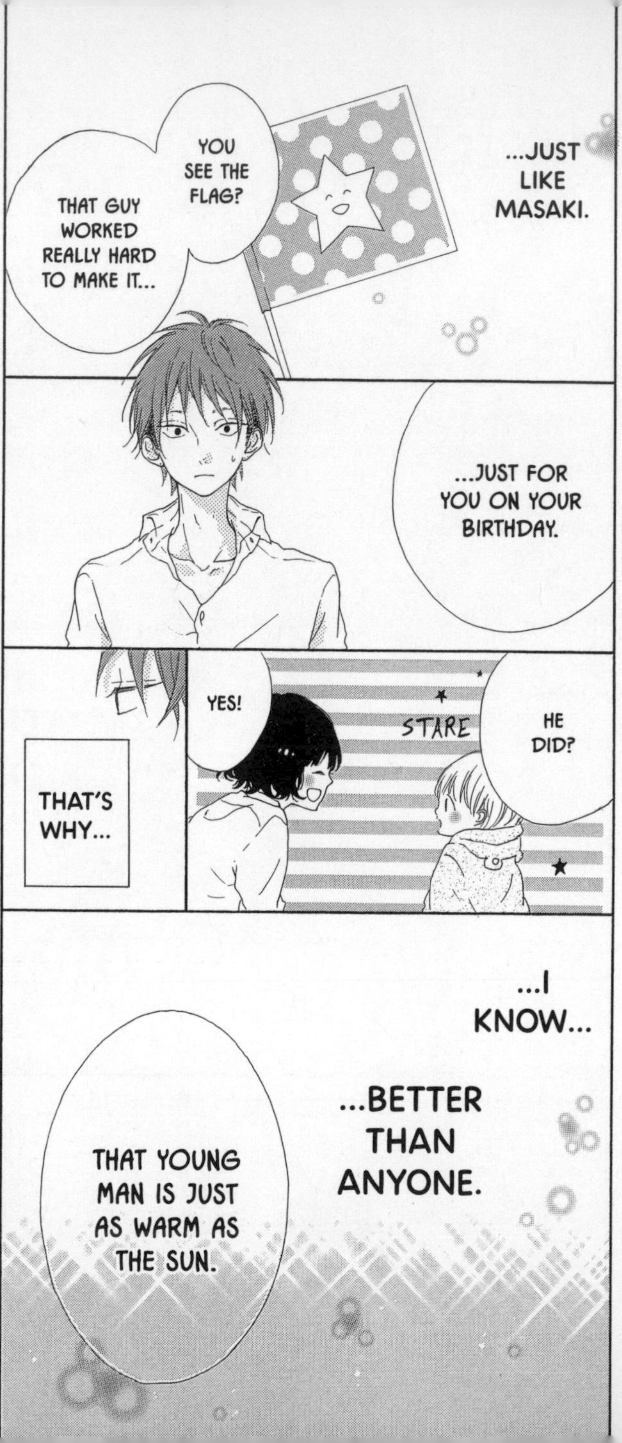
...JUST LIKE MASAKI.
YOU SEE THE FLAG?
THAT GUY WORKED REALLY HARD TO MAKE IT...
...JUST FOR YOU ON YOUR BIRTHDAY.
HE DID?
STARE
YES!
THAT'S WHY...
...I KNOW...
...BETTER THAN ANYONE.
THAT YOUNG MAN IS JUST AS WARM AS THE SUN.
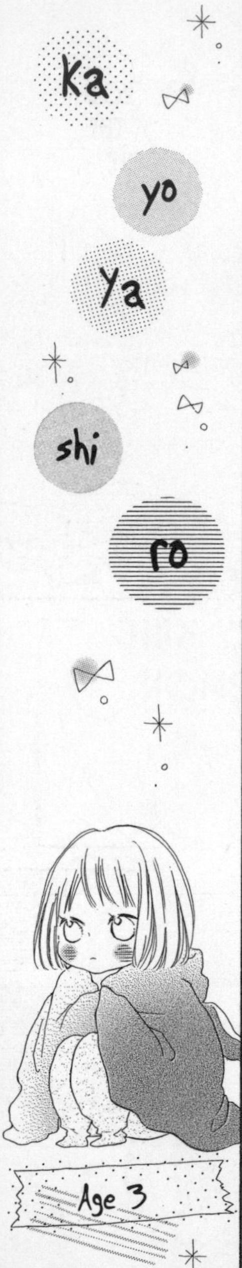
Ka
yo
Ya
shi
ro
Age 3

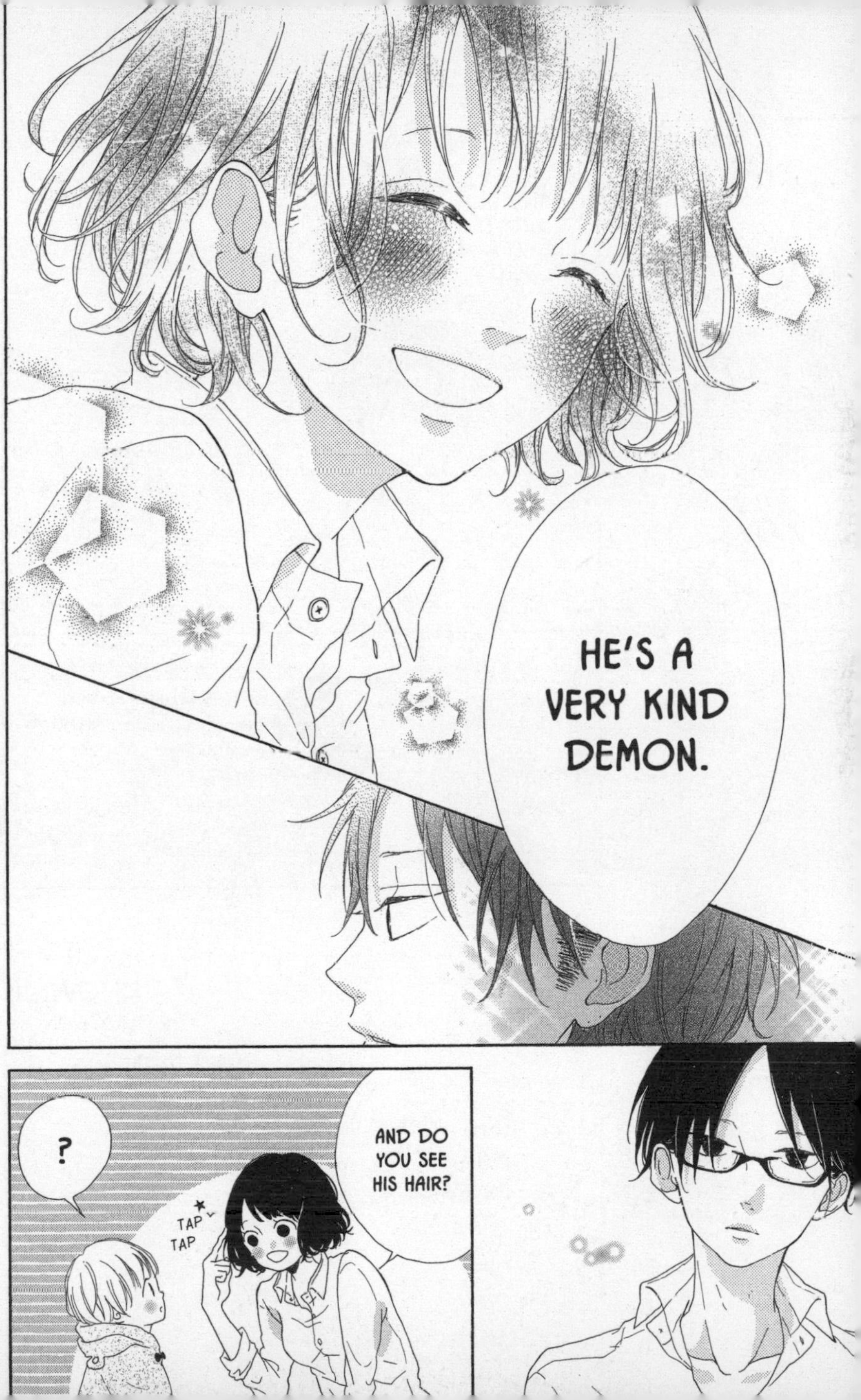
HE'S A VERY KIND DEMON.
AND DO YOU SEE HIS HAIR?
?
TAP TAP

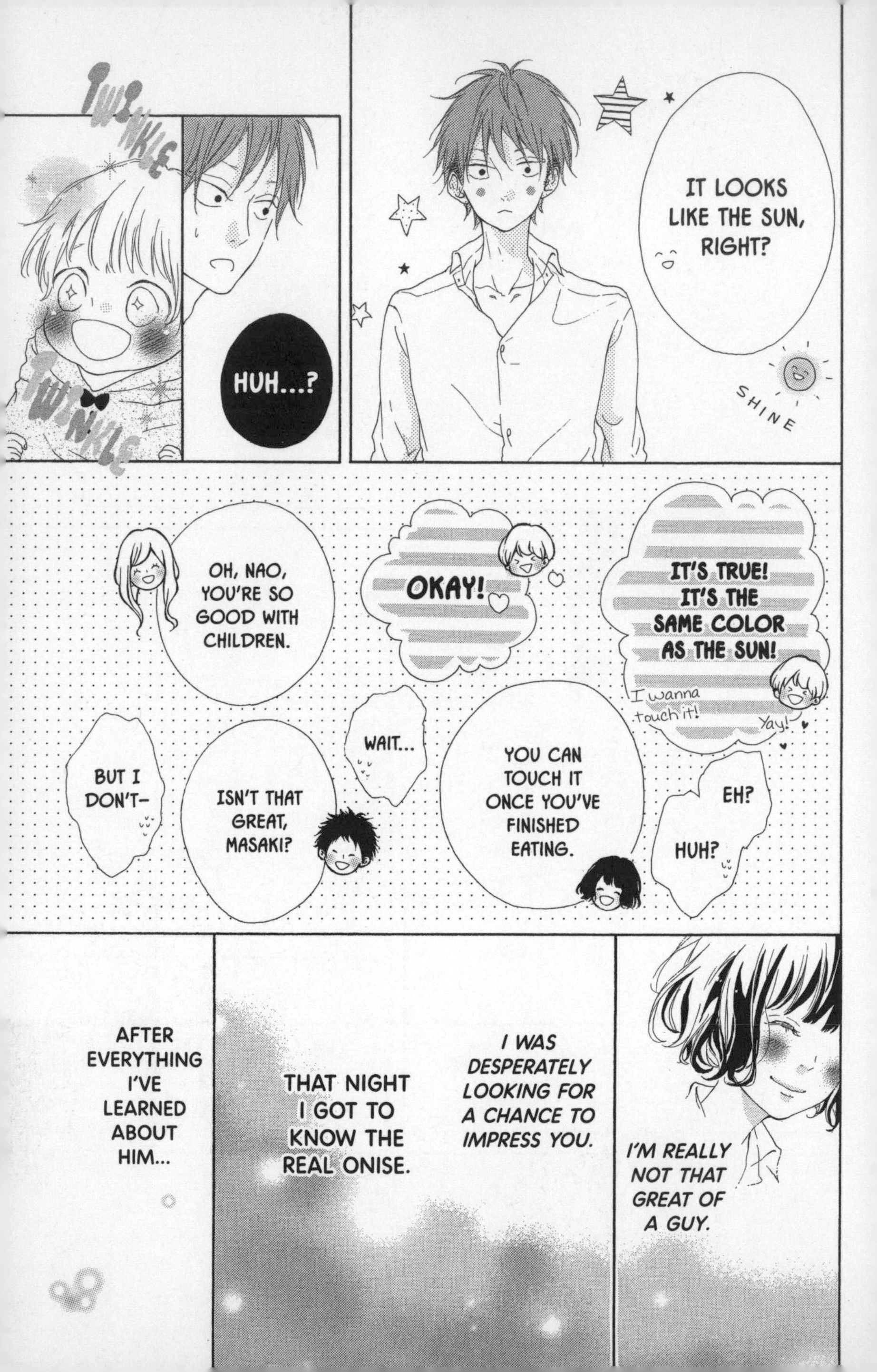
IT LOOKS LIKE THE SUN, RIGHT?
SHINE
TWINKLE
HUH...?
TWINKLE
IT'S TRUE! IT'S THE SAME COLOR AS THE SUN!
I wanna touch it!
Yay!
OKAY!
OH, NAO, YOU'RE SO GOOD WITH CHILDREN.
EH?
HUH?
YOU CAN TOUCH IT ONCE YOU'VE FINISHED EATING.
WAIT...
ISN'T THAT GREAT, MASAKI?
BUT I DON'T-
I'M REALLY NOT THAT GREAT OF A GUY.
I WAS DESPERATELY LOOKING FOR A CHANCE TO IMPRESS YOU.
THAT NIGHT I GOT TO KNOW THE REAL ONISE.
AFTER EVERYTHING I'VE LEARNED ABOUT HIM...

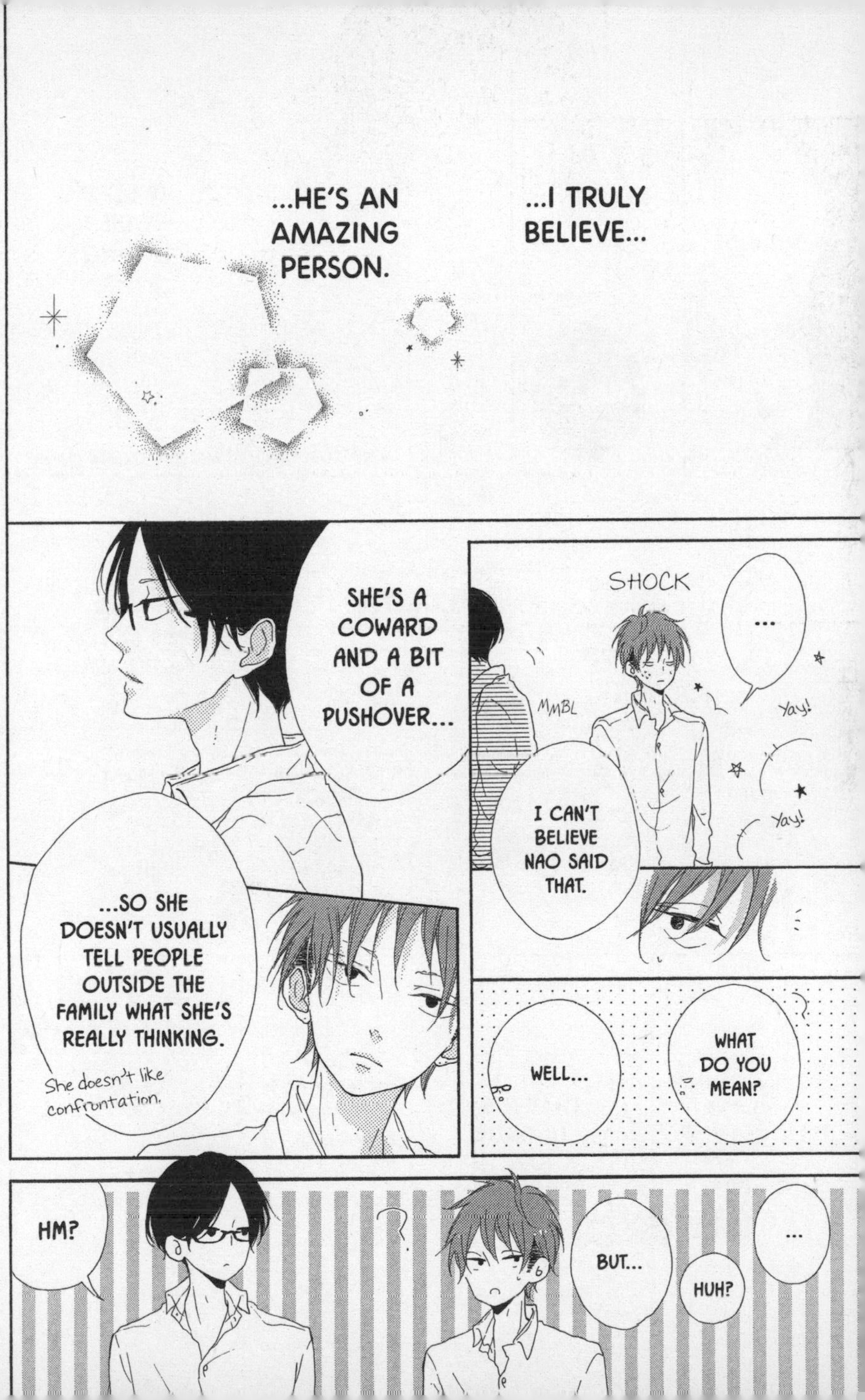
...I TRULY BELIEVE...
...HE'S AN AMAZING PERSON.
...
Yay!
Yay!
SHOCK
MMBL
I CAN'T BELIEVE NAO SAID THAT.
WHAT DO YOU MEAN?
WELL...
SHE'S A COWARD AND A BIT OF A PUSHOVER...
...SO SHE DOESN'T USUALLY TELL PEOPLE OUTSIDE THE FAMILY WHAT SHE'S REALLY THINKING.
She doesn't like confrontation.
...
HUH?
BUT...
HM?

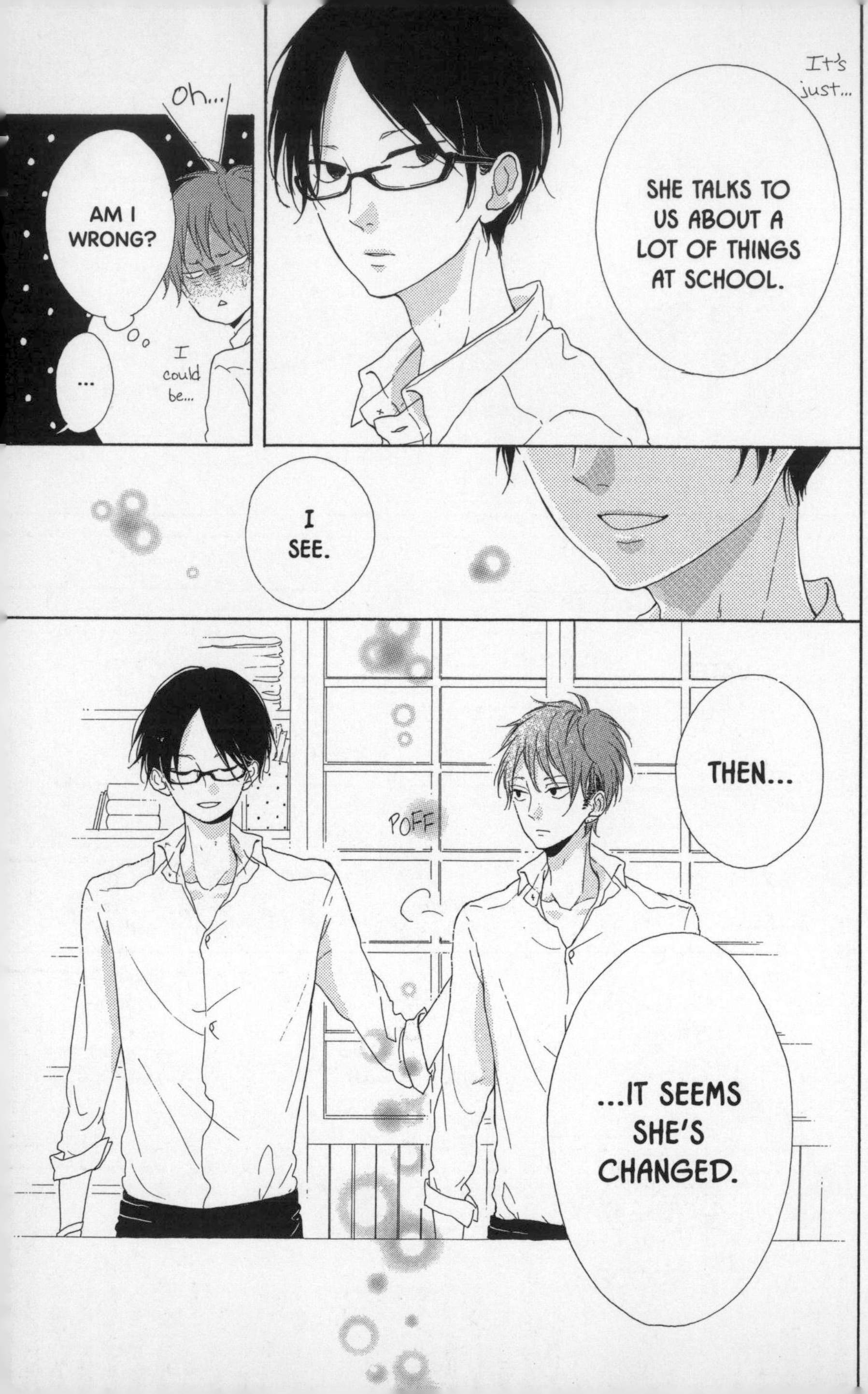

It's just...
SHE TALKS TO US ABOUT A LOT OF THINGS AT SCHOOL.
Oh...
AM I WRONG?
...
I could be...
I SEE.
THEN...
POFF
...IT SEEMS SHE'S CHANGED.

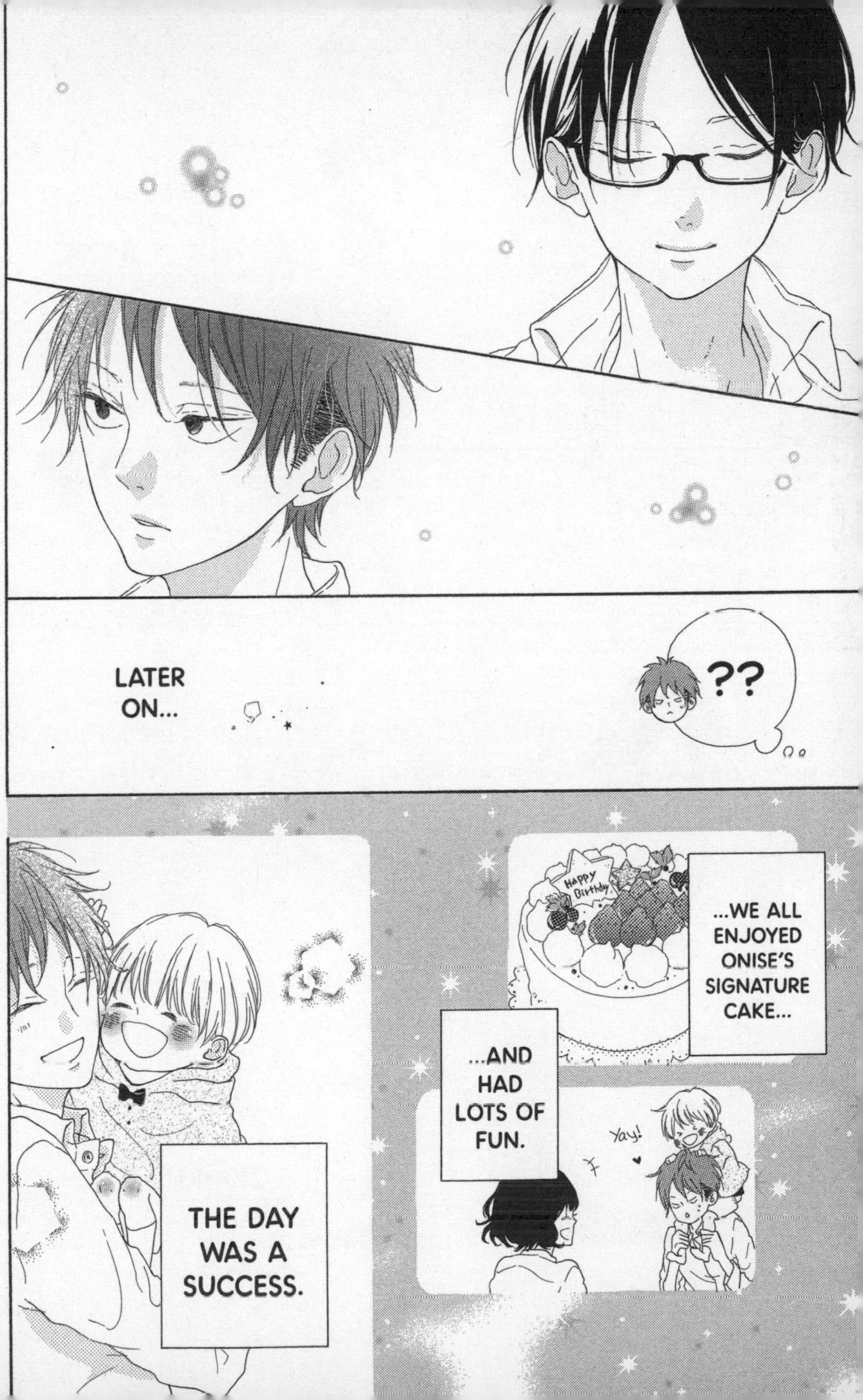
??
LATER ON...
...WE ALL ENJOYED ONISE'S SIGNATURE CAKE...
Happy Birthday
...AND HAD LOTS OF FUN.
Yay!
THE DAY WAS A SUCCESS.

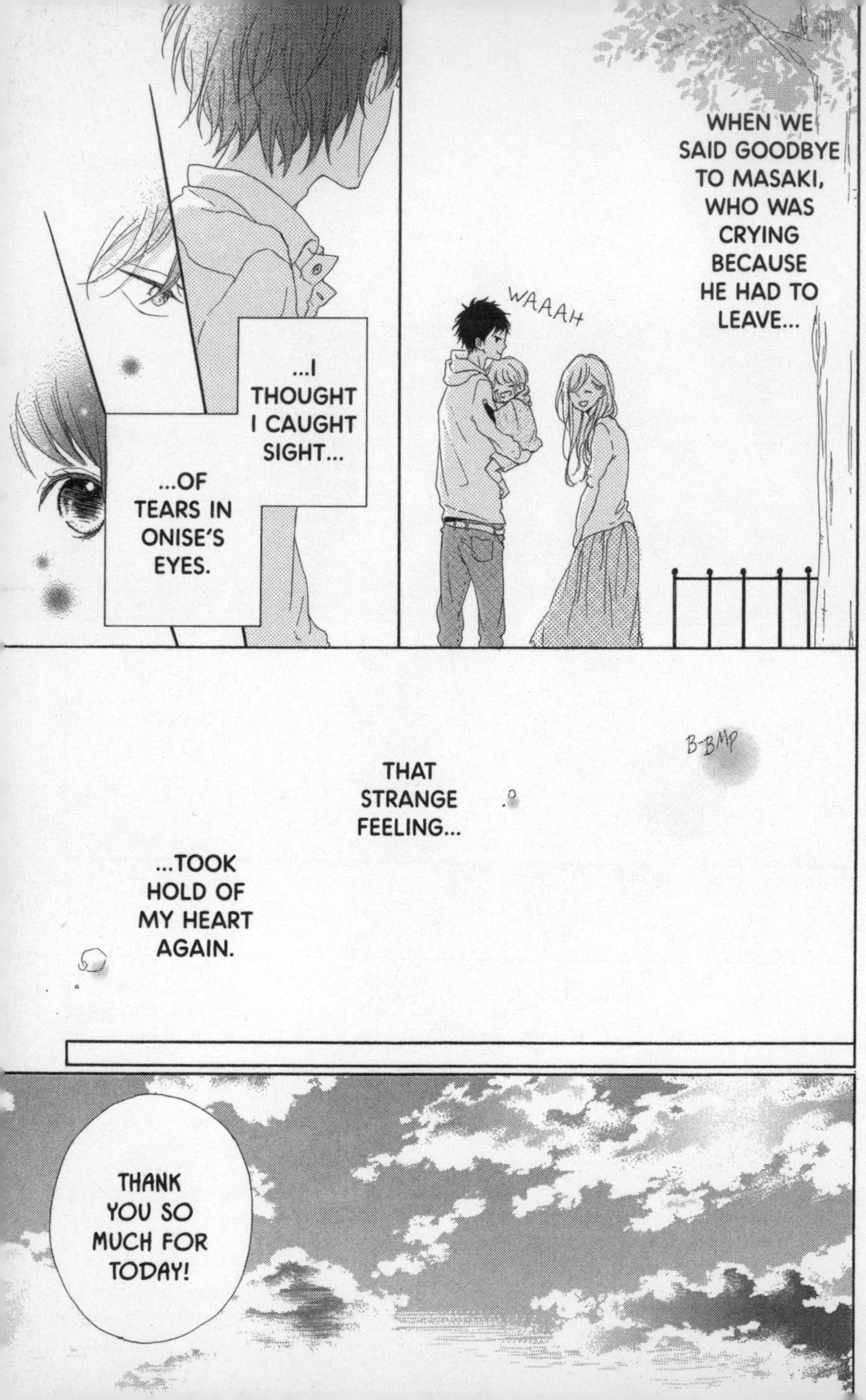
WHEN WE SAID GOODBYE TO MASAKI, WHO WAS CRYING BECAUSE HE HAD TO LEAVE...
WAAAH
...I THOUGHT I CAUGHT SIGHT...
...OF TEARS IN ONISE'S EYES.
B-BMP
THAT STRANGE FEELING...
...TOOK HOLD OF MY HEART AGAIN.
THANK YOU SO MUCH FOR TODAY!

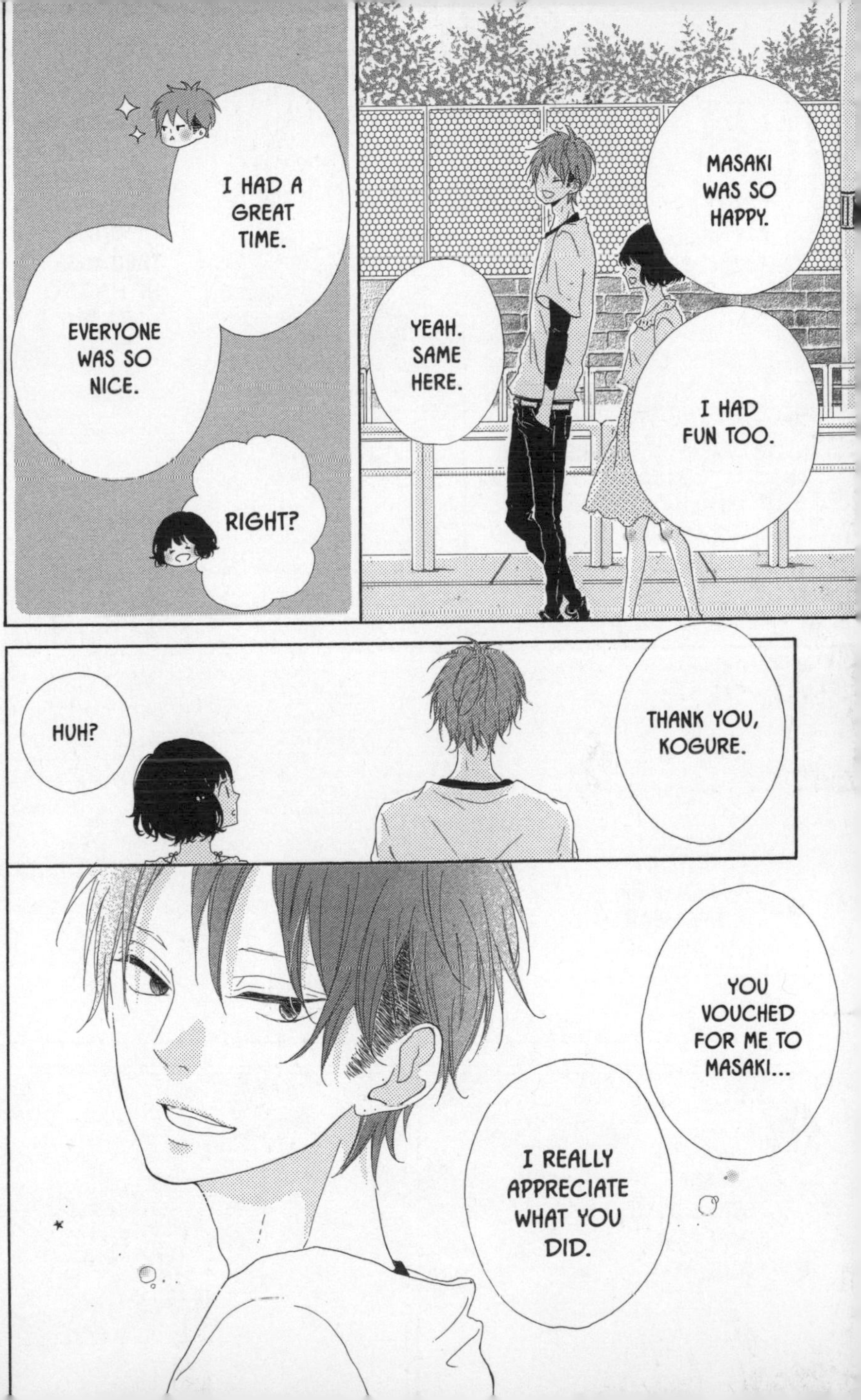
MASAKI WAS SO HAPPY.
YEAH. SAME HERE.
I HAD FUN TOO.
I HAD A GREAT TIME.
EVERYONE WAS SO NICE.
RIGHT?
THANK YOU, KOGURE.
HUH?
YOU VOUCHED FOR ME TO MASAKI...
I REALLY APPRECIATE WHAT YOU DID.

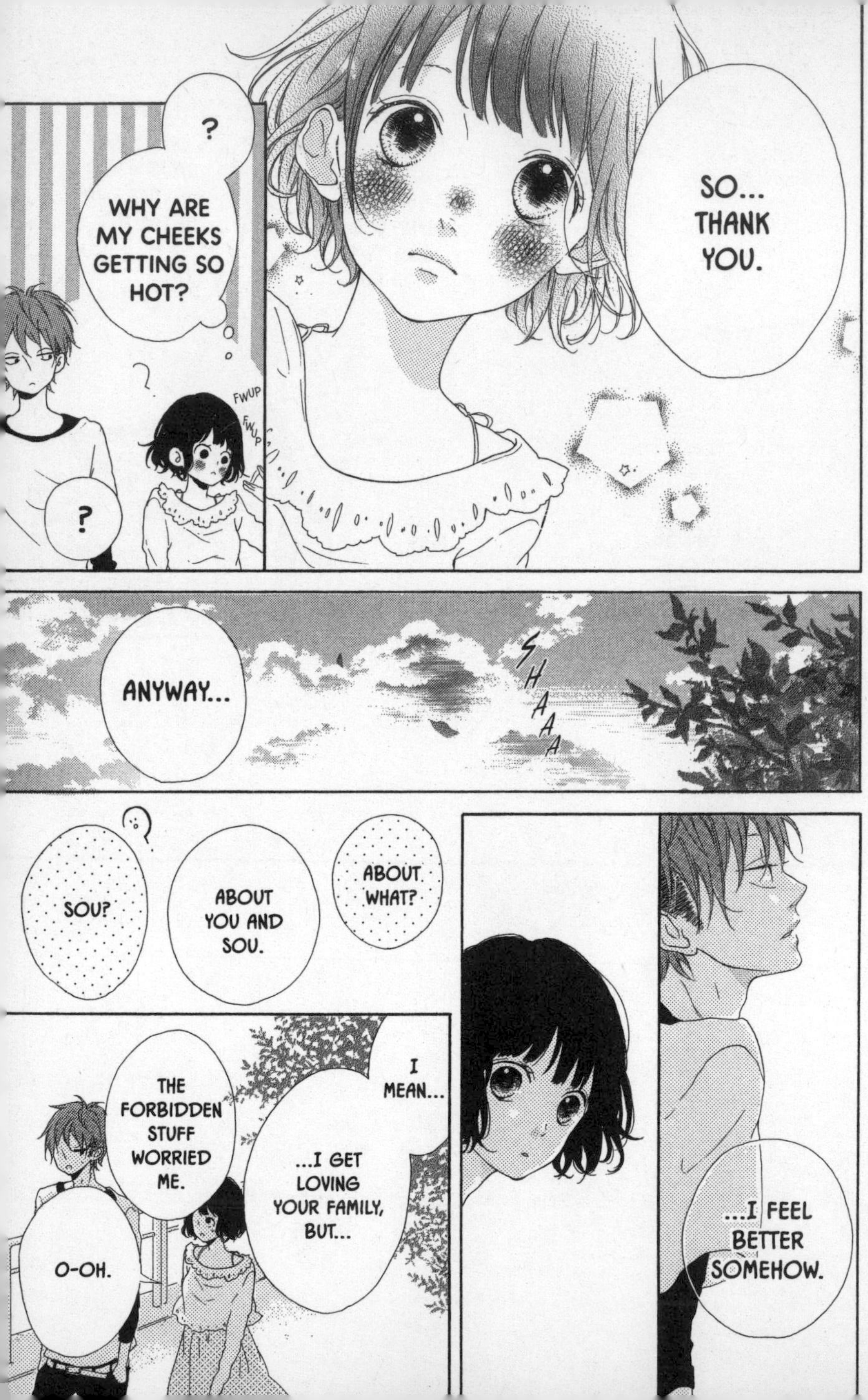
SO... THANK YOU.
?
WHY ARE MY CHEEKS GETTING SO HOT?
FWUP FWUP
?
ANYWAY...
SHAAA
...I FEEL BETTER SOMEHOW.
ABOUT WHAT?
ABOUT YOU AND SOU.
SOU?
I MEAN...
...I GET LOVING YOUR FAMILY, BUT...
THE FORBIDDEN STUFF WORRIED ME.
O-OH.

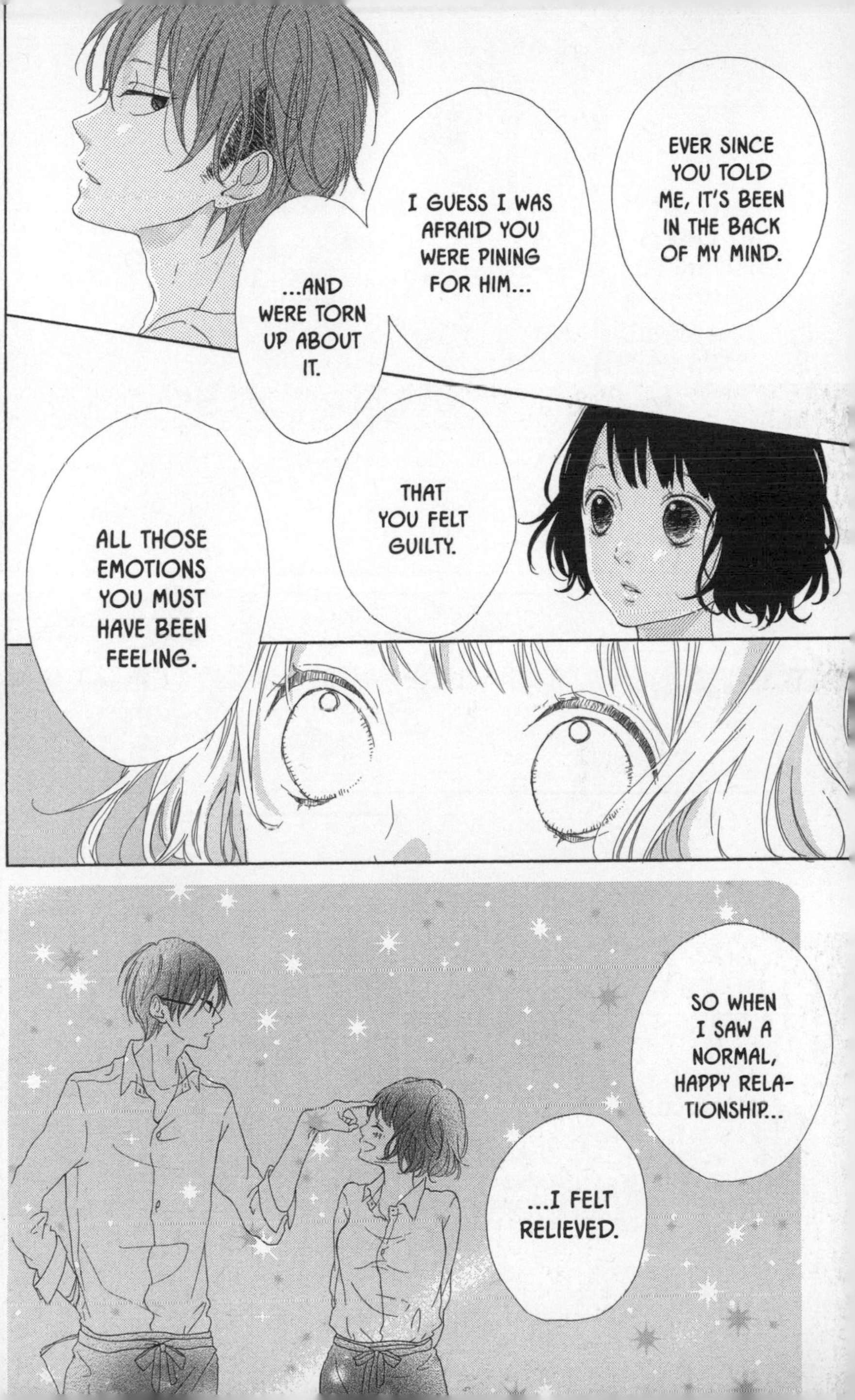
EVER SINCE YOU TOLD ME, IT'S BEEN IN THE BACK OF MY MIND.
I GUESS I WAS AFRAID YOU WERE PINING FOR HIM...
...AND WERE TORN UP ABOUT IT.
THAT YOU FELT GUILTY.
ALL THOSE EMOTIONS YOU MUST HAVE BEEN FEELING.
SO WHEN I SAW A NORMAL, HAPPY RELA-TIONSHIP...
...I FELT RELIEVED.

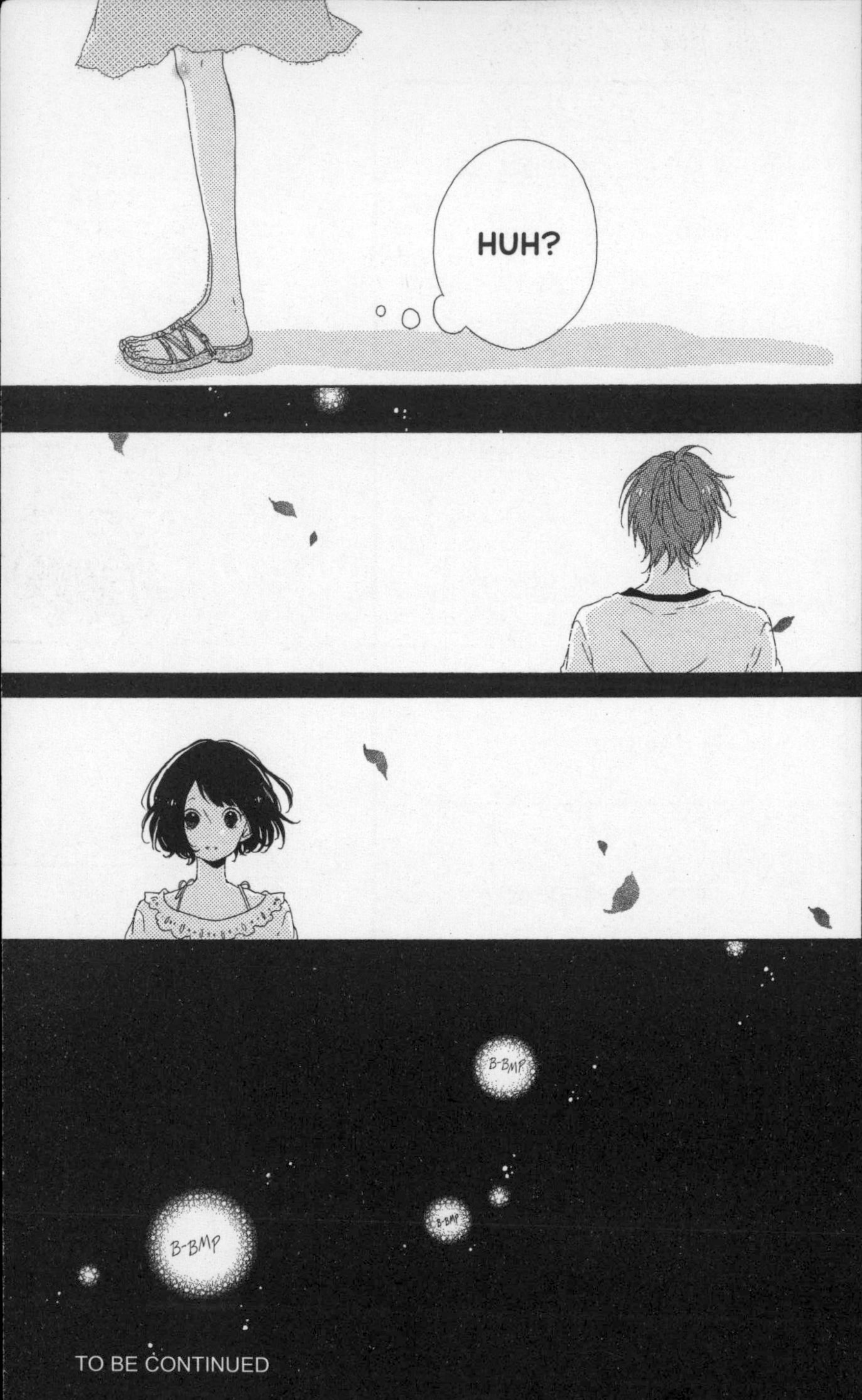
HUH?
B-BMP
B-BMP
B-BMP
TO BE CONTINUED

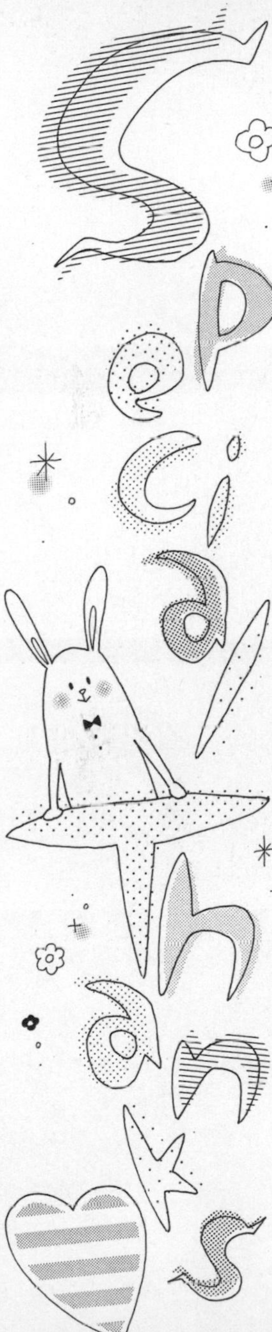
Special Thanks

Thank you for reading all the way to the end! I know it's far from perfect, but I'll keep working diligently to write about Nao and Onise in a way that you enjoy!

So then, I hope you will stick around for volume 2. (･ᴗ･)*｡

See you again!

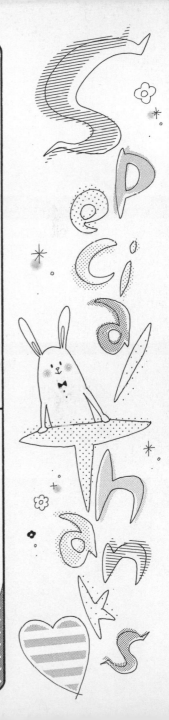

FIND SHOJO BEAT ON SOCIAL MEDIA:

TWITTER: @SHOJOBEAT

FACEBOOK & TUMBLR: OFFICIALSHOJOBEAT

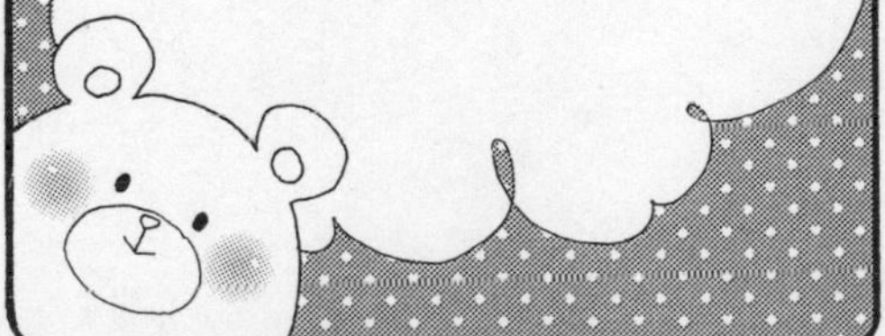

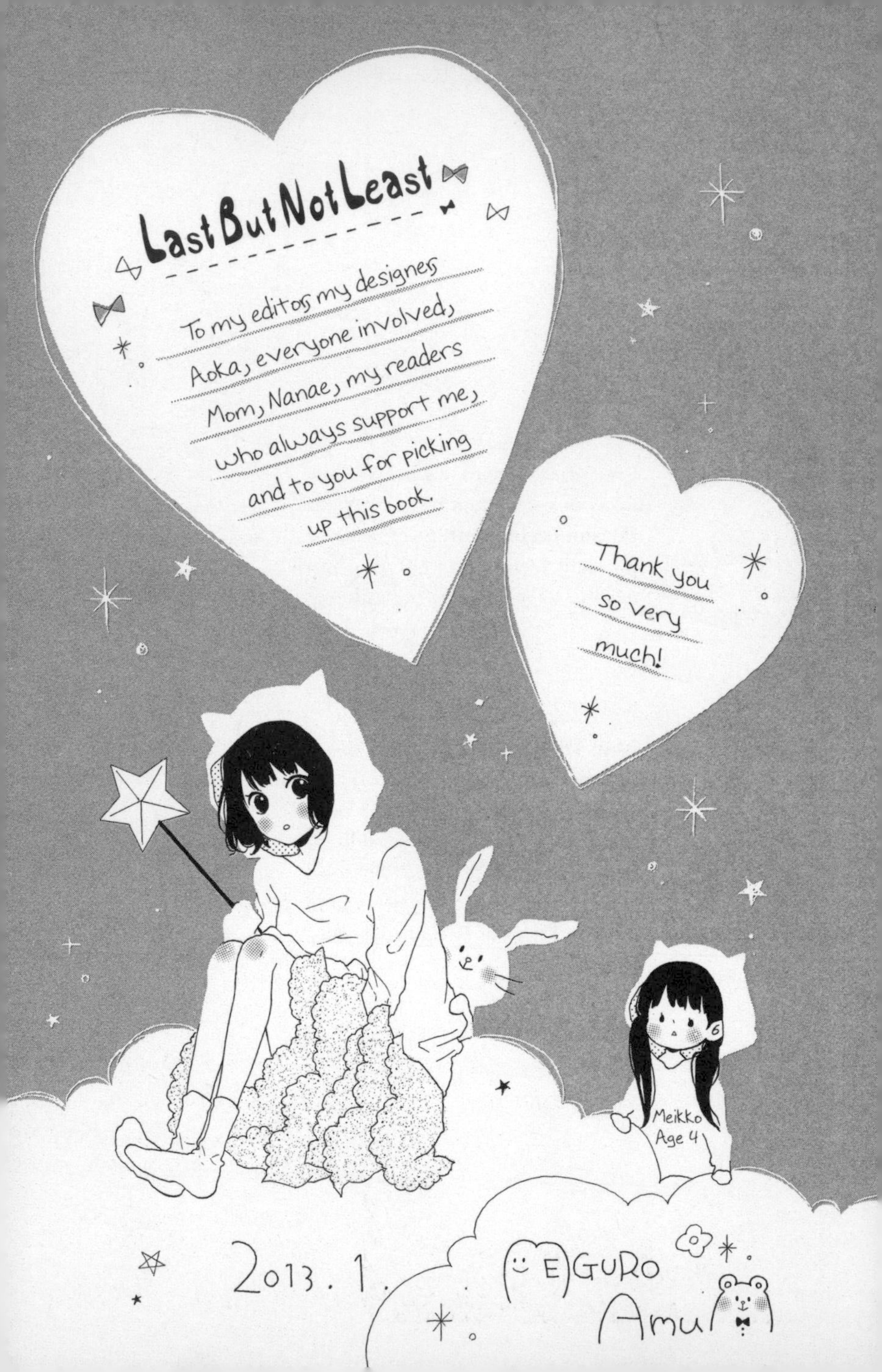
Last But Not Least
To my editors, my designers, Aoka, everyone involved, Mom, Nanae, my readers who always support me, and to you for picking up this book.
Thank you so very much!
Meikko Age 4
2013. 1.
MEGURO Amu

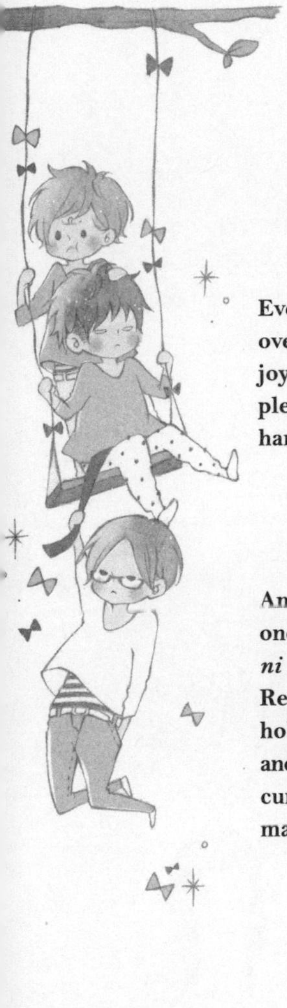

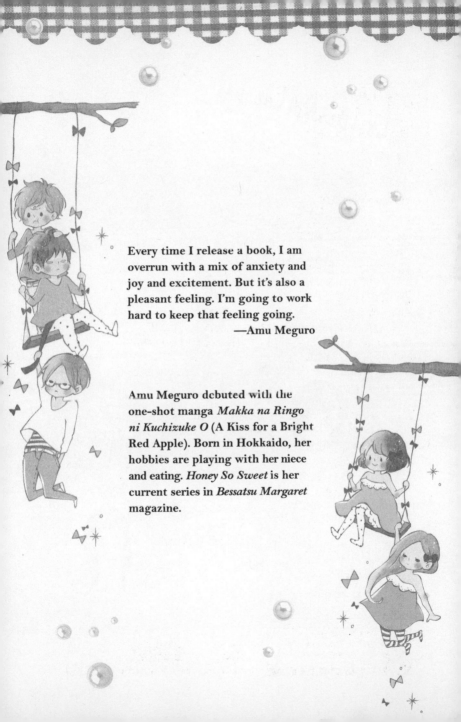

Every time I release a book, I am overrun with a mix of anxiety and joy and excitement. But it's also a pleasant feeling. I'm going to work hard to keep that feeling going.

—Amu Meguro

Amu Meguro debuted with the one-shot manga *Makka na Ringo ni Kuchizuke O* (A Kiss for a Bright Red Apple). Born in Hokkaido, her hobbies are playing with her niece and eating. *Honey So Sweet* is her current series in *Bessatsu Margaret* magazine.

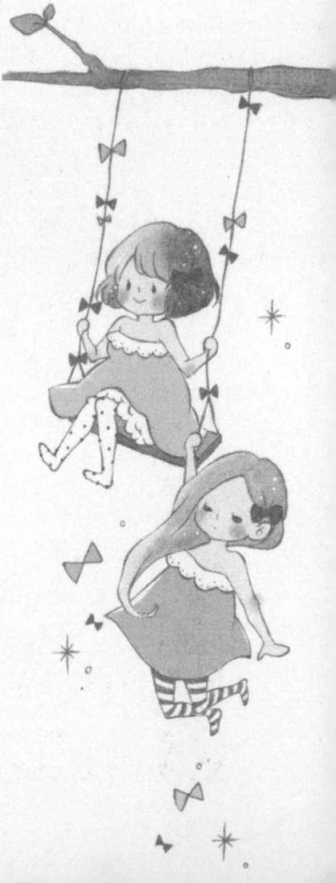

Honey So Sweet

Shojo Beat Edition

Volume 1

STORY AND ART BY
Amu Meguro

Translation/Katherine Schilling
Touch-Up Art & Lettering/Inori Fukuda Trant
Design/Izumi Evers
Editor/Nancy Thistlethwaite

HONEY © 2012 by Amu Meguro
All rights reserved.
First published in Japan in 2012 by SHUEISHA Inc., Tokyo.
English translation rights arranged by SHUEISHA Inc.

Printed in the U.S.A.

Published by VIZ Media, LLC
P.O. Box 77010
San Francisco, CA 94107

10 9 8 7 6 5 4 3 2 1
First printing, January 2016

 www.viz.com

 www.shojobeat.com

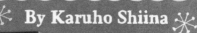

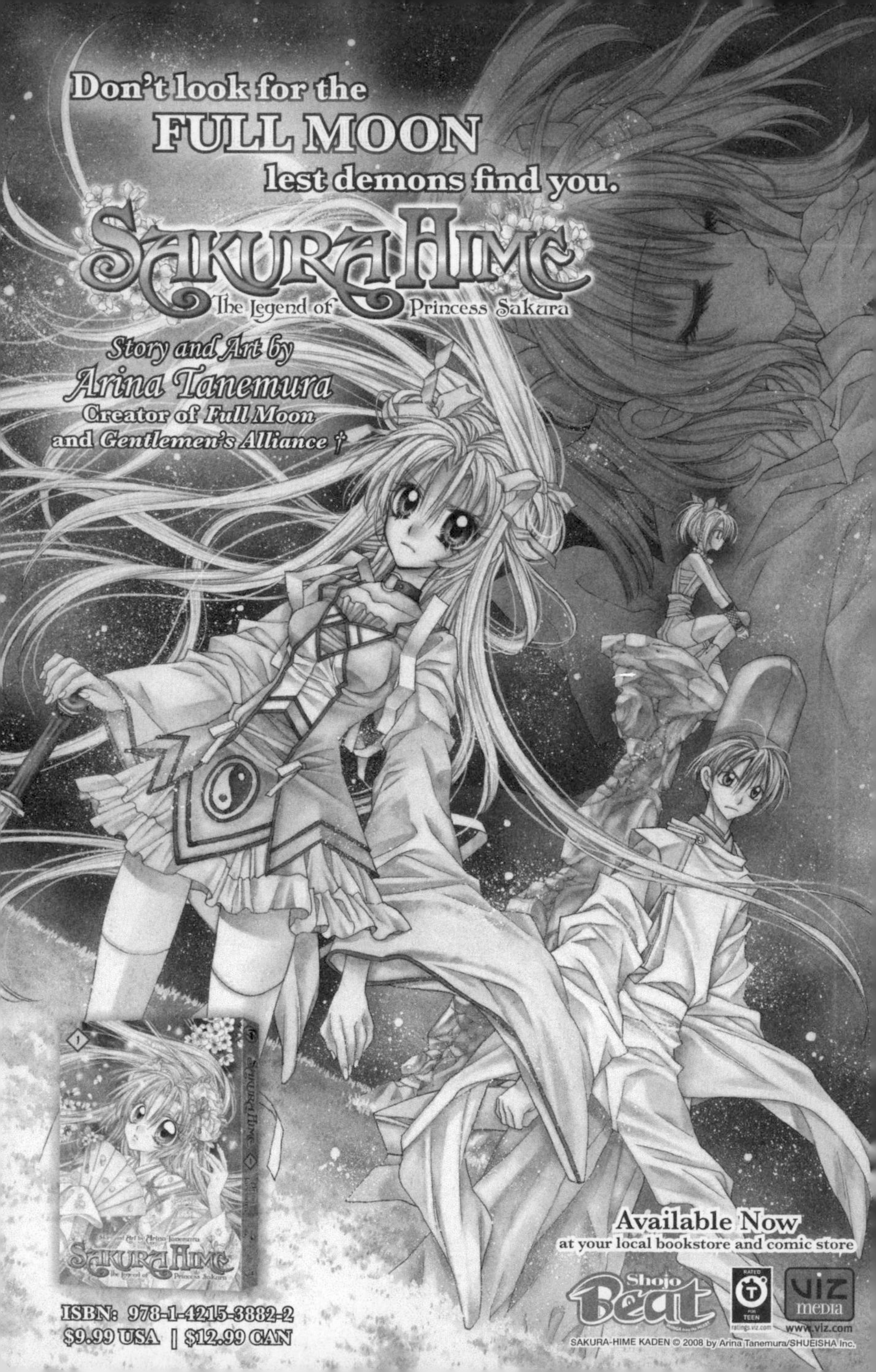

Don't look for the
FULL MOON
lest demons find you.
SAKURA HIME
The Legend of Princess Sakura
Story and Art by
Arina Tanemura
Creator of Full Moon
and Gentlemen's Alliance †
Available Now
at your local bookstore and comic store
ISBN: 978-1-4215-3882-2
$9.99 USA | $12.99 CAN
Shojo Beat
RATED T FOR TEEN
ratings.viz.com
VIZ media
www.viz.com
SAKURA-HIME KADEN © 2008 by Arina Tanemura/SHUEISHA Inc.

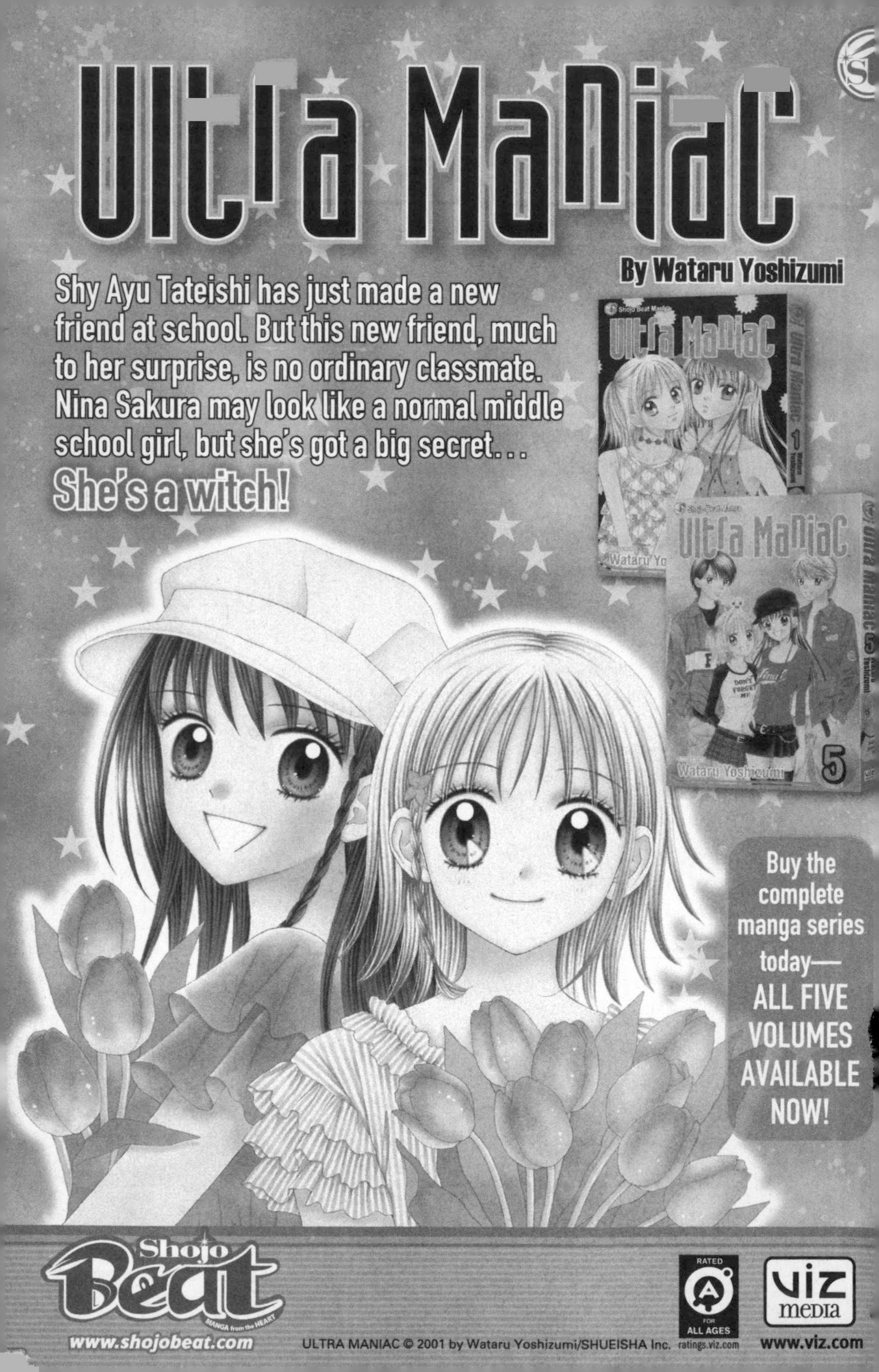
Ultra Maniac
By Wataru Yoshizumi
Shy Ayu Tateishi has just made a new friend at school. But this new friend, much to her surprise, is no ordinary classmate. Nina Sakura may look like a normal middle school girl, but she's got a big secret...
She's a witch!
Buy the complete manga series today— ALL FIVE VOLUMES AVAILABLE NOW!
Shojo Beat
MANGA from the HEART
www.shojobeat.com
ULTRA MANIAC © 2001 by Wataru Yoshizumi/SHUEISHA Inc.
RATED A FOR ALL AGES
ratings.viz.com
VIZ media
www.viz.com

You may be reading the wrong way!

This book reads right to left to maintain the original presentation and art of the Japanese edition, so action, sound effects and word balloons are reversed. This diagram shows how to follow the panels. Turn to the other side of the book to begin.

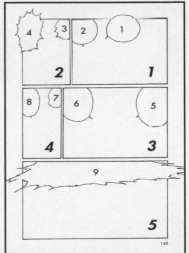